# NEW GERMAN CINEMA AND ITS GLOBAL CONTEXTS

## Contemporary Approaches to Film and Media Series

*A complete listing of the books in this series can be found online at wsupress.wayne.edu.*

**General Editor**

Barry Keith Grant
*Brock University*

# NEW GERMAN CINEMA AND ITS GLOBAL CONTEXTS

## A TRANSNATIONAL ART CINEMA

EDITED BY
MARCO ABEL AND
JAIMEY FISHER

AFTERWORD BY ERIC RENTSCHLER

Wayne State University Press
Detroit

ISBN 9780814348901 (paperback)
ISBN 9780814348918 (hardcover)
ISBN 9780814348925 (e-book)

Library of Congress Control Number: 2024930158

On cover: Sylvie Winter and Del Negro atop the World Trade Center in *Sylvie*. © ZDF/ Klaus Lemke. Used by permission. Cover design by Michel Vrana.

Published with the assistance of a fund established by Thelma Gray James of Wayne State University for the publication of folklore and English studies.

Wayne State University Press rests on Waawiyaataanong, also referred to as Detroit, the ancestral and contemporary homeland of the Three Fires Confederacy. These sovereign lands were granted by the Ojibwe, Odawa, Potawatomi, and Wyandot Nations, in 1807, through the Treaty of Detroit. Wayne State University Press affirms Indigenous sovereignty and honors all tribes with a connection to Detroit. With our Native neighbors, the press works to advance educational equity and promote a better future for the earth and all people.

Wayne State University Press
Leonard N. Simons Building
4809 Woodward Avenue
Detroit, Michigan 48201-1309

Visit us online at wsupress.wayne.edu.

# CONTENTS

# ACKNOWLEDGMENTS

In late summer 2018, when Wayne State University Press had just published our coedited volume *The Berlin School and Its Global Contexts: A Transnational Art Cinema*, we began pondering the idea of putting together a parallel volume—both a sequel and prequel of sorts—on the New German Cinema, which had long been canonized as the last of the great "classical" European new waves but which, we thought, had undeservedly suffered an overly long period of critical neglect. The time, in other words, seemed ripe for another look at what is generally considered the second golden age of German filmmaking (the cinema of the Weimar Republic being the first), not least also because its afterlife in post-unified Germany and an increasingly globalized post–Cold War cinephilic culture appeared to us as ghost-like: no longer alive, as evidenced by the dearth of scholarly attention to it in the last quarter century, but also not quite dead. That New German Cinema is not quite dead is demonstrated by the fact that several filmmakers associated with the Berlin School—whom we consider to comprise German cinema's third golden age—more or less explicitly position themselves in relation to, among others, their West German predecessors of the 1970s. Moreover, someone like Dominik Graf, arguably Germany's greatest genre filmmaker, time and again hails the ghosts of the *Autorenkino* around the "holy troika" of Fassbinder, Herzog, and Wenders in his often polemical salvos on the state of contemporary German filmmaking.

In this sense, then, we thought that revisiting New German Cinema would be a project whose stakes would be located not merely in a debate about the past (what *was* New German Cinema?) but also in an ongoing contemporary conversation about the present and future of German cinema—about what directions might become available, perhaps, as a result of revisiting a reframed, reimagined New German Cinema reconsidered and reconceived through a transnational purview as a means to revisit both canonical filmmakers and lesser known ones whose status as

New German Cinema filmmakers has long been tenuous at best. To realize this project, which we knew would exceed our individual capacities, we reached out to colleagues both in German film studies and beyond to solicit their contributions to our idea. We are grateful to *everyone* who initially responded with enthusiasm, even though several colleagues whom we had lined up as contributors had to pull out of this project due to the effects the coronavirus pandemic had on their lives. We are also grateful to those colleagues who participated on the panels focusing on this volume's topic that we organized for the German Studies Association Conference in Portland, Oregon, in fall 2019: being able to get an early sense of where some of our authors would be taking their contributions helped us shape this volume. We thank our editor at Wayne State University Press, Marie Sweetman, for all her support and guidance, as well as Barry Keith Grant, editor of the Contemporary Approaches to Film and Media Series, for his feedback and willingness to work with us on making adjustments to this project based on very helpful reports we received from two anonymous peer reviewers, to whom we are grateful as well. Last but not least, we want to thank our contributors for their excellent work: *New German Cinema and Its Global Contexts: A Transnational Art Cinema* would not exist without you.

We would like to dedicate this volume to one colleague who is, alas, sorely missing from this volume due to his unexpected passing on December 4, 2019: Thomas Elsaesser. His indelible scholarly legacy will continue to shape conversations on the history of cinema, including New German Cinema, for years to come.

# INTRODUCTION

## New German Cinema and Its Global Contexts—A Transnational Art Cinema

*Marco Abel and Jaimey Fisher*

Film scholars and critics have long regarded New German Cinema (NGC) of the 1970s and 1980s as a chronologically later, if perhaps not the latest, European new wave to have emerged after World War II.[1] While underappreciated and underperforming commercially in Germany, filmmakers such as the famous male troika of Rainer Werner Fassbinder, Werner Herzog, and Wim Wenders—as well as several female directors including Margarethe von Trotta, Helma Sanders-Brahms, and Helke Sander, to name but a few—received much attention abroad. As Thomas Elsaesser writes in his landmark study on the topic, "One of the more puzzling aspects of the history of the New German Cinema is . . . the discrepancy between the directors' reputation abroad, and their status in Germany itself. To over-simplify perhaps, one could say that the New German Cinema was discovered and even invented abroad, and had to be reimported to be recognized as such" (1989, 300). In fact, it was film critics in New York City who coined the term "New German Cinema," underscoring the fundamentally transnational and/or global character of the "movement" from its inception.

Indeed, by the mid-1970s, the West German left-liberal government deployed many of these films as canny kinds of cultural emissaries, particularly through its sprawling network of Goethe-Instituts throughout the world, now seen as a core element of the films' successes. The historic importance of the export of these films and critics' responses to them abroad highlight something that Rosalind Galt and Karl Schoonover emphasize—namely, the traveling character of art cinema—but these mechanisms, as NGC makes clear, were operational well before the more recent films that their important collection foregrounds (2010, 6–8). For example, as early as spring 1972—the year that saw the release of NGC classics such as Herzog's *Aguirre, der Zorn Gottes* (*Aguirre, the Wrath of God*), Wenders's *Die Angst des Tormanns beim Elfmeter* (*The Goalie's Anxiety at the Penalty Kick*), and Fassbinder's *Die bitteren Tränen der Petra von Kant* (*The Bitter Tears of Petra von Kant*)—cineastes in New York City could explore "seventeen features and twelve shorts under the then novel title 'New German Cinema' at the Museum of Modern Art," a showcasing organized by the Goethe-Institut (Sandford 1982, 16).[2] By funding films that were self-consciously critical of both German history in general and the Federal Republic in particular, the West German government aimed to premiere and promote a new post-1968 nation that was a proud beacon for forward-looking democratic ideals. Indeed, to use Herzog's famous quip, NGC was quickly regarded as the first "legitimate" German cinema since the Weimar years of Fritz Lang and F. W. Murnau.[3] While not shared by all NGC filmmakers, this assessment was at the time promoted by the governing coalition of the Social Democratic and the Free Democratic Parties under the leadership of Chancellor Willy Brandt as a means to aid its efforts to solidify West Germany as both a properly democratic nation that its Western allies could trust and as the only Germany with a claim to be the "legitimate" heir to the German nation's historical, artistic, and intellectual accomplishments. Unique to the history of German cinema, the "curious set of circumstances in the FRG [Federal Republic of Germany] . . . fostered a national cinema inordinately at odds with its nation," as Eric Rentschler astutely comments on the fact that so many of the films associated with NGC express a "critical realism," the alternate images of which amount to a veritable "counter-cinema" (1980, 154)—albeit one that "doesn't have a national audience," as another commentator observes (quoted in Davidson 1999, 4).[4]

Due to the initial reception of New German Cinema, which tended to focus on German history as well as the country's contemporary context, much of the early scholarship on these films and directors approached this period through the lens of *national* cinema—so much so that in some circles German cinema was, and perhaps still is, considered the most "national" cinema among the various new waves.[5] At times, NGC seems to comprise a body of films difficult to appreciate outside the confines of the national, beyond what they show about Germany or how they express a distinctly German subjectivity and indeed identity. As the influential German film historian Hans Helmut Prinzler writes in his foreword to Beat Presser's *Aufbruch ins Jetzt: Der Neue Deutsche Film*, while the filmmakers associated with NGC were inspired by the French New Wave as well as British realism, their films "told different stories, and those concerning German history were told differently," centering the "search for one's own identity" (2019, 13).[6]

This focus on the films' national aspects rather than their clearly transnational origins and engagements, it can be argued, came at considerable cost to the legacy of NGC. Few critics, for example, would highlight the emphatically and/or consistently national aspects of the French New Wave or New Hollywood. When film scholars gradually began to investigate film history from a more global, internationalist, and indeed transnational perspective from the mid-1990s on, the films of the NGC seemed to be gradually forgotten. As Lutz Koepnick puts the matter, "Beginning in the late 1990s, scholarship on German cinema was quite eager to engage with the role of the popular in German film culture. The predominant focus was no longer on the good objects of New German Cinema or Weimar expressionism, but on the films of the Nazi era or the 1950s, the work of German exiles in Hollywood or the heritage and consensus films of the post-Wall era" (2013, 553). More polemically put, we might say that a backlash of sorts occurred—perhaps especially within German film studies—against the excessive privileging of NGC as a "good object" for German (film) studies scholars to study and, ultimately, to celebrate. This development allowed such academics to examine this cinema at a level of "art," if not "high art"—a value that historically has played a privileged role in German culture.[7] Countering this tendency—not least, perhaps, because of its potential to open the door for feelings of pride in this *national* accomplishment to emerge and become "legitimate" and legitimated—the field started to rethink the history of German cinema by putting greater emphasis on its *popular*, which is to say: genre, tradition, rather than continuing to focus on the *Autorenkino* (cinema of authors) of the NGC.[8] Perhaps we could say: precisely because of the perception that the focus on the *Autorenkino* as a "good object" has led to a celebration of German cinema as a *national* cinema of which one can be proud, scholars turned toward Germany's long-standing tradition of *popular* genre filmmaking (which has frequently been denigrated by critics and scholars alike) and its more overt international influences in order to complicate, if not to undo, the troubling view that equated the *Autorenkino* as (high) art cinema with NGC, NGC with "legitimate" German cinema, and the latter, in turn, with German *national* cinema—with the disconcerting consequence that through the positing of this synecdochic relationship between NGC's *Autorenkino* and the West German nation-state the latter emerged as the warrant that enabled the German *nation* to reemerge as "good" at its core. Understandably, the concern was that this celebration of German national cinema was just a short step away from (unintentionally) offering a justification for nationalism. NGC thus fell out of favor with scholars so much so that, on average, one might be justified in claiming that, of all the great new waves, it is these films that have suffered the most in reputation, causing them to recede for all but a small cadre of German film historians.

This state of affairs is likely what well-known film critic Hanns-Georg Rodek had in mind when writing a remarkable review of an exhibition of photos at the Bayerischen Akademie der Schönen Künste in Munich by the prominent Swiss photographer Beat Presser, who over several decades had taken photos of key NGC protagonists (filmmakers, actors, and technicians alike). Rodek argues that, even in Germany itself, New German Cinema "is increasingly becoming terra incognita. A German is more likely to have seen *Nosferatu* (1921 [*sic*!]) than *Messer im Kopf* (1978), *Metropolis* (1926) rather than *Supermarkt* (1974)" (Rodek 2019). This likelihood that NGC films are unknown to contemporary Germans is paralleled by the fact that, as Rodek points out, "for most of these filmmakers there exist no monographs [in German]. There is a twenty-five-year-old history by Thomas Elsaesser and a small Reclam book with three dozen descriptions of films and a four-dozen-pages-long survey, but no historian has ever set out to write a full account of this period."[9] Rodek makes an important point, even if one does recognize that vital work has been carried out by Anglophone scholars of NGC that, in total, amounts to around twenty books on the period. Notably, however, the vast majority of these books were published decades ago.

We agree with Rodek that it is high time to revive interest in this period—once considered Germany's second golden age after the Weimar period—but we aim to do so within updated frameworks. We seek to address this lacuna in recent film scholarship with a novel approach, one that comprehends the films' self-consciously national themes within broader transnational understandings and engagements. We take Galt and Schoonover's collection (2010) as an inspiration but also explore an emphatically earlier moment than they and their contributors do, not least to demonstrate that these global operations—rather like globalization itself—were well underway and even accelerating in the 1970s. Similarly, many scholars have implored German film studies to look beyond the merely national to comprehend how cinema made in Germany participates in more global circuits of commerce and art and the many intersections therein. For example, in a *German Studies Review* forum on the state of German film studies, Sabine Hake bemoaned the fact that "German film studies continues to be defined by the demarcating effects of the national in terms of its self-understanding and self-presentation" (2013, 644) and advocated that scholars need to open up their "work on German cinema *as* European cinema to the entire range of research questions and methodologies available in film and media studies on both sides of the Atlantic" (651). And Koepnick pointedly argued in the same forum that with "the rise of cultural studies and postcolonial theory, the normative concept of national cinema as art cinema in the last years of the twentieth century increasingly appeared, not simply as a specter from the past, but as precarious strategy to contain non-Western images within a predominantly white, male, and Eurocentric framework" (2013, 653). Our volume heeds these criticisms and applies a more outward-looking approach to German cinema of the late 1960s to the mid-1980s. By reframing these films with a global lens, the collection seeks to make the period freshly available to conversations about not only global cinema (of and beyond that time period) but also contemporary Germany, of which the most important instantiation are the films by the so-called Berlin School. In celebrating the Berlin School group of filmmakers, critics have investigated and established their debt to global art cinema (as demonstrated in our coedited volume on the topic), but their debt to their predecessors in the NGC is still insufficiently explored.[10]

Our anthology aims to approach these celebrated years of German art films from multiple innovative angles. First, the essays address the inter- and transnational aspects of these films to illuminate them anew. It seems surprising that while many scholars have, over the years, acknowledged the role of inter- and transnational film culture in the creation of a notion of "New German Cinema," this insight has usually not carried over to analyses of individual films or directors.[11] Second, the contributions herein seek to expand our notion of these years beyond the predictable canonical films of NGC, in part to help rethink conventional notions of art cinema. As Rentschler noted in a 2012 essay entitled "Reconsidering New German Cinema"—another source of inspiration for the present volume—the "canon" of films from this period that are regularly viewed and taught has hardly changed since it was expanded to include work made by female, and usually feminist, filmmakers in the late 1970s (119). Notably, in that same essay, Rentschler suggests a line of research—and teaching—that would reconsider and reconceptualize what national cinema is and how it operates. Reminding us that the "new German cinema . . . confronted the aporias of the German past and in the process renewed German film, transforming bad history into a legitimate cinema . . . renown[ed] for resolutely personal voices, idiosyncratic visions, and formal alternatives" (120), he holds that a "course today on post-war German cinema will want to take leave of the spirited partisanship from several decades ago and to reconsider the heady terms of its heroic master narrative" (121). He suggests that scholars, when considering NGC, ought to "extend the sampling of texts beyond a rarefied ensemble of art films to consider shorts and nonfiction films, to factor in popular features as well as avant-garde undertakings" (122).

Our volume takes up these challenges by posing questions such as: What international interests and influences affected filmmaking in Germany in this period? How did the films function, and how were they received, within what inter- and transnational circuits of production, distribution, and exhibition? How can such an updated understanding of these films as part of a world cinema system help in rethinking art cinema and its relationship to the nation? And rather than entirely getting rid of the very notion of "national cinema," this volume instead embraces Rentschler's qualified defense thereof when he, citing Andrew Higson on national cinema in general, concludes that it "is essential that we think of national cinema not just in terms of films that were produced in the FRG" (2012, 122). By pairing a range of German films, including, perhaps somewhat controversially, some made in East Germany, with interlocutors from countries such as Poland, Chile, the United States, New Zealand, France, the Czech Republic, and Italy—whether in the form of films from those countries or in terms of intellectual movements and arguments—*New German Cinema and Its Global Contexts: A Transnational Art Cinema* is the first sustained attempt to examine NGC not only through a more globally oriented lens but also from a perspective that expands the canon of NGC by folding in West—and East—German filmmakers who are usually not considered representatives of NGC.

For example, the volume includes Nora M. Alter's essay on Harun Farocki, whose stock among critics and scholars has risen since the initial waves of work on NGC that excluded his films from discussion. Alter attends to his little-analyzed attempt at directing a feature film, *Betrogen* (*Betrayed*, 1985) and its transnational fate. Farocki's abrupt turn from his famously rigorous film essays to a crime thriller with a film noir tone highlights the dynamic boundaries of art versus (and with) transnational genre. The volume also includes an analysis of animation (see Jennifer Lynde Barker's contribution), which has heretofore not been considered in discussions of NGC. The conventional categories of art cinema seem once again surprisingly blurred: the animated films Barker examines are artistically highly ambitious works that were shown at film festivals, cited highbrow influences, won prestige prizes, and so on—precisely the purview of conventional art cinema.

In exploring the boundaries of NGC as an art cinema, the volume also turns to filmmakers rarely discussed in the scholarship on NGC. Hester Baer's essay, for instance, takes up the work of Claudia von Alemann, Jeanine Meerapfel, and Ula Stöckl, considering them within the context of transnational feminism and the institutional framework of the Ulm School of Design, founded by Alexander Kluge and Edgar Reitz. Feminist cinema has in fact been a calling card of NGC, a rarity among the sundry new waves, and scholars are increasingly appreciating its importance, as prominent German critic Rainer Gansera indicates in his review of Beat Presser's book of interviews, *Aufbruch ins Jetzt*, a companion piece to the latter's photo exhibition. Gansera observes, "Until this day the *Autorenfilm* has not been able to shake the bad name it was given [by West Germany's conservative government in the 1980s]. This makes one blind to an essential aspect of NGC, which comes through well in [Presser's book of interviews with the NGC protagonists]: namely, that the *Autorenfilm* opened the doors for the *Frauenfilm* [films made by women]" (2019).

To be sure, this is not an agreed-upon assessment. On the one hand, Jutta Brückner, NGC director of films such as *Ein ganz und gar verwahrlostes Mädchen—Ein Tag im Leben der Rita Rischak* (*A Thoroughly Demoralized Girl: A Day in the Life of Rita Rischak*, 1977) and *Hungerjahre* (*The Hunger Years: In a Land of Plenty*, 1980), seems to lend support for Gansera's argument, arguing, "Feminist film practice has been influenced largely by German women. We had so many opportunities compared to women in other countries to develop a style of feminist filmmaking. The new West German auteurs' films are very distinctive, so this is true of the feminist branch as well" (quoted in von Zadow 1998, 97). And Miriam Hansen lamented a long time ago the fact that the "American-styled New German Cinema canonized [a number of men] but rarely extends to [female filmmakers]" who, she rightly pointed out, "are," or at least *were* in 1983 when her essay originally appeared in the first and only European feminist film journal, *frauen und film* (founded by Helke Sander), "conspicuously absent from the pantheon of New German auteurs" (1993, 293). Yet Julia Knight reminds us that the establishment of NGC as an *Autorenkino* actually functioned "at a number of levels to inhibit serious consideration of the work of women filmmakers" (1992, 68), not least because their films, "based to a considerable degree on autobiographical material" (65), was considered more a "cinema of personal experience"—that is, documentary in nature—than a "cinema of self-expression" that the concept of the *Autor* privileged. Furthermore, as is well known, auteurism (whether in its original French or its significantly altered German form) "privileges the notion of *individual* authorship" (65), whereas many women filmmakers "adopted collective working methods" (66). So, while it is true that West German women became "the most active national group of women filmmakers" (Frieden et al. 1993, 3), it is perhaps less the case that the *Autorenkino* "opened the door" to women filmmakers than that the latter *forced* the door open. Baer's account of how the Ulm School of Design shaped early West German feminist filmmaking offers compelling insights into the struggle of West German women filmmakers in the 1960s—a discussion that works in concert, we think, with Ervin Malakaj's contribution herein, in which he revisits an important debate *within* West German feminist filmmaking that took place in the early 1980s.

The volume also deliberately extends the geographic purview of the contributions eastward from New German Cinema's usual western confines, with essays on Hansjürgen Pohland's adaptation of Günter Grass's *Katz und Maus* and its relationship to the celebrated Polish cinema of these years (see John E. Davidson's contribution), as well as student films made at the East German film school, the Hochschule für Film und Fernsehen "Konrad Wolf" in Potsdam-Babelsberg (essay by Ilka Brombach). Other contributions engage works by filmmakers who are lesser known (both in Germany and abroad) and at times not (yet) received as part of NGC, such as Klaus Lemke (see Marco Abel's essay) and Roland Klick (contribution by Brad Prager). Simultaneously, the book aims to shed new light on selected works by some of the most famous directors associated with NGC, such as Fassbinder (see essay by Ian Fleishman) and Herzog (Margaret Strair's essay), as well as offer insights into films by lesser-known directors such as Werner Schroeter (Jaimey Fisher's contribution), Peter Lilienthal (the focus of Claudia Sandberg's essay), as well as animated films by Boris von Borresholm and Wolfgang Urchs (Jennifer Lynde Barker's essay).

The essays in the collection take up a broad range of marginalized figures, often-forgotten facts, and contested counter-narratives, all with an eye toward thinking New German Cinema anew and, indeed, in a more transnational context. The set of films, filmmakers, casts and crews, as well as broader film culture that made and makes up NGC was always a somewhat woolly grouping, a usefully open set, and it is our hope that the essays herein help us reconsider what these works and personnel have meant in the broader West and East German context as well as in the European and global cultural landscape.

Setting the stage for our volume by drawing out some of the stakes of its film-historiographical interventions—to wit, that *New German Cinema and Its Global Contexts* not only seeks to revisit New German Cinema in order to rediscover what it was but also to imagine both what it *could have been* had its canon formation proceeded along different lines and what it *might yet become* as a result of the interventions assembled herein—Marco Abel's essay "(Don't) Look Back on *Sylvie*: Klaus Lemke, D. A. Pennebaker, and the 'Lightness' of a 'Left without Leftism'" draws attention to a long-neglected West German film of the 1970s: Klaus Lemke's *Sylvie* (1973). With his seventh feature, shot between his two classic Hamburg films, *Rocker* (1972) and *Paul* (1974), this enfant terrible of German cinema returned to Munich in order to shoot what is arguably one of the "lightest" films not only of his career but also of (New) German Cinema. This "lightness"—which Abel considers a crucial political affect—is the result of a transformation in Lemke's point of cinematic orientation and completely alien, or other, to the then dominant "heaviness" of NGC and art cinema in general. Whereas Lemke's early work was, like that of his peers from the so-called New Munich Group of the mid- to late 1960s, deeply indebted to Howard Hawks's films, *Sylvie*'s primary point of cinematic departure is D. A. Pennebaker's "direct cinema" landmark film, *Dont Look Back* (1967). Whereas Hawks taught Lemke and his New Munich Group friends how the act of narrating a story has to become the real adventure of a film, so Pennebaker taught Lemke that the goal of a film is to get as close as possible to the subjective experience of the protagonists—without any consideration for a story. Through his encounter with Pennebaker's film, Lemke ended up making what Abel characterizes as a "left film without leftism": a film in which the "concentrated irrationality of life," as Lemke puts it, is affectively *intensified* (rather than intellectually contained) with the help of the film's own irrationality that, in this case, is rendered sensible by, among other aspects, the film's radical shifts of setting—from Munich to New York to eventually Hamburg; the impossibility of the love story itself, in which a fashion model from Munich falls in love with a sailor from Hamburg; and mood, which occurs perhaps most intensely on the streets of New York City, where Sylvie, and the film itself, undergoes a crucial transformation. What Lemke—through his transnational cinematic encounters with first Hawks and then Pennebaker—stumbled upon in the making of *Sylvie*, Abel shows, was the political affect of "lightness": an affect in which inhered the *potential* history of another—an "aesthetic"—left that has largely been forgotten by German film historiography. It is this left—a left without leftism—that, in Abel's view, should be recovered as a crucial corrective to the film-historiographical dominance of the "heavy" political left as cinematically embodied by what has film historiographically been codified as "New German Cinema."

Turning to another often overlooked Munich-based filmmaker whose aesthetic dispositions, like Lemke's, were deeply shaped by Hollywood genre cinema as well as conventional art cinema, Brad Prager discusses how Roland Klick is frequently considered at the fringes of NGC, in something of a self-imposed distance. Indeed, Klick himself often highlights the contrastive "Americanness" of his films, by which he seems to mean their sensuality and emphasis on the physicality of the body. Prager argues in "A Relentless Forward Movement: The German and Un-German Cinema of Roland Klick" that the New Munich Group, to which Klick is occasionally seen to belong and that also includes Lemke, Rudolf Thome, and the duo May Spils and Werner Enke, underscores the need to rethink the distinction between popular and so-called art/art house films.[12] Klick can also be said to have a more market-oriented mentality than many of the NGC directors, openly disdaining (like Lemke) the state subsidy system and suggesting it fostered contempt for film audiences and their pleasures. He especially delighted in skewering some of the Young German Film and New German Cinema directors like Alexander Kluge, whose work he saw as intended for elitist audiences and as extractive in that it took stories from communities without working in forms they would want to engage. Although Klick pledged allegiance to US genre films, Klick's first substantive work, *Bübchen* (*Little Vampire*, 1968), nonetheless shows the influence of François Truffaut and Jean-Luc Godard—especially with the latter, Klick at least provisionally shared a common ancestor with many of the NGC directors. There were also important links to Italy's innovative postwar waves, as Klick worked as a production assistant for Federico Fellini, and many of his German actors claimed to have learned their trade in Italy, as with Klaus Kinski, Mario Adorf, and Gisela Hahn. Klick's *Deadlock* (1970), however, moves further toward genre in its variation on the western, manifesting the influence of both Henri Clouzot's *Le salaire de la peur* (*The Wages of Fear*, 1953) and Sergio Leone's *Il buono, il brutto, il cattivo* (*The Good, the Bad, and the Ugly*, 1966), a direction confirmed by his 1974 film *Supermarkt* (*Supermarket*).

Harun Farocki's substantive oeuvre has received increasing scholarly attention in the last twenty years, and in her essay "The Many Betrayals of Harun Farocki's *Betrogen*," Nora M. Alter adds an important chapter to this revival by analyzing Farocki's sole foray from his now widely celebrated nonfiction films into directing/writing a fictional feature. His turn from what seemed high-art film essays to fiction filmmaking—indeed, to *genre* film—manifests an intriguing development in Farocki's career, given that he would later add a surprise sidebar to his esteemed work as a script collaborator on the features of his student and friend Christian Petzold. In the arc of the NGC era, *Betrayed* also marks a particularly interesting moment because Farocki—one of the most celebrated filmmakers and critics of the era—regarded it as a break with the challenging and little-seen nonfiction films he had been making. Alter details how this self-declared break also included his abrupt resignation from *Filmkritik*, one of the most important German film journals in this era and a forum for and/or influence on many of NGC's key filmmakers that in the late 1960s was also the venue for a film-critical debate between the so-called "political left" and the "aesthetic left" that Abel's essay revisits in his discussion of Lemke and the New Munich Group. But Farocki not merely resigned as editor of this journal but also took leave of his long-standing production team, to which he returned, however, after *Betrayed* did not find much resonance with either critics or audiences. Alter examines these broader film cultural issues as well as the film itself, which intriguingly manifests some of Farocki's interests as articulated in his writings of the time, which often draw on global film movements, especially in their turn to film noir as well as to Robert Bresson's cinema. For example, the film offers a cleverly conceived critique of consumerism and middle-class society in its Hitchcockian tale of a man killing a woman he loves and then replacing her with her sister, who is more willing to play the game of mainstream family values. Its themes of modernity, exchangeability, and malleable identities in a noirish package look both backward to Alfred Hitchcock and forward to Farocki's work with Petzold, not least to *Phoenix* (2014). For Alter, the film's poor reception is linked to the mutating film landscape in the late NGC period, when there were many changes indeed.

Turning to a very different genre, Jennifer Lynde Barker begins her essay "Gnomic Animation: Decrypting the German New Wave" with the frequently forgotten fact that the Oberhausen Manifesto, rare for its kind of dramatic declaration, included animation alongside cinema filmmakers. This inclusion among its signatories is an occasion for Barker to rethink the predominating narratives of NGC, one of the key goals of our volume. Citing the tradition of avant-garde animation in the Weimar period, Barker explores the innovative role that animation played in the (earlier) Young German Film and in (central) European art cinema in general, including especially the work of Boris von Borresholm and

Wolfgang Urchs.[13] This work featured, Barker recounts, "juxtapositions of styles, postmodern pastiche, [and] existentialist absurdist themes" with an aesthetic that drew on graphic design from around the globe, new waves around Europe, and modernist approaches from the prewar era. These animated films notably share many of the familiar themes of NGC (anti-authoritarianism, engaging the German past, critiquing the culture industry), but with an animated aesthetic that lent itself to transnational influence and collaboration. For instance, Borresholm's career was full of collaborations with Eastern European émigrés amid their flight from the Eastern Bloc.[14] Borresholm, who won the Filmband in Gold (then West Germany's highest award for film) in 1980, had an unusual career arc that included publishing books (for example, on Goebbels's propaganda machine); serving as a dramaturge and editor; and then as a filmmaker producing newsreels, educational films, and documentaries. Borresholm and Urchs were both part of a Munich group that met regularly and included Peter Schamoni—director of one of the first features of Young German Film, *Schonzeit für Füchse* (*No Shooting Time for Foxes*, 1966), who subsequently would produce the New Munich Group duo May Spils and Werner Enke's *Zur Sache, Schätzchen* (*Go for It, Baby*, 1968)—and Kluge. Borresholm and Urch's first film (with Schamoni collaborating on the script) in fact premiered at that fateful Oberhausen festival in 1962: *Die Gartenzwerge* (*The Garden Gnomes*) skewers West German conformity, consumerism, and material smugness. Some actual garden gnomes were injured in the production of this film, as their destruction at the outset is then a point of departure for an animated portion in which the little figures crawl out from under the ubiquitous rubble, their war-time helmets metamorphosing into nightcaps. Urchs opened an animation studio with the earnings from the German Film Prize for *Garden Gnomes*, which produced other works that make up this largely neglected chapter of 1960s and 1970s German film history.

While Werner Herzog is probably the best-known NGC director who shot in South America (in *Aguirre, the Wrath of God*, *Fitzcarraldo* [1982], and *Cobra Verde* [1987], among others), Claudia Sandberg explores a lesser-known director, the Jewish German-Uruguayan Peter Lilienthal, whose work engaged the contemporary situation in Latin American in much greater detail. The self-proclaimed "South-American bird" among the NGC directors, Lilienthal had his start at West German regional state broadcasters SWR and SFB directing dramas, and his first film, *Malatesta* (1969), won the German Film Award and was in competition at Cannes. A whole series of Lilienthal's films from the early 1970s through the 1980s and even into the 2000s included collaborations with Latin American artists, among them recurring work with Antonio Skármeta, who would go on to win the national literature prize of Chile. Lilienthal's 1973 *La Victoria*—co-produced by NGC mainstays Filmverlag der Autoren and ZDF's *Das kleine Fernsehspiel*—was the turning point in this direction of collaboration: the film, in its open effort to rework the Eurocentrism of most German cinema even when shot abroad, cannot be read without the filters of transnationalism. The film documents Salvador Allende's efforts to fight inequality and offer a stable new socioeconomic foundation to the poor in Chile by following a woman from the provinces arriving in Santiago, seeking work and starting a new life there. Sandberg compares Lilienthal's film (shot with Chilean cast and crew) to a near-contemporary film by Raúl Ruiz, *Palomita blanca* (1973/1992), which was, like *La Victoria*, shot in the last months of Allende's government. While Ruiz's film is a fictional social satire/romance, both films thematize Chile's deep "social divides and patriarchal structures" and the ways that women's political participation can address them. Sandberg even addresses the fate of these films post-coup and their later legacy in Chilean memory culture.

John E. Davidson, in turn, draws our attention to another fascinating transnational connection subtly informing the history of New German Cinema—one that looks in the diametrically opposite direction from Sandberg's critical purview: Poland. In "*Katz und Maus*: A West German Project in Poland by Pohland," Davidson investigates one of the earliest recipients of subsidies from the Kuratorium junger deutscher Film (Board of Trustees for Young German Film). Although the Kuratorium is seen as an important milestone in the creation and rise of NGC, Hansjürgen Pohland's adaptation of Günter Grass's novella *Katz und Maus* (*Cat and Mouse*) is today largely ignored. The film serves, in Davidson's hands, as both a case study for international East-West co-productions and evidence that *Vergangenheitsbewältigung* (coming to terms with the past), which many see at the heart of NGC, was actually "an international activity." Moreover, Davidson makes the case that Pohland's adaptation was a "key text in mid-1960s West German cultural politics." To name just two intriguing aspects of the text investigated in the essay, both the location shooting in Gdansk and the West German/Polish co-production—one of the very few in this era—underscore the transnational nature of coming to terms with the past. To comprehend this complexity, Davidson gives context to Polish/West German cultural relations at the time—citing, for instance, that Polish films tended to be more viewed in West Germany than East—and then investigates a number of co-productions between Western and Eastern Europe, which sought, with primarily Western capital, to exploit what was understood as the "permeability" of the "Iron Curtain," at least at specific historical moments. For example, one of the only West German/Polish co-productions at its time, *Ósmy dzień tygodnia* (*The Eighth Day of the Week*, 1957) was directed by Aleksander Ford, the mentor of Andrej Wajda and Roman Polański, and starred Zbigniew Cybulski, the Polish "James Dean," as well as German actors like Sonja Ziemann. It was produced by Lodz-born Artur Brauner, who would be a force in West German cinema in general for decades. Having established this context, Davidson turns to Pohland's film, which he sees as reflecting tensions in West German politics at the time, including tensions around the associations of refugees and Western tourism to the Eastern Bloc.

Like Davidson, Ilka Brombach also looks eastward to uncover New German Cinema's transnational contexts and adds an important perspective—one from East Germany—in her essay "Babelsberg Freedoms: The Films of the Babelsberg Film School, European New Waves, and New German Cinema." Although NGC is often regarded as solely a West German phenomenon, Brombach shows how some of the student work originating from the Film School "Konrad Wolf" in Babelsberg was engaged, very early, with the (Western) European new waves, including Italian neorealism and (especially Left Bank) Nouvelle Vague. Part of this East German story is one of regular border crossing: before the Berlin Wall was built in 1961, the Konrad Wolf film students regularly crossed over into West Berlin to see foreign films that were not (legally) distributed in East Germany, particularly "the Italians" at the Filmbühne Steinplatz. This allowed the East German students—including some, like Jürgen Böttcher, who went on to become key figures at DEFA, the East German state-controlled film studio—to incorporate the increasing intersection of political and aesthetic experimentation in these new waves. Another notable and often neglected aspect of this East German wave was an engagement with innovative documentary, especially, as Brombach argues, with the essay films of Chris Marker, a unique figure among the Left Bank French New Wave. Marker had a clear influence on West German filmmakers like Farocki and Hartmut Bitomsky, but his impact in the Eastern Bloc countries is less well understood. Intriguingly as well, these East German films took up some of the often-neglected innovations afforded by other Eastern European movements like the Czech New Wave, including how to achieve freedom, personally and aesthetically, within an all-too-often intervening system. Brombach's argument provides another case in which the two Germanys can illuminate anew the presumed institutional underpinnings of global art cinema: most often, as in Galt and Schoonover, it is festivals that are mentioned (2010, 5–6), but film schools also played and play a crucial role in art cinema's inherent cosmopolitanism.[15]

While Brombach's essay mines the archive of *East* Germany's sole film school, Hester Baer turns in her essay, "The Ulm School and Feminist Film History," to *West* Germany's first film school to engage with one of NGC's most celebrated aspects—its strong feminist component—and explains how conventional understandings do not quite do it justice. Although the feminist filmmakers and theorizing around the dffb (Deutsche Film- und Fernsehakademie Berlin [German Film and Television Academy Berlin]) are well known, Baer shows how the feminist film history of the Ulm School adds to this legacy substantively. The Ulm School of Design (Hochschule für Gestaltung) started primarily as a design school, with links to the Bauhaus, and by the time film schools were being founded in Germany, it actually had a significantly higher ratio of women in its classes than the more famous dffb. Baer focuses on the work of Ulm students such as Claudia von Alemann, Jeanine Meerapfel, and Ula Stöckl, whose work complicates conventional key categories of NGC (as well as art cinema in general) such as authorship, national cinema, and conspicuous issue-orientation. Some of their early films manifest the influence of then Ulm teachers Alexander Kluge and Edgar Reitz, particularly in filmic "miniatures" made at the school that were formally rigorous and politically inclined. Moreover, the careers of all three emphasize how engaged they were with global forces and political movements. For example, having grown up in Argentina as the child of Jewish émigrés, Meerapfel (president of the Akadamie der Künste [Academy of the Arts] in Berlin since 2015) has made work ranging from a focus on Jews in divided Berlin to the psychological consequences of the Argentine military dictatorship. Alemann made films on the 1968 Paris uprising, Vietnam, and the challenges facing women working in the German metal industry. She also made feature films, including *Die Reise nach Lyon* (*Blind Spot*, 1981), which Baer argues is among the most aesthetically important feminist work of this era.

Also shedding light on the role feminism played in and for the history of NGC is Ervin Malakaj, who in his contribution "On Debility in Helma Sanders-Brahms's *Die Berührte*" turns to one of the key women filmmakers now associated with NGC. *Die Berührte* (*No Mercy, No Future*, 1981), however, proved controversial for many West German feminists. Rather than depicting, as many feminist films of the time did, how women's liberation can be accomplished through female agency, Sanders-Brahms's film refuses to affirm such optimism about the future and instead zooms in on what Malakaj calls "strategic debility" as an institutionalized technology of power that suppresses the very self-actualization that the women's liberation movement pursued. To draw out the stakes of the film's refusal to "celebrate agential prowess," Malakaj situates *No Mercy, No Future* in the broader context of feminist filmmaking in Europe, comparing it in particular with Chantal Akerman's *Jeanne Dielman, 23 Quai de Commerce, 1018 Bruxelles* (1975)—the film that now tops *Sight and Sound*'s influential (and controversial) once-a-decade poll of the one hundred greatest films of all times (2022 version) and that, like Sanders-Brahms's, examines "women's daily routines under heterocapitalist patriarchy."[16] Important to Malakaj's argument is his attention to intersectionality: his detailed reading of *No Mercy, No Future* reveals how it simultaneously proffers a critique of strategic debility that allows it, at times, to express "something akin to intersectional struggles against heterosexist and racist oppression" and falls short of its aims "when considering the representational strategies of the men of color in the film."

Margaret Strair, in her essay "Enigmatic Soundscapes: Werner Herzog's *Kaspar Hauser* and Jane Campion's *The Piano*," offers a new angle on the question of national cinema and New German Cinema by focusing her (auditory) attention on film sound. This novel approach affords new insights into one of the (conventionally) central figures of NGC, Werner Herzog, who has become renowned for his fruitful combination of outsider figures and breathtaking landscapes. But, as Strair demonstrates, in Herzog's *Jeder für sich und Gott gegen alle* (*The Enigma of Kaspar Hauser*, 1974), the sounds of society and national culture play a central role in constructing the eponymous protagonist's outsider status. Building on Carol Flinn's groundbreaking work on the sonic aspects of some of the NGC works, Strair shows how, in global art cinema in general, sound can function to construct "displacements, homelessness, and alienation."[17] For her, a rich analogue for these mechanisms is Jane Campion's international breakthrough *The Piano* (1993). In *The Piano* as well, sound functions to convey the outsider status of the protagonist, Ada, a contentious character particularly parallel to Hauser in her strong opinions on musical aesthetics. In both films, the complex interplay between diegetic and nondiegetic sounds situates the protagonist in a world not their own and highlights what kind of border crossing the respective plots will require of them. This border crossing becomes, in fact, a kind of psychological and even ontological crisis for both Kaspar and Ada. The tension in these films between sound and image emphasizes not only the outsider status of Kaspar and Ada but also how this estrangement in a strange land queries and eventually undercuts the cultural traditions of which such music—and the filmmakers and their films—are a key part. Both films have, as Strair shows, a common ancestor in Romantic painting and art, and both Julia Kristeva and Laura Mulvey illuminate how these themes, in Campion's feminist work, intersect gender and its inflection in colonialism—this constellation would look very different, as Strair explores, in the film's darker original ending.

Ian Fleishman analyzes a later and telling moment of NGC in his essay "New Hollywood Fassbinder: Genre and Gender in Sam Peckinpah's *Cross of Iron* and Rainer Werner Fassbinder's *Querelle*" by engaging a film that is usually regarded as ending the cycle, Fassbinder's *Querelle*—the last film he made before his untimely death on June 10, 1982, an event that, "in retrospect," as Gerd Gemünden puts it in a special issue on Fassbinder's work in *New German Critique*, can be said to have "brought with it also the demise of the New German Cinema" (1994, 6). Fleishman takes as his point of departure an intriguing cinematic counterfactual, a filmic road almost taken: apparently, among others, Sam Peckinpah, John Schlesinger, Roman Polański, and Martin Scorsese were all considered for *Querelle*, a film that now seems indelibly associated with Fassbinder—it is an origin story that raises questions about the traditional association, if not complete identification, of art cinema and auteurist filmmaking. In fact, the producers were struggling to find a commercially viable director who could persuade the Gallimard rights holder to green-light the project. For example, Werner Schroeter worked on an early screenplay draft but was rejected for not being commercial enough for these Gallimard guardians. Fleishman uses these unusual production conditions to consider the tendencies of NGC as compared to those of New Hollywood, which, as Fleishman persuasively argues, had a somewhat different relationship to genre than most NGC work. Fleishman engages with Thomas Elsaesser's analyses of New Hollywood, which are of particular interest for the present collection in light of Elsaesser's groundbreaking and still influential work on NGC. Elsaesser highlights, at the turbulent intersection of American genres and New Wave vagaries, the contradictions of the conventionally active US male protagonist and how he might fare in the era of Vietnam defeat and a broader demythologization of the American dream. Precisely such contradictions of masculinity structure the narratives of both Peckinpah's *Cross of Iron* (1977) and *Querelle*, with both probing a militarized mode of the male and both exploring the role of homosociality and homoeroticism in such forms. Both films are preoccupied with community—and its potential for downfall—among men (largely) in the absence of women. In this framing and then close analysis, Fleishman demonstrates how, despite its national cinema reputation, NGC was well imbricated in global constellations.

Bringing this volume's exploration of New German Cinema's transnational art cinema connections to a close, Jaimey Fisher's "Institutionalizing Passion as Shocks to the System: Michel Foucault and Anti-Psychiatry in Werner Schroeter's *Day of the Idiots* and Milos Forman's *One Flew over the Cuckoo's Nest*" takes up one of the most influential directors of this period but one who is not nearly as well known, especially internationally, as Fassbinder, Herzog, and Wenders. Elsaesser described Schroeter as "German cinema's greatest marginal filmmaker" (1989, 204), and Fassbinder celebrated him as Germany's "best kept secret" (quoted in Riley 2010). One of the things that made Schroeter so remarkable was his consistently transnational mode of working. From some of his earliest work, like *Salomé* (1971, shot in Lebanon) to his most famous films, *Nel Regno di Napoli* (*The Kingdom of Naples*, 1978) and *Palermo oder Wolfsburg* (*Palermo or Wolfsburg*, 1980), to his late films shot in France and Portugal, Schroeter worked in, and engaged with, distant cultures. The film that Schroeter made in the wake of *Palermo or Wolfsburg*, entitled *Tag der Idioten* (*Day of the*

*Idiots*, 1981), continued this deliberate engagement. Even the recent mini-wave of interest in Schroeter, this film—which won Schroeter one of his three Filmbänder in Gold—has not invited any sustained engagement. While *Day of the Idiots* extends his transnational inclinations with French lead Carole Bouquet (most famous for the James Bond film *For Your Eyes Only* [1981]), it also engages with global art cinema in another way: it manifests aspects of the anti-psychiatry movement important globally at that time. In the same year that his conversation with Foucault was published, Schroeter made a film focused on some of Foucault's key themes: discipline and normalization in mental health facilities. In exploring how mental health and especially institutionalization allegorize the young's struggles with modern society, *Day of the Idiots* demonstrates the influence of both Frederick Wiseman's *Titicut Follies* (1967) and especially Milos Forman's *One Flew over the Cuckoo's Nest* (1975). Taken together with *Titicut* and *Cuckoo's Nest*, *Day of the Idiots* confirms this emplotment of madness as metaphor for modern struggles in global art cinema of the late 1970s and early 1980s.

When we solicited contributions to *New German Cinema and Its Global Contexts*, we were still living in a different world—one that now seems little more than a distant memory. Since December 2018, when we launched this project, the COVID-19 pandemic changed life as we knew it, and Russia's invasion of Ukraine shook the world to its core. The biopolitical shock to our collective system also impacted the final shape of this volume. Many of our contributors, understandably, fell behind—as did we; some were ultimately unable to deliver their contributions, notwithstanding several extensions to the submission deadline; and sadly, one of our planned contributors, Thomas Elsaesser, passed away. Given Elsaesser's stature in the many fields in which he worked, this also felt like a sea change for German film studies and film studies in general. Rather than considering the absence of various contributions a shortcoming (in the end, it is of course the reader who has to judge this), we think that in these missing essays inheres the promise of additional exciting work to come—perhaps to be published in other essay collections and journal issues that might, we hope, step into the intellectual space we envision our volume will open up.

In his essay "Reconsidering New German Cinema," Eric Rentschler, to whom we purposefully give the last word in this volume in his capacity as one of the most influential scholars of German film and German studies in general, encouraged scholars to "introduce new intertexts, historical constellations, and theoretical incentives that might help us review this body of work and reassess the dominant wisdom about [New German Cinema]" (2012, 122). We believe that this volume is the first to have heeded this appeal by centering the question of how filmic and intellectual-political interlocutors from outside Germany have impacted the accomplishments of NGC and/or how the former can help us rethink what New German Cinema was and thus realize, perhaps, what it can still become as a film-historical category.

## Notes

1 In his useful transnational and comparative study, Geoffrey Nowell-Smith flags immediately that NGC came later than the other main European new waves and also Brazil's Cinema novo, "at the end of the period" (2008, 1).

2 Elsaesser writes that the "crystallization point, where the name 'New German Cinema' acted as both a label of identification and a mark of quality, was reached very quickly. Within the space of eighteen months all major film journals had published either analyses of the 'phenomenon' of the New German Cinema or in-depth studies of its leading figures" (1989, 291). The first wave of academic interest in NGC manifested itself in a series of special journal issues, including *Literature/Film Quarterly* 7.3 (1979), *Wide Angle* 3.4 (1980), *Quarterly Review of Film and Video* 5.2 (1980), *New German Critique* 24/25 (1981–82), and *Discourse* 6 (1983). During this time, the earliest books on the topic appeared as well. In addition to Sandford's book: Peter W. Jansen, *The New German Film* (Munich: Goethe-Institut, 1982); James Franklin, *New German Cinema: From Oberhausen to Hamburg* (New York: Twayne, 1983); Timothy Corrigan, *New German Film: The Displaced Image* (Bloomington: Indiana University Press, 1983; rev. ed., 1994); Klaus Phillips, *New German Filmmakers: From Oberhausen through the 1970s* (New York: Ungar, 1984); and Eric Rentschler, *West German Film in the Course of Time: Reflections on the Twenty Years since Oberhausen* (Bedford Hills,

NY: Redgrave, 1984). Also noteworthy is Renate Möhrmann, *Die Frau mit der Kamera: Filmemacherinnen in der Bundesrepublik Deutschland* (Munich: Hanser, 1980)—the first book focusing on the contributions female filmmakers made to NGC, which were "proportionately [greater than in] any other national cinema," as Elsaesser points out (quoted in Frieden et al. 1993, 3).

3 "WE HAVE LEGITIMATE FILM CULTURE IN GERMANY ONCE AGAIN" (Herzog 1988, 117).

4 "I know of no other 'national cinema' that has less support or interest from the people of that nation than the New German Film. . . . What good is a national cinema if it doesn't have a national audience?" Remarks made by Karl-Heinz Laabs, tone master and head of a Berlin-based commercial video and film production, in a conversation with John E. Davidson.

5 Even in the mid-1990s, when interest in NGC began to cool, this approach can still be observed in what is arguably the best study on Fassbinder, Thomas Elsaesser's *Fassbinder's Germany: History, Identity, Subject* (Amsterdam: Amsterdam University Press, 1996). And in the same year that Elsaesser's book on NGC appeared, Anton Kaes published his immensely influential *From Hitler to Heimat: The Return of History as Film*, in which he traces the changing role history plays in NGC from its early years, during which the filmmakers "polemically challenged the existing amnesia as well as the repression of the past," to later years, when films, with their greater emphasis on "silently suffering female main characters," focused more on "individual life stories and the history of everyday life (rather than political history)" (1989, 198).

6 Unless otherwise noted, all translations from German-language sources are ours.

7 German culture is, of course, not the only one in which the notion of "high art" (versus popular or "low" art) has played an important role in shaping national discourse. Yet the suspicion, if not opposition, to popular culture is deeply rooted in the German intelligentsia and is often associated with the Frankfurt School around Theodor Adorno and Max Horkheimer. It should be pointed out, however, that in the locus classicus of this anti–popular culture discourse (of which film would be a prime example), Horkheimer and Adorno's "Culture Industry" chapter, the authors do *not* simplistically denigrate "low art" and celebrate "high art"; rather, the target of their critique is the culture industry's *erasure of the difference* between the high and the low, as a result of which all cultural expressions become one undifferentiated mush. As they write, "The

split between ['light art' and 'serious art'] is itself the truth: it expresses at least the negativity of the culture which is the sum of both spheres. The antithesis can be reconciled least of all by absorbing light art into serious or vice versa. That, however, is what the culture industry attempts" (2022, 108). The field of cultural studies continues to stubbornly ignore this crucial part of their allegedly elitist dismissal of popular art.

8 It is important to understand the fundamental difference between the better-known *cinéma d'auteurs* and the *Autorenkino*. The former—famously developed in the pages of the *Cahiers du cinéma* and then popularized outside of France by Andrew Sarris in the United States and Peter Wollen in the pages of *Screen* in the UK—points in a *retrospective* gesture to a body of work by a filmmaker, locating in their oeuvre a unifying "signature." The latter, in contrast, is based on an *a priori* claim to authorship, even before a filmmaker has ever had the chance to develop an oeuvre. As Julia Knight helpfully summarizes a complex set of circumstances, "Unlike the French concept of 'auteur' which was applied to a director retrospectively on the basis of an existing oeuvre of work, the status of *Autor* was conferred on the film-makers both conceptually and institutionally *before* they had even made their first films" (2004, 28). To put it simply: young German filmmakers found themselves after 1966 in the odd position of having to declare themselves as authors *before* ever having made a feature film in order to receive state-aided subsidies to finance their projects. This is one of the main reasons why Elsaesser asserts that the *Autorenfilm* "does not name a particular genre of films or range of subjects, but is first of all a political concept" (1989, 303).

9 The books Rodek has in mind are Elsaesser's *New German Cinema: A History* (1989) and Norbert Grob, Hans Helmut Prinzler, and Eric Rentschler, eds., *Neuer Deutscher Film* (Leipzig: Reclam, 2012).

10 See Marco Abel and Jaimey Fisher, ed., *The Berlin School and Its Global Contexts: A Transnational Art Cinema* (Detroit: Wayne State University Press, 2018).

11 We have in mind here the volume of work, consistent over the last decades, on Werner Herzog, in both the United States and Germany.

12 Spils and Enke's *Zur Sache, Schätzchen* (*Go for It, Baby*, 1968) is one of the biggest box office hits of all time in German film history. It is all the more noteworthy, then, that the duo is rarely mentioned in discussions of NGC, just as Spils is virtually never included in discussions of West Germany's women's filmmaking. It is obvious that their historical exclusion from NGC has to do with the perceived lightness if not frivolity of their commercially successful films. As for Klick, even though Dominik Graf

and Johannes Sievert's cinema-historical documentary *Verfluchte Liebe deutscher Film* (*Doomed Love: A Journey through German Genre Films*, 2016) situates him alongside filmmakers such as Lemke and Thome, as Prager mentions, we think it is best not to think of him part of a group whose name was coined by the well-known Munich-based film critic Enno Patalas, who also co-founded West Germany's most important film journal, *Filmkritik*. For more on Lemke and the New Munich Group, see Abel's essay herein.

13 The relationship between so-called Young German Film and NGC is a point of debate among scholars. Elsaesser's contention that NGC does *not* hearken back as far as 1962 (that is, to the Oberhausen Manifesto) and instead is distinct, especially "in terms of the politics of film-making, as well as in terms of style and subject matter," from the Young German Film of the early to mid-1960s is well-nigh canonical (1989, 2). Davidson, in contrast, seeks to "avoid making this distinction [between Young German Film and NGC] precisely because it reinforces a false split between the political/economic and cultural/aesthetic sides of NGC" (1999, 36). Doing so allows him to draw attention to "the *Kulturpolitik* (cultural politics) of NGC, which," he claims, "remains relatively consistent from the beginning of the 1960s to the end of the 1980s" (36), and show how NGC, "as a realm of neocolonial knowledge production" (33), has "consistently [been] involved in re-creating an 'othered' German identity in order to integrate Germany into the [neocolonial] West more fully and resolidify the West in the face of continuing crises" (9).

14 The impact Eastern European émigrés had on West German cinema in the 1960s and 1970s might be worth a study in its own right. In addition to their influence on Borresholm's career, we can also think of Eastern European émigré filmmakers such as the Croat Vlado Kristl, whose anarchic attitude and experimental dispositions gradually turned him away from, if not against, some of the stalwarts of Young German Film such as Kluge and Peter Schamoni, with whom he initially connected at the 1962 International Short Film Festival Oberhausen; the Bulgarian Marran Gosov, whose presence in Schwabing (Munich) in the 1960s impacted the history of the New Munich Group; or the Czech Zbyněk Brynych, whose films *Engel, die ihre Flügel verbrennen* (*Angels with Burnt Wings*, 1970) and *Die Weibchen* (*Little Women*, 1970), a horror thriller with a transnational cast, as well as the episodes he shot for the West German television crime series *Der Kommissar* (four episodes between 1969 and 1970) and *Derrick* (thirty-seven episodes between 1975 and 1994), left a

mark on West German cinema and television that to this day has largely been ignored.

15 For an excellent account of this inherent cosmopolitanism of film schools, see also Madeleine Bernstorff, "Transnational Learning," *Rosa Mercedes* 3 (December 2021), https://www.unl.edu/english/graduate-directory. Bernstorff traces the various transnational aspects of the dffb from its early years (which Harun Farocki witnessed firsthand as a member of the school's first class) to the present.

16 Lending support to our claim that NGC has fallen off the contemporary critical radar more than any of the other new waves, the poll includes only one NGC film in its top one hundred: Fassbinder's *Angst essen Seele auf* (*Ali: Fear Eats the Soul*, 1974). *Aguirre, the Wrath of God* placed 118th, Wenders's late NGC films *Himmel über Berlin* (*Wings of Desire*, 1987) and *Paris, Texas* (1984) are tied for 185th.

17 See Caryl Flinn, *The New German Cinema: Music, History, and the Matter of Style* (Berkeley: University of California Press, 2004).

## Works Cited

Davidson, John E. 1999. *Deterritorializing the New German Cinema*. Minneapolis: University of Minnesota Press.

Elsaesser, Thomas. 1989. *New German Cinema: A History*. New Brunswick: Rutgers University Press.

Frieden, Sandra, et al., eds. 1993. *Gender and German Cinema: Feminist Interventions*, vol. 1: *Gender and Representation in New German Cinema*. Providence: Berg.

Galt, Rosalind, and Karl Schoonover. 2010. "Introduction: The Impurity of Art Cinema." In *Global Art Cinema: New Theories and Histories*, edited by Rosalind Galt and Karl Schoonover, 3–27. New York: Oxford University Press.

Gansera, Rainer. 2019. "Aufbruch ins Jetzt." *filmdienst.de*, October 21. https://www.filmdienst.de/artikel/38615/aufbruch-ins-jetzt-neuer-deutscher-film.

Gemünden, Gerd. 1994. "Introduction: Remembering Fassbinder in a Year of 13 Moons." *New German Critique* 63 (Autumn 1994): 3–9.

Hake, Sabine. 2013. "Contemporary German Film Studies in Ten Points." *German Studies Review* 36.3: 643–51.

Hansen, Miriam. 1993. "*Frauen und Film* and Feminist Film Culture in West Germany." In *Gender and German Cinema: Feminist Interventions*, vol. 2: *German Film History / German History on Film*, edited by Sandra Frieden et al., 293–98. Providence: Berg.

Herzog, Werner. 1988. "Tribute to Lotte Eisner." In *West German Filmmakers on Film: Visions and Voices*, edited by Eric Rentschler, 115–17. New York: Holmes & Meier.

Horkheimer, Max, and Theodor Adorno. 2002. "The Culture Industry: Enlightenment as Mass Deception." In *Dialectic of Enlightenment: Philosophical Fragments*, translated by Edmund Jephcott, 94–136. Stanford: Stanford University Press.

Kaes, Anton. 1989. *From Hitler to Heimat: The Return of History as Film*. Cambridge: Cambridge University Press.

Knight, Julia. 1992. *Women and the New German Cinema*. New York: Verso.

———. 2004. *New German Cinema: Images of a Generation*. New York: Wallflower.

Koepnick, Lutz. 2013. "German Art Cinema Now." *German Studies Review* 36.3 (October): 651–60.

Nowell-Smith, Geoffrey. 2008. *Making Waves: New Cinemas of the 1960s*. New York: Continuum.

Prinzler, Hans Helmut. 2019. "Was damals geschah." Foreword to *Aufbruch ins Jetzt: Der Neue Deutsche Film*, by Beat Presser, 10–21. Basel: edition achsensprung.

Rentschler, Eric. 1980. "Introduction: Critical Junctures since Oberhausen. West German Film in the Course of Time." *Quarterly Review of Film and Video* 5.2: 141–56.

———. 2012. "Reconsidering New German Cinema." In *Teaching Film*, edited by Lucy Fischer and Patrice Petro, 119–25. New York: Modern Language Association of America.

Riley, John. 2010. "Werner Schroeter: Flamboyant, Experimental German Filmmaker." *Independent*, June 7. https://www.independent.co.uk/news/obituaries/werner-schroeter-flamboyant-experimental-german-film-director-1993050.html.

Rodek, Hanns-Georg. 2019. "Zwanzig Jahre deutsches Kino gehören nicht einfach in die Tonne." *Die Welt*, June 6. https://www.welt.de/kultur/kino/article194880317/Der-Neue-Deutsche-Film-und-wie-er-vor-dem-Vergessen-gerettet-wird.html.

Sandford, John. 1982. *The New German Cinema*. New York: Da Capo.

von Zadow, Ingeborg. 1998. "Interview with Jutta Brückner: Feminist Filmmaking in Germany Today." In *Triangulated Visions: Women in Recent German Cinema*, edited by Ingeborg Majer O'Sickey and Ingeborg von Zadow, 95–102. Albany: State University of New York Press.

# 1

# (DON'T) LOOK BACK ON *SYLVIE*

## Klaus Lemke, D. A. Pennebaker, and the "Lightness" of a "Left without Leftism"

*Marco Abel*

> Hawks had shown us how narration itself—that is, how a film is being told—has to become the real adventure of a film. Then Pennebaker and *Dont Look Back* appeared, and suddenly the only goal was to get as close as possible to the subjective experiences of the protagonists—without care for any story.
>
> —Klaus Lemke

## Klaus Lemke and New German Cinema

At one moment in their extensive conversation about Klaus Lemke's oeuvre, Peter Przygodda (best known for his work as editor of numerous Wim Wenders films), Martin Müller (who handled sound on some one hundred German films, including many by Wenders), and Christopher Roth (director of, among other films, *Baader* [2002]) briefly address how Lemke's films in the early 1970s were viewed by the West German film establishment. "In 1970/71," a time that was "politically dark" and that saw the emergence of "the seriously socially conscious red flag films," as Müller puts it, critics accused Lemke's films of being "frivolous," "escapist," and "unserious" (Przygodda, Müller, and Roth 2006, 64). Müller and Przygodda, who both frequently worked with Lemke, recall that whenever they arrived on a Wenders film set or that of another New German Cinema

(NGC) stalwart, Volker Schlöndorff, after having just completed a Lemke production, they had to endure a belittling attitude ("You and your Lemke-gang") precisely because of the perceived frivolity of Lemke's films, which did not fit in with the serious, politically conscious attitude that dominated NGC at the time. Interestingly, however, Roth—the youngest of the three interlocutors and editor of Lemke's *Zockerexpress* (1988)—responds to Przygodda's comment about how they were greeted on NGC film sets by pointing out that Wenders "is hardly [a] profound political filmmaker either," to which Müller adds: "Nicht unbedingt politisch, aber uns fehlte der Trübsal des Lebens" ("Not necessarily political, but we lacked the sorrow of life"). Wenders, in other words, may not have been the most profoundly political of the NGC filmmakers, but at least his films oozed a kind of existential dread and the very *Trübsal* characterizing his films' (male) protagonists; and the heavy weight of this melancholic mood, it is implied, lend Wenders's films at least a veneer of gravitas and political importance. In sharp contrast to Wenders's films (not to mention to those by the more overtly politically minded NGC filmmakers such as Rainer Werner Fassbinder, Schlöndorff, or the feminist directors emerging from the dffb such as Helma Sanders-Brahms and Helke Sander), Lemke's films were, in Przygodda's words, characterized by a "leichte Schulter" (meaning, to paraphrase the Beatles' "Hey Jude," a shoulder that does not have to carry the world's weight): they were made without pretending to have a serious message, political or otherwise.

What this moment in their conversation intimates is an intriguing distinction between two kinds of "political affect": on the one hand, one defined by heaviness, seriousness, earnestness, and existential sorrow and, on the other hand, one characterized by a sense of lightness, triviality, frivolity, and nonchalance. Film historically, the former is inextricably associated with the West German political left of the "long 1968," not least with the NGC, whereas the latter has long been denounced (by the so-called political left and the film historiography that would come to codify its cinematic articulation) as apolitical or unpolitical, if not as politically right-wing.[1] My hypothesis is that this particular affective parsing of the political (and, specifically, of the meaning of the political "left") not only prevented film critics at the time from considering Lemke (among others) as part of the then still emerging NGC but also, in the long run, caused a film-historiographical erasure of Lemke (and others) from official film history.[2] What follows is, to be sure, partly speculative, as I seek to introduce the possibility that the political affect we find in Lemke's films can be productively considered as that of a "left without leftism," which is to say a critique of the "political left" from a decidedly *affectively* left point of view, one that, borrowing from Enno Patalas, I suggest calling the "aesthetic left."[3]

To introduce this idea—a fuller development of which will have to wait for another time—I will focus on what is in my view one of the greatest West German films of the early 1970s, one that in its sheer *lightness* has no equal in the NGC context: Lemke's seventh feature, *Sylvie* (1973). Seemingly ironically, at the very moment when critics in New York City started noticing films made by newly emerging filmmakers from West Germany who clearly exhibited an affinity for US culture, Lemke goes unnoticed—and this even though *Sylvie* not only can be said to offer some of the most remarkable images of Manhattan of the time but also is among the earliest West German films partly shot in the United States, beating Wenders (*Alice in den Städten* [*Alice in the Cities*, 1974]) and Werner Herzog (*Stroszek*, 1977) to the punch.[4] Yet that Lemke went unnoticed by the New York City intelligentsia is not surprising considering that the film critics who would soon coin the "New German Cinema" label zoomed in precisely on what Herzog would eventually proudly proclaim as these films' "legitimacy"—a newly legitimate, and legitimated, (West) German cinema by which an interested audience abroad was offered a window on a new, post-1968 attitude toward German history and its (contemporary) people.[5] Conversely, it was precisely the perceived absence of legitimacy in the sense just defined that prevented most West German film critics from giving Lemke's films serious attention, as a result of which, I suspect, the cultural arms of the newly elected left-liberal West German government were not inclined to help promote his films abroad.[6] In hindsight, it is possible to recognize in this omission of Lemke—who, as Przygodda holds, was to many West German viewers actually better known than Wenders[7]—from the left-liberal establishment's efforts to redress West Germany's image abroad as one of the earliest moments of rupture between this anarchic filmmaker and the state-subvented (West) German filmmaking culture that he would subsequently denounce as "feudalistic state cinema" ("feudalistisches staatskino"), a "Stalinist art film system" ("stalinistisches Filmkunstsystem") (quoted in Suchsland 2012), and a "state cinema cuddled into helplessness" ("BIS ZUR HILFLOSIGKEIT VERHÄTSCHELTES STAATSKINO").[8] And given the important role Alexander Kluge played in establishing this subvention system, Lemke's polemics would often refer to this stalwart of canonical New German Cinema: "That Alexander Kluge's prayers in the 1970s for subvention of the 'cultural good film' were answered de facto meant the annexation [of West German cinema] to the state-run cinema of the GDR. Even though Kluge merely intended to provide his Schwabing-boys, whose films no one wanted to see, a villa in Tuscany. But aside from this: I LOVE KLUGE" (*Süddeutsche Zeitung* 2020).[9] But Lemke's near-erasure from (West) German film history of the 1970s now also affords us the chance to reimagine what NGC could have been and, perhaps, still can be—*can be* in the sense of this volume's overall effort to revisit NGC from the point of view of its global contexts in order to rethink, or even redefine, an era of West German filmmaking that once was hailed as the last great European new wave but that today is arguably the least known.

To focalize this discussion, I will look back at *Sylvie*, a beautiful yet woefully underappreciated (and critically neglected) film. Taking my cue from something Lemke shared with me in a conversation, I will filter this revisionary glance through D. A. Pennebaker's seminal direct cinema (or cinéma vérité) film *Dont Look Back* (1967) because it bridges Lemke's films from the 1960s such as *48 Stunden bis Acapulco* (*48 Hours to Acapulco*, 1967) and his short films such as *Kleine Front* (1965) and *Henker Tom* (1966), which are grounded in his obsession with Howard Hawks's films and Jean-Luc Godard's *À bout de souffle* (*Breathless*, 1960) and the films he started making in the early 1970s, including *Sylvie*, about which Thomas Groh once enthused: how "breathtaking and infinitely exhilarating, how young, how free, how agile this almost forty-year-old film is still today, how it jumps right into the promise of a free life" (Groh 2012). Concurring with Groh's exuberant assessment, Dominik Graf adds that *Sylvie* not only exemplifies the ZDF's *Kleine Fernsehspiel* of the 1970s "more beautifully than it has ever been: light, melancholic, loving" (2009, 41), but also can be considered an example of direct cinema (or cinéma vérité), a movement of which Lemke "was, in a way, the German branch" ("er war sozusagen die deutsche Dependance") (Graf 2010).[10] *Sylvie*, as I will argue, implements what Lemke learned from Pennebaker and ended up providing viewers with a vision of life that, rather than being escapist, expresses a more intensively imagined engagement with the present—something that the past-obsessed NGC and its supporters were perhaps not quite ready for.[11]

## *Dont Look Back*

Much has been written about Pennebaker's landmark film in which he follows Bob Dylan on his 1965 tour in England, just when the musician famously (and controversially) was replacing his acoustic guitar and protest songs/folk music roots with an electric guitar to reinvent himself as a rock singer of increasingly indecipherable lyrics. Yet the enduring appeal of and influence exerted by *Dont Look Back*, which saw its theatrical release only in 1967, may be as much due to Dylan's undeniable charisma as to the director's instinctual receptiveness to the artist's desire to "[act] out his own life," as Pennebaker once put it (quoted in Levin 1971, 240).[12] To act out one's life means to *perform* it, and Keith Beattie, in his book on the filmmaker, convincingly argues that in refusing the "separation of front/onstage and backstage and the 'dual selves' implied by this separation" (2011, 13), *Dont Look Back* ultimately insists that "*the performed self is the real or authentic self*" (14). This rejection of an "authentic self"—the assertion that any "real self" is the effect of a performance, that is: that truth is performative—flew in the face of not only the values of the era's left-liberal folk music community but also the conventions of a documentary filmmaking tradition in which privileged access to the "private" (backstage) side of one's subject is supposed to reveal the truth of the public self. The film's refusal to cater to these values and conventions formally manifests itself in its denaturing, if not replacement, of a documentary's traditional emphasis on telling "by the process of 'showing'" (Beattie 2011, 14–15)—that is, in the film's "experiment in formal emancipation" that "exhibits a typically counter-cultural disregard for formalized language" (Saunders 2007, 60, 59). These critical assessments of Pennebaker's innovations are echoed by the director, who claims that *Dont Look Back* "is not documentary at all by my standards. It throws away almost all its information and becomes purposively kind of abstract and tries to be musical rather than informational" (quoted in Levin 1971, 243).

Perhaps the most radical example from *Dont Look Back* demonstrating the above is the (in)famous "song contest" between Dylan and Donovan.

From the film's start, Donovan's name is present, first when Dylan, noticing the Scottish folk singer's name in a newspaper, exclaims, "Donovan? Who is this Donovan?" and subsequently when Dylan's entourage seems to egg him on, perhaps with the (good-natured) intention of spurring on a rivalry between the two young artists. In any case, the film's structure arguably primes viewers to expect a sort of "high noon" moment between the two by the time we finally get to their face-to-face meeting in Dylan's suite at the Savoy Hotel in London. As throughout the film, Pennebaker deviates in this scene from documentary conventions in that he neither provides the names of the people present in the room nor offers directorial commentary to set the stage and possibly also to counter the impression given by the film's structure that Dylan was merely waiting for the opportunity to upstage Donovan—which would certainly be in line with some of Dylan's behavior we have witnessed up until this moment.[13] Instead, Pennebaker lets his camera roll fly-on-the-wall style as Donovan begins to play "To Sing for You." Pennebaker shoots Donovan's performance from an unobtrusive medium, slightly low-angle position, yet quickly pans to audience members in the room as they respond to the (somewhat shyly delivered) performance, whether laughing with apparent encouragement, as folk musician Derroll Adams does, or nasally proclaiming, "Yeah, that's a good song, man," as Dylan, wearing sunglasses, does, leaning forward in his chair and smiling. After focusing for a few more bars on Donovan earnestly delivering a song dripping with calm, warm, friendly, and rather insipid sentiment, the camera pans back to Dylan, as Pennebaker must have noticed Dylan's leg moving leisurely in rhythm to the tune (the camera tilts downward slightly to foreground this), holding the shot for the next thirty-five seconds, thereby allowing us to focus on Dylan's subjective experience of listening to Donovan, before the camera pans back to the latter just in time to mark the performance's ending.

After some applause while the camera quickly pans from Donovan to Adams (who shouts, "Well done!") and back to Donovan as Dylan takes the guitar from him, Donovan asks Dylan to play "It's All over Now, Baby Blue," a song from his recently released record *Bringing It All Back Home* (1965), which marked Dylan's transformation "from a polite leading light of the marginal folk scene into an incendiary figure in the cultural mainstream" (Bowcock 2016). At just this moment—and to me this remains one of the more remarkable moments in both music and film history—Pennebaker zooms in onto an extreme close-up of Donovan's face, looking screen left and talking with Dylan about the tuning. The younger singer clearly admires Dylan, and we might speculate that he is likely requesting this song precisely because he recognizes that its affect is diametrically opposed to that of his own song: cool, sneering, aggressive, yet expressed with innovative lyrical wit rather than with the simplistic metaphors and rhymes of his own ditty. Knowing what he is about to subject himself to and asking for it anyway, Donovan is essentially (albeit unconsciously) setting himself up for a moment that would (justly or not) end up defining his career, notwithstanding his protestations to the contrary. For if one recalls anything about his career (unless one is a Donovan fan), it is the *impression* one gets from watching what follows that Donovan emotionally and intellectually experiences Dylan's ensuing performance with a complex mixture of awe and admiration, on the one hand, and humiliation and a sneaking sense of inferiority and defeat, on the other.

Like a lion waiting in the tall grass to pounce on prey, Dylan, after first double-checking ("You wanna hear that tune"?), proceeds to deliver—all the more forcefully in its cocky nonchalance—the "most toxic of strummed kiss-offs" that, unlike Donovan's unthreatening sentimentality, exudes "not a snowball's chance in hell of reconciliation," as the song was once memorably described in *Q* magazine (quoted in "Bob Dylan's Best Songs" 2015). Whereas Pennebaker's camera remained in a medium shot while recording Donovan, it quickly zooms in from a medium shot of Dylan strumming his guitar to an extreme close-up of Dylan's face, as if intuiting what would become one of the most iconic moments not just of the film but also in all of rock music history: Dylan commandingly gazing around the room, nodding and smiling, fully aware of the genius of "Baby Blue"—indeed, of it effecting, right then and there, an incorporeal transformation in the body of popular music, unequivocally declaring that from now on he would be a *rock*, not a folk, singer.[14] And this incorporeal transformation is rendered physically sensible precisely in Donovan's face, onto which Pennebaker intuitively pans right at the end of Dylan's first intoning of the song's refrain.[15] We see Donovan taking a deep drag on his cigarette, holding his breath (one wonders whether he ever exhaled) as he first slightly smiles and then visibly clenches his jaw. After a medium close-up of Adams followed by a medium shot of Donovan, the camera zooms back in on a close-up of Dylan's face as he completes one of his

FIGURE 1.1. *Dont Look Back*—Dylan taking down Donovan. (Screengrab)

masterpieces, delivered with the sex-drugs-and-rock-and-roll attitude of a *rock* star rather than the pedagogical yet conciliatory manner of a left-liberal folk singer. Dylan now turns his head toward Donovan, directly addressing him with his eyes and (let's say warmly) laughing to punctuate the song's end as the camera zooms back out to a medium shot before immediately panning to and zooming in on another extreme close-up of Donovan's face: it's all over now, indeed!

It is hard to believe that this scene was *not* a setup—that it did not result from a conspiracy between Pennebaker and Dylan to cash in on the film's "narrative" arc relating to Donovan that commenced early on. And yet, by all accounts, there was nothing staged about it, nor did the two protagonists perceive there to be any tensions between them (at least according to their public statements in response to questions about this moment). Yet, while it may very well be the case that Dylan did not intend to demonstrate that his talent was far superior to Donovan's, and while it may also be true that Donovan might not have been cognizant of just what this moment might mean for him, it seems difficult to deny the camera's objectively rendered visual evidence of Donovan's subjectively experienced affect. And I think it is precisely this aspect of the film that influenced Lemke. Pennebaker insisted that he "never gave Dylan any kind of directions" (quoted in Levin 1971, 259). Yet not giving directions does not mean an absence of staging.[16] As the director put it himself: "That's just a thing I know how to do—construct a dramatic thing in which I'll find a way to make Dylan break through. But it's Dylan that breaks through, not me. I just do the thing to make it work" (261). Put differently, the thing Pennebaker knows how to do is *framing*, which according to Ilona Hongisto's innovative rethinking of documentary filmmaking "is the performative practice with which documentary cinema participates in and contributes to the real as process" (Hongisto 2015, 12).[17]

While there are many moments in *Dont Look Back* that one could point to, in the end it seems there is none better than its most famous one to exemplify what Pennebaker meant when stating "What I want to tell you about is the mood, I guess, not the information" (quoted in Levin 1971, 243). His lens, or his way of framing, we might say, abstracts the informational clichés from the reality in front of it to render sensible a pure image of reality—but one whose purity is permeated by artifice (from the always self-consciously performing Dylan to the technologically innovative camera Pennebaker used, having jury-rigged it precisely in order to be as imperceptible and to appear as nonprofessional as possible).[18] What Pennebaker exposes us to, then, is neither Dylan's authentic intention (we have no access to it) nor Donovan's authentic interpretation of what transpired (ditto) but rather this moment's authentic mood, its affective force. Or, in Lemke's words cited in the essay's epigraph, through how he stages the scene, Pennebaker presents us with the subjective experience of his protagonists.

## *Sylvie*

After a series of short films and his first features, *48 Hours to Acapulco* and *Negresco****—Eine tödliche Affaire* (*Negresco*, 1968), which, like his short films, were still impacted by his love for genre cinema, Lemke took a new turn with two German television films, *Mein schönes kurzes Leben* (1970) and *Liebe, so schön wie Liebe* (1971), both of which featured Sylvie Winter, who at the time was Lemke's girlfriend (they broke up prior to shooting *Sylvie*, however). Winter was one of West Germany's most famous photo models, often seen nude on the cover of mass-market magazines such as

*Stern* and *Quick* (a fact that *Sylvie* repeatedly, and humorously, plays with, each time only to have Sylvie deny that it is her nude image we see on the cover of *Stern*); and together with the even more famous model Uschi Obermaier, she was for a while "the girlfriend of the left" because both were open to experimentation, "to trying things out, to testing how one's own life could unfold in the most exciting way. That would make the two the perfect girls for the left at the time. Two girls without well-defined politics, from a different, attractive world" (Philippi 2006, 151, 152).[19] With the New Munich Group (NMG) mostly having run its course by 1970, Lemke seemed to be looking for a new direction, one that would lead him to making less constructed films than those he had made under the influence of Hawks and Hollywood genre cinema, always filtered through the lens of early Godard.[20] For his films, this primarily meant a further reduction of concern with plot. Whereas *Acapulco* and *Negresco* as well as his "RAF" film, *Brandstifter* (1969), were still organized around recognizable storylines (even if those would have hardly passed muster from a classical Hollywood perspective), the black-and-white *Mein schönes kurzes Leben* and especially the colorful *Liebe, so schön wie Liebe* are essentially films that subordinate plot to the filming of situations and most of all the people themselves. This strategy would become the hallmark of *Rocker* (1972), a film that today is recognized as one of the best (West) German films of the time (and beyond) and that Lemke views as transformative for himself. As he puts it, though "we always wanted to get rid of this intellectual thing[,] I only managed to do so with *Rocker*—but then for real and for good" (quoted in Abel 2019, 310). In Lemke's view, these real-life rockers "could not do anything wrong [because they] were the real Americans," whereas "*we* were no real guys [but were rather] already the dream of a dream of American cinema" (302, 307). With *Rocker*, that is, Lemke turned his back on staging pre-planned ideas, albeit not least out of necessity, since the rockers did essentially just do their own thing, something Lemke and his team did their best to capture and, whenever an opportunity arose, infuse with an idea here and there in order to lend what he was filming a semblance of form.

In this regard, *Sylvie*—telling the story of the jet-setting and food-loving photo model Sylvie falling (sort of) in love with the temporarily cab-driving sailor Paul (Paul Lys), who in the end returns to sea, leaving Sylvie behind—was a step back, as Roth argues in his conversation with Müller and Przygodda (Przygodda, Müller, and Roth 2006, 66), for *Sylvie* is more staged and controlled by Lemke than both its predecessor and its successor, *Paul* (1974). Yet from my perspective, notwithstanding the undeniable greatness of both *Rocker* and *Paul*, it is *Sylvie* that opened an entirely new horizon for (West) German cinema precisely because of its lightness of touch—a palpable degree of nonchalance regarding subject matter and the filming itself that is thoroughly singular and sets *Sylvie* apart from *Rocker* and *Paul*. The greatness of the latter two, *Milieustudien* of sorts, resides in how they capture a way of speaking that must have struck West German television viewers as unusual at the time, given the country's television and film productions' penchant for having actors mostly speak *Hochdeutsch* (High German) and act as if on a theater stage.[21] And this uncommonly colloquial use of language prominently features in *Sylvie* as well, especially thanks to the presence of Paul Lys, a former sailor who, like everyone else in the film—Sylvie, her real-life photographers Guido Mangold and Werner Bokelberg as well as Del Negro, with whom Sylvie shoots in New York City—more or less plays himself.[22] But whereas *Rocker* and *Paul* are primarily in love with a fresh use of German language—that is, these films are about an auditory love affair between Lemke and his subjects—*Sylvie* is a love affair with *looking*. It is a film about encounters that transpire because of and in the acts of looking performed by both the people themselves and Lemke's camera (handled by Lothar Elias Stickelbrucks). And through how this looking is staged, as well as through how the people looked at both each other and the world, Lemke renders sensible their subjective experiences for us, thereby also exposing us to a different idea about living, about life—an idea affectively embodied in *how* Lemke, as he likes to put it, confronts the "concentrated irrationality of life with even more irrationality in film" ("der geballten Irrationalität des Lebens noch etwas Irrationaler im Film daherzukommen").[23]

Differently put, with *Sylvie*, Lemke implements the insight, gleaned from *Dont Look Back*, that it is not necessary to be smarter than his films. As Lemke memorably puts Pennebaker's importance for his career, he "liberated us from the prison of a wrong life. The wrong life was the fact that we thought we would have to be smarter than our films."[24] It would be a mistake, however, to think that the result of this would be the mere capturing of life "as it is": to wit, a naïve realism. Indeed, Hans C. Blumenberg argues that notwithstanding "all the authenticity of language . . . and milieu, Lemke is nevertheless not a realist director, nor does he apparently want to be one. Almost always the cinema fantasies of his protagonists (which are of course also his own) prevail, and the figures escape from the everyday into a beautiful dream world. Lemke films are about the truth of dreams" (1979). Of the many examples one could give from *Sylvie* to evidence this logic, I'd like to discuss three: the first occurs shortly after Sylvie and Paul meet in Munich; the second consists of the film's entire middle section, set in New York City (which I will discuss last); and the last is the very end, when Sylvie and Paul part ways at the dock in Hamburg.[25]

### *Girl Meets Boy; or, The Lightness of Longing for Longing*

After Sylvie gorges herself on snails and champagne at a stuffy restaurant in which both waiters and patrons appear predictably scandalized by the model's charmingly unselfconscious disregard for bourgeois behavioral codes of fine dining, she gradually wakes up on the backseat of Paul's cab as he is studying a map to figure out how to get her home to Grünwald. At this moment, the shot/reverse shot sequence does not yet stage their gazes as an encounter, for Lemke films this interaction from an objective point of view. (Likewise, when Sylvie hails Paul with an unladylike whistle a few moments earlier, Lemke does not give us a point of view shot from either of their perspectives.) However, once Paul asks a group of bikers for directions inside a snack bar, one of the most terrific "falling in love" scenes in German film history occurs—albeit one that is noticeably characterized by the very *asymmetry* of feelings that will characterize their relationship for the rest of the film. As Paul interacts with the bikers (echoes of *Rocker*, Lys's first appearance in a Lemke film), the camera slowly zooms through the group and in on Sylvie, who nonchalantly and with great appetite messily scarfs down a burger (has there ever been a film in which a beautiful female lead is seen to eat with as much abandon as *Sylvie*?), thereby humorously undercutting the sex appeal with which this male-gaze voyeuristic zoom-in-on-close-up would otherwise imbue her. In other words, this is not Paul's gaze but the camera's. When the camera cuts to a reverse shot of Paul, his gaze, when he notices her across the room, is impossible to read, yet it is not that of a would-be lover. But when the camera cuts back to Sylvie in a medium shot, we notice her taking increasing interest in what she sees. For several seconds, the shot remains motionless, showing Sylvie slightly repositioning her posture, before it slowly zooms in on her, only to stop on an extreme close-up of her face as she cracks a smile: it is as if Sylvie—both the character and the real person, the distinction between them indiscernible—cannot help but laugh at the very idea that she is a sex symbol. At this moment, Lemke cuts again to a reverse shot, this time on a close-up of Paul, who is mostly obscured by one of his interlocutors but not enough to prevent us from registering him now taking greater notice of Sylvie. The ensuing reverse shot, a medium close-up of her, is almost

FIGURE 1.2. *Sylvie*—Sylvie meets Paul. (Screengrab)

comical in that it evokes the cliché of the kind of softcore sex films popular in West Germany at the time, with Sylvie (who, according to Lemke, loved to eat in real life) demonstratively licking her burger before taking another bite, then checking whether her actions continue to capture Paul's attention.[26] They do, as we see in the next reverse shot. Something appears to be happening between the two—a sensation furthered by Lemke's first use of the Rolling Stones' accordion ballad "Back Street Girl" (1967) on the soundtrack.

The scene ends with lighthearted banter between them (Sylvie: "I gradually get the impression you are a bit slow." Paul: "I'll smack you!") and him carrying her back to his cab after she passed out when playfully trying to hit him. But rather than taking advantage of Sylvie's intoxication, he drives her to his mother's apartment, where Sylvie wakes up the next morning, overhearing him spinning a sailor's yarn to (truthfully) convince his disapproving mother that the sexual implications of her question of whether he "picked up a drunk girl on the street" are entirely unwarranted. Paul's denial ("But Mama!") in fact rang true for the extra-diegetic Paul as well: according to Lemke, Lys never considered Winter sexy (Philippi 2006, 153). Indeed, it seems that Lemke picked Lys as Winter's partner for this very reason: going after a dynamic, he chose a dyad with a particular potential for tension, then pushed them together to observe the results, intuitively shifting the tension back and forth, very much as Pennebaker responded to the dynamics resulting from the sundry tensions between Dylan and his interlocutors, not least but by no means exclusively Donovan.

This boy-meets-girl moment is emotionally as real as any in cinema, yet it is also staged as a cinematic fantasy, a performance. In the restaurant scene, we see Sylvie eating with an almost childlike relish that gives us the (illusory) impression that we are present with the "real" Sylvie—un-self-mediated for the (male) gaze, as an enthusiastic consumer (of food), rather than an object to be consumed by the (male) gaze.[27] This lends this moment a texture of "reality," of intimacy, with her as a real person who is not acting or seducing. Her beginning to eat seductively for Paul's gaze, then, signifies a turn: she makes herself into a performer, and we see that this happens precisely because she takes an interest in Paul (in however abstract a way). As is the case during the three lengthy photo shoot sessions (the "Daisy Duck" shoot in Hamburg, the sequences on the streets of New York City, and the wedding dress shoot in Frankfurt, with Paul a reluctant and not overly competent aide to Mangold) that interrupt the nearly nonexistent plot development, she commands the attention of the male gaze both diegetically and extra-diegetically, yet she does so precisely because of her "girl-next-door" aura, which is as much a performance as Dylan's offstage behavior in *Dont Look Back*, albeit of a different, considerably more muted kind. In a way, it is Lemke's camera and use of the Rolling Stones' music that turn her into the equivalent of a rock star, with Paul as her interested yet always slightly distant groupie. But whereas in the photoshoot scenes Sylvie is performing professionally—she has products to sell—here she is performing only for Paul's eyes: she does not have anything to sell. Rather, what the camera registers in the apparent, albeit nevertheless illusory, slide of registers in how she eats (from a "real" unselfconscious eating that carries over to the first shots of her eating the burger to a clearly performative eating) is that she is undergoing an incorporeal transformation *in Paul's eyes*, from a drunken cab fare to a strange but glamourous woman who looks (but does not exactly behave) like a movie star. She seems to appear to him, at this moment, as if in a dream—but not a dream he has for himself, one that he wants to realize in his real life; rather, it is as if he enters *her dream* of living a normal life, free from photo model glamour, and is willing to step outside himself to explore this dream, to look around in it, to observe, without ever truly "buying" into it.[28] Which is also to say: the film itself communicates that the two are never likely to become a couple because it does not stage this moment as a love-at-first-sight one. Nevertheless, it makes us fall in love with the *idea* of their love—perhaps not least also because we witness the "real" Sylvie breaking through in how she eats in these two scenes.

It is in this manner that the film presents its (West) German viewers of the time with a specter of a different life—one that the film renders sensible by refusing any psychologizing of its protagonists, explanations for their behaviors, or attempts to convince us that their actions are realistic, let alone "right" or meaningful. Instead, we are presented with the realism of a dream that is anchored in the real world of real people who act out one possible version of their lives. This is neither a world, as is the case in Wenders's films, where the (especially male) characters are driven by the urge to find themselves—to discover who they are—nor one in which they are oedipally trying to reject the (post-)fascistic (West) German society into which they were born and in which dreams of a better world are always shot through with a pedagogical and moral dogmatism that blocks these protagonists' affective lives so much that neither they nor the films themselves are capable of affecting viewers with a vision of a desirable world. It is through the absence of a leftist "heavy" critique of the state of affairs that *Sylvie* offers an affectively palpable (left-)utopian sensation that is not merely escapism precisely because of how these real people fabulate just ever so slightly refracted versions of themselves—that is, because of the "becoming of the real character[s] when [they start] to 'make fiction', when [they enter] into 'the flagrant offence of making up legends' and so [contribute] to the invention of [their] people" (Deleuze 1989, 150). Whereas many NGC films of the time emphasized the need to juxtapose truth to the lies of the parents (fathers), *Sylvie* (similarly to yet also different from *Rocker* and *Paul*) refuses this dialectic—one predicated on positing a preexisting truth that, however, "necessarily expresses the dominant ideas or the point of view," if not of the colonizer, as Deleuze holds in relation to a filmmaker such as Pierre Perrault (150), then of those defining the terms of cultural and political discourse and, in a way, delimiting what lives are and are not permissible to imagine.

Importantly, Deleuze's propositions regarding the "powers of the false" (fabulation) are offered in the context of a discussion of the "direct cinema of Cassavetes and Shirley Clarke, . . . 'the cinema of the lived' of Pierre Perrault, [and] the '*cinéma-vérité*' of Jean Rouch" (1989, 150). Deleuze highlights that this cinematic invention frees fiction from a model of truth that has penetrated it like a parasite and in so doing frees cinema to "rediscover the pure and simple *story-telling function* which is opposed to this model [of truth]" (150). While I am not suggesting that *Sylvie* is of a kind with the cinema of either Perrault or Rouch—the contexts are obviously dramatically different—I submit that in its own context *Sylvie* (and Lemke's cinema in general) can be productively seen through Deleuze's notion of "minor cinema," not least because what it opposes to "fiction is not the real" but the "story-telling function of the poor, in so far as it gives the false the power which makes it into a memory, a legend, a monster." In so doing, such cinema grasps less "the identity of a character, whether real *or* fictional, through his objective and subjective aspects" but rather "the becoming of the real character" (150). When the real Sylvie and Paul, enacting refracted versions of themselves, become other to themselves at the snack bar, they merge the before and after of their transformation in this passage from one corporeal state to another—that is, when they begin "to tell stories without ever being fictional." The director himself, Deleuze crucially continues, "for his part becomes another when there are 'interposed', in this way, real characters, who wholly replace his own fictions by their own story-telling" (150). The snack bar scene is the start of the real Paul Lys telling stories that are clearly very much his own (or slightly improvised versions thereof), which captivate the real Sylvie Winter playing a version of herself, just as the real Sylvie playing a refracted version of herself puzzles, yet in so doing fascinates, the real Paul playacting a version of himself.

For example, as he is driving Sylvie to the airport, the reality of his excitement while telling her his stories of drunken sailor debauchery in the United States is palpable precisely in *how* Paul talks: whatever Lemke's instructions might have been, how (if not also what) Paul speaks would hardly have occurred without the real Paul Lys performatively breaking through his character, indeed without his "becoming of the real character"—something Lemke's camera cinematically enhanced through a fortuitous moment of technical imperfection: as we listen to Paul underlining his excitement with giddy laughter and an emphatic "Du machst dir kein Bild" ("You can't picture this"), the shot is so washed out that we quite literally cannot see them.

FIGURE 1.3. *Sylvie*—"You can't picture this." (Screengrab)

Then, to the tune of the Stones' 1967 song "Connection" ("I can't make no connection . . ."), the scene cuts to the two at Munich airport, where Paul excitedly continues to fabulate while Lemke energetically shoots their hurried walk toward the gate as if they were rock stars: "There you hear the Rolling Stones and one is positively in the middle of it all. . . . And then, two hundred women. I tell you: that was something! Two hundred women in the middle of the venue. Outside they grilled cows and inside they fucked." While it is possible that this is scripted, it very much *feels* like the real Paul speaking: it is his language, his way of speaking. And at this moment, having arrived at his story's conclusion, which Sylvie, who is trying to catch her plane, barely registers, they stop, and *he* kisses her. It is the film's sole moment when Paul shows such a sign of affection for or interest in her. (In the film's penultimate scene on the train, for instance, Paul, who according to Lemke was always a "Top-Alkoholiker" ["serious alcoholic"], prefers to get plastered instead of embracing Sylvie's amorous hopes.)[29] But: is this not Paul acting as if he were in a dream, exploring how it would feel to really be Sylvie's boyfriend and to live a glamorous life?

Yet Paul is ultimately not swayed by this vision: while he does not judge Sylvie's life, he instead simply asserts (at film's end) that he belongs on the ship setting out for open waters. The truth he utters at this moment is itself performative (and thus transformative): he performs the authenticity of the sailor's life *as* his life and in so doing becomes akin to a lone western hero who, having transformed the community he temporarily entered, leaves it behind (Lemke's love for westerns by Hawks et al. is well documented). But his performance, which is real in the same way Dylan's performance in Pennebaker's film is real, is indistinguishable and constitutive of his "true" being; it is also performative in that it effects in Sylvie tears that in their glycerinian, artificially rendered glory suggest a utopian moment inhering in the affect of longing itself: Sylvie—as real person cum protagonist cum real person—longing for an intense sensation of the lightness of longing itself, rather than for the heaviness of longing for a specific object of desire that could truly fulfill this longing but that one can never have. This lightness inhering in a longing for longing itself—an intransitive desire—is precisely what is largely absent from the (West) German cinema of the time, as it is dominated by a transitive yearning *for* something very specific, for the realization of a preexisting idea. This, I think, is precisely what renders this intransitive form of longing radical: because it

FIGURE 1.4. *Sylvie*—Sylvie and Paul say goodbye at Hamburg Harbor. (Screengrab)

is contentless (and thus affectively "light"), it is not even reducible to that which in many ways intensifies Sylvie's feeling for Paul so much that she temporarily believes she is really in love with him.

### *New York, New York (with Munich on Her Mind)*

This intensifier is New York City. As Graf perspicaciously observes, *Sylvie* shows, among other things, "how a little bit of affection transforms into what is supposed to be love in the absence of the other. Only in New York does Sylvie fall in love with the man who kissed her in Munich and who she hopes will wait for her there" (2009, 43). Crucially, however, it is Sylvie's subjective experience of the sheer energy of New York that makes her change her mind and, contrary to her answer to Paul's inquiry at the airport whether she will come back—"no"—she decides to fly back to Germany with a stuffed animal as a present for Paul, who is waiting to pick her up, after Del (and Lemke) push things a bit too far with their guerilla-like staging of photoshoot scenes on the streets of New York as they gradually head northward from Manhattan's southern end. She does so ultimately less because she is under the illusion that Paul is the right guy for her than because Paul affords her the chance to experience the *sensation* of longing precisely because of his amorous disinterest in her—a dynamic of longing that can be said to mirror Lemke's own relationship to the United States, which, as Christoph Hochhäusler intimates, had already been in "Lemke's previous films simultaneously an impossible and ever-present vanishing point [as] a highly stylized cinema fantasy" (2018). That is, just when the West German context defining NGC constrained (left) desire with morally and pedagogically motivated, near-compulsory reference to the country's fascist past, "America" functioned for Lemke as a dream, through the cinematically playful actualization of which he performatively sought to liberate the affective potential inhering in the (utopian) force of intransitive longing.

The first appearance we see of New York City may still be one of the most astonishing images ever shot of the Big Apple—even five decades afterward. After Sylvie's "no" to Paul's question and a brief shot subtly moving in on his face as he looks off-screen to where Sylvie disappeared, with an expression that is virtually impossible to read, a cut occurs, on the other side of which we are . . . well, elsewhere. As famous as the image of what we see is today—and not only due to the events of September 11, 2001—at the time of the film's release the World Trade Center's Twin Towers had not yet assumed the iconic force they eventually would. Perfectly centered, the towers momentarily appear as otherworldly as the famous monolith in Stanley Kubrick's *2001* (1968). Indeed, as the image is shot from a helicopter gradually spiraling around and up the towers only to reveal a strange dance-like scene on one of the towers' rooftop, the massive buildings assume a dreamlike quality. Or rather: it is as if they were in Paul's mind's eye, as if what we objectively see—one of the first ever (moving) images of the World Trade Center, shot just before it opened to the public—renders sensible his subjective experience of the very city of which he breathlessly told Sylvie just moments before.

This subjective intensification of the objective, documentary-like presentation of what were then the world's largest buildings infuses *Sylvie* with the kind of images only rarely found in (West) German cinema of the time, or ever. For it is not just the images' content that effects an aesthetic accentuation that infuses the film with a nearly mythological force but also how Lemke and his team stage and frame it. The first image is accompanied by the barely audible diegetic sound of the wind and street noise well below the helicopter as it silently hovers in the air; and then, after circling around the buildings as if cautiously examining these mysterious objects, while the sound of sirens emanating from the streets grounds the sublimity of the visual force exuded by the towers, the wind's noise strengthens, and at just this moment an extra-diegetic *tick-tick-tick* of a hi-hat sound kicks in—the start of The Temptations' recently (February 1973) released "Masterpiece." Now atop the roof, the camera in the helicopter zooms in on what turns out to be a photoshoot, with Sylvie dancing and leaping through a space still visibly under construction. Then a cut to Sylvie and Del Negro sitting on the edge of the roof, with Manhattan in the background, as Sylvie starts taking photos of Del making faces, neither heeding the view they are privileged to see. As if to counteract their seeming disregard—maybe even lack of respect—for their mise-en-scène, Lemke's camera (now also on the roof) tilts up above their heads and zooms in on

FIGURE 1.5. *Sylvie*—Sylvie and Del on the rooftop of the World Trade Center. (Screengrab)

the skyline in the background anchored by the Empire State Building just when Del suggests to Sylvie that they get back to work. The scene ends with another shot from the helicopter circling around the roof, with Sylvie and Del recommencing the shoot.

I describe this remarkable scene—one that is truly singular in the history of cinema—in some detail because it embodies a will to take risks and to experiment, to roll with the punches, as it were, that could have been a first step on a path that, in the end, was largely *not* taken by NGC. Using a direct cinema approach (finding ways for the camera to be virtually invisible to the protagonists), Lemke films Sylvie and Del in a way that would not have given them the chance to know how exactly they would be filmed from the camera high up in the helicopter, just as Dylan and his entourage were largely, but not completely, unaware of being filmed; and this "largely but not completely" logic is what performatively undermines any distinction between an "authentic" and "performing" Dylan, instead rendering sensible his and his interlocutors' subjective experiences that are always-already the effect of performing-the-real, just as Lemke energizes his fictional/ized scenes, imbricating them with the real and vice versa to a point of near indiscernibility.[30]

This mix of staging and improvising, directing and capturing whatever transpires when you put highly performative people who are not actors per se in front of the camera, is put to remarkable effect throughout the film's middle section in New York. But it is perhaps nowhere better at work than, first, in the scene taking place in front of the Federal Hall National Memorial and, second, in the penultimate New York scene, which arguably facilitates Sylvie's return to Munich and thus Paul, after in a previous scene she manages to get him to call her (which costs, as we learn from him, the day's wages from his work as a cab driver) in her room at the famous Chelsea Hotel. From there, she imparts to Paul her experience of New York by holding her phone over the balcony of her hotel room: "Did you hear this? That was an American police siren. It sounds like in a war here," she says in what might be a sonic declaration of love of sorts on her part, for at this moment she ingeniously shares with him the objective reality of her linguistically unrepresentable subjective experience of a city that the real Sylvie Winter intimately knew from her previous visits.[31]

Indeed, Sylvie Winter's knowledge of New York City deeply impacted the making of *Sylvie*, as Müller confirms, "for we," unlike Sylvie, "were just naïve guys from Munich who never had seriously been outside of Munich."[32] Yet while Sylvie was able to guide Lemke and his team based on her experience, the film's trajectory—its mood—was also deeply informed by Lemke's own dreams of America, the realization of which he took a first stab at with the making of *48 Hours to Acapulco*, a film they shot while being initially under the false impression that "Acapulco was on the Caribbean side" (Abel 2019, 296).[33] But this dream of America, and specifically of New York City, ended up in a certain degree of disillusion. However, as if the movie gods had taken mercy on the great "cowboy" of German cinema, this disillusion ended up leaving a mark on *Sylvie* in an affectively positively charged way.[34] After the thrill of working with the Hells Angels in Hamburg (*Rocker*), Lemke felt that there was only one way of topping this experience: shooting in New York at the Chelsea Hotel. Yet his experience of the famous hotel disappointed him: "At the hotel bar a few old hippies. No girls. And it rained. Rain fell like a prayer from the heavens: let's just get away from here! In the cab with Martin Müller. And suddenly 'Angie' from the Stones played for the first time on the radio. And that was it. The photo model Sylvie falls in love with a cab driver from Munich, who is thousands of miles away. And whom she hardly knows."[35] A heavenly gift indeed: "Angie" was released on August 20, 1973, literally during the shooting of the New York scenes.

Braiding real life and fiction—with the former in the form of the Stones' song itself being a fiction of sorts, in symmetrical relationship to the fictions Lemke stages in New York that are always on the verge of disappearing into the real-life surroundings in which he embeds them—Lemke translates the song's mood and, I speculate, his own subjective experience of hearing this masterpiece for the first time into Sylvie's gradually shifting encounter with the city. He does so across a series of scenes in which he intensifies their reality effect to a breaking point.[36] For example, the lengthy "Bonnie and Clyde" scene in front of the Federal Hall National Memorial on Wall Street was staged in a way that Sylvie (the real person-cum-actress) was aware of, even if as viewers we might wonder whether this is improvised or acted, whether Lemke really incited his team to stage a fake robbery that would trigger the action of real members of "New York's Finest": we first see Sylvie emerging from the building, holding a gun and wearing a white suit, bandana, and fedora, and eventually witness how several cops arrest her and her partner (also in a white suit)

FIGURE 1.6. *Sylvie*—Playing Bonnie and Clyde. (Screengrab)

after having also arrested a Black preacher. Several scenes later and further uptown, however, we witness Sylvie getting (fake) mugged by a group of local teenagers in what would turn out to be the final big photoshoot scene in New York—and this time Sylvie was *not* in on the plan.[37]

After she had already expressed increasing irritation with Del earlier in their hotel room (prior to her calling Paul) because he kept taking photos of her, she "loses her shit," as it were, when discovering that he (but really Lemke) *staged* what to her momentarily *felt* like a real attack, yelling: "Let me go. What is that shit, Del? Leave me alone! What is that shit? What are you doing? Was machst Du eigentlich? Ich dachte, wir machen Bilder." Replying to Del's "We're taking some photos," Sylvie continues, enraged: "But this is not New York. Da glaubt jeder, man wird auf der Strasse überfallen. Du spinnst wohl! Was glaubst Du eigentlich, das Du für Dein Geld noch alles kriegst. Du bist wohl wahnsinnig," capping her expression of real anger by spitting.[38] And when Del, who does not seem to know quite what to do (just as the three teenagers linger awkwardly in the background, waiting for Del to pay them), seems to want to take more photos, she tells him: "Hör auf! Gleich knallt's!" ("Stop! I'm fed up!"), leaving Del to sheepishly turn away before the camera zooms in on Sylvie's face, capturing her *real* anger at him but also at Lemke, as her brief glance toward the camera suggests (figure 1.7, frame 6). Indeed, as Müller explained to me, the guys who mugged her were quite harmless but looked somewhat dangerous. But "Sylvie was not aware of the plan and therefore was really mad at Klaus, for this did not correspond with her idealistic image of NYC. She really vented, and even the teenagers were quite embarrassed, saying, 'Yes, ma'am, sorry, ma'am.'"[39]

This quiet moment may be one of the film's most compelling, perhaps not least because it seems that Sylvie—both the real person and the fictionalized version of her—is so fully *in the present*. The exhaustion that registers on her face and body is palpable and real (regardless of whether she also performs based on directorial suggestions), in a way that seems exactly analogous to the reality of the awe and pain Donovan's clenched jaw renders sensible in response to Dylan's performance of "Baby Blue." While Lemke's staging is of course different than Pennebaker's by virtue of the simple fact that the latter was not shooting a however thinly constructed fictional story, it nevertheless exhibits what Lemke learned from *Dont Look Back* in that he managed to intuit the real manifestation of subjective experiences of highly performative people and capture the expressions thereof in the interstices of their main activities—for example, Sylvie's brief moment of laughter when the real New York cops, acting as themselves, arrest her; her eyes throwing daggers at Del as well as the crew in the off-space; the stress manifesting on Del's face as he is yelling ("Get outta here!") at bystanders in Times Square to create enough space to pretend to take photos of Sylvie but likely also for Lemke's camera to really shoot Sylvie's actions; and various quiet moments of introspection, in which Sylvie (which version?) seems to be completely with herself, whether while sitting in front of a storefront with a plush animal she just purchased or on the subway. Everything merges in what seems like an impossible mix of anarchic street realism and highly staged fictionalizing, where the fictional character "Sylvie" becomes real precisely when Sylvie Winter "starts

FIGURE 1.7. *Sylvie*—Sylvie getting mugged. (Screengrab)

to 'make fiction', when [she] enters into 'the flagrant offence of making up legends'" (Deleuze 1989, 150) based on her own lived experiences. Put differently and with reference to how Pennebaker describes his own filmmaking, Lemke creates (often in haphazard, spontaneous ways) dramatic scenes that allow the condition of possibility for the real persons enacting refracted versions of themselves to break through. Yet it is not the director who breaks through; it is not the director's preexisting vision or message he wants to communicate that gets realized at this moment. Rather, it is Sylvie Winter, Del Negro, and Paul Lys who are breaking through their performances *by way of* their performances, immanently.

## Conclusion

Documenting New York City by capturing the subjective experience of his actors qua real people, Lemke time and again catches them in the act of fabulating themselves. This capturing—or rather framing—is an active gesture on Lemke's part (as it is on Pennebaker's), for his strategy to repeatedly put them in juxtaposition against a particular *real* setting cannot be separated from the fictional storytelling, just as Pennebaker's direct cinema mode of observing profilmic reality cannot be separated from the performative quality of that reality. The result of this is that Lemke, as a filmmaker, "becomes another" precisely because of how in these fabulating moments "real characters . . . wholly replace his own fictions by their own story-telling" (Deleuze 1989, 150). The radicalness of *Sylvie*, then, resides precisely in how, thanks to the lessons Lemke learned from Pennebaker, the film introduces into NGC a heretofore unimaginable attitude toward the world: the imbrication of the real with artificiality *in the name of realism*. The result of this unique mode of filmmaking, which has been largely ignored if not dismissed in the historiography of (West) German cinema, not least of NGC, is precisely the rendering sensible of an affective lightness and nonchalance in the context of the aftermath of the events of 1968 and the abyss they constituted. This is also to say that, contrary to Blumenberg's claim that Lemke is not a realist, he is a realist filmmaker precisely in Bazin's sense, namely, in that realism is not primarily a function of indexicality (and thus authenticity) but rather an accomplishment that results from an attitude toward the world.[40] The Bazinian point about Italian neorealism—to only refer to his most famous example—is not that films such as Roberto Rossellini's *Roma, città aperta* (*Rome, Open City*, 1945) or Vittorio De Sica's *Umberto D* (1952) are realist because they document—objectively re-present—fragments of profilmic reality of postwar Rome, but rather because they organize those fragments of reality in accordance with a particular attitude toward the world typical of the period, what he calls a "spiritual adherence to their time" (Bazin 2009a, 220). In so doing they render sensible something that may otherwise not be accessible to us due to the "habits and preconceived notions of all the spiritual detritus that [our] perception has wrapped it in" (Bazin 2009b, 9). They abstract clichés from a subject's way of seeing reality and thereby render different or strange not only that reality to the subject but also the subject to themselves.

To me, the critical term "aesthetic left" Patalas coined—and that was mobilized clearly in the context of the NMG films of the mid- to late 1960s, including Lemke's—names in a different context what Bazin located in neorealism.[41] And just like the latter was instantly attacked in Italy not just by the ruling conservative party but also the Italian Communist Party (for allegedly sullying Italy's image in the world), so the NMG (and the aesthetic left) was quickly attacked by the (West) German film establishment *on the political left*.[42] Yet *that* the "aesthetic left"—and Lemke's films were among those for which the term was positively deployed—was received with considerable irritation marks *something*. And perhaps this *something*, in all its complex forms of articulation, was the desire of those who had, to paraphrase Jacques Rancière, a part in the count to prevent those who had no part in the existing "distribution of the sensible" from issuing their disagreement.[43] And they—those who had a part in the count—did this precisely by linking the latter's aesthetics, *as* the antithesis to left politics, to the realm of the ideological enemy: the United States (capitalism) and Hollywood (escapism). It may, then, not have been coincidental that the young filmmakers of the NMG were attacked as right wing for the simple reason that they, like the Young Turks of the Nouvelle Vague such as Godard and François Truffaut, loved filmmakers such as Hawks and John Ford.

But perhaps the films of the "aesthetic left"—of which I posit *Sylvie* as a prime example that emerged just when NGC was on the verge of assuming hegemony, at least among the film critical establishment—constitute a subterranean tradition of an *other* left politics, the rendering sensible of which might require a genealogical tracing in Michel Foucault's sense that will have to be done another time. Just briefly by way of concluding, though, the aim of such a genealogy would be twofold: (1) to grasp the present—that is, to understand or produce some sort of knowledge about the character of contemporary reality; and (2) to transform that reality by opening up new possibilities for thought and action. These two aims must be understood together, in the sense that genealogical (aka critical) inquiry in the Foucauldian sense aims to transform the present by grasping more fully what it is. Or, as he writes, "The critical ontology of ourselves . . . has to be conceived as an attitude, an ethos, a philosophical life in which the critique of what we are is at one and the same time the historical analysis of the limits that are imposed on us and an experiment with the possibility of going beyond them." To do this one has to ask "what place is occupied by whatever is singular, contingent, and the product of arbitrary constraints" in "what is given to us as universal, necessary, obligatory" (Foucault 1984, 50, 45). That is, what artifacts of the present, which appear as necessities (in terms of, for example, the canonical story about NGC and about what counts as "left" cinema in the historiography of [West] German cinema), are, in fact, merely contingent limitations on what we can do or think? I wonder if such a genealogical, experimental tracing—of which my discussion of Pennebaker's influence on Lemke's *Sylvie* is meant to function as but one example—might be able to produce, as it were, a politics of the left against the left—or, with a nod to Jacques Derrida's claim that Walter Benjamin's thought was "messianic without messianism" (1994, 181), of *a left politics without leftism.*

## Notes

The epigraph is from Marco Abel, phone conversation with Klaus Lemke, personal audio file, October 26, 2019. During this conversation, Lemke read a brief text he had written in response to my question about what films had influenced him in the making of *Sylvie*. I quote the continuation of his answer below. Translations from all original German-language sources are mine throughout.

1 For more on the notion of the "long 1968" in the context of German film history, see Christina Gerhardt and Marco Abel, eds., *Celluloid Revolt: German Screen Cultures and the Long 1968* (Rochester, NY: Camden House, 2019).

2 Lemke and others associated with the New Munich Group barely make an appearance in the major film history books focusing on (West) German cinema. Perhaps symptomatically, whereas the original edition of Hans Günther Pflaum and Hans Helmut Prinzler's canonical *Film in der Bundesrepublik Deutschland* (Munich: Hanser Verlag, 1979) had brief

entries on Lemke as well as NMG directors May Spils and Rudolf Thome, in the revised edition (Bonn: Inter Nationes, 1992) only Thome retains an entry. Tellingly, in an interview, Prinzler admits that it would never have occurred to him and his co-director Michael Althen to include Lemke's *Rocker* (1972) in their film *Auge in Auge—Eine deutsche Filmgeschichte* (*Eye to Eye: All about German Film*, 2008) had it not been for Dominik Graf's insistence to use it as one of the examples around which to structure their version of German film history. As Prinzler puts it, they would never have thought of it because "it was contrary to what today counts as canonical or important films" (quoted in Schultz 2008).

3 Enno Patalas, "Plädoyer für die Ästhetische Linke," *Filmkritik* 7 (1966): 403–7. Patalas coined this term to describe a film *critical* position, one that in my view aligns with the films of the NMG (among others) and that, in any case, I find productive in conceptualizing a certain tendency of West German film that emerged in the mid-1960s and that continued to exist beyond, albeit mostly subterraneously. For an important investigation of what "left" was around 1968 that informs my own thinking about "leftism," see Andreas Christoph Schmidt's four-part television documentary *Was war links?* (2003).

4 Wenders was actually in New York City during the time Lemke shot his film, preparing *Alice in the Cities*, as Martin Müller told me. Marco Abel, interview about *Sylvie* with Martin Müller, personal audio file, February 9, 2021. Michael Pfleghar shot *Die Tote von Beverly Hills* (*Dead Woman from Beverly Hills*, 1964) and *Serenade für zwei Spione* (*Serenade for Two Spies*, 1965), which were both produced by Hansjürgen Pohland, partly in the United States and, like Lemke a few years later, in a semi-guerilla style.

5 In the mid-1970s, Herzog frequently referred to the films of the New German Cinema as "legitimer deutscher Film" ("legitimate German film") (quoted in *Der Spiegel* 1975, 188).

6 It was at roughly the same time that Roland Klick found his film *Deadlock* (1970) uninvited by the 1971 Cannes Film Festival. As Brad Prager recounts in this volume, the behind-the-scenes maneuverings of the Export Union of German Films prevented the film's premiere at the festival. Rumor has it that the well-networked Alexander Kluge—Adorno student, Oberhausen Manifesto signatory (1962), and a stalwart of both the Young German Cinema of the mid-1960s and its successor, the NGC—was involved. See Harald Mühlbeyer, "Zwischen den Stühlen," https://ray-magazin.at/zwischen-den-stuehlen/.

7 "Some people knew Lemke better than Wenders. But in the so-called German film scene Klaus did not play a role [kam Klaus nicht vor], even

though he made one film after the next" (Przygodda, Müller, and Roth 2006, 65).

8 Klaus Lemke, text messages from May 31, 2014 and June 3, 2019, respectively.

9 In Lemke's Twitter-German, the quotation reads: "Alexander Kluges erhörte Prayers nach Subvention für das 'Kulturgut Film' in den 70ern waren de facto der Anschluss an das Staatskino der DDR. Obwohl Kluge eigentlich nur vorhattte: Seinen Jungs in Schwabing, deren Filme niemand sehen wollte—doch ne Villa in der Toskana zu verschaffen. Aba daz mal beiseite: I LOVE KLUGE."

10 A word on the terminology of "direct cinema" and "cinéma vérité": As Jeanne Hall explains, the "term 'cinema verité' was used by early film critics to denote both the French and North American schools of the movement. . . . Thus, although Erik Barnouw refers to the French school as 'cinema verité' and the North American as 'direct cinema' in his widely used textbook, most contemporary documentary scholars . . . use the former term for both" (1998, 251 n.1). Summarizing the differences between direct cinema and cinéma vérité, Barnouw argues that the "direct cinema artist aspired to invisibility[, whereas] the *cinema verité* artist was often an avowed participant [in profilmic action]. The direct cinema artist played the role of involved bystander; the *cinema verité* artist espoused that of provocateur" (1974, 255).

11 To be sure, it is quite understandable why, at the time, working through the past was deemed more important, indeed necessary, than a focus on the present *as* present. And yet, one can acknowledge the need for this working through of the past while also insisting on the (unintentional) cost that came with this attitude toward filmmaking, if not life itself.

12 Robert Polito recounts the relationship between the time of shooting and the delayed release in his essay included in the film's Criterion DVD release and proposes to view it as "out of sync, prophetic, timeless" (2015). We might say that both the film itself and what it depicts—Dylan *becoming* Dylan—render *Dont Look Back* untimely, in that what we see is as much about this specific moment of Dylan touring the UK in April and May 1965 as it is about giving us a glimpse of the future Dylan, the one who would go electric and be harassed by parts of his audience for doing so, the one who would make a string of landmark records in the mid-1960s, of which *Bringing It All Back Home* (1965), which had just been released prior to Dylan's tour, would be the clarion call—but also in that the film itself invented a new form of filming "the real," one that

insists on authenticity's performativity as much as on this performativity's authenticity.

13 Pennebaker credits his former college roommate William Gaddis and his novel *JR* for "the idea of not saying who's talking so you have to figure it out" (quoted in Polito 2015).

14 As per Deleuze and Guattari, an incorporeal transformation is effected by a statement that is applied directly to bodies and is inserted into the subject's actions and passions, thereby altering and determining a body's specific social meaning. The statement "You are an illegal immigrant" applies differently to the same body than a statement such as "You are an undocumented citizen." The literal body remains the same in either case; the social body, however, vastly differs because of the statements' different forces. In Dylan's case, his literal body remains the same, yet his performance makes a statement that alters his social meaning, first just for his immediate audience (and most specifically for Donovan) but eventually also for the public, even before the film's public release, which in a way only retroactively shows the moment of incorporeal transformation, rendering it, if you will, corporeal (in the sense that the cinema is a body too). See Gilles Deleuze and Félix Guattari, *A Thousand Plateaus*, trans. Brian Massumi (Minneapolis: University of Minnesota Press, 1987), especially chapter 4.

15 Polito convincingly argues that Pennebaker "was gifted at intuiting the dramas around highly performative people and focusing them at oblique angles to their main activity" (2015).

16 In this context it is worth recalling André Bazin's (often ignored) insistence that "in art, realism can obviously be created only out of artifice" (2009a, 227).

17 Hongisto convincingly contests the representationalist ontological assumptions governing most accounts of the documentary form and instead reconceptualizes documentary filmmaking as expressive (in Deleuze's sense): "The aesthetics of the frame calls attention to two levels of expression: the exhibiting agency of the real and documentary renditions of it. What is more, these levels are seen as immanent to one another in the event of filmmaking. The entanglement allows reorienting the work of the documentary from explicating what already is to facilitating the vibrant becoming of the real in its myriad manifestations" (2015, 17).

18 For Pennebaker's account of his shooting methodology, see Polito 2015.

19 Obermaier is most famous for her role in the Kommune 1 but also was part of the NMG universe, starring in Rudolf Thome's *Detektive* (1968)

and *Rote Sonne* (*Red Sun*, 1969) as well as in Martin Müller's short films *Zinnsoldat* (1968) and *Die Geschäftsfreunde* (1969).

20 For more on the New Munich Group, see Marco Abel, *Mit Nonchalance am Abgrund: Das Kino der "Neuen Münchner Gruppe" (1964–1972)* (Bielefeld: transcript Verlag, 2024).

21 For more on Lemke's thoughts on language use, see Abel 2019, 299. A decade later, Dominik Graf would be the first West German filmmaker to systematically experiment with Lemke's approach to staging dialogue, especially in his episodes for the West German TV series *Der Fahnder* (1984–2005). He also reminds us that Klaus Theweleit "once identified the West German youth language of the political sixties—its language-altering witty agitprop idiom—as a reason for why a more liberated left scene was so appealing" (2010).

22 Lemke himself makes a brief appearance too, standing behind Paul when he pays for a rather costly telephone call he just made from Munich to Sylvie at the Chelsea Hotel in New York. Virtually the only professional actor in the film is Ivan Desny, playing the businessman who, after asking Sylvie to marry him, completely disappears from the film. Del Negro was in real life a painter and actor who played Brother Gaspar in Werner Herzog's *Aguirre, der Zorn Gottes* (*Aguirre, the Wrath of God*, 1972). A brief article identifies Lys as an "abgemusterte Seemann"—a signed sailor who is ashore (*Der Spiegel* 1973).

23 Abel, phone conversation with Klaus Lemke, October 26, 2019.

24 Abel, phone conversation with Klaus Lemke, October 26, 2019.

25 Not available commercially, the film is available on YouTube: https://www.youtube.com/watch?v=evb5CtjAfYk&t=714s.

26 The famous "lusty dining" scene in Tony Richardson's *Tom Jones* (1963) might also come to mind (thanks to Joy Castro for pointing this out to me). Lemke attributes Winter's love for eating to her experience growing up after World War II in the American Zone, where soldiers regularly fed her hamburgers (Philippi 2006, 151).

27 Philippi suggests that in the restaurant scene Sylvie consumes with abandon because of her nervous excitement about her date with the businessman (which never comes to pass). "At no moment is this nervous excitement [Aufregung] an act designed to solicit attention from others. This act [Spiel] is just for Sylvie herself" (2006, 151).

28 The real Sylvie Winter would soon quit modeling and acting (*Paul* was her last film). In the 1980s, she moved as Gayan Sylvie Winter to Santa Fe, New Mexico. She has since published several New Age advice books.

29 Simon Hauck, “Filmklassiker: Paul,” June 5, 2018, https://www.filmdienst.de/artikel/12493/paul.

30 Part of the scene's magic may well be the very chutzpah involved in shooting it. According to Müller, who was on the rooftop to do the sound, it was cameraman Stickelbrucks who contrived the World Trade Center scene, for thanks to previous experience in New York he knew how one could get into the building, which was not yet open to the public. Having arranged for Sylvie Winter, Del Negro, and Müller to be up on the roof, Lemke and his cameraman were in the helicopter shooting the Twin Towers in a way that would soon become impossible due to security reasons. Stickelbrucks also knew local companies that employed policemen who in their spare time made money by appearing in films in their uniforms, as in the scene shot in front of the Federal Hall National Memorial discussed below (Abel, interview about *Sylvie* with Martin Müller).

31 According to Lemke, they stayed at the same hotel room in which Bob Dylan stayed. In the bathroom, they even found part of a poem by Dylan Thomas stuck underneath the sink (Abel, phone conversation with Klaus Lemke, personal audio file, January 19, 2021).

32 Abel, interview about *Sylvie* with Martin Müller.

33 In his brief essay on one of his favorite scenes in German film history (the helicopter scene just discussed), Hochhäusler observes that *48 Hours to Acapulco* “had also already been partly shot in America or rather Mexico, but in this film Lemke's America was hardly more than a highly stylized cinema fantasy” (2018).

34 Lemke often calls his interlocutors “cowboy.”

35 Klaus Lemke, personal email, October 22, 2019. In his follow-up phone conversation with me about the making of *Sylvie* (January 19, 2021), Lemke stated that Uschi Obermaier was in the cab as well.

36 Lemke, however, never uses “Angie.” Instead, he keeps splicing “Back Street Girl” into the soundtrack.

37 Bridging this penultimate New York scene and her return to Munich is one more brief scene in which she and Del ride the subway. The mood is downcast, with Sylvie looking like a regular (and exhausted) woman rather than a model. They board the train, which is populated by real New Yorkers, who eventually witness Sylvie adding to the graffiti inside the subway car, writing “Paul,” accompanied by a few hearts. There is no dialogue and only original sound, except for the brief fade in and out of a few bars of “Back Street Girl.”

38 What Sylvie speaks in German is, first, “What are you doing? I thought we shoot photos,” and then, “Everyone will think one is being robbed

on the street. You are crazy. What else do you think you can get for your money? You must be mad."

39 Abel, interview about *Sylvie* with Martin Müller.

40 See also Daniel Morgan, "Rethinking Bazin: Ontology and Realist Aesthetics," in *The Film Theory Reader: Debates and Arguments*, ed. Marc Furstenau (New York: Routledge, 2010): 104–30.

41 Indeed, Frieda Grafe's review of *Acapulco* was perhaps one of *the* key aesthetic statements of the "aesthetic left," declaring that *Acapulco* "is made against all those important [wertvollen] and especially important [besonders wertvollen] films that derive the justification to exist from extra-filmic ideas" (1967, 679).

42 A review of *Sylvie* characterizes the film as "culinary, consumable cinema," asserting that this is exactly what Lemke tries to make because he "does not want to change the world but to entertain" (*Frankfurter Rundschau* 1973). Leaving aside the question of what Lemke wanted at the time, I simply note the presence of the era's leftist dogma, namely, that only cinema that cannot be consumed—that would provide significant challenges to one's digestive system—can possibly change the world. My thesis is that this idea was misguided, and my hypothesis is that the "aesthetic left" offered a counter-idea, or at least a counter-intuition, to this leftist dogma, opposing it from a perspective that I suggest theorizing as *affectively left*.

43 This language is present throughout Rancière's work. He famously argues, for example, that "politics exists wherever the count of parts and parties of society is disturbed by the inscription of a part of those who have no part" (Rancière 1999, 123).

## Works Cited

Abel, Marco. 2019. "An Interview with Klaus Lemke: 'Being Smart Does Not Make Good Films.'" In *Celluloid Revolt: German Screen Cultures and the Long 1968*, edited by Christina Gerhardt and Marco Abel, 292–321. Rochester: Camden House.

Barnouw, Erik. 1974. *Documentary: A History of the Non-fiction Film*. Oxford: Oxford University Press.

Bazin, André. 2009a. "Cinematic Realism and the Italian School of the Liberation." In *What Is Cinema?* translated by Timothy Barnard, 215–49. Montreal: Caboose, 2009.

———. 2009b. "The Ontology of the Photographic Image." In *What Is Cinema?* translated by Timothy Barnard, 3–12. Montreal: Caboose.

Beattie, Keith. 2011. *D. A. Pennebaker*. Urbana-Champaign: University of Illinois Press.

Blumenberg, Hans C. 1979. "Alle Träume werden wahr." *Die Zeit*, April 6. https://www.zeit.de/1979/15/alle-traeume-werden-wahr.

"Bob Dylan's Best Songs: It's All over Now, Baby Blue." 2015. *borntolisten.com*, January 15. https://alldylan.com/bob-dylans-best-songs-its-all-over-now-baby-blue-8-audio-video/.

Bowcock, Simon. 2016. "*Don't* [*sic*] *Look Back*, Bob Dylan and the Invention of the Rockumentary." *The Guardian*, May 17. https://www.theguardian.com/music/2016/may/17/dont-look-back-bob-dylan-invention-rockumentary.

Deleuze, Gilles. 1989. *Cinema 2: The Time-Image*. Translated by Hugh Tomlinson and Robert Galeta. Minneapolis: University of Minnesota Press.

Derrida, Jacques. 1994. *Specters of Marx: The State of Debt, the Work of Mourning, and the New International*. Translated by Peggy Kamuf. New York: Routledge.

*Der Spiegel*. 1973. "Lemke-Film: Neues, wildes Kino-Leben?" October 22. https://www.spiegel.de/kultur/lemke-film-neues-wildes-kino-leben-a-aad71cc4-0002-0001-0000-000041843165.

———. 1975. "Lorbeer für die Wunderkinder." November 17, 182–92.

Foucault, Michel. 1984. "What Is Enlightenment?" In *The Foucault Reader*, edited by Paul Rabinow, 32–50. New York: Pantheon Books.

*Frankfurter Rundschau*. 1973. "Sylvie." December 18.

Graf, Dominik. 2009. "Die Frau, die weint und winkt: *Sylvie* von Klaus Lemke." In *Schläft ein Lied in allen Dingen: Texte zum Film*, edited by Michael Althen, 41–43. Berlin: Alexander Verlag.

———. 2010. "Independence Day." *Süddeutsche Zeitung*, July 29.

Grafe, Frieda. 1967. "48 Stunden bis Acapulco." *Filmkritik* 12: 679–80.

Groh, Thomas. 2012. "Versprechen eines freien Lebens." *taz*, November 28. https://taz.de/!537536/.

Hall, Jeanne. 1998. "'Don't You Ever Just Watch?' American Cinema Verité and *Don't* [*sic*] *Look Back*." In *Documenting the Documentary: Close Readings of Documentary Film and Video*, edited by Barry Keith Grant and Jeanette Sloniowski, 237–53. Detroit: Wayne State University Press.

Hochhäusler, Christoph. 2018. "Konfetti 1: Hochhäusler." *Dirty Laundry*, April 22. https://somedirtylaundry.blogspot.com/2018/04/konfetti-1-hochhauser.html.

Hongisto, Ilona. 2015. *Soul of the Documentary: Framing, Expression, Ethics.* Amsterdam: Amsterdam University Press.

Levin, G. Roy. 1971. *Documentary Explorations: 15 Interviews with Filmmakers.* New York: Doubleday.

Philippi, Anne. 2006. "Mädchen injeindeutiger Position." In *Inside Lemke: Ein Klaus Lemke Lesebuch*, edited by Brigitte Werneburg, 144–57. Cologne: Schnitt—der Filmverlag.

Polito, Robert. 2015. "Everyone Loves You for Your Black Eye." DVD release of *Dont Look Back*. Criterion Collection.

Przygodda, Peter, Martin Müller, and Christopher Roth. 2006. "Der Hundedieb taucht 30 Jahre später in Ibiza auf. . . ." In *Inside Lemke: Ein Klaus Lemke Lesebuch*, edited by Brigitte Werneburg, 46–87. Cologne: Schnitt—der Filmverlag.

Rancière, Jacques. 1999. *Dis-agreement: Politics and Philosophy*. Translated by Julie Rose. Minneapolis: University of Minnesota Press.

Saunders, Dave. 2007. *Direct Cinema: Observational Documentary and the Politics of the Sixties*. New York: Wallflower.

Schultz, Sonja M. 2008. "Diese deutsche Schwere." *critic.de*, June 27. http://critic.de/interview/diese-deutsche-schwere-2044.

Suchsland, Rüdiger. 2012. "Es ist alles faul und falsch!" *artechcok*, April 12. https://www.artechock.de/film/text/interview/l/lemke_2012_2.html.

*Süddeutsche Zeitung*. 2020. "SMS von Lemke," July 16. https://www.sueddeutsche.de/kultur/gehoert-gelesen-zitiert-sms-von-lemke-1.4969091.

# 2

# A RELENTLESS FORWARD MOVEMENT

## The German and Un-German Cinema of Roland Klick

*Brad Prager*

Roland Klick's films are typically described in terms of how they distinguish themselves from New German Cinema. Relative to New German Cinema's stereotyped Germanness, characterized by its cerebral themes and slow rhythms, Klick prefers to describe his work in terms of its Americanness. He and those who study and classify his films emphasize their unbridled sensuality, which they argue was largely missing from the more widely and internationally acclaimed German productions of the late 1960s and early 1970s. In interviews Klick sometimes speaks about "the left"—by which he likely means German filmmakers who rose to prominence around the time of the 1968 movement—in terms of its hostility to sensuality (*Sinnesfeindlichkeit*).[1] Klick asserts that his films, by contrast, are physical, bodily events, and they need to be experienced rather than understood (Wildermann 2013).

In Dominik Graf and Johannes Sievert's cinema-historical documentary *Verfluchte Liebe deutscher Film* (*Doomed Love*, 2016), Klick makes several appearances as one among many filmmakers associated with the New Munich School, which also includes Klaus Lemke and Rudolf Thome, who all reinforce the overall argument that German film history needs to be rewritten to account better for the distinction between the popular films of that era and the internationally acclaimed but drearier films of the New German Cinema.[2] The latter's aesthetics, according to the documentary's argument, are centered on the wholesale renunciation of their audience's pleasure; New German Cinema essentially disdained its spectators. Klick reserves special contempt for the “art for art’s sake” aesthetic of those filmmakers who benefited from the 1967 German Film Funding Act (*Filmförderungsgesetz*), which established a national film-funding bureau and provided subsidies for filmmakers.[3] In Klick’s view, only the market guarantees creative freedom, and the fact that German filmmakers took government support for granted merely led to a culture of censorship. In Frieder Schlaich’s interview film *Das Kino des Roland Klick* (1997), Klick complains that some German filmmakers had so deeply internalized the domestic funding process that they went so far as to discourage him from earning money at the box office on the basis that doing so risked undercutting the subsidy system. Cinema should, Klick asserts, stand on its own two feet.

Klick and the filmmakers who are part of his cohort contended that New German Cinema was dead on arrival. The group penned manifestos proclaiming that recent German films were as lifeless as the old ones.[4] Enumerating the differences, filmmaker by filmmaker, Andreas Martin Widmann argues that Klick had no use for Rainer Werner Fassbinder’s theatrical tableaus, Wim Wenders’s long takes, Hans-Jürgen Syberberg’s Wagnerianism, Werner Herzog’s fascination with the sublime, and Volker Schlöndorff’s literary adaptations (2018, 114). Widmann decries such propensities as “shtick,” adding that films by those filmmakers tend to be stiff and humorless. The directors interviewed in *Doomed Love*, on the other hand, boast that they are the inheritors of the legacy of truly entertaining German films such as those of Fritz Lang, including his Mabuse films, his spy films, and even his later adventure films such as *Das indische Grabmal* (*The Indian Tomb*, 1959). In Schlaich’s interview film, Klick refers to *Deadlock* (1970), his commercially successful production that resembles an American western and that was filmed in Israel’s Negev Desert, asserting that it was not made with the aim of earning money but was instead concerned with its audience’s pleasure. Klick compares his own motivation to that of the Rolling Stones, naïvely citing them as an example of artists who are more interested in their enjoyment of music than in making money.

Asserting that his aesthetics represent the authentic inheritance of the freedom of the 1960s, Klick declares that his motto was “*Physis* is *Geist*,” a conflation of Greek and German terms. Klick boasts that his films feature an unusually strong emphasis on physicality, and in *Doomed Love* the

German film star Mario Adorf recounts a pertinent anecdote from the set of *Deadlock*: Adorf risked life and limb because Klick, fixated on getting precisely the right take, demanded that the truck that was chasing him not veer from its course and that Adorf instead jump at just the right moment into a sandy hole, giving a starker impression of having been run over. Klick put Adorf at risk for the sake of acquiring a convincing continuous take. Stories along these lines are not all that distinct from those Herzog recounts when he reminisces about the production of *Auch Zwerge haben klein angefangen* (*Even Dwarfs Started Small*, 1970). Herzog's entirely nonprofessional cast ran around in front of moving vehicles to secure uncut takes such that audiences could, as Herzog likes to say, "trust their own eyes."[5] Moreover, like Herzog's, Klick's actors were frequently nonprofessionals drawn from society's margins: just as Herzog boasts of having cast true eccentrics and street musicians, such as Bruno Schleinstein, who starred in *Jeder für sich und Gott gegen alle* (*The Enigma of Kaspar Hauser*, 1974), Klick cast Charly Wierczejewski, a penurious youth with little or no acting experience, to play Willi, the lead role in *Supermarkt* (*Supermarket*, 1974).[6]

In his book-length study of Klick, Ulrich von Berg writes that German films around 1970 were popular with students but "not with the regular guys" (1993, 15). Von Berg cites a couple of exceptions, including the earliest films by Fassbinder and Peter Fleischmann's *Jagdszenen aus Niederbayern* (*Hunting Scenes from Bavaria*, 1969). The belief that films should be made for wide audiences rather than intellectuals is often connected to the question of whether German cinema should adhere to the more plot-driven American model. Klick explains, "My films are not American, but Americans make films right. And if you make films right, they look American" (quoted in Busche 2014, 6). His advocates tend to liken his feature films to major works of US cinema, and in *Doomed Love*, film scholar Lisa Gotto remarks how surprising it is that *Supermarket* appeared years before Martin Scorsese's *Taxi Driver* (1976), which touches on similar themes. According to Norbert Grob, Klick expressed enthusiasm in 1974 for Nicholas Ray, Raoul Walsh, and Samuel Fuller. Drawing on the example of Walsh's *White Heat* (1949), Klick says that some of those directors' works were made with "great precision" and that they serve as models for him. He adds, "These are films that I really learned from watching, sometimes ten times over" (1984, 16).

Although Klick maintains that there are pronounced differences between his approach and that of the major auteurs of the New German Cinema, one could just as convincingly argue in favor of overlaps and continuities. Claudius Seidl writes that Klick "admired American cinema for its brashness and speed, for the physical presence of its heroes, and for the evidence it gave of what was visible and happening. And he hated German cinema. He detested the so-called Young German Film, even though Wim Wenders and Rainer Werner Fassbinder, who were his contemporaries . . . loved and respected American cinema for almost exactly the same reasons" (2010). Klick rejected the major trends in German film at the time, yet he shared much in common with the most prominent German directors: Fassbinder's films can surely be said to emphasize sensuality; Wenders's films drew inspiration from the same American directors as Klick's; and Herzog's films were made with a sense of adventure in mind—they are films to be experienced rather than understood. Although some of the filmmakers of the New German Cinema conform to the caricature Klick and others put forward in *Doomed Love*, the standpoint expressed in that documentary can hardly be said to capture the varied dimensions of the many German films that were receiving international acclaim in the late 1960s and early 1970s.[7]

Many of these ideas about Klick's work build on the impression—one that is promulgated by Klick himself—that his films, unlike those of the New German Cinema, depict life as it actually is. If the most prominent German filmmakers associated with the 1970s each have their shtick, Klick's work, by contrast, has an aura of authenticity. When Klick speaks about his own film *Supermarket*, for example, he claims that the film's story has an authentic basis, and that it is meant to return a narrative to the community from which it was taken, particularly to the junkies and downtrodden people who inspired it. Klick argues that if a filmmaker draws on others' lives and fates, then he or she has an obligation to return something to them. In Schlaich's *Das Kino des Roland Klick*, Klick contends that this sense of accountability makes him unlike Alexander Kluge, who only produces films for refined viewers in ivory towers. Kluge, whom television executives have labeled a *Quotenkiller* (ratings killer), who is among the authors of the original Oberhausen Manifesto, and whose works are generally aimed at highly literate audiences, is among Klick's favored scapegoats—his perceived elitism makes him a better foil than Wenders or Herzog.

*Ludwig* (1964), one of Klick's early short films, which he shot in the upper Franconian region near Hof an der Saale, where he spent his early childhood, can be described as a highly Germanic film. Slightly less than fifteen minutes long, it focuses on an afternoon and evening in the life of its eponymous small-town pariah. The Franconian town at the film's center is presented as a desolate landscape in which unsupervised children entertain themselves by kicking a balloon around a grubby street. Even the youngest residents know to make fun of Ludwig, a gawky outcast played by Otto Sander in his first film role. Klick turns his camera's attention to a crew of locals who are out for the evening—a provincial group not dissimilar to those who can be seen hanging around wasting time in Fassbinder's *Katzelmacher* (1969). They have little to do but badger those who pass by, and their interest eventually turns to tormenting a cat, an activity that foreshadows the sadistic cruelty depicted in Klick's first feature-length film, *Bübchen* (1968).[8] *Ludwig* was produced in the same year as Herzog's fourteen-minute *Spiel im Sand* (*Game in the Sand*, 1964), in which children buried a rooster up to its neck in sand. Owing to its gloomy setting, it has been labeled an "anti-*Heimat* film" and can, in that sense, be seen alongside Fleischmann's *Hunting Scenes from Bavaria* and Schlöndorff's *Der plötzliche Reichtum der armen Leute von Kombach* (*Sudden Wealth of the Poor People of Kombach*, 1971).[9] It thus falls well within a lineage of German films and either resembles or anticipates several early works of New German Cinema.

If Klick's earliest films show any indications of international influence, they come across more clearly in his forty-nine-minute *Jimmy Orpheus* (1966). In many respects that film resembles works of the French New Wave, and cinematographer Robert van Ackeren's use of light and shadow recalls portrayals of Paris in François Truffaut's best-known films from the 1960s. From certain standpoints, the film can be said to echo thematically Jean-Luc Godard's works, particularly *Vivre sa vie* (*My Life to Live*, 1962) and *Bande à part* (*Band of Outsiders*, 1964), films that also served as touchstones for New German Cinema, particularly for Fassbinder's *Liebe ist kälter als der Tod* (*Love Is Colder Than Death*, 1969).[10] In *Jimmy Orpheus*, which originally had the working title "Eine Nacht" ("One Night"), Kristoff, the film's main character, is down and out—a working-class guy who wanders the streets seeking women's company. He eventually meets a woman who remains unnamed in the film and may be a prostitute. She is flirtatious and playful in a way that recalls the performances of Godard's muse Anna Karina, and Klick's many editorial stylizations, including fast-forwards, inserts, and a decidedly unserious car chase, all call to mind the hallmarks of Godard's playful and self-reflexive early films.

The many international influences on *Jimmy Orpheus* hardly make Klick's film *un*-German, however: to the contrary, they are absolutely consistent with what numerous other Germans, particularly Fassbinder and Schlöndorff, did. Many of Klick's films are thus as Germanic as they are divergent from New German Cinema. Klick positions himself against a cultural mainstream, but coming to terms with his various stylistic choices is a complex matter. He resisted what he perceived to be the cold, alienating, and overly mannered style of New German Cinema, eventually declaring his allegiance to faster-paced American genre films, yet in drawing on styles and motifs from French cinema, as in the case of *Jimmy Orpheus*, he was doing what many of his fellow filmmakers had done. *Bübchen*, which appeared two years after *Jimmy Orpheus*, is similarly in line with the work of his German contemporaries. *Deadlock*, however, can be seen to mark a noteworthy breakthrough: rather than looking again to the works of Truffaut and Godard, Klick, as he worked on that major internationally produced project, chose to echo the relentless forward narrative velocity of Henri-Georges Clouzot's French-Italian action film *Le salaire de la peur* (*The Wages of Fear*, 1953). Having been provided with the freedom and opportunity to film a screenplay on which he had long been working, Klick chose as his model a thrilling film that was known for heaping action upon action.

## Klick's Feature Films

Klick says that *Bübchen*, about an adolescent boy who kills his baby sister while their babysitter is otherwise occupied, was inspired by a true story he came across in a newspaper. Klick had been working as a production assistant for Federico Fellini in Rome, but, according to von Berg, he read the story about the murder, got on the next train back to Germany, and wrote his first version of the screenplay in sixteen hours (von Berg 1993, 69). *Bübchen* remains very much in the spirit of New German Cinema: there are similarities to major New German Cinema films including Schlöndorff's

*Mord und Totschlag* (*A Degree of Murder*, 1967), which played at Cannes in 1967, and to Johannes Schaaf's *Tätowierung* (*Tattoo*, 1967), which played at the Berlin Film Festival that same year and which is a similarly unsparing depiction of bourgeois domesticity. Patrick Wildermann describes *Bübchen* as Klick's thoroughly personal film about growing up under the narrow constraints of the polite middle class and notes that it was filmed in the director's parents' home in Neumünster (2013, 2). *Bübchen* can, in this sense, be interpreted as a moralizing film, one that asks whether West German parents are adequately looking after their children. The couple featured in the film leave their son and daughter in the hands of a negligent babysitter, a neighbor's daughter, so that they can attend a Mardi Gras celebration, and they later fail to notice that their infant child has gone missing. Monika, the flirtatious babysitter whom Andreas Busche, noting an overlap with French cinema, calls a "Bardot surrogate," abandons her charges, preferring to drive around with her boyfriend (2014, 10). The film indicts everyone equally and offers no palliative to its dark moral universe.

In Schlaich's *Das Kino des Roland Klick*, Klick asserts that *Bübchen* should not be seen as social-critical because it refuses to point an accusatory finger.[11] If there is an immediacy to *Bübchen*, it may come from the impression that the film lacks a narrative anchor. The invisibility of Klick's style—specifically that there are no overdetermined montages and few, if any, self-reflexive long takes—suggests neither that there is a grand image maker at work nor that we are seeing the film's world from any one of its character's individual standpoints.[12] Klick is correct that his technique exhibits neither deliberately Eisensteinian montages nor complex Hitchcockian assemblies. In *Doomed Love*, many German film stars describe how they learned their filmmaking techniques in Italy. Performers such as Klaus Kinski, Mario Adorf, and Gisela Hahn learned from Italian filmmakers by acting in Italo-westerns and Mafia films. Klick, however, had apprenticed under Fellini as an uncredited production assistant on *Satyricon* (1969), a work by a filmmaker who tends to produce meaning through camera movement and the composition of his frames rather than by relying on dialectical editing strategies. Fellini uses the entirety of the frame's depth, a realist approach associated with Italian postwar filmmakers such as Roberto Rossellini and Michelangelo Antonioni.[13]

In one long and wordless stretch of *Bübchen*, we are led to the body of the murdered girl, and the junkyard in which the scene is set recalls the construction site at the end of Schlöndorff's *A Degree of Murder*, where a body was similarly discarded. But if *Bübchen* bears a resemblance to films made by Klick's German contemporaries, then *Deadlock*, which Klick also wrote and directed, represents a turning point. To some extent, the choices that inspired *Deadlock* may have resulted from events in Klick's personal life: not long after the birth of their son, his wife died in a car accident, and he is said to have immersed himself in the production of *Deadlock*, which was shot in Israel, where the aftereffects of the 1967 Arab-Israeli war could still be felt. Von Berg quotes Klick as having said that after his wife's death he had "every reason to seek solitude" and that he drove around Spain, Italy, Yugoslavia, and North Africa, eventually making his way to Israel because a film festival there was playing *Bübchen*. "I took a rental car in Tel Aviv and saw a salt camp in the desert on the road to Eilat" (von Berg 1993, 82–83). That location, in the Negev Desert, became the film's set, and Busche (2014) explains that the production found itself close to the front, sometimes requiring the protection of the Israeli military. The film's wartime backstory resembles several production anecdotes told by Herzog, who more than once filmed in North African and Central American conflict zones.

According to von Berg, the film's Israeli setting was intended to resemble Mexico but was not meant to be old-fashioned—not out of the nineteenth century or the gold rush era but rather an abandoned location with a modern touch (1993, 82–83). Although the film's locality is never named, one of the first things we see on-screen is a briefcase filled with stolen American cash. One of the characters makes a fleeting reference to the robbery having taken place in or near Santa Cruz, but this is of little help given how many US and Mexican places are known by that name. Mario Adorf's character, Charlie Dump, explains that he has been working for the North American Mining Company and claims he has received a "citation from Congress" for killing, but none of this confirms for viewers precisely where the film is meant to be set.

*Deadlock* resembles a western and opens with a long shot of Kid, played by Marquard Bohm, who also worked with Klick's contemporaries Lemke and Thome on the cutting-edge films *Brandstifter* (1969) and *Rote Sonne* (*Red Sun*, 1969), wandering through the desert. The camera distance and the longer shot lengths in this opening sequence are calculated to highlight both the breadth of the unpopulated landscape and the protagonist's diminutive size within it. The score, although it was written by the German experimental rock band Can during their early years, resembles, at least in this first sequence, music composed by Ennio Morricone insofar as it sets a mood similar to that of Italo-westerns from the 1960s. Von Berg reflects on whether *Deadlock* should be considered a genre film or an *Autorenfilm*, but it should surely be understood as both: it is a genre film insofar as it meets, trades on, and even satirizes many of the major tropes of the western, but it is simultaneously a manifestation of its director's personal vision (1993, 86). At the same time that Robert Altman was putting his stamp on the western with *McCabe & Mrs. Miller* (1971), Klick was stylizing his personal vision for the genre in Israel.

With its particularly lean premise, *Deadlock* would today be considered a high-concept film. Norbert Grob describes it as a "chamber-play for two cars, two guns and five people" (1984, 18), and von Berg similarly characterizes it as "an apocalyptic endgame with three men, two guns, and a Chevy pick-up" (1993, 20). In its streamlined approach, the film recalls Sergio Leone's *The Good, the Bad, and the Ugly* (1966), and Klick was certainly familiar with the structure and aesthetics of Italo-westerns, yet von Berg also remarks on the influence of Clouzot's *Wages of Fear* (1993, 20). That film's plot had a relentless and American-style forward narrative movement. Its reputation as a masterwork is predicated on its riveting premise and its unforgiving stretches of tension. The film piles action upon action, and it is little wonder that it was remade by the American director William Friedkin in 1977 (under the title *Sorcerer*) as a follow-up to *The French Connection* (1971) and *The Exorcist* (1973). Von Berg writes of the interconnection between Clouzot's film and *Deadlock* as though the link were self-evident: in describing some of *Deadlock*'s psychedelic motifs, he writes, "Right at the beginning [of *Deadlock*] there is a sequence that can be interpreted as Kid's fever dream, after he has been shot, which makes it clear that this film is just as close to contemporary underground cinema as *The Wages of Fear* (an old favorite of Klick's)" (1993, 84). Von Berg's mention of underground cinema is likely meant as a reference to Alejandro Jodorowsky, whose *El Topo* (1970), a wild fever dream of a film that draws on the tropes of the western and was produced in Mexico, was released at nearly the same time.

As in *The Good, the Bad, and the Ugly*, one of *Deadlock*'s major motifs concerns how cruel its protagonists can be to one another. If the film is considered a chamber play, then it features only three roles, each of them marked by brutality and greed: the pathetic caretaker Charles Dump (a "desert troglodyte") and two gunslingers—the paternalistic Mr. Sunshine and Kid, his protégé who stands in allegorically for the younger, hipper generation.[14] Sunshine is played by Anthony Dawson, a major Scottish star who, prior to 1970, had worked for Alfred Hitchcock and on more than one James Bond film. Throughout *Deadlock*, the three men continually turn the tables on one another. Dump initially seems to be in control, but the briefcase full of cash and the gun are soon wrested from him, and Kid and Mr. Sunshine, who eventually wage war on one another, turn Dump into their plaything. In one sequence, they force him to play a song on a xylophone while they shoot out its keys. Dump ends up unsuccessfully pleading for his life, reduced to declaring his own worthlessness.

The film's desolate mise-en-scène highlights its motif of human cruelty: the world depicted in *Deadlock* has a postapocalyptic appearance, and an overladen delivery vehicle belonging to the film's postman suggests that there is little apart from civilization's detritus to be found anywhere in *Deadlock*'s universe. Its ambiance presages the deserted spaces of George Miller's *Mad Max* (1979). Here as there, the world consists mostly of trash and broken furniture. Atop one of the roofs in Dump's compound stands a deteriorating, larger-than-life highway sign featuring a cowboy whose arm has broken off. As a fragmentary image of a once-whole masculinity—a manly, gunslinging culture that used to exist—the billboard is of a piece with the film's retooling of the western. *Deadlock* is a "no longer epic" western, and its protagonists are unlikely ever to be made whole.

The women's lot is worse than that of the men: the only women in the film are Jessy, who seems to lack the power of speech, and Corinna, an older woman whose only lines are delivered as angry rants. Jessy, who is eventually revealed to be Dump's daughter, is depicted as almost feral, and Dump appears to offer her sexual services to Kid. *Deadlock*'s troubling treatment of its female figures would have been more at home in a grisly horror film than a western, and the film's sexism can only be rationalized if it is treated as a deliberate and satirical exaggeration of the western film's widely known sexist tropes.

As one of two female roles in *Deadlock*, Jessy may call to mind Linda, the only woman featured in Clouzot's *Wages of Fear*. Although Linda eventually speaks, she is virtually silent when we first encounter her, cleaning the floors of a saloon. Clouzot's male characters acknowledge her with little more respect than they would accord a dog. In one sequence the film's main character, a Frenchman named Mario, departs town, headed out on the mission that gives the film its premise. Linda runs after the car while he and Mr. Jo drive away, begging Mario not to leave her. Watching the sequence alongside *Deadlock*, it is hard not to think that Klick had it in mind as he wrote and directed a similar sequence in which Jessy runs alongside Kid and Mr. Sunshine's truck while the gunslingers drive away, pleading with Kid to take her along. In both scenarios, the local woman is, with comparable abandon, spurned and mistreated by the film's two tough guys.

In Clouzot's film, the fictional town of Las Piedras is located in an unnamed Latin American country, and from the perspective of the European characters who are marooned there, it, like the setting of *Deadlock*, looks like the ends of the earth. Although this town is more populated than

FIGURES 2.1 AND 2.2. *Wages of Fear* and *Deadlock*—Women spurned and mistreated by tough men. (Screengrabs)

*Deadlock*'s setting, few roads lead in or out, and a slow-moving donkey in the town's only street produces a traffic jam. In *The Wages of Fear*, the Southern Oil Company runs everything, and the film's principal characters find themselves stranded, lacking the resources to leave. Their only chance to make an exit from the town involves accepting a hazardous contract to transport nitroglycerine via truck from one company worksite to another. Reflecting some of these same themes, the setting of *Deadlock* is essentially a truck stop: trucks represent the characters' only access to a civilization that lies elsewhere, a world that neither we nor they are allowed to see.

There are several other similarities between the films: Jo or "Mr. Jo," the older gangster featured in *The Wages of Fear*, resembles *Deadlock*'s Sunshine or "Mr. Sunshine," and the films' two pairs of men—one younger, one older—are embroiled in analogous Oedipal struggles. In both cases the older man is ultimately revealed to be the weaker, less stable one. These paternal figures are each, at first, depicted as being so tough that they are not afraid to hand a gun over to a rival, confident that none will have the courage to pull the trigger. But the clearest connection between the films comes when, in *Deadlock*, Dump, the property manager, meets his end. He tries to flee while being chased across a desert plain by Kid and Sunshine in a truck. Unique to Klick in this case is his sequence's triangular editing—a montage that includes alternating close-ups of each of the three men, their faces exhibiting varying degrees of anger, bloodthirstiness, and fear. But at the moment Dump is overrun, the resonance between the two films grows unmistakable. Mr. Jo, at a climactic moment in *The Wages of Fear*, ends up in a pool of oil, his legs flattened by the truck's tires, an injury that eventually does him in. Whether Klick is consciously or unconsciously reproducing Clouzot's sequence, he similarly takes his time depicting this major character's demise. The importance of imitating this shot may have been a factor in why he insisted on having Adorf put himself in real danger during filming.

The two films' conclusions also share a similar spirit of excess. In *The Wages of Fear*, Mario, the sole survivor of the film's perilous expedition, drives back to Las Piedras in the hopes of enjoying the money he has earned, finally ready for a chance at happiness with Linda. But Clouzot, rather than permit his viewers a happy ending, has Mario, who had only barely escaped death's clutches, take an altogether gratuitous plunge off a cliff. In *Deadlock*, Klick's gunslingers end up facing off with one another

FIGURES 2.3 AND 2.4. *Wages of Fear* and *Deadlock*—Men meet their ends beneath the wheels of trucks. (Screengrabs)

at the edge of town. Without any particularly good reason, Mr. Sunshine kills Jessy and Corinna, but in doing so he appears to drive himself mad. A series of close-ups of his screaming mouth agape could have been seamlessly integrated into Jodorowsky's *El Topo*. Klick's film, like Clouzot's, is marked by an atmosphere of vanquished masculinity. Historically, many westerns were hopeless—frontiers are harsh, and dreams of happiness are always already made to be crushed. A hallmark of the genre is that its protagonists have been beaten and broken long before the films' narratives began. Klick's film is surely no remake of *The Wages of Fear*, and it should not be mistaken for one, yet that film, along with *The Good, the Bad, and the Ugly* and *El Topo*, can be viewed as intersecting intertexts that overlap with Klick's unusually international and relentlessly forward-moving auteurist western.

Some elements of *Deadlock*'s reception highlight that it appears to have been made in opposition to New German Cinema. Although the film was a success domestically, it struggled for inclusion at the Cannes Film Festival, which would, in the years immediately afterward, welcome new works from Herzog, Wenders, and Fassbinder. Juliane Liebert (2019) explains that when *Deadlock* was first invited to Cannes in 1971, the Export Union of German Films (Export-Union des Deutschen Films) filed a petition to prevent the film's inclusion on the basis that it was a "*Zerrbild*" ("caricature") of film culture in Germany. The petition was presented while Klick was on his way to the festival and *Deadlock* was pulled from the competition at the very last minute. As Klick tells the story in Sandra Prechtel's documentary *Roland Klick: The Heart Is a Hungry Hunter* (2012), some prominent figures had done everything in their power to ensure that the film was not shown because they felt it would undermine German cinema's hard-won recent reputation. The forces arrayed against him achieved their goal, even though "the entire Croisette was already paved with *Deadlock* posters."[15] According to Klick's own account, "There was a special screening . . . but no one came because of an unexpectedly dramatic rainfall. Only one man watched the film with his girlfriend—the great Chilean surrealist Alejandro Jodorowsky, who shortly afterwards released the strange western *El Topo* and has since then been an ardent admirer of the film" (Peters 2014a). Klick's tale of his rebuff at Cannes contributes to the perception that the German film industry organized against him. Influenced by French thrillers and Italo-westerns, Klick, who aspired to make films for mass audiences rather than for ivory towers, felt he was destined to remain an outsider.

## The End: After *Deadlock*

*Deadlock* was an exciting and original film, but Klick may still be best known for his follow-up film *Supermarket*, which was shot in 1973 in the port neighborhood of Hamburg. *Supermarket* deals with Willi, a young man who lives in Hamburg's streets, commits a series of crimes, and falls for a prostitute. Its aesthetics represent a departure from *Deadlock*, and Klick traded in the earlier film's semi-apocalyptic desert universe for the grit of Hamburg. Harun Farocki, enamored of the film's approach to realism, observed, "The streets have neither been cleared nor are they left as they are; the images are neither constructed nor found. . . . The *Berlin Evening News* [*Abendschau*] wouldn't do it any other way" (1974, 435).

*Supermarket* reflects a blend of international influences. At the film's beginning, Willi commits a petty crime, which is foiled by a group of young kids—a sequence that recalls the young children at the beginning of *Ludwig*. An unfortunate figure, he is simply and idly moving through the streets when the police, whose attention has been drawn to him for no apparent reason, pick him up. He is stylized somewhat as Malcolm McDowell was during that era, and one would hardly be wrong to associate this character's misanthropy with figures connected to England's Angry Young Men movement and ultimately with the British New Wave, including the protagonists of Tony Richardson's *The Loneliness of the Long Distance Runner* (1962) and Lindsay Anderson's *If* (1968), both of which center on disaffected young men who turn to violence. If Wierczejewski's Willi is said to resemble characters played by McDowell, who starred in *If*, viewers might also be tempted to think of Stanley Kubrick's *A Clockwork Orange* (1971), which premiered in Germany in March 1972, particularly during the sequence in which Willi returns with an affluent man to an apartment that features a gaudy fountain and gaudy décor, all of which calls to mind how out of place McDowell's character Alex was when he found himself in Frank Alexander's bourgeois home.

Critics and historians who would highlight Klick's enduring fascination with the United States and its films may note that he proceeded to make a documentary about the Kentucky Derby entitled *Derby Fever USA* (1978), which he then followed with the feature film *White Star* (1983), a work he shot largely in English in order to accommodate the American stars Dennis Hopper and David Hess. Stories from the filming of *White Star* center largely on Klick having to rewrite the film around Hopper's unpredictable behavior, his cocaine habit, and his refusal to learn his lines. Klick also remains known for having been replaced by producer Bernd Eichinger as the director of *Wir Kinder vom Bahnhof Zoo* (*Christiane F.*, 1981). Klick had begun to cast the film with indigent young people and drug users who lived in and around the train station, attempting to repeat the success of having discovered Wierczejewski, but Eichinger eventually handed the film over to Uli Edel, leaving Klick's fans to imagine a great film that might have been.[16] Not long after, Klick gave up making feature films, and in *Doomed Love* he explains that he grew tired of applying for funding. The process, he says, started clinging like lead to his legs. According to Peters, "Klick turned his back on Germany and did not make another film, at least not under his own name" (2014b, 18). Peters remarks that a DVD box set of Klick's films was released in Germany to coincide with the director's seventy-fifth birthday, but these films are still not available to most American audiences. What was important in his major works was emulating the rousing and sometimes relentlessly forward-moving narratives of American films—Klick's belief in piling action upon action, an attempt to make films with the same dynamism and fire as the Rolling Stones, a British band under the influence of American rock-and-roll, made music. To achieve that, however, Klick studied, drew upon, and emulated French and Italian films, as had many of his German contemporaries.

## Notes

1 Klick's comment in German is: "Was ich an der ganzen linken Bewegung, wenn sie überhaupt noch existiert, bis heute falsch finde, ist diese Sinnesfeindlichkeit" (quoted in Busche 2014). This and all other translations from German are my own.
2 On this dichotomy, put forward in *Doomed Love*, see Rentschler 2019.
3 The subsidy situation is discussed at length in Elsaesser, especially chapter 1, "Film Industry—Film Subsidy," (1989, 8–35).
4 In the film *Doomed Love*, an article is shown on-screen with the declarative headline: "The Old Film Is Dead—Is the New Film Too?" ("Der alte Film ist tot—der neue auch?"). A second Oberhausen Declaration is mentioned by Rentschler. See Eric Rentschler, "The 2013 Berlinale," *ArtForum* 51.9 (May 2013), https://www.artforum.com/print/201305/the-2013-berlinale-40444. The text of that second, untitled Oberhausen Declaration in 1965, signed by Jean-Marie Straub, Thome, Lemke, and others is reprinted in Scott MacKenzie, ed., *Film Manifestos and Global Cinema Cultures: A Critical Anthology* (Berkeley: University of California Press, 2021), 153–54.
5 Herzog uses the phrase frequently. For example, see *High Profiles* 2012.
6 According to Harald Peters, Klick had found Wierczejewski by chance in a run-down flat for unemployed people in Hamburg (2014b, 18).
7 Rentschler makes precisely this point: "What is so vexing about Graf and Sievert's overarching thesis is their employment of a straw man and a false opposition. To maintain that the only genre created by New German Cinema is the *Autorenfilm* is to ignore the Berlin worker films, the wave of anti-*Heimatfilme*, the noteworthy variations on the American as well as the spaghetti western, the spate of literary adaptations, road movies, subversive melodramas by Fassbinder and others, and, of course,

its inordinately successful and internationally resonant historical retro films" (2019, 228).

8 The film was also released by Alpha-Filmverleih under the title *Der kleine Vampir* (*Little Vampire*). For purposes of this essay, I am referring only to the film's better-known title *Bübchen*.

9 See Busche (2014, 8), who writes that at the time of *Ludwig*'s release critics loved it and praised it as the first "anti-*Heimatfilm*." *Ludwig* won prizes at short film festivals in Tours and Cracow.

10 See Laura McMahon, "Imitation, Seriality, Cinema: Early Fassbinder and Godard," in *A Companion to Rainer Werner Fassbinder*, ed. Brigitte Peucker (Malden, MA: Blackwell, 2012), 79–100. Schlöndorff also drew heavily on French filmmakers, particularly Jean-Pierre Melville. See Hans-Bernhard Moeller and George Lellis, *Volker Schlöndorff's Cinema: Adaptation, Politics, and the "Movie-Appropriate"* (Carbondale: Southern Illinois University Press, 2002), 11–13.

11 On this point, see also von Berg (1993, 70); and Lisa Haegele, "Beyond the Left: Violence and the Politics of Affect in Roland Klick's *Bübchen* (*Little Boy*, 1968)," *The Sixties* 10.1 (2017): 45–62.

12 The concept of the "grand image maker" or mega-narrator who is not the film's intradiegetic narrator but rather the perspective of the film's assembler is borrowed from Gaudreault and Jost (2000, 58).

13 In Sandra Prechtel's documentary, *Roland Klick: The Heart Is a Hungry Hunter* (2012), Klick says that he watched Antonioni's *La Notte* (1961) twelve times and did classroom presentations on it as a student.

14 The description "desert troglodyte" is attributed to Friedrich Luft in von Berg (1993, 88).

15 See also Peters 2014a.

16 The drama of the film's casting and the missed opportunity are described in von Berg (1993, 131–38) and in *Roland Klick: The Heart Is a Hungry Hunter*.

## Works Cited

Busche, Andreas. 2014. "Aus dem Archiv: Roland Klicks Exile on Mainstream." *Splatting Image*, May 26, 2. http://www.splatting-image.com/?p=284.

Elsaesser, Thomas. 1989. *New German Cinema: A History*. New Brunswick: Rutgers University Press.

Farocki, Harun. 1974. "Supermarkt." *Filmkritik* 213 (September): 435.

Gaudreault, André, and François Jost. 2000. "Enunciation and Narration." In *A Companion to Film Theory: An Anthology*, edited by Robert Stam and Toby Miller, 45–63. Oxford: Blackwell.

Grob, Norbert. 1984. "Umsonst ist nur der Tod: Gesehenes, Gelesenes, Gedachtes—Die Filme des Roland Klick." *epd Film*, no. 10: 15–18.

*High Profiles*. 2012. "Depth of Field: Werner Herzog." March 27. https://highprofiles.info/interview/werner-herzog/.

Liebert, Juliane. 2019. "Anarchie ist Ordnung." *Süddeutsche Zeitung*, July 3. https://www.sueddeutsche.de/kultur/kino-jubilaeum-anarchie-ist-ordnung-1.4509570.

Peters, Harald. 2014a. "Er war zu verrückt für den deutschen Film." *Die Welt*, July 9. https://www.welt.de/kultur/kino/article129932835/Er-war-zu-verrueckt-fuer-den-deutschen-Film.html

———. 2014b. "Junger Mann, so geht das hier nicht." *Die Welt* (Berlin edition), July 9, 18.

Rentschler, Eric. 2019. "An Elegy for German Cinema: Dominik Graf's Doomed Loves and Open Wounds." *New German Critique* 46.3: 207–33.

Seidl, Claudius. 2010. "Das Unglück des Helden ist das Glück des Films." *Frankfurter Allgemeine Zeitung*, March 21. https://www.faz.net/aktuell/feuilleton/kino/momente-des-deutschen-films-vi-das-unglueck-des-helden-ist-das-glueck-des-films-1954920.html.

von Berg, Ulrich. 1993. *Das Kino des Roland Klick*. Essen: edition filmwerkstatt.

Widmann, Andreas Martin. 2018. "Verloren im Supermarket: Jenseits des Neuen Deutschen Films—Kino und Karriere von Roland Klick." *Lettre International* 123: 112–17.

Wildermann, Patrick. 2013. "Der unbeugsame Roland Klick." *Tagesspiegel*, February 9, 2. https://www.tagesspiegel.de/kultur/deutsches-kino-der-unbeugsame-roland-klick/7760164.html.

# 3

# THE MANY BETRAYALS OF HARUN FAROCKI'S *BETROGEN*

*Nora M. Alter*

In October 2017, the Kino Arsenal theater in Berlin screened a series of films by the late filmmaker artist Harun Farocki. That the Arsenal would host a retrospective of the director's work was not surprising as Farocki had a long-standing relationship with the independent film institute, which not only had shown many of his films but for which he had curated several programs in his capacity as film critic. The lineup in 2017 included well-known classics such as *Nicht löschbares Feuer* (*Inextinguishable Fire*, 1969) and *Bilder der Welt und Inschrift des Krieges* (*Images of the World and the Inscription of War*, 1988), as well as recently restored prints of *Zwei Wege* (*Two Paths*, 1966) and *Etwas wird sichtbar* (*Before Your Eyes: Vietnam*, 1982). At the time of the retrospective, Farocki was a "star" in both the German filmmaking world and the international art scene. From 1966, when he began his career, to his death in 2014, he made over one hundred media works. Over forty of these were produced by 1982—the year of Rainer Werner Fassbinder's death, which critics often use to mark the end of New German Cinema. And yet, until the 2000s, Farocki was, in his words, "Germany's best known unknown filmmaker" (2004, 177). He worked on the margins of the West German film world in relative obscurity; despite that, in addition to his filmmaking, he was a prolific writer and critic as well as the editor from 1974 to 1984 of the German-language film journal *Filmkritik*. Thomas Elsaesser recalls that he first knew Farocki as a writer and only later as a filmmaker.

The question arises as to why a West German film director who has achieved such a level of international prominence and recognition today was virtually ignored during the heights of New German Cinema and its immediate aftermath. Farocki's exclusion raises questions about the codes in play and the rules of the game that allowed some to be part of the club while others were kept out. Further, what changed to cause Farocki to be suddenly catapulted into success whereas the brilliance of others has waned? There are no simple or easy answers but, I argue, Farocki's decades-long peripheral status coincides with myriad circumstances involving questions of politics, genre, and distribution platforms.

During the first phase of his filmic career, while Farocki was still a student at the dffb (Deutsche Film- und Fernsehakademie Berlin / German Film and Television Academy Berlin), he was a political activist. He made unapologetic films such as *Die Worte des Vorsitzenden* (*Words of the Chairman*, 1968), protesting the visit of the shah of Iran to Berlin, and *Wie nimmt man einem Polizisten den Helm ab* (*How to Remove a Police Helmet*, 1969), which called for direct action. A member of the inaugural class at the dffb, he joined the Dziga Vertov Student Group, which temporarily took over the film academy. His classmates at the dffb included Helke Sander, Helma Sanders-Brahms, Skip Norman, Wolfgang Peterson, Hartmut Bitmosky, and Holger Meins—none of whom became part of the core NGC team, although both Sander and Sanders-Brahms were sometimes included due to tireless efforts by feminist critics and academics to expand the canon and permit voices from the so-called margins to be heard. However, it is interesting to note that initially it was these two filmmakers' treatment of women's issues and stories that were lauded rather than earlier films' subjects such as Farocki's protest against the Vietnam War in *Ihre Zeitungen* (*Their Newspapers*, 1968) on which Sander served as assistant director, or the economic plight of guest workers as in Sanders-Brahms's *Die industrielle Reserve-Armee* (*The Industrial Reserve Army*, 1971). At the time, positions on gender equality and representation were a safer bet than an anti–US stance or economic questioning. Farocki's openly Marxist position and his direct critique of capitalism as well as US imperialism were quite simply too radical for North American critics to include in their formation of NGC. Although Danièle Huillet and Jean-Marie Straub occupied a position similar to Farocki's, the opacity of their films made their politics less obvious, leading critics to focus more on their formal interventions. Simply put, Farocki's brand of radical politics was not compatible with the promotion and export of West German cinema around the globe.

The second significant obstacle preventing Farocki from being part of NGC had to do with the type of films he made. For the first twenty years, he worked primarily in nonfiction, making essay films, observational documentaries, and agit-prop films. And whereas Wim Wenders, Werner Herzog, and Fassbinder all made essay films, these were all clearly demarcated from their fictional features in terms of both length and distribution. Instead, Farocki sought to make feature-length essay films such as *Erzählen* (*About Narration*, 1975), *Zwischen zwei Kriegen* (*Between Two Wars*, 1978), and *Before Your Eyes: Vietnam* that interwove documentary and fiction to produce histories of labor, narrative theory, image production, and media spectacle. These multi-layered interventions contain multiple densely interwoven strands of narrative that are difficult to follow and did not appeal to international (or even national) audiences that expected clearly defined generic offerings.

Finally, further inhibiting Farocki's entry into the international cinematic scene was the fact that beginning in the 1970s and through to the early 1990s his main source of funding and distribution was through West German television networks. Even though television had more cultural power and prestige than in the United States, it was still viewed as a lesser medium than film in terms of both social status and aesthetic properties. Farocki lacked the backing of major funding sources that would have permitted him to make films that attained the production levels of NGC directors. Additionally, television production hindered the international distribution of Farocki's films, and it was not until the 1990 that a subtitled video cassette of *Images of the World and the Inscription of War* was distributed in North America.

To return to the 2017 retrospective at the Arsenal, there was one significant surprise in the program: a film that no one in the audience (many of whom were personal friends of Farocki or specialists who had carefully studied his oeuvre) had seen. This was Farocki's only fictional feature film, *Betrogen* (*Betrayed*, 1985), a noir-style thriller. On that fall evening, the audience filed into the theater with some trepidation, unsure of what we were going to see. After all, Farocki had publicly decried the film, even calling it "silly" (2009, 225). There was a fear that this would indeed be an embarrassment from a filmmaker whom many revered as Germany's equivalent of Godard. The response after the screening was one of perplexity, for instead of the anticipated discomfort and unease, we were pleasantly surprised by how good *Betrayed* was. The question then immediately arose as to why this film had been obscured institutionally and repressed personally by Farocki.

*Betrayed* constitutes an anomaly in Farocki's oeuvre for a number of reasons, not least of which is that he completely disavowed the entire project. During his lifetime, few knew about the existence of *Betrayed*, and even fewer had ever seen it. Farocki usually refused to discuss the work, and in one of the rare instances in which he did address it, he did so with marked disdain: "I had to take more criticism and scorn for this film than for any other one. . . . Today I don't want to see or show *Betrogen*. Some of it is really silly" (2009, 225). And it was in part because of the failure of *Betrayed* that he turned to making documentary films. As he states unequivocally: "The attempt to make a feature film that adheres to rules was a complete failure. Hence documentary films" (2017, 304).

But the 2017 Arsenal audience was neither the only nor the first one to be impressed by the film. In a 1986 review of noteworthy films from 1985, film journalist Kraft Wetzel cited one significant "surprise": Harun Farocki's *Betrayed*. Prophetically, Wetzel, who extolled the film's virtues, was aware that "it will be overlooked" and that "film historians will be puzzled by this [oversight] in thirty years" (1986, 18).[1] Moreover, despite Farocki's stance of seeming indifference approximately twenty years after the film's release, at the time of its making, Farocki's position on *Betrayed* was just the opposite. He had invested all his resources—material and emotional—into its production. He was convinced that it would catapult him to success in the field of feature filmmaking. Though he was prolific as both an independent filmmaker and a writer, Farocki yearned for the international fame of those other West German filmmakers such as Fassbinder, Herzog, and Wenders, whom he had decried in his writings. Clearly, he was not satisfied with being merely "the best-known unknown filmmaker in Germany."

In advance of the production of *Betrayed*, in November 1983, Farocki wrote a letter to his friends, colleagues, and staff at *Filmkritik* to say goodbye. He had never abandoned the journal for any of his other film projects and had consistently used it as a venue to promote his work. Farocki's stated reasons for resigning are understandable and to a certain extent predictable: problems with understaffing, financial instability, and the general institutional precarity of the "independent" film, television, and writing culture in West Berlin. The letter is written in the tone of a somewhat exhausted and beleaguered individual who quite simply cannot continue under these circumstances. Toward the end, he states, "With my departure, I would like to impart the futility of this endeavor" (Farocki 1983). Such hopelessness from someone who had devoted the past twenty years of his life to building and being part of an extremely tight-knit community was surprising, for there were always hard times. However, it is perhaps more understandable considering the new film project he was about to undertake—a project that would lead to many such breaks. After his farewell to *Filmkritik*, Farocki's writerly output slowed considerably: in 1983, he published no fewer than thirty-three pieces, whereas in 1984 he wrote two and in 1985 only one. His departure from *Filmkritik* was but one of several goodbyes during that period. But perhaps even more significant than leaving *Filmkritik* was his dismissal of his steadfast production team: as he was embarking on his most ambitious project to date—a commercial feature with a professional cast and crew—there was no place for personal friends and colleagues.

*Betrayed* opened at the Nineteenth International Hof Film Festival in October 1985. In subsequent years, it had a limited festival run, with screenings at the Edinburgh Film Festival (August 1986), Journées cinématographiques d'Orleans (November 1986), and the International Festival for New Cinema in Montreal (November 1987). It was broadcast on television in 1989 and screened once in Berlin at the FSK Kino in 1990, after which point, for all intents and purposes, it disappeared. Upon its premiere, the reception of *Betrayed* was rather neutral. Up to this time, Farocki was known primarily as a writer, editor, and maker of experimental documentary films and television programs. Viewers were surprised when instead of yet another powerful essayistic meditation and ideological critique they witnessed unfolding on-screen a film noir thriller involving a love story gone bad, false identity, and murder. As Wetzel remarks, "With a dreamlike certainty, Farocki uses material from everyday life that had formerly appeared as 'big themes' in his essay films about National Socialist economics. The truth of complicated facts is presented in an amazingly simple way with suggestive metaphors" (1986, 18).

Although noted at the time as not uninteresting, *Betrayed* was not picked up for international distribution and quickly sank into obscurity. This lack of immediate acclaim by the professional film public led Farocki to pen a short text in October 1985, “Ich habe genug!” He opens with the harsh pronouncement, “I don’t want to meet any more film people [*Filmmenschen*]” (2019b, 445). He continues with an acerbic critique against filmmakers, filmgoers, writers, critics, and students alike. “The film people call themselves filmmakers . . . as if they were craftsmen, as if a film was an everyday useful object like a shoe. As if it was easy to make a film. As if film came from being something useful into being an art by itself” (445–46). The rejection of *Betrayed* and Farocki’s bitter disappointment resounds throughout the essay.

Five years later, when *Betrayed* was screened at the FSK Kino, its reception was even worse. Instead of being overlooked, it provoked scathing critiques that ensured that its revival would be short-lived. As noted by critic Katrin Bettina Müller (1990), “When diving for hidden treasures, many rusty cans have seen the light of day. With the screening of Farocki’s 1985 feature *Betrayed*, previously unscreened in Berlin, the FSK Theater was hoping to resurrect a previously commercially censored film that might have the potential for being mentally stimulating. However, the dusting off of this film canister was not worth it.” Another critic concludes that the film is “totally blah [blaß] and very boring” (Glomb 1990).

The critical panning of *Betrayed* impacted Farocki enormously: not only was he unwilling to discuss or screen it, he attempted to erase it from his life. As a visit to his archive attests, Farocki was incredibly meticulous and saved every piece of information, correspondence, and documentation for each of his projects in a double system of files that were organized by both the title of the project and the calendar year. In these files, there are informal notes and comments, screenplays, and reviews, as well as bills for food and transportation, funding applications, and personal letters in the form of postcards (he loved receiving postcards) and faxes, including copies of those he sent.[2] He was obsessed with the establishment and careful organization of a record of his life and work. As a documentary filmmaker, Farocki knew well the proleptic significance of an archive.

It is therefore striking that all files, logbooks, and binders connected to *Betrayed* during the time period of its making (roughly 1984–85) are missing—except for one significant letter by Ingo Kratisch. Kratisch,

Farocki's cinematographer, had at the time already made several films with him, including *Before Your Eyes: Vietnam*, *Ein Bild* (*An Image*, 1983), and *Jean-Marie Straub und Danièle Huillet bei der Arbeit an einem Film nach Franz Kafkas Romanfragment "Amerika"* (*Jean-Marie Straub and Danièle Huillet at Work on a Film Based on Franz Kafka's "Amerika*," 1983). And after *Betrayed*, he resumed working with Farocki until the latter's death. In the brief letter, Kratisch asks Farocki why he has dismissed his entire loyal production team of the past several years and instead contracted a new team of workers and producers for *Betrayed*. The tone of the letter is marked less by confrontation than by confusion and hurt. Kratisch voices that he feels let down and *betrayed* by Farocki.

Unlike his other films, for which Farocki served as the primary producer with financial support cobbled together from various sources, including television, *Betrayed* had external backing from Helmut Wietz, whose production company, Common Film, retained the rights to the film. Additional co-producers included the Bayerische Rundfunk, Helmut Herbst, and Adolf Winkelmann. For the first time in his career, Farocki gave up his authorial rights to make this feature. He put everything into it and broke with his Berlin-based network of friends, colleagues, and workers.

Despite a generous production budget and a cast of professional actors and crew, *Betrayed* was a commercial failure. A contemporary viewing without the specific historical context does not provide any clues for why it failed. At face value, it seems like a perfectly viable film; indeed, critic Piero Scaruffi even included it on his list of top movies from 1985.[3] *Betrayed* is a finely crafted noir thriller and is not overtly genre-bending. The narrative revolves around a case of stolen identity and duplicitous role-playing. It is evocative of Petzold's *Phoenix* (2014), for which Farocki cowrote the screenplay. The plot had its roots in a newspaper story Farocki had read that related the case of a man who killed his wife and for a while successfully substituted her sister in her place. In his review essay, "Vertauschte Frauen" ("Exchanged Women") in *Filmkritik* in 1980, Farocki focuses on examples in film and literature in which one woman replaces another and the substitution goes undetected.[4] He begins with Agnés Varda's *Le bonheur* (*Happiness*, 1965): "In *Happiness* a woman is substituted for another, and the exchange goes without a hitch. A story is rarely told about the substitution of a woman in which the exchange doesn't work" (Farocki 2019c,

261). He discusses thematically similar films and novels, ranging from William Irish's *I Married a Dead Man* (1948) to François Truffaut's *Mississippi Mermaid* (1969). Farocki concludes by citing a newspaper article about a British soldier in Singapore who killed his wife and replaced her with her sister. The sister successfully takes on the identity of her murdered sibling; however, she has four children whom she must now adopt as if she were the surviving sister of the dead woman. It all goes according to plan.

Here we find the germ of Farocki's *Betrayed*. As he recalls, "I carried this newspaper clipping around with me for a long time. The paper has become yellowed and wrinkled over time" (Farocki 2019c, 264).[5] Farocki explains the recourse to a newspaper or factual story for inspiration: "Poe wrote stories in such a way that life is only communicated by the metaphors that are contained within them. That is the beauty of newspaper stories too" (264). For Farocki the stripped-down or "operational" language of factual reporting may be read simultaneously as a metaphor that symbolically points to something else.[6] In this instance, through an exchange of identity, performance and appearance become the reality. He concludes: "An exchange is also a ghost—one existence takes over another. There is an arrangement behind this, that is the rule of the game. So that the process of illusion-disillusionment is not empty, the illusion must establish and assert its own reality. The exchange is a powerful metaphor. That one person can step into the outline of another and has to live something out of the life of the other: that is too good an idea to easily become a good story" (264). (It is interesting to note that Farocki never mentions Daniel Vigne's immensely successful *Le retour de Martin Guerre* [*The Return of Martin Guerre*, 1982], which centers on a soldier [played by Gérard Depardieu] who returns from war and takes on another's identity.)

*Betrayed* is contemporaneously set in late 1970s/early 1980s Hamburg after its successful rebirth following West Germany's "economic miracle." The film pays meticulous attention to details of everyday life and the changing landscape of the country. The protagonist, Jens (Roland Schäfer), works as a *Klimatechniker* (air-conditioning technician)—a postwar American import reinforcing notions of US imperialism that even extends to controlling and regulating the environment. In his profession, he makes enough money to buy—thanks to a new mortgage system for financing—a contemporary condominium by the sea. Anna (Katja Rupe), his love interest and future wife, is employed in a high-end club, where she supplements her bar income as an "escort" to wealthy clients. When he is not working, Jens spends his time watching Anna at work and grows increasingly obsessed with her until he finally makes contact. The film focuses on his desire.[7] Anna's sister, Edith (Nina Hoger), lives alone with her two young children. She is on the run from the law (we are not quite sure why) and studies court cases in preparation for her own defense. Anna provides her with both financial assistance and help caring for the children.

Jens's marriage to Anna is doomed from the onset. She does not respond well to her new isolated existence in the modern apartment. In contrast to the vibrant life of bars and clubs, here she wanders through the various empty rooms without a purpose. The contrast between the two spaces is stressed by the lighting; the nightclub is shot in warm colors and earth tones, whereas the apartment is represented in cool lighting to stress its soulless character. The new building is without a history and provides the ideal stage on which to begin a new life. The functional and antiseptic nature of the building mirrors the middle-class marriage in which Anna finds herself, and it is only a matter of time before she returns to her former haunts. Anna's nightly absences and emotional distance fan a jealous fury in Jens. He seeks her out and tries to force her to return home with him. She wavers and, seeming to acquiesce to his demands, gets into his car to return to their home. However, as Jens begins to rail against her and become enraged, she gets out.

What happens next is ambiguous. Farocki masterfully films the key scene from the perspective of someone in the car, closely aligned with Jens's point of view. We see Anna walking in the road in front of him; there is then a cut to a shot of her purse, which she has left on the car's passenger seat. Jens reaches for the bag, and in that instant, it is not clear whether he swerves the car intentionally to hit her or temporarily loses control as he goes for the purse. Consciously or not, Jens has mortally injured Anna. However, instead of taking her to a hospital to get medical attention, he lets her die. He then disposes of her corpse, though it is not revealed how or where.

The next step in the plot is to convince Edith, who is about to lose her children, to move in with Jens and assume Anna's identity. In exchange for the charade, he will provide her and the children with a safe home and a solidly middle-class existence. *Betrayed* then portrays a series of sequences

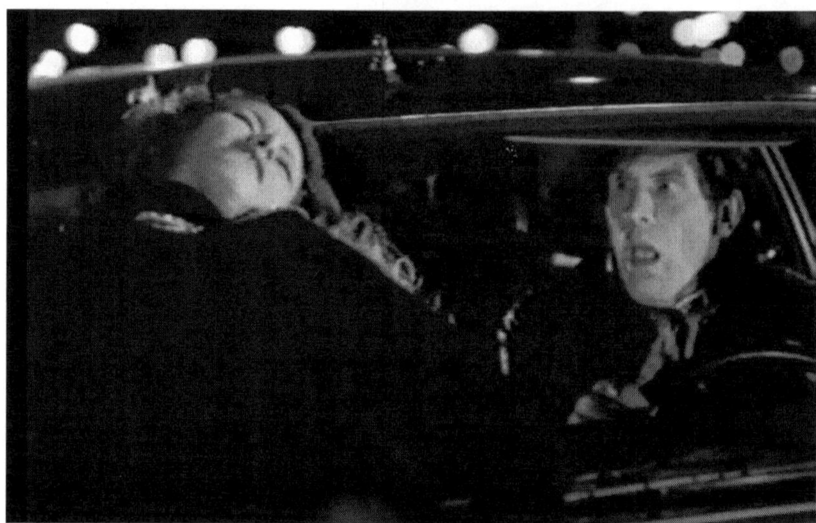

FIGURE 3.1. *Betrayed*—Car accident. (Screengrab)

in which the successful masquerade is performed. Edith slips into Anna's role and files an application for herself and her husband, Jens, to adopt her missing sister's children. The custodial exchange works without a hitch, and even later, when the social worker visits the children in their new home, the family manages their performance perfectly. Everything goes according to plan except for one glitch: one character sees through the façade.

From the outset of the film, Jens is not the only person interested in Anna. There is a strange clownlike figure, Eddi, who exists at the margins of the bar, sometimes selling flowers and cigarettes. Eddi's significance is underscored as Farocki opens *Betrayed* with a shot of him organizing his wares on a display board that he wears. Eddi thinks of himself as Anna's special friend and carries her photograph with him. Around the time of Anna's marriage and departure from the club, he enters a mental institution for treatment. Upon his release, over a year later, he returns to the bar and sees Edith acting Anna's role. As Edith and Jens leave the club, he immediately recognizes the deception and calls out, "No!" followed by "You have forced her down, you have snuffed her out."

Eddi's last words echo uneasily as he collapses in a paroxysm on the ground: "I have picture . . . have picture . . . picture." The next shot is of him receiving electroshock therapy, succeeded by a close-up of a crowbar

FIGURE 3.2. *Betrayed*—Eddi's accusation. (Screengrab)

prying up a cobblestone. The camera pulls away and pans out, and in the film's final scene a police crew digs and searches the banks of the Elbe, suggesting that they are looking for Anna's corpse.

As this lengthy description reveals, the plot is quite compelling, a fact that several critics immediately acknowledge. However, they are quick to condemn Farocki for ruining an otherwise great story. According to one, "In some films, doing without the usual narration is a creative convenience rather than an avant-garde choice. With Farocki it is worse: a first-class story falls by the wayside" (Simonoviescz 1990, 53). Though the genre elements are brought into play—crime, passion, emotion, deception, melodrama, and suspense—they are not properly calibrated and do not fit together. And Farocki, who had so carefully studied the rules of filmmaking, was betrayed by the commercial failure of the film.

*Betrayed* is about mimicry, acting, and simulation. All the agents in the film are engaged in forms of performance and role-playing. Their interactions are part of an intricate game that revolves around capital and commodity exchange. If Edith wants financial security for herself and her children, she must adopt a new role and adhere to certain conventions and guidelines. The same bourgeois contract was offered to Anna, who refused to play by the rules. An early exchange between Jens and Anna reveals her self-awareness as a commodity. Jens, like a spectator or voyeur, comes to "watch" Anna every night.

Finally, she sits down to talk to him but first demands that he buy her a drink since "that is what is done if one wants a woman's attention." Jens criticizes this ritual, and they have the following exchange regarding payment for a woman's time and attention. Jens sanctimoniously declares, "I find whores more honest. Here the girls act as if men had a chance; they act as if they are really in love with men," to which Anna retorts, "Men know that women will pretend to be in love with them when they spend money on them. That is what they pay for. One also goes to the movies even though one knows that the actors don't really die." In other words, we willingly pay for our illusions to be upheld. For Anna, Jens, and Edith, their livelihood depends on the successful performance of their roles, just like in a film. Games and role-playing are integral features in Farocki's oeuvre, extending from prominent works such as *Leben—BRD* (*Life in the FRG*, 1990), *Deep Play* (2007), and the four chapters comprising *Serious Games* (2009–10) to children's games in the five short films of *Einschlafgeschichten* (*Bedtime Stories*, 1976–77). In his autobiography, Farocki remembers significant moments in cinema and their impact on him. For example, in his early twenties, he recalls seeing Paul Newman in the role of Eddie in

FIGURE 3.3. *Betrayed*—First drink. (Screengrab)

*The Hustler* (1961), observing: "His false play consisted in showing that he belonged to them. As well, I participated in a false play and paid close attention to see that the others also played by the rules" (Farocki 2017, 49).

In *Betrayed*, as with Newman's character, role-playing and acting have become a profession. For Anna, Jens, and Edith, their livelihood, like that of all hustlers, depends successfully deceiving the clientele. To that extent, they are no longer, according to game theoretician Roger Caillois, players but rather workers. Mimicry is instrumentalized.[8] Farocki underscores, in a Lacanian gesture, that desire is produced in consumers of the game even as they are aware of being taken. It becomes like going to a film—the grandest of illusions. From his memories of Newman to his navigation of everyday life in *Betrayed*'s narrative, Farocki underscores parallels between filmmaking and game-playing. Cinema is about successfully creating different imaginary worlds in which the spectator momentarily loses him- or herself despite the knowledge that the world on-screen is not real: *Je sais bien, mais quand même . . .* ("I know very well but nevertheless . . ."). In an explicit nod to Lacan, Farocki demonstrates that Jens, by violating the implicit rules and conventions of fantasy through his attempt to possess his fetishistic object of desire, is doomed to failure. In *Betrayed*, human relations are harshly reduced to economic transactions in which both parties know the value of the negotiated goods. One has to pay to play the game.

The story of Jens and Anna is thus transformed into a metaphor for cinema and a metonym for life more generally. Yet the question remains: what accounted for *Betrayed*'s failure at the box office? The narrative was compelling, but how it was told, its form, was decried as being too "avant-garde." As one critic laments: "The artificiality is intentional" (Müller 1990), while another charges that "Farocki's characters are so artificial to the extent that their dialogue is ready to be printed, thereby diminishing any interest in either them or the newspaper article from which their story was taken" (Glomb 1990). Specifically, critics responded to a stylized form of acting and the distanciation effect that Farocki developed from Brecht. The actors act in a way that reflects on itself and draws attention to the fact that they are playing roles that have been crafted for them by society. Such a method is intended to break the fourth wall with the audience and to produce a new state of social awareness. However, in the case of *Betrayed*, the actors' performances were roundly condemned as "abysses that open up with every word. The unspeakable hides behind the banality. The actors themselves don't believe the lines they deliver" (Müller 1990). The actors are faulted for breaking the conventional code of make-believe and drawing attention to the fact that they are acting and not *believing*.

Two years prior to the making of *Betrayed*, Farocki had worked as an actor with Brechtian filmmakers Huillet and Straub in their film *Klassenverhältnisse* (*Class Relations*, 1983). In this adaptation of Franz Kafka's *Amerika*, Farocki plays the role of Delamarche. Farocki details their rigorous rehearsal process and work with actors in his *Jean-Marie Straub and Danièle Huillet at Work on a Film Based on Franz Kafka's "Amerika."* Every phrase, word, and syllable is meticulously calibrated and rhythmically measured so that the lines achieve at once a natural but stilted delivery. Because Huillet and Straub repeated exactly Kafka's original literary language from the novel, the formality of the exchanges is already built into the dialogue. In the case of *Betrayed*, with its contemporary setting and original corresponding screenplay, the awkwardness of the dialogue manifests in both Farocki's scripted language and the delivery of the lines.

The Brechtian alienation effect is further reinforced by Farocki's recourse to an acting technique based on *gestus* that further reveals the embeddedness of bourgeois ideology. For example, the fatal act of leaving her purse in the car underscores Anna's willingness to abandon a particular way of life and to resume her status outside of society. Additional Brechtian influences in *Betrayed* manifest in the execution of the narrative, which instead of flowing smoothly unfolds in a series of, at times, disjointed episodes. It is left for the viewer to connect the dots and fill in the gaps; thus, it is never shown how or where Jens disposes of Anna's corpse or why Eddi is institutionalized. As one anonymous reviewer remarks in a blurb used to promote the film, "The most important aspects of his film take place between the images, that is to say in the black holes between edits."[9] Other critics were not as generous in their assessment: "Instead of just telling a story, Farocki (and he shares this with many German filmmakers) insists on an analysis. For most other German films this comes at the expense of the narrative; however, Farocki's script stands on its own, only his narrative style ruins what could have been brilliant" (Simonoviescz 1990, 53). Early on, Farocki perfected a Brechtian filmmaking style in essay films such as *Inextinguishable Fire, Eine Sache, die sich versteht. 15 mal*

(*Something Self-Explanatory (15x)*, 1971), *Between Two Wars*, and *Before Your Eyes: Vietnam*; however, the translation of these effects into a feature film was not successful. The response to this unconventional presentation of the story, combined with an artificial style of acting, led to the following withering assessment: "They act as if they were in a 20-Minute TV series between commercials" (53).

In addition to Brecht, another important influence on Farocki at the time was Robert Bresson. Immediately prior to making *Betrayed*, Farocki had been deeply immersed in researching the films of Bresson both for a television broadcast, *"L'Argent" by Bresson*, and for a special issue of *Filmkritik* devoted to the French director. In his contribution to that issue, "Bresson ein Stilist" ("Bresson a Stylist"), Farocki singles out several characteristics that distinguish the director.[10] First, he notes that "Bresson never uses long shots, and never provides an overview of the entirety before focusing in on a small detail" (Farocki 2019a, 438).[11] And in *Betrayed* Farocki too eschews establishing shots and compositions that would provide a totalizing view. The film begins with a disorienting over-the-shoulder shot of Eddi arranging cigarettes and flowers, followed by a cut to parts of Jens's light-blue car with partially obscured words printed on it, followed by a cut to the bar, in which Anna is first presented from the back, her face reflected, but barely discernible, in a mirror. After this rapid series of shots, the camera moves back, and a totality of the sequence is provided. The reveal is slow, like the erotic stripteases performed in various clubs in Hamburg's Reeperbahn (red light) district where *Betrayed* is set.

Another of Bresson's stylistic tendencies that impressed Farocki is the French director's way of "tight cutting," a narrow editing style that further pronounces the fact that the totality is assembled out of shards and fragments. Reviewers comment on Farocki's editing style both positively and negatively: as Müller (1990) recognizes, "In the interface between shots, the blind spots of perception, the truth lurks." In his essay in *Filmkritik*, Farocki notes that for Bresson, one of the most critical exchanges is the "look." *Betrayed* is replete with long shots of characters gazing at each other or gazing into an off space, their eyes filmed unblinkingly by the camera. Jens watches Anna; Anna watches Jens watching her; their dialogues are punctuated by long periods of silence in which the camera focuses on eyes that gaze off-screen.

Additionally, Farocki remarks that Bresson's films are replete with figures on society's margins who don't fit in. Anna is an outsider who cannot conform to bourgeois life and considers Jens's apartment a prison. She frequently runs away and is most at "home" with other transients in bars and nightclubs. In the penultimate sequence of *Betrayed*, a former lover of Anna's encounters Edith, in the guise of Anna, with Jens in the bar where Anna used to perform. He immediately detects that something is off because she looks like "a housewife playing at being a whore." He condemns her for selling out and adopting a bourgeois lifestyle, reminding her of a blood pact the two had made earlier to save each other if either were to become middle class.

Finally, it is the most peripheral of all the characters, the half-mad Eddi, who plays a critical role in shattering the otherwise perfect illusion. Like the stock figure of the village idiot, he is the one able to see through the deception with a preternatural insight. As in Bresson's films, these others function to signal the falsity and duplicity of standardized middle-class norms, and West Germany's rush to embrace social conformity is condemned.

*Betrayed* becomes a mixture of Brecht and Bresson that results in a highly stilted artificial performance in which characters play clichéd roles

FIGURE 3.4. *Betrayed*—False Anna. (Screengrab)

in a well-worn narrative that begins with an attempt to convert a prostitute with a heart of gold. From the "facts" of a newspaper article, Farocki creates a metaphor for the postwar West German "consumer society." In addition to the deliberate staginess of the performances and the disorienting delivery of lines by the actors, what seems to have irritated audiences and critics was a heavy-handedness and condescension that suggested Farocki's spectators were too stupid to reach their own conclusions. As Glomb (1990) observes, "The audience is more intelligent than the filmmaker thinks." This sentiment is echoed by Simonoviescz, who sees Farocki's deliberate slow placing and alienation effects as stemming from the worst kind of didacticism. He wonders why, "with such an abundance of ideas . . . Farocki saw the need for slow-motion pace and alienation. There is enough social reality that one can read from the pictures without having to draw attention to the social relevance through didactic pauses or underlining" (1990, 53).

When *Betrayed* was first released in 1985, NGC was waning, although it still had a few good years left. NGC was a term originating in America that applied to the West German film industry based in Munich and not Berlin. Farocki had always been an outsider and even a staunch critic of many of the filmmakers associated with NGC. In his writings as editor of *Filmkritik*, he disparages, for example, Wenders's *Falsche Bewegung* (1975) and Herzog's *The Enigma of Kaspar Hauser* (1974).[12] It is not surprising that Farocki attributes *Betrayed*'s poor reception to the NGC aficionados taking their "revenge." And yet, stylistically and thematically, *Betrayed* seems to be related to those films that Farocki so disdained. Farocki was filming by the rules of a type of independent European avant-garde cinema. Unfortunately for him, by the time *Betrayed* was released, its time had come to an end. Audiences were tired of that type of film. As Simonoviescz astutely noted, "Farocki is not alone in German cinema. Instead of a story, we keep seeing explanations of reality, as if the filmmakers didn't trust the audiences to be able to read their pictures" (1990, 53).

By 1985, NGC was passé, and the Oberhausen Manifesto was under attack. Already by the beginning of the 1980s, a new type of film was in demand, as evidenced by the international success of work by one of Farocki's former student colleagues at the dffb, Wolfgang Petersen's *Das Boot* (1981), and Edgar Reitz's vastly popular television series *Heimat* (1984). National and international audiences were looking for a new product that embraced formal cinematic conventions and did not stress the viewer with an alienating and off-putting style. They desired a new cinema that was brighter, more contemporary, and global in its appeal—in short, more like Hollywood. In 1985, such a film was presented at festivals at the same time as Farocki's—Doris Dörrie's "light-hearted" feminist comedy, *Männer* (*Men*, 1985). *Men*, a first feature film by a new generation of West German filmmakers, presented itself as the antidote to the gloom and doom of the immediate postwar era. It signaled that West Germany had overcome its past and was ready to move on and focus on contemporary concerns like other Western nations.

A decade after the premiere of *Betrayed*, two significant events changed Farocki's cinematic trajectory and catapulted him out of obscurity. The first was the production of his first dual-screen installation, *Schnittstellle* (*Interface*, 1995), commissioned by the Lille Museum of Modern Art; the second was his collaboration with Christian Petzold on the latter's *Pilotinnen* (*Pilots*, 1995). Both projects were pivotal for Farocki. *Interface* marked the beginning of his career in the art world, a third life in which he soon became an international "art star." Farocki's work on *Pilots* initiated a close working relationship with Petzold that resulted in a dozen feature films. Whereas for the art world, Farocki's politics shifted from a rigid Brechtian critique of capitalist principles to a less conspicuous Flusserian-influenced media archeology, in his partnership with Petzold Farocki continued his denouncement of bourgeois liberalism. Farocki sought to play by the rules of the game in 1985, but his timing was off; by 1995 new alignments ensured that he would finally be recognized.

## Notes

A version of this essay was previously published in *Harun Farocki: Forms of Intelligence*, by Nora Alter. Copyright © 2024 Columbia University Press. Reprinted with permission of Columbia University Press.

1 Unless otherwise noted, all translations from German are my own. Farocki quotations are in his original English.
2 Farocki would use fax technology for his most personal and intimate correspondences to ensure that there would always be a record.

3 Piero Scaruffi, "Best Films of the 1980s," 7.0 Harun Farocki, *Betrogen/Betrayed*, https://www.scaruffi.com/cinema/chro980.html.
4 Originally published in *Filmkritik* 282 (June 1980): 274–79.
5 An earlier version of *Betrayed* may be found in Farocki's unpublished and undated screenplay *Zwei Schwestern* (*Two Sisters*).
6 The term "operational language" comes from Roland Barthes's *Mythologies*, a text that Farocki reviewed in 1965. Farocki translates the concept of a ready-made "operational language"—that of Marxist economic theory—to film and settles on the form of nonfictional or documentary rather than poetic or fictional film to transcode his transmission of abstract political thought. The language of newspapers becomes equivalent to the language of documentary.
7 As Petzold recollects when he studied with Farocki, they would watch many films with shots of naked women, "but the films that got us excited were always about the one who desires" (2023, 248).
8 Caillois observes, "A characteristic of play, in fact, is that it creates no wealth or goods, thus differing from work or art." Work should be "an occasion of pure waste." He continues, "As for the professionals—the boxers, cyclists, jockeys, or actors who earn their living in the ring, track or hippodrome or on the stage . . . it is clear they are not players but workers" (2001, 5–6).
9 This insight may have been offered by Farocki, who tended to promote his films in the form of reviews or interviews with himself, often using the alias Rosa Mercedes.
10 This was, incidentally, Farocki's last contribution to the journal written before he resigned from the editorial board, but it was published several months later.
11 Originally published in *Filmkritik* 327 (March 1984): 62–67.
12 See Harun Farocki, "Jeder für sich und Gott gegen alle," *Filmkritik* 227 (November 1975): 515–16; and Harun Farocki, "*Falsche Bewegung*. Ballade vom Nihilismus," *Filmkritik* 227 (November 1975): 521.

## Works Cited

Caillois, Roger. 2001. *Man, Play, and Games*. Champagne-Urbana: University of Illinois Press. First published in 1958.

Farocki, Harun. 1983. "Brief vom 8. November 1983." Sammlung Johannes Beringer.

———. 2004. "Making the World Superfluous: An Interview with Harun Farocki." In *Harun Farocki: Working on the Sightlines*, edited by Thomas Elsaesser, 177–89. Amsterdam: Amsterdam University Press.

———. 2009. "Written Trailers." In *Harun Farocki: Against What? Against Whom?* edited by Antje Ehmann and Kodwo Eshun, 220–41. London: Koenig Books.

———. 2017. *Zehn, zwanzig, dreißig, vierzig: Fragment einer Autobiographie*. Berlin: Harun Farocki Institut/n.b.k.

———. 2019a. "Bresson ein Stilist." In *Harun Farocki: Ich habe genug! Texte 1976–1985*, edited by Volker Pantenburg, 438–43. Berlin: Harun Farocki Institut/n.b.k.

———. 2019b. "Ich habe genug!" In *Harun Farocki: Ich habe genug! Texte 1976–1985*, edited by Volker Pantenburg, 445–46. Berlin: Harun Farocki Institut/n.b.k.

———. 2019c. "Vertauschte Frauen." In *Harun Farocki: Ich habe genug! Texte 1976–1985*, edited by Volker Pantenburg, 261–67. Berlin: Harun Farocki Institut/n.b.k.

Glomb, Ronald. 1990. *Volksblatt*, February 15.

Müller, Katrin Bettina. 1990. *Die Tagezeitung*, February 15.

Petzold, Christian. 2023. "'As if We Were Dreaming It': Christian Petzold's *Undine*." Interview with James Lattimer. In *Christian Petzold: Interviews*, edited and translated by Marco Abel, Aylin Bademsoy, and Jaimey Fisher, 244–51. Jackson: University Press of Mississippi.

Simonoviescz, Andre. 1990. "Mord in Werbeblock." *Tip Berlin*, no. 4 (February 15–28): 53.

Wetzel, Kraft. 1986. "Was antwortet der Neue Deutsche Film auf Zimmerman und Hollywood?" *Film*, no. 5: 16–22.

# 4

# GNOMIC ANIMATION

## Decrypting the German New Wave

*Jennifer Lynde Barker*

The Oberhausen Manifesto is one of the few documents of its kind authored by animation filmmakers alongside their cinema colleagues, yet few people connect animation with New German Cinema. This is not surprising, given that animation is often associated with advertising, industry, and children's stories rather than political critique or experimentation. But while German animation did have a solid presence in advertising and children's entertainment, it also had prewar avant-garde roots that were back in bloom by the late 1950s. In fact, two signatories of the manifesto, Boris von Borresholm and Wolfgang Urchs, were responsible for directing and producing a collection of remarkable, award-winning animated films throughout the 1960s that defined West German animation for national and international audiences. Featuring eccentric juxtapositions of styles, postmodern pastiche, existentialist absurdist themes, and ironic cynical appraisals of human frailty, they took their cue from international graphic art design, European cinematic new waves, and prewar modernism.

While this work has seldom been read in relation to the larger movements of Young German Cinema (YGC) or New German Cinema, it most obviously falls into the former category as it is already in motion in 1962 and peaks in the late 1960s.[1] In fact, animation was surprisingly pervasive in YGC films as a hybrid technique, as Franziska Bruckner (2018) has thoroughly documented.[2] However, its trajectory continues through the 1970s, so it makes little sense to read it as something other than contiguous, especially as it features the same principles. That such distinctions can be useful but restrictive is obvious, and the political intent of privileging a New German Cinema emerging from the 1968 youth and counterculture movements was surely compelling to the American critics who coined the term in the mid-1970s. Yet no enfant terrible of animation emerged from 1968; there were only the ones who continued to rage against the machine as of old. Thus, when focusing on animation from this period and in relation to NGC, it makes more sense to refer to it as a *new wave*—beginning in the late 1950s and continuing through the 1970s. It is a subcategory of film that helps to provide an illuminating perspective on the traditional understanding of the NGC, achieving an important reassessment that Eric Rentschler has advocated: the need to "complicate the master narrative that attended the movement and summarily shortchanged films made in the FRG before 1962 and after 1985"—so that we can "conceptualize different chronologies and different narratives" and discover "unacknowledged connections and continuities" (2012, 123).

Canonized as they were by auteur theory, the films of the younger generation—Rainer Werner Fassbinder, Werner Schroeter, Wim Wenders, Margarethe von Trotta, and others—have remained more prominent than the work of the Oberhausen Manifesto signatories (save Alexander Kluge and Edgar Reitz). Lack of availability and a more liminal and hybrid nature has also led to these works' neglect. As Ralph Eue observes, much of the work of the YGC was not systematically collected or even lost, "so for decades one was confronted with the historical curiosity that the time of the Oberhausen Manifesto is equally one of the most famous and one of the least known epochs in German film history" (2012, 3).[3] And while distinctions between young versus new can be useful, they essentially point to the same impulse: what the manifesto describes as "a new film language" conveying "concrete intellectual, formal, and economic conceptions" (Oberhausen 2014, 153). In terms of the animation, it shares with NGC an anti-authoritarian focus, critiques the German past and present, decries the culture industry, challenges popular narrative filmmaking, and offers a pronounced formal innovation. It is distinctive, however, in being less personal and self-tortured—less about the self and more about the continuity of the self with others. Thus, a history of animation provides both an alternate chronology and narrative for the NGC period.

It is the very lack of personal obsession or narrative focus and alienating modernist representations that makes the animated works ironically accessible to a global audience and distinctive as a film form. With their aesthetic rejection of realism they are able to uniquely "remap and redefine reality," as Rentschler notes—one of the desired goals of the NGC (2012, 120). They do so through abstract, surreal representation and symbolic (nonnarrative) structures that make character identification difficult. Thomas Elsaesser has described narrative force as an essential characteristic of the NGC—it was able to create "a narrative image of an entire country" that was appealing to those outside of Germany (1989, 6). Its tortured self-critique was likely what the West wanted to see at the time. But in German new wave animation, there is no pretense that the characters on-screen are human, or that we share much in common with their poetic adventures or the abstract landscapes they inhabit. What we do share is an existential core of understanding that to be human is to suffer and that the destructive abuse of power is eternally recurring. This narrative abstraction emphasizes the transnational potential of the films, as they speak to the universal. The films also align themselves with international graphic art trends from various new waves and the traditions of cosmopolitan modernism. Indeed, Borresholm's career can only be read in light of his collaborations with Eastern European émigrés and their flight from the restrictions of official state Communist cultures.

## Wolfgang Urchs and Boris von Borresholm

There were two animators who signed the Oberhausen Manifesto in 1962—Wolfgang Urchs and Boris von Borresholm. Borresholm (1912–89) was a renaissance man, born in Essen, who studied theater. He translated works by Sartre, Cocteau, Anouilh, and Giraudoux into German and wrote the important book *Dr. Goebbels: Nach Aufzeichnungen aus seiner Umgebung* (1949), which examines Goebbels's role in the Nazi propaganda machine. In post–World War II Berlin he was a dramaturge, editor, critic, and the editor in chief of *Fox Tönende Wochenschau*, an influential weekly newsreel program. His newsreels, educational films, and documentary work were connected to his anti-Nazi stance, with titles such as *Der 20. Juli 1944 vor dem Volksgerichtshof* (1954) and *Völker hört die Signale* (1958), which focus on Nazi culpability and accountability for their crimes. Borresholm first began working on animation in the 1950s, writing for two

Gerhard Fieber films and co-directing and writing *Der Spielverderber* (*The Spoilsport*) with Ferdinand Diehl in 1959. Thus, he trained with two famous German animators, both of whom represented a tradition of realism Borresholm soon rejected. In breaking with these traditions, the avant-garde work of Herbert Seggelke, Ferdinand Khittl, and Flo von Nordhoff surely proved inspirational. In particular, Seggelke's *Eine Melodie—vier Maler* (*One Melody—Four Painters*, 1955) and Khittl's *Das magische Band* (*The Magic Tape*, 1959) were brilliant films that self-consciously deconstructed animation production, interrupted master narratives, and highlighted the influence of contemporary art by Jean Cocteau and others. Borresholm received the Filmband in Gold in 1980, West Germany's highest award for filmmaking. He died in Berlin on November 9, 1989, the very day that the Berlin Wall ceased to divide East from West.

Wolfgang Urchs (1922–2016) was born in Munich but grew up in Dutch Guyana and India before attending school in Germany. He trained in graphics and painting and began working on commercial and documentary films in the postwar period, including *Schuman Plan* (1953) and *Der weiße Rabe* (1955). Like most early animators, he taught himself his craft doing commercial work and improvised by drawing on exposed X-ray film from hospitals. Urchs was part of a group in Munich that included Borresholm, Peter Schamoni, Alexander Kluge, and others who met together regularly at the Schwabinger Nest and who authored the Oberhausen Manifesto as a protest against the established industry's production excesses. This group provided fertile ground for artistic collaboration, establishing Munich as not only a center of film culture but also the epicenter for much of the best animation of the 1960s.

Their first film together, *Die Gartenzwerge* (*Garden Gnomes*), premiered at the International Short Film Festival Oberhausen in 1962. Borresholm wrote (with Schamoni) the script and produced the film while Urchs directed and animated. It is a fitting film for the announcement of a new German cinema, a biting critique of an older German generation that had enabled the fascism of the war only to then fall into the cultural fascism of postwar capitalism and consumerism. It neatly manifests the Frankfurt School critiques of Theodor Adorno and Max Horkheimer about the dangers of the culture industry, which uses popular culture to control the masses and enforce conformity.[4] *Garden Gnomes* is a blunt critique of postwar West Germany and its mindless conformity and empty consumerism. The film begins with an almost literal critique of "Papas" (and thus Papas kino) as real ceramic garden gnomes haphazardly littering the screen begin to break apart and are trashed. It is essentially a blueprint for what the Oberhausen Manifesto protests: the economic bloat and conventionality of a failed West German film industry. By opening the film with real objects, the film frames its critique with material familiar from everyday experience. With their cheeky poses on the screen mimicking their kitschy presence in suburban landscapes, the gnomes also introduce an ironic absurdity about the banality that led to fascism as well as a "littleness" and hollowness of personality. They establish a conformist landscape and cultural mediocrity that is then explicitly tied to the war as the film moves into drawn animation, with gnomes climbing out from under the rubble, their helmets transforming into nightcaps. Resembling little Deutsche Michel, they work to rebuild the city like the Trümmerfrauen did with real German cities after 1945. In their nightgowns and caps, they represent affable, hard-working, generic types who are also naïve, gullible, self-congratulatory, and prone to obeying orders.

FIGURE 4.1. *Garden Gnomes*—A garden gnome as Deutsche Michel. (Screengrab)

A competitive capitalistic world ensues with the innovation of transportation and other commercial goods. One Michel transforms into a gnome with a red cap who soon advertises himself all over town. An especially striking moment visually captures the transition from individual to copy. As the chief gnome is driven in his big car, he enters a crowd of observers who are just shapes—a field of empty signifiers. His car is slowly swallowed up by this crowd, his face ever more elusive, while in the foreground a building appears with his image on a poster. As the drive continues, he is eclipsed by the crowd and his own image, with the poster finally replacing him. It is a keenly wrought visual metaphor of mass consumption and cultural fascism. The rest of the film provides further critiques as tourists swarm into other countries, and gnomes grow fat on their economic prosperity, mindlessly consuming objects, food, culture, art, and each other. At this point, they turn back into ceramic gnomes and fall into the dustbin of history. We have thus circled back to the beginning of the film, underscoring a common critique in these films: that fascism was not a singular or linear event but is a universal, eternal threat.

*Das Unkraut* (*The Weed*, 1962) is livelier and more colorful than *Garden Gnomes* but focuses just as clearly on symbolic critique. A film about bureaucracy and passing the buck, it is a morality tale admonishing viewers to take responsibility for maintaining society. The abstract buildings and landscapes contain depth and expression infused by the color palate, and the substance of the gnomes has given way to sketchiness. This makes the characters interchangeable and nondescript, essentially cardboard cutouts of people—a further manifestation of the empty signifiers glimpsed in *Garden Gnomes*. The film's true focus is the graphic field around them, in particular the weed that grows and transforms throughout. It is the real star, as the title suggests, and the characters merely provide straw man opposition to its total ascendancy. Thus, the film not only critiques the vapid, selfish population who refuse to make the world a better place but also contains a stealthy appreciation for the vitality, perseverance, and wild beauty of the weed. If read in relation to the manifesto, the weed represents the filmmakers themselves, who destroy an indifferent citizenry to make way for a strange, new, vibrant citizen.

## Urchs and T.C. Trickstudio

Urchs opened T.C. Trickstudio in 1962 with earnings from the German Film Award for *Garden Gnomes*. This studio produced his short animated works *Die Pistole* (*The Pistol*, 1963), *Kontraste* (*Contrasts*, 1964), *Maschine* (*The Machine*, 1966), and *Nachbarn* (*Neighbors*, 1973), as well as his live-action feature film *Zeit für Träumer* (*Time for Dreamers*, 1969). Urchs's style transformed from film to film—he freely took as influence the work of John Hubley at UPA, the Zagreb School, and others, mixing childish sketching with abstractions, cutouts, caricatures, and more. His was an impure, postmodern mixture that yet always cohered in a distinctive way. Urchs continued to make animation through the 1980s, including two popular feature films—*In der Arche ist der Wurm drin* (*Stowaways on the Ark*, 1987) and *Peterchens Mondfahrt* (*Peter in Magicland*, 1990)—and the children's television series *Janoschs Traumstunde* (*Janosch*, 1986–90). His studio is perhaps best remembered for its contribution to the ZDF "Mainzelmännchen"—six gnome-like cartoon broadcasting mascots created by Wolf Gerlach. In contrast to Hans Fischerkoesen's 1950s beloved and bewhiskered Hessischer Rundfunk mascot, Onkel Otto, these beardless youth embody a NGC vibe and one can imagine them shouting to Onkel Otto: "Papas kino is DEAD!"

Premiering at Oberhausen in 1963, *The Pistol* is a surreal mixture of drawings and cutouts. The main character of the film is the titular pistol, which represents the cynically endemic violence of humankind. Like *Garden Gnomes*, the film rejects the idea of progress. Violent and unrelenting, the pistol moves of its own volition and is a villain without scruples. Everything challenges the pistol: language, nature, sustenance, creatures, power, time. But neither the arts nor sport civilize it; nothing tames its cruel and competitive nature. The film interestingly uses letters as transformative elements, perhaps the influence of Jan Lenica, including alpha, beta, and delta. While the gun is primarily a disembodied object, people are also implicated in its supremacy. We see an eye that also shoots and an ear that hears the shots. An antiwar film, it could as easily be critiquing the Algerian or Vietnam wars as World War II: the military images are universal, and the film invokes the circularity of the pistol wrecking destruction, being unhinged by language, and proliferating violence again.

*Contrasts* screened in 1964 at the Berlin IFF, where it won a Silver Bear. It focuses on a woman restlessly updating her house in order to deconstruct the pretentions of the bourgeoisie to chic modernity. It contrasts past and present and shares with the surrealists of the 1930s a love of cultural detritus. It begins with the most bourgeois of mise-en-scènes, a traditional drawing room with piano, and proceeds through myriad transformations to bring it up to date, a process that ultimately fails. Featuring cutouts, drawings, collage, cell and silhouette animation, it contrasts black and white with vivid colors, and uses color and design to express psychology and emotion. Thus, when the woman smells flowers, she is suffused with their color and presence (likely a tactic from Lenica) and her psychology is displayed with X-ray vision. Her mind is filled with the detritus of civilization and her judgment of her husband is seen as an internal procedure. In the end, her pretensions judge her, and she literally derails the film and rewinds it by climbing backward up the sprocket holes in the frame. Ultimately restoring order for its characters, *Contrasts* is most engaging when it presents a meta-awareness and verbal play about the process of representation.

*The Machine* screened at the Berlin IFF in 1966 and won another German Film Award. While *Contrasts* deliberately juxtaposed the past with the present, *The Machine* is more firmly rooted in modernity. The film begins boldly with black lines on white space, a geometric design reminiscent of Mondrian. A realistically drawn man with a suit and bowler hat (nod to Magritte) sits alone drawing stick figures until an angel kisses his head. Struck by inspiration, he designs and manufactures machines that create a variety of items, from clothes to weapons of destruction. Along the way, he eliminates his competition and invents mass production and monopoly, solidifying his control until at last artificial intelligence prevails and the machine decapitates him. As in many of Urchs's films, its allegory is soon clear, concisely moving from the invention of useful machines to the destruction wrought by them. But the style builds an engaging complexity—like the bold use of lines or the mathematical scribbling that precedes each advancement in the capitalist system. The animation's imaginativeness softens its didacticism. The music, by regular collaborator Hans Posegga, also adds depth to the film's historical and eternal drive, offering a pastiche of medieval, sacred, and modern.

Urchs made two more animated shorts of note: *Die Gouvernante* (*The Governess*, 1970) and *Nachbarn* (*Neighbors*, 1973). Combining animation and live action, *The Governess* is set in windy isolated mountains, which lends an aura of horror reinforced by credits dripping like blood down the screen. The nineteenth-century scenario contrasts with 1920s jazz in a disconcerting fusion that typifies Urchs's juxtaposition of traditional and contemporary. In their bourgeois drawing room, the live-action parents move through drawn backgrounds; after producing two children they look for help at the Governess Bazaar. This market is filled with statues that depict various "types," but instead they program a machine to construct a Frankenstein's monster from their assorted preferences. A Viking with striped socks and a helmet, she utterly commandeers their children while they faff around collecting butterflies and knitting. While picturesque, this lifestyle ossifies them—from dancing atop abstract art and smudged paint they decline into butterfly-clad bodies. The parents' shocking awakening is also their death, as their frightening children trample them with a troop of Viking youth. *The Governess* critiques neo-Nazi youth, but from the perspective of an indifferent and apathetic bourgeois culture.

Three years later, *Neighbors* has a stripped-down aesthetic with only ten lines and two minimal faces as its basic image. While featuring a variety of styles, fonts, mobile ink, and cutouts, it focuses closely on an exchange between two faces eyeing each other from opposite windows. The film has a clear affinity with Norman McLaren's *Neighbors* (1952), though the styles differ greatly. Both films create allegories of national cooperation aimed at an international audience, with two neighbors competitively and selfishly upping the ante with each other—from irritating noises to intellectual pursuits and physical violence. In McLaren's film, the two are evenly matched, but in Urchs's, one neighbor is more accomplished and adaptable than the other; he even reaches enlightenment through meditation, emitting light from an Eye of Providence on his forehead. Urchs may intend this esoteric symbol variously—as the compassionate watchfulness of God, Jeremy Bentham's symbol for the Panopticon, or the Bavarian Illuminati, an Enlightenment secret society that sought control over public life and political power.

In the end, the inferior neighbor resorts to violence, starting a fight that ends with them gruesomely ripping off each other's skin and shooting each other's skeletons in the head. Afterward, the camera pulls back slowly

FIGURE 4.2. *Neighbors*—Two neighbors, dead in the desert. (Screengrab)

to reveal the setting to be a desert surrounded by plants reminiscent of the landscapes of Henri Rousseau. Then the communal credits roll—the studio name followed by a list of individuals, an anti-auteur approach that identifies a film community. The scene is lush, barren, and macabre: it might be the stage of human history from Cain and Abel onward, engendering continual competition, drama, and bloodshed. Like McLaren's work, it is certainly a Cold War critique: both give us a vision of primal hatred and destruction, coolly observed by a natural world whose beauty only inspires conflict. But unlike McLaren's film, which ends with the directive to "love your neighbor" written in multiple languages, Urchs's postmodern irony and detachment reign supreme: stupidity, he seems to say, is inevitable.

## Borresholm and Lux-Film

Borresholm founded his studio Lux-Film in 1961 in Munich, where he produced some of the most important German animation in the 1960s and 1970s, much of it by émigrés. In 1964, he also created *Puppets*, a recut version of *The Spoilsport* (1959).[5] The subject matter is classic Borresholm, as are the Shakespearean references to *Julius Caesar* and the use of documentary-style live-action film. The movie is pedagogical and didactic, typical for an antifascist film at the time. It uses a puppet narrator who frees himself from his strings to explain the eternal return of tyrants, seducers, and charlatans, and the blockheads (*Holzköpfe*, which the puppets literally are) who are easily led by them. The film takes a look at the behind-the-scenes world of puppets between performances where history, literature, and legend exist simultaneously—a kind of postmodern space where Mephistopheles, Hitler, and the Pied Piper of Hamlin mirror one another. Borresholm uses footage from speeches by Goebbels and others to reveal public gullibility and to urge people to stay "wired" against the appealing lies of mass seducers. The didactic tone belies a fear of the continuation of dictatorships, and while the topic is very German, it is also pitched on a global scale: certainly the building of the Berlin Wall in 1961 was a reminder that the tyrants had not really been defeated.

While Urchs's work reflects an international sensibility in terms of his style and influences, Borresholm facilitated a transnational influence in Germany by hiring and promoting the work of Eastern European artists, including Jan Lenica, Vlado Kristl, Bohumil Štepán, and Kristina Böttrich-Merdjanowa. His sponsorship of these artists was a bold, important move—not least because some of them became teachers in the new university film programs. Each brought with them distinctive knowledge and experiences from countries with important traditions of graphic art and animation, but having resisted Communist rule, they focused more on representational freedom than national identity. Only Lenica and Kristl had much experience with filmmaking, and it seems likely that Borresholm aided a good deal with shaping the films. Though there is scant record of how the process worked, the collaboration is clear in terms of his consistent interest in antifascism, cultural critique, literariness, allegory, surrealism, and experimental style. Borresholm has sometimes been critiqued for not being an auteur, but part of his ethos was a rejection of dictatorial control; really, he was a bricoleur. This approach, along with his background in editing and translation, lent itself to nurturing the artistic visions of others. With an eye for talent, he helped produce animated shorts crucial to the development of German animation.

Borresholm produced several films by Lenica, all masterpieces of the era. Jan Lenica (1928–2001) was born in Poznan, Poland, worked as a graphic artist, editor, and critic after the war at *Szpilki* satirical magazine, and began making movie posters in 1950. His work in the Polish school of posters is perhaps what he is best remembered for. His graphic art style permeated his animation, which combined a linear regularity with lush colors. He began making films in collaboration with Walerian Borowczyk, including *Był sobie raz . . .* (*Once upon a Time . . .*, 1957) and *Dom* (*House*, 1958). Between 1959 and 1963 Lenica was in Paris and Poland, making the stunning existential films *Monsieur Tête* (1959), *Nowy Janko Muzykant* (*New Johnny the Musician*, 1961), and *Labyrinth* (1962). He then directed several animated films with Borresholm at Lux-Film, including the short films *Die Nashörner* (*The Rhinoceros*, 1963), *A* (1965), *Die Hölle* (1971), *Landscape* (1975), and the feature film *Adam 2* (1968). Lenica eventually moved to Germany for good, serving as the chair of animated film at Kassel University from 1979 to 1985 and professor at Berlin Hochschule der Künste from 1986 to 1994. His work provides a good case study for how filmmakers could fit into both Young and New German Cinema: his style and approach were consistent, but his films became more personal and historically reflective in the 1970s. *Landscape* in particular deconstructed his wartime experiences in grotesque but beautiful images—"visual oxymorons," as Steve Weiner notes (1992, 9).[6]

*The Rhinoceros* was Lenica's first film in Germany. Based on the play by Eugène Ionesco, it is an absurdist tale of conformity and despair, and focuses on the problem of dissidence in a world of growing submission. At first this transformation is, as in *Garden Gnomes*, sourced in the culture industry and consumption, but it soon becomes more extreme, as the film's hero, a drinker and iconoclast, discovers that people are transforming into rhinoceroses—inhuman and brutish. Its style is more minimalist than Lenica's earlier films but still features a two-dimensional plane of representation eschewing perspective for a contrast of elements. It adeptly encapsulates thoughts as images; for example, the hero's desire is projected as an image of wine, which then fills a glass, his drinking producing a cornucopia of colorful flowers bursting from his mind to convey his bliss. On another occasion, newspaper content manifests around him as images, transforming his face into a skull as the violent stories imprint on his psyche. Riffing on the symbolic function of the rhinoceros, people appear

FIGURE 4.3. *The Rhinoceros*—The protagonist's face becomes a skull as the violent images he sees in the newspaper transform his psyche. (Screengrab)

to be what they are: a man's internal organs become a machine and the hero becomes an insect when he acts like a pest. In another sequence, alphabetized filing cabinets contain objects that correspond to their letters. The visual universe Lenica develops here concisely, playfully, and eerily displays its impact with graphic and visceral punch.

A deceptively simple allegorical film, *A* begins with a quote—"Into a calm and solitary life a monster insinuates itself." This monster is as symbolic as one can get: the letter A. Lenica plays around with letters in several films—the building blocks of language and communication made manifest and intrusive in the visual field. As in *Monsieur Tête*, when people talk nonsense, it takes on a life and image of its own and works to poison others. *A* focuses this idea into an abstract allegory of how an isolated individual can be irritated and even destroyed by the invasive language, ideas, and intentional hatred of others. The man tries cajoling, seducing, flattering, and arguing with the letter, to no avail. As the letter A taunts and tortures the writer in his room, seemingly to death, the soundtrack creates a frantic and ominous atmosphere. After a triumphant victory, A implodes and disperses. Eventually the man rises again, only to be faced with the next letter in the alphabet. The inevitable existential struggle against oppression continues, in a way that has not changed in the slightest.

Lenica's *Adam 2* (1968) is an underappreciated masterwork of animation. It also appears to be the only animated feature film associated with NGC. Lenica worked for years on it with his longtime collaborators Borresholm, Renate Rühr (editing/camera), and avant-garde composer Josef Anton Riedl. It was released the same year as the classic *Yellow Submarine* (George Dunning, 1968), but few people have seen it, even though it is just as momentous, brilliantly stylized, surreal, and surprising. Of course, Riedl is not the Beatles. Rather, his experimental music offers a modernist *Verfremdungseffekt* to the film. *Adam 2* is challenging, and while its ongoing complexity of development is focused on a metaphorical coherence, that metaphor is somewhat inscrutable. His heavy reliance on Adam Mickiewicz's poetic Polish masterpiece *Dziady* (1822) caused one critic to dismiss the film, claiming, "The Polish obsession deformed the film" and it was thus "indecipherable" (Weiner 1992, 8). Such a critique highlights the obsession with nationalism that plagued the twentieth century and continues to guide thinking about identity and affinity, not to mention the problem of which nations are "relevant" or "European"—all conversations that were in play at Oberhausen, as Heide Fehrenbach outlines.[7] Yet one need not know much about *Dziady* to appreciate the scope and significance of *Adam 2*. Its obsession with the number 44, for example, need be no more specific than that of A. It is a sign, and like all signs, has multiple interpretive possibilities based on contextual understanding. If one reads or researches *Dziady*, it becomes clear that 44 refers to a Polish savior (Trencsényi and Kopeček 2007).[8] If one does not, then the film's references to Goethe's *Faust*, Alban Berg's *Wozzeck*, and *Superman* suggest other readings. An anti-epic odyssey, *Adam 2* offers a version of Prometheus, and 44 is the number on the box he steals from God, leading him on an endless retreat from divine wrath.

This remarkable film mixes high and low culture, collages old and new, contrasts heavy outlines, black-and-white backgrounds and rich bursts of vivid colors, and riffs on pop art, art nouveau, and psychedelia. The inherently cosmopolitan nature of (post)modernist representation mirrors perhaps the openness of the modern world, its lack of clear national boundaries—especially for émigrés whose lives are an amalgamation of experiences and traditions.[9] So, Adam 2 fantasizes about his place in the world and locates himself in a nexus between classical and modern heroes and antiheroes—the biblical Adam, Faust, Konrad (from *Dziady*), Superman. Lenica tells the "strange, ghostly, egregious, utterly incredible and yet true story of his life" and does so while invoking de Chirico, Topor, Lichtenstein, Karel Zeman, Heinz Edelmann, Jules Verne, Einstein, and Rousseau. In his distinctive style he incorporates Ben Day dots, spaceships, botany, numerology, time travel, torture, television's impact, shipwrecks, cross-country biking, alternate (blockhead) worlds, and angelic ascension. The mundane mixes with the surreal as *Adam 2* provides historical and thematic scope, satirical critique, and postmodern play in a way perhaps unprecedented in animated features.

While Borresholm worked most extensively with Lenica, three other artists also made important films with him. Bulgarian-born Kristina Böttrich-Merdjanowa (1933–2012) is best remembered for creating the opening credits for the long-running German television series *Tatort* in 1969.[10] She also made one film with Borresholm—*Autoportrait* (1966). Produced jointly by Lux-Film and T.C. Trickstudio, and consistent with their output, *Autoportrait* represents issues with conformity and the endless circularity of its destructive force. The film is allegorical, with "auto" being a pun on both "cars" and "self." It contrasts a flowering natural world with a dark and smoggy city full of angry cars, which resemble hedgehog-like creatures with teeth. The film portrays the modern city as a perversion of the natural order, with a cow feeding gas to cars instead of milk and a constant devouring that is devoid of nourishment. There is one live-action image in the film, of teeth, which anchors the idea of devouring and the imminence of violent altercations in reality.

Born in Zagreb, Vlado Kristl (1923–2004) made a number of films there, including *Don Kihot* (*Don Quixote*, 1961), one of the masterpieces of the early Zagreb School of animation. It screened in Oberhausen in 1962, putting Kristl at the center of the manifesto movement. He also emigrated to Munich in 1962, where Borresholm produced his film *Die Utopen* in 1967. *The Utopians* is quite different from his earlier animation, bearing more of an affinity with Borowczyk. Using drawings and cutouts, it is a chaotic melding of images, angles, and movements. The first half resembles a frantic fidgeting and restless searching filled with

FIGURE 4.4. *Addendum to Orwell*—Two "buttheads." (Screengrab)

crudely drawn images: open mouths, multiple eyes, symbols, machines, a man's hypertensive outline, a dog cavorting. The people in the film are joined to each other as bodies with three eyes and two mouths—perhaps the not-quite-utopians of the title. The film's second half features a faceless man cutting people apart with a sword, a kind of fascist destroyer of difference and enforcer of normality. In the end, the body parts hang from hooks, dripping blood—an image that resonates with Lenica's *Adam 2* and the political ravages of the late 1960s.

Czech artist Bohumil Štepán (1913–85) made collage poster art in Prague before emigrating to Munich in 1969 after the failure of the Prague Spring. While he worked primarily in illustration and poster design, he also made at least one film with Borresholm, *Die Ordnung* (*The Order*, 1971). It is a film that features Štepán's characteristic surreal collage and, much like Borresholm's "blockheads," uses butts to express the inanity of "buttheads" who simply follow orders. In keeping with the other films Borresholm produced, it focuses on the problem of conformity. This ideological consistency provides a clear legacy for Borresholm's production and translation of the work of others in the NGC period.

## Conclusion

In their animated and experimental work, Borresholm and Urchs created a body of work that critiques and satirizes the Nazi past and the conformist present and contributes to the growing body of postmodern work emerging after World War II. Their allegorical gnomes, buttheads, and blockheads speak to the ongoing tide of thoughtlessness that they believed formed the basis for fascism. Their work still resonates, perhaps because of its allegory and abstraction and its correspondence to and support of international modernist art movements that align it with a specific national critique of German culture after the war, made manifest in Oberhausen in 1962. One final film serves to underscore their oft forgotten achievements and highlights the quixotic nature and impact of Borresholm's work. Half of Borresholm's last credited film, *Addendum to Orwell* (1985), appears to form the basis for Munich's Kraut disco band Pollyester's video *Change Hands.*[11] *Addendum to Orwell* is a kind of palimpsest of late 1960s Munich animations and a pastiche of styles, including art from Štepán, Lenica, and Urchs. As such, it does seem like a fitting addendum to their work and objectives, not to mention Orwell's. In its unexpected reincarnation as music video, their animation finds renewed life advocating resistance to blind obedience.

## Notes

1 This is due to changes in film distribution that made the expensive production of animation difficult to continue into the 1970s.

2 Bruckner analyzed the data for fifty-four short films by Oberhausen Manifesto filmmakers between 1958 and 1969, twenty-nine of which contained some kind of animation (minimal, hybrid, or fully animated). See especially her analysis on pages 38–43.

3 Translations here and elsewhere are mine.

4 Max Horkheimer and Theodor W. Adorno, *Dialectic of Enlightenment: Philosophical Fragments*, trans. Edmund Jephcott (Stanford: Stanford University Press, 2007).

5 Franziska Bruckner briefly makes the argument for this edited rerelease in "Oberhausen Revisited" (2018, 42).

6 Production information for Lenica's films is often complicated. Weiner and also Marcin Gizycki (2017) note that *Landscape* was developed at Harvard University, though filmportal.de states it was produced and written by Borresholm. Gizycki also reports that Lenica made an earlier version of the French-produced *Ubu et la Grande Gidouille* (1979) as *Ubu Roi* in 1975 in Germany.

7 See especially Fehrenbach's discussion of "Red Oberhausen" and anti-Polish slurs (1995, 222–24).

8 Trencsényi and Kopeček assert that the most reasonable explanation for naming the savior as "forty and four" is that Mickiewicz believed 44 was the numerical value of the letters of "Adam" in Hebrew. See especially pages 409 and 418.

9 Lenica was finally given a hyphenated status as Polish-German in the updated reference work *Animation: A World History* (Bendazzi 2016, 194–95)—a step in the right direction.

10 Merdjanowa sued for authorship in 2009, but her claim could not be proven based on the lack of records.

11 *Nachtrag zu Orwell* is credited as the source for the video from Schamoni Films. Filmportal.de lists Borresholm as the director.

## Works Cited

Bendazzi, Giannalberto. 2016. *Animation: A World History*. Vol. 2. New York: CRC.

Bruckner, Franziska. 2018. "Oberhausen Revisited: Animierte und hybride Tendenzen im 'Jungen Deutschen Film.'" In *Im Wandel . . . Metamorphosen der Animation*, edited by Julia Eckel, Erwin Feyersinger, and Meike Uhrig, 35–67. Wiesbaden: Springer.

Elsaesser, Thomas. 1989. *New German Cinema: A History*. New Brunswick: Rutgers University Press.

Eue, Ralph. 2012. "Begrüßung." In *Provokation der Wirklichkeit: 50 Jahre Oberhausener Manifest. Das Wiener Symposium*, edited by Ralph Eue and Christian Schulte, 3–4. Vienna: Synema-Publikationen.

Fehrenbach, Heide. 1995. *Cinema in Democratizing Germany: Reconstructing National Identity After Hitler*. Chapel Hill: University of North Carolina Press.

Gizycki, Marcin. 2017. "Freedom outside Reason: The Animated Cinema of Jan Lenica." Harvard Film Archive, December 2. https://harvardfilmarchive.org/programs/freedom-outside-reason-the-animated-cinema-of-jan-lenica.

Oberhausen Manifesto, 2014. In *Film Manifestos and Global Cinema Cultures: A Critical Anthology*, edited by Scott MacKenzie, 152–53. Berkeley: University of California Press. First published in 1962.

Rentschler, Eric. 2012. "Reconsidering New German Cinema." In *Teaching Film*, edited by Lucy Fischer and Patrice Petro, 119–25. New York: MLA.

Trencsényi, Balázs, and Michal Kopeček. 2007. *National Romanticism: The Formation of National Movements*. Budapest: Central European University Press.

Weiner, Steve. 1992. "Jan Lenica and *Landscape*." *Film Quarterly* 45.4 (Summer): 2–16.

# 5

# DOCUMENTING THE EVERYDAY IN ALLENDE'S CHILE

## Peter Lilienthal's *La Victoria* and Raúl Ruiz's *Palomita blanca*

*Claudia Sandberg*

The Jewish German-Uruguayan director Peter Lilienthal (1927–2023) was an integral part of the West German artistic community of the 1970s and 1980s, and he worked with the same film personnel that gave New German Cinema (NGC) its signature style.[1] Quite a bit older and less feted than some of NGC's protagonists, Lilienthal found himself to be "the South American bird" among them (Lilienthal 2006, 112). While the self-taught and aspiring German filmmakers were brought up in the postwar rubble years that defined their language, motifs, and stories, Lilienthal drew from other sources and experiences. He had been exposed to ostracism as a ten-year-old in Nazi Berlin and spent his formative years in Uruguay among a European émigré community. Back in West Germany after World War II, Lilienthal was employed at the Südwestdeutscher Rundfunk and the Sender Freies Berlin in the 1960s, where he directed several dramas and plays. His first feature, *Malatesta* (1969), won the German Film Award and was nominated for the Golden Palm in Cannes. Colleagues such as Hark Bohm and Laurens Straub articulated their appreciation for Lilienthal's experience, views, and interests, which reached far beyond German and European borders. Straub remembers that he looked up to Lilienthal and felt privileged that he supported the projects and ideas of younger colleagues. He notes in the documentary *Gegenschuss: Aufbruch der Filmemacher* (*Reverse Angle: Rebellion of the Filmmakers*, 2008), which he co-directed with Dominik Wessely: "Then there is Lilienthal. He is a gentleman, an urban gentleman. . . . He is involved in the Latin American conflict. . . . He is the man who can tell you who Fidel Castro is."

Lilienthal's family suffered hostility and degradation before their eventual escape from Nazi Germany, and when they returned to post–World War II Germany the country demanded that remigrants enter a pact of silence about the recent past. Thus Lilienthal spent his youth among nostalgic and traumatized adults, experiences that played a role in his motivations, expressions, and ethics as a Jewish artist. His early plays and dramas, such as the *Martyrium des Peter O'Hey* (*Martyrdom of Peter O'Hey*, 1964) or *Abschied* (*Farewell*, 1966), which communicate grief, loss, and paralysis in implicit formats, allude to the fate of the Jewish German population and critique the young FRG as unwilling to address this theme.[2] By the 1970s, he had redirected his gaze away from German matters. In advocating for the needs of groups and communities in Latin America, where violent right-wing dictatorships repressed one country after the other, Lilienthal's filmmaking had acquired a political focus and a realist style.

In his influential study *New German Cinema: A History*, Thomas Elsaesser refers to Lilienthal as an expert who "has one of the most solid reputations and track records as a left-liberal director with an excellent knowledge of Latin American issues" (1989, 113). Indeed, Lilienthal was one of the few filmmakers who brought the cultures of Central and South America to West German screens. He had firsthand insights into Latin America's political, social, and cultural history and was well known in the region's artistic-intellectual circles.[3] The features *La Victoria* (1973), *Es herrscht Ruhe im Land* (*Calm Prevails over the Country*, 1975), *Der Aufstand* (*The Uprising*, 1979), *Das Autogramm* (*The Autograph*, 1984), *Der Radfahrer von San Cristóbal* (*The Cyclist of San Cristóbal*, 1987), and the documentary *Camilo—Der lange Weg zum Ungehorsam* (*Camilo—The Long Road to Disobedience*, 2007) were made in collaboration with Latin American artists and evidence Lilienthal's work's affiliation to non-Western sociocultural movements and cinematic tendencies.[4]

The landscapes of South America fascinated other contemporaries too, most notably Werner Herzog. His *Aguirre, der Zorn Gottes* (*Aguirre, the Wrath of God*, 1972), which stars Klaus Kinski as Spanish conquistador in the search of El Dorado in the Peruvian jungle, is regarded as the film that initiated the NGC. *Aguirre* maps the struggles of a delusional male protagonist who wants to succeed against all odds, a Herzog archetype who was, as Brad Prager puts it, "concerned with revolutionary choices including anarchic revolt or operatic self-display" (2020, 234). With *Aguirre, Fitzcarraldo* (1982), and *Cobra Verde* (1987), Herzog discovered these spaces as an imaginary toolset to choreograph European colonial history. According to John Davidson (1993), Herzog's megalomaniac heroes in the New World displayed a West German self-image as a formerly "colonized" country that in the post–World War II era reclaimed its position among the European *Kulturnationen* (culture nations) and flexed its neocolonial muscles. His work with Denis Reichle, *Ballade vom kleinen Soldaten* (*Ballad of the Little Soldier*, 1984), which focuses on the Miskito Indians, a native tribe that took part in guerrilla activities with the Sandinistas in 1979, is another rerouting of German cultural and political discourses to foreign spaces. Herzog and Reichle connected Miskito Indians to soldiers fighting in World War II, which fed the revisionist discourse of collective German victimhood.

Herzog's "white" sketches of the Global South, in other words, his historically and geographically rerouted, stylized, and self-referential engagements with the West German present, were widely popular at the time. To put the spotlight on a Lilienthal film is to challenge subjectivities, thematic interests, and sociopolitical spaces that have been accepted as legitimate German cinema all along. In this chapter, then, I invite readers to contemplate the NGC in relation to Jewish concerns, ethical practices, and artistic expressions. For this aim, I analyze the film *La Victoria*, which was the beginning of Lilienthal's long-term engagement with Latin American politics and societies. It is an example of his cinema that to a large degree reflects the desire of sharing resources in a like-minded community. The film was co-financed by the Filmverlag der Autoren and the ZDF program *Das kleine Fernsehspiel*. The director-activist, who fought Eurocentric tendencies, was one of the co-founders of the Filmverlag. Affiliated with the ZDF as a commissioned filmmaker, he also helped give shape to the thematic and aesthetic scope of *Das kleine Fernsehspiel*. Democratic television at its best and a vital outlet of NGC, the program featured the work of women filmmakers such as Jutta Brückner, Ulrike Ottinger, and Helma Sanders-Brahms. It hosted graduation projects and became the preferred forum for political and experimental work of all formats.[5] Over the years, many of Lilienthal's films were screened on *Das kleine Fernsehspiel*, and the director, in collaboration with program director Eckart Stein, managed to bring the work of several Latin American artists to this site.

*La Victoria* cannot be understood if not read through a transnational lens, namely, as a film that was part of the adventurous spirit, thematic scope, and committed nature of Chilean progressive cinema before its sudden exodus in September 1973. Lilienthal was invited to Chile by the Goethe-Institut Santiago at the beginning of the 1970s. The country, under the leadership of the party alliance Unidad Popular (Popular Unity, UP), headed by Chile's first elected socialist president, Salvador Allende, was in the midst of a profound social and economic restructuring process, including renationalizing important industry sectors and expropriating big landowners. Subsequently ordering the building of affordable housing for the poor, among many other ideas, the objective was to encourage a more even and fair distribution of resources among the Chilean population. *La Victoria* evolved into a project that documented these activities. The film tells the story of a woman from the provinces who arrives in the Chilean capital, Santiago, to look for work, signs up to become a teacher in the literacy campaign, and works with women groups at the fringes of the city. *La Victoria* was undertaken with a Chilean cast and crew. Its vibrant cinematic language and documentary style echo the approaches of a young and rebellious generation of filmmakers eager to promote the UP reforms.

*La Victoria* observes Chilean politics and cinema from an extraterritorial place, which becomes evident when considering another film made in this era, *Palomita blanca* (*Little White Dove*, 1973/1992), made by the bad boy of Chilean cinema, the young visionary artist Raúl Ruiz, then still fairly unknown to foreign audiences. His take on the romance between a girl from a modest family and a young man from the upper echelons of society is a signifier for the experimental, audacious, and somewhat absurd nature of the Chilean socialist mission. The film coincides thematically and aesthetically with *La Victoria*, unsurprisingly so. They were shot simultaneously, during the final months of the Allende administration. Their directors were acquainted with each other, and members of the crews worked on both film sites. Ruiz even had a cameo appearance in *La Victoria* (see figure 5.6). The films convey the affective and vibrant atmosphere of the Allende era and at the same time, remark on the deep social divides and patriarchal structures of Chilean society. In different styles, Lilienthal and Ruiz explore women's political participation and ideological leaning tied to conditions they found at home and at work. Their works establish a critical intervention to the filmscape of these years.

To begin my analysis, I will briefly explore the role of Chilean artists in raising the profile of Latin American independent cinema at the end of the 1960s and outline filmmaking efforts aligned to Allende's social program. The following close reading of Lilienthal's and Ruiz's work reveals a society that negotiated traditional values and progressive forces, dealing with machismo attitudes and a highly rebellious youth culture. These dynamics explicate, underpin, and challenge socialist reform ideas. The conclusion offers a brief assessment regarding the fate of these films after the coup d'état and their importance in Chilean memory culture after the country's return to democracy in 1989.

## Chilean Progressive Cinema, Raúl Ruiz, and the Year 1973

In Chile at the end of the 1960s, cinema was off to a flying start. Enabled by a beneficial legal and economic framework, Chilean artists and functionaries were at the forefront of setting up a continental network of cineastes (Cortínez and Engelbert 2011, 45–47).[6] As a result, the national filmscape became thematically more diverse and aesthetically playful and daring. There was a great deal of anticipation that the socialist government would prioritize the advancement and expansion of the filmmaking sector.[7] During their three-year reign between 1971 and 1973, the UP failed to give the cultural industry a precise course, however. The production company Chile Films was handed over to the filmmakers and reflected many of the disputes and battles that divided the political allies. Director Miguel Littin noted these difficulties: "There was no program or project. . . . The cinema did not manage to capture the complex wealth of the reality. Moreover, the existing structures of cinema dated from before the Popular Unity, . . . they certainly no longer fitted the [current] circumstances and didn't allow the flowering of a new cinema" (1976, 56). In effect, cinema remained a largely self-organized venture. Filmmaker-activists formed the Committee of Support for Popular Unity, helping to diffuse ideas of the Chilean left. Many traveled to workers' groups and farmers in the provinces with the intention of instigating discussions about the expectations and hopes they connected with the new government. The New Chilean cinema, according to Tomás Cornejo, was "a coincidence of aesthetic, political and social interests of a handful of youngsters" (2013, 14).

Ruiz was an exceptional talent and a key figure in Chilean cinema from the 1960s through to the Allende years whose auteurial signature emerged early on. He started his career in the pre-socialist era. The short *La maleta* (*The Suitcase*, 1963) and the feature *El tango del viudo* (*The Tango of the Widower*, 1967) see the young director capturing images of daily life in people's gestures and habits, employing nonlinear narrative formats and playing with surrealist elements (Goddard 2013, 18). The radical changes in the Chilean political landscape in the early 1970s had made him, like most of his colleagues and friends, turn attention to the emancipation processes that were underway. Rather than succumbing to propagandistic formats and ideas, Ruiz kept to his surrealistic style and continued to observe the common people in demystifying and/or humorous ways. In documentaries and shorts such as *Ahora te vamos a llamar hermano* (*Now We Are Going to Call You Brother*, 1971), *La expropriación* (*The Expropriation*, 1971), and *El realismo socialista* (*Socialist Realism*, 1973), the director foresaw that lofty intellectual debates about progress and enlightenment often misjudged the realities and needs of workers and peasants (González 2020). The features *Tres tristes tigres* (*Three Sad Tigers*, 1968), *Nadie dijo nada* (*Nobody Said Anything*, 1971), and *Palomita blanca* constitute what Ruiz himself referred to as "cinema of inquiry" (1970, 63). These films take place in private spaces and shady bars and feature extensive dialogues about meaningless issues. They sketch out misconceptions, absurdities, petit bourgeois behavior, or alcoholism—transgressions of established or imposed norms that Ruiz found to be essentially Chilean (Cortínez and Engelbert 2011, 120).

*Palomita blanca* was planned as a commercial production. Enrique Lafourcade's homonymous novel (1971), a contemporary Romeo and Juliet story set in the tumultuous time of the presidential election, was hugely successful with Chilean audiences and promised to be the right material for a popular film (Cáceres 2019, 219–27). Producer Prochitel envisioned a blockbuster that would lift Chilean film into the spheres of international distribution and exhibition. Though Prochitel knew that Ruiz had little experience with large-scale productions, they recognized that he was *the* Chilean artist who could put quirky personalities and popular stories on the big screen (Cáceres 2019, 226). Hence, generously provided with financial resources and technical equipment, Ruiz enjoyed an artistic carte blanche arrangement. He gathered around him a team of trusted friends and talented artists, including Sergio Trabucco (producer), Silvio Caiozzi (photography), Carlos Piaggio (editor), Valeria Sarmiento (assistant editor), and Pepe de la Vega (sound), who gave the film its look and feel.

As a venture that was pushed by various cultural and political actors and financed by private businesses, *Palomita blanca* is evidence of the popularity of film and changing social dynamics in Chile at the time. When Lilienthal first arrived there in 1972, he experienced this country in a transformational moment that had created an environment where artisanal, experimental, and communal modes of filmmaking thrived. Looking back on this adventure, the director would say that his sojourn in Chile during the Allende era was a life-altering experience that guided his cinema into the future: "I developed an ever-increasing skepticism towards the inclination to protect myself with my artificialities. From then on, I let myself be carried by the unexpected and unpredictable" (Lilienthal 1984). In befriending Antonio Skármeta, a literature professor and author, he was introduced to members of the Chilean artistic avant-garde, among them Ruiz.[8] Lilienthal and Skármeta initially drafted a script for a film about a cyclist that was based on a short story of Skármeta's, and Lilienthal found funds for this project in West Germany.

*La Victoria* would become interlinked with concerns of Lilienthal's Chilean crew. Its producer, Helvio Soto, was a filmmaker in his own right. Works such as *Voto+Fusil* (*Vote and Rifle*, 1971) and *Metarmorfosis del jefe de la policía política* (*Metamorphosis of the Chief of the Political Police*, 1973) observed problems and inconsistencies in Chile's social and political landscape. Soto's sensibility for marginalized populations was certainly reflected within *La Victoria*. Silvio Caiozzi was engaged to do the camera work. He photographed most feature films and documentaries that were made in Chile between 1968 and 1973 and was well adapted to approaches of combining fictional and documentary modes as incursions into debates about the socialist modernization project.[9] Caiozzi's participation in *La Victoria* and *Palomita blanca* created crossovers in the two films' visual styles that I will explore below.

Both films picked up the heated political atmosphere in Chile: things came to a head in March 1973, when the parliamentary elections were about to take place. The country experienced a surging inflation rate and major food shortages. There were long queues for food in front of the shops. Worker strikes and political protest marches happened on a daily basis. Alfredo Barría Troncoso notes that the increasingly unsettled political and social situation guided filmmaking approaches and interests: "It was so important to give space to the immediate events that the fictional elements had to yield to a montage of still shots and extracts from different sources" (2011, 38). The young artists attentively observed the social and political events. There was a sense that the UP government could collapse at any time, which added importance to the idea of documenting this time and its protagonists.

The urgency of recording this era in the present tense was inscribed into *La Victoria*'s and *Palomita blanca*'s textures, although the directors had divergent perceptions about the longevity of the socialist undertaking. Ruiz's observations have a rather satirical nature. Zooming in on the behavior of his fellow Chileans in this exceptional political moment, he distrusted their capacity to understand or have an interest in working for the collective. His film suggests doubts whether the socialist experiment would return fruitful results. Lilienthal, on the other hand, who had come to Chile for the first time, was enthusiastic about Allende's win, the repatriation of previously foreign-owned companies, educational and housing reforms, and the confident presence of various social actors in the public sphere. This might be a place where his desires for a just society with a humanist face were about to become reality.

The films explored their ideas by foregrounding the experience of female protagonists. Lilienthal, preparing for shooting, decided to modify the script. The story of a cyclist became that of a secretary, whose journey was set against the background of a Santiago embroiled in a flurry of flags, music, and posters. The Chilean film crew befriended one of the socialist candidates, Carmen Lazo, and received permission to film her election campaign. They accompanied her when she met with inhabitants of a shantytown district in the capital's outer suburbs. Lazo becomes one the film's main protagonists, always surrounded by enthusiastic crowds. Thus an empathetic émigré director's observations of Allende's Chile record the country's social and political movements in big, colorful brushstrokes.

FIGURE 5.1. *La Victoria*—Clockwise: Marcela Carrasco arrives in Santiago, which is brimming with life; socialist politician Carmen Lazo visits a shantytown; one of the many rallies that took place in March 1973, just before the parliamentary elections; Carmen and Marcela during an election campaign. (Screengrabs)

Meanwhile, Ruiz was busy with selecting the leads for *Palomita blanca*.[10] Following a huge casting call, young adults, many of whom came from remote provinces and humble backgrounds, traveled to Santiago and patiently waited their turn to audition in the offices of Chile Films. Ruiz talked to dozens of candidates, among them numerous women. They shared their aspirations and dreams with the director, which he brought into the portrayal and relations of the main protagonist María and her partner Juan Carlos, with the idea of making the film a generational portrait.

## Gender, Youth, and the Public Sphere

*La Victoria* and *Palomita blanca* test Allende's utopia against the everyday Chilean reality in a texture of quotidian activities and gestures. A lot of this critique was channeled into images around gender relations and politics. In this sense, the films work as a conversation with one another: *La Victoria* seems to be informed by lofty and bold ideas of emancipation and empowerment that *Palomita blanca* calls into question. *La Victoria*'s female lead, Marcela Carrasco (Paula Moya), had just passed her exams as

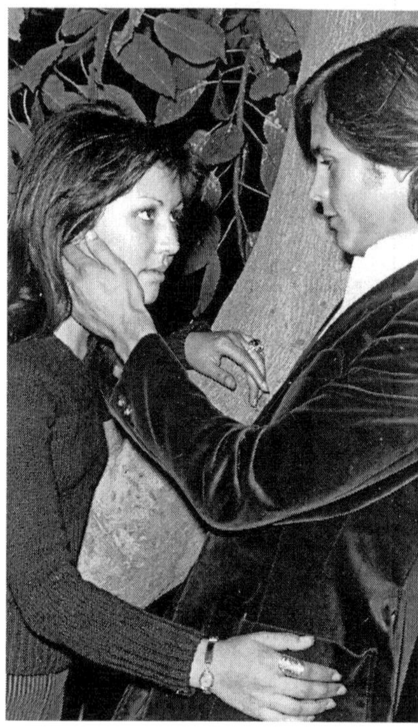

FIGURE 5.2. *Palomita blanca*—Beatriz Lapido and Rodrigo Ureta as María and Juan Carlos. (Screengrab)

a typist in a small town and ventures to Santiago to find employment. She works day jobs in private firms and governmental offices, ignoring inappropriate looks and fending off sexual advances by male peers and superiors. A colleague lectures her on proper conduct as part of the white-collar, female workforce: "Miss Carrasco, this is an office and not a fairground, and you are a secretary and not a drayman. A secretary never shouts. And a secretary never forgets herself. A secretary is not extravagant. A secretary should never talk more than necessary."

Many other scenes capture gender discrimination at work or picture scenarios in which mothers work and study while having to manage childcare at the same time. During the UP government there was insufficient funding for programs such as childcare facilities.[11] There is a dialogue in which workers organize a strike. The female colleagues coordinate their participation in shifts so as to provide support for the care of their children. In another instance, we see a female student in a classroom accompanied by her son, who carefully places a cup of coffee next to her typewriter

FIGURE 5.3. *La Victoria*—Marcela is tested on her typing skills at a lawyer's office. The small role of the lawyer is played by Lilienthal's Chilean friend and the film's co-scriptwriter, Antonio Skármeta. (Screengrab)

and sits down beside her. In documenting the double burden of Chilean women, Lilienthal's film latches on to concerns and politics addressed by West Germany's second wave feminists, including female directors such as Helke Sander, who co-founded the *Kinderläden* (cooperative childcare centers).[12]

*La Victoria* does not intend to victimize its female protagonists. Quite the opposite: the film illustrates that they have agency in the driving of social and political activities for—but also against—Chilean socialism. Wealthy women took to the streets because they feared losing their privileged position within the existing gender and class hierarchy. The girlfriend of Marcela's uncle, who deals luxury goods on the black market, is a materialistic and egocentric figure. In one of her chats with Marcela, the politician Lazo drops a comment about "the rich women who do not get up early." Her comment alludes to the right-wing movement *Poder Feminino* (female power), an undertaking that united women of middle and upper classes who, among other activities, protested food shortages by banging pots and pans in the so-called *cacerolazos*.[13] Apart from these referential remarks to initiatives in conservative social circles, the film's female leads embody the somewhat utopian idea that women of all classes recognized the need to promote changes within the social fabric. Marcela accompanies Lazo on her tours through the shantytowns, volunteers as a teacher in the literacy campaign, and organizes financial support for the children of a colleague who became victim to a confrontation with the police. The daughter of a miner in the north of Chile, Lazo was a trained primary school teacher and politically active since her early youth. While female politicians were underrepresented in the UP government, Lilienthal has Lazo act against this condition. She serves as a role model for female empowerment who relates well to problems that women face. In a scene that includes footage of the politician's meeting with women in the shantytown, they discuss topics ranging from the district's access to water and electricity to ideas of how to cook potatoes. These images show a self-confident female leader who listens to those whose concerns had never been addressed.

Less optimistic about the political aptitude of Chile's lower social classes, *Palomita blanca* draws their image between joy and despair. The sixteen-year-old protagonist, María (Beatriz Lapido), lives with her godmother (Bélgica Castro) in a small flat. María's alcoholic mother and stepfather often verbally and physically abuse the young woman. These are references to problems that plagued Chile's poorest populations, including improper housing, domestic violence, and alcohol addiction. At the same time, the sparsely furnished rooms are a communal space where family, friends, and neighbors drop in and enjoy each other's company. María meets Juan Carlos (Rodrigo Ureta) at a music festival. They spend the night together, and he takes her on a ride to the sea where they go swimming naked. Finely dressed, tall, and white-skinned, oozing the physical appearance of the upper crust, Juan Carlos lives in an extravagant mansion in Santiago's elegant neighborhood Providencia. For María, Juan Carlos represents the world of the rich and famous, an unfamiliar terrain that she finds fascinating.

The film is set on the eve of the presidential elections in 1970, and these political events serve as a noisy backdrop to the story, for example, when a radio broadcast of the election results is projected loudly into María's empty room. María's family seems not impressed by the prospect of a socialist president. In a voice-over, María declares that her parents support the conservative candidate, Jorge Alessandri, and describes herself as "a bit Alessandrista" too, while the camera pans across a scene of men from different political camps battling each other with sticks on the roof of a house.

The young woman's adoration of the handsome Juan Carlos is nourished by flickering images of a TV soap opera that María and her mother follow religiously. Scenes from this telenovela appear at various points throughout the film, and María, her family members, and even the staff in Juan Carlos's household are shown glued to the screen.[14] Unlike the outspoken and headstrong Marcela of *La Victoria*, who in one scene decisively turns off the TV—which could be read as a choice to take matters into her own hands and not succumb to illusions—María is a timid girl who indulges in writing romantic letters. She tells Juan Carlos's sister that she has feelings for him because "he reminds me of the many films that I have seen." María's character resonates with Siegfried Kracauer's *kleine Ladenmädchen* (little shopgirls), unmarried women employed in white-collar jobs who, exploited, underpaid, and underprivileged, are consumed by fantasies of a glamorous upper-class lifestyle (Kracauer 1977).

FIGURE 5.4. *Palomita blanca*—Clockwise: watching television is a favorite pastime for María and her mother; telenovela scenes appear frequently in the film; María sits in the dark, looking at TV idol shown in the previous picture; a woman at a hairdresser's reads a magazine, with posters of pop stars behind her. (Screengrabs)

Parallel to Kracauer's ruminations about the escapist and trivial nature of Weimar cinema, Ruiz's film provides a critique of a Chilean visual culture that aligns closely with capitalist social and economic logics. His criticism is personified through a character in the film whom we see walking about in front of an open window and thinking aloud. Functioning as didactic device, this is also the continuation of the stick-fighting scene I mentioned previously: "What happens when a girl from the subjugated class goes out with someone from the dominant class? Without doubt, for a time she feels fulfilled with his dreams, his goals, because she is influenced by the values of the dominant class by the media." Without abandoning sympathy for his character, Ruiz portrays María as a member of a susceptible audience that is lacking agency in their lives.

While both films portray Chilean society as marked by the vicissitudes of class divides and gender inequalities, their visual styles convey a youthful energy. Not relying on well-planned shot compositions, many scenes contain immediate and spontaneous responses from characters, including impromptu dialogues. The handheld camera becomes a wandering eye through a lively urban Santiago, where the films evoke the light-heartedness of Jean-Luc Godard's *À bout de souffle* (*Breathless*, 1960). Engaging the poorest participants as protagonists and filming within their everyday spaces, the pictures—reflecting the politically and ethically committed New Latin American cinema—signal the movement's neorealist heritage. Similar to Roberto Rossellini's *Roma, città aperta* (*Rome, Open City*, 1945) or Vittorio De Sica's *Ladri di biciclette* (*Bicycle Thieves*, 1948), which depict the Italian city in "a moment of decisive transition in the tumultuous aftermath of World War II" (Shiel 2006, 1), *La Victoria* and *Palomita blanca* find Chile in a profound renovation that sweeps through political, social, and cultural spheres.

In this panorama, *La Victoria* represents an urban snapshot that blurs margins and center. In what symbolizes a democratic public sphere in its spatial manifestation, we see political parties, workers' groups, and trade unions occupying public spaces and making political claims. The film opens with the long shot of a ceremony that takes place on the grounds of a sports stadium. Youths march in formations carrying red flags, cheered on by hundreds of spectators in the stands in support of the UP allied parties. In the next scene, people cross train tracks and wait at the station, among them Marcela waiting for her uncle, who works as a cook on a passenger train. This is the beginning of a film that has its main protagonist discover Chile's uneven and unequal social and economic structure. Caiozzi's camera—in busy inner-city shopping districts, quiet suburban streets, spacious houses of the well-to-do, classrooms, governmental offices, and favelas on the urban fringes of Santiago—presents Chile's population in a multitude of faces and a peaceful and purposeful mobility of bodies, cycles, and cars.

*La Victoria* approaches marginalized groups as able and emancipated members of Chilean society who have a right of political integration. A number of scenes are shot with residents of Nueva Palena, a shantytown at the outer fringes of Santiago, known to be a former squatter settlement that was politically and socially self-organized.[15] The film title points to another emblematic neighborhood, La Victoria, in the south of the Chilean capital, where in the late 1950s two thousand homeless workers, unable to find affordable housing, occupied abandoned farmland and set up makeshift homes.[16] Within a decade, persevering against the attacks of a hostile state, the tent city had developed into a *barrio* (neighborhood) encompassing a social infrastructure that included medical services and educational institutions.

Where *La Victoria* attends to socially and economically disenfranchised individuals and groups, Ruiz's film celebrates the contemporaneous Chilean youth culture that he himself is part of. With a cast and crew made up of members barely thirty years old, alleged love affairs on the set, and alcohol consumed during and after shootings, this might have transferred into the film's experimental style and inserts that appear as if made in an altered state of consciousness. The narrative is lined with scenes of events, gatherings, and images that function as an escape from the prescribed story line and breathe an air of rebellion. Among such narrative diversions are an orgy to which María is invited, a random monologue of one of María's professors that takes over five minutes of film time, and the close-up of a young man in a concert who vigorously shakes his head until his look changes to a frightful stare. Ignacio López-Vicuña notes that "*Palomita blanca* restores to the viewer not only the colors of 1970s Chile but also the sounds, the music, the slang, the diverse social registers and cultural tensions of that immensely vital time just before the military coup" (2009, 161). Ruiz knew the hot spots of the Chilean urban scene: the Parque Forestal in downtown Santiago, the discotheque El Hipopótamo in Vitacura, and the Galería Drugstore in Providencia, a famous mall that housed clothes stores and music shops.

The director has Juan Carlos and María meet at the most enigmatic venue of Chilean hippie culture, the music festival Piedra Rojas. Known as the Woodstock of Chile, the event took place in October 1970, ran over three days, and drew thousands of music lovers of all socioeconomic spheres. Patrick Barr-Melej notes that Chilean *hippismo* (hippie culture) "crossed class lines in a classist society . . . it was ad-hoc, improvised, and decentralized, though shaped by national and transnational circumstances and trends" (2017, 7). In a sequence that is accompanied by the song "Tema de los Titulos" ("Title Theme") and part of the soundtrack that Chile's hippest rock band of the time, Los Jaivas, had composed, we see María and her friend making their way through the crowd of youths who sit on the lawns, talk, smoke, and listen to live music. Close shots capture dancers enthralled by the music.

By lingering on the spaces, tastes, and ideas of young Chileans, *Palomita blanca* highlights the country's rampant social and political conflicts as generational. Older Chileans were anxious that radical or esoteric ideas, many of which were adopted from Europe and the United States, would

FIGURE 5.5. *Palomita blanca*—Chilean youth used to frequent Galería Drugstore. (Screengrab)

corrupt the local youth. María's parents beat her up because her boyfriend, Juan Carlos, was a siloist—belonging to a movement that adhered to Western interpretations of Marxism and believed in transcendental meditation and anarchy. Branded by the UP as immoral political adversaries, the police often broke up siloist meetings and conferences (Barr-Melej 2017, 8). Chilean hippies embody these tensions between Old Left and New Left, a counterculture that aimed to overcome the values, teachings, and expectations of an older generation.

With a focus on the life worlds of their protagonists, the films arrive at almost opposite conclusions. Ruiz's María remains powerless; her romantic relationship cannot change her social status. Lilienthal's Marcela, however, is a symbol for the potential of Chilean socialism to suture historical class barriers and create a more socially cohesive society.

Where the films evaluate the capacity and willingness of different groups and classes to become engaged in the socialist reform processes, they also evoke a sense of community apart from any ideological-political-didactic program. *Palomita blanca* reflects an ephemeral and accidental nature of community (Ríos 2019, 52). The chaotic episodes that dot the film's narrative and visual arrangement mark community as a dissonant experience and/or space. Ruiz appears in *La Victoria* as a party guest smoking and drinking in a crowded kitchen, scenes that were filmed in the house of renowned Chilean photographer Paz Errázuriz in Providencia (Cáceres 2019, 269). The energy present in these images corresponds to the atmosphere in María's home in *Palomita blanca*, populated "with people who enter and leave the frame, are behind the camera, with sound from outside the scene" (Ríos 2019, 52).

Unsurprisingly, in the film of a Jewish director who was used to negotiating his space in various national, cultural, and linguistic spaces, community comes into being through communicating, listening, and reflecting. When Marcela does a day job in a glamorous lawyer's house and lunches with the family or Carmen Lazo meets with shantytown women, there is the sense that encounters between individuals from diverse walks of life are exchanges of insights, talents, and resources. Another such discussion unfolds in a humble makeshift building that accommodates the shantytown school. Here, a group of women who have signed up to teach literacy skills to adults attend a workshop. The tutor presents a photo that depicts a family of three generations seated around a table and represents the word

FIGURE 5.6. *La Victoria*—Raúl Ruiz in the background of a party scene, filmed in the house of famous photographer Paz Errázuriz. (Screengrabs)

*home*. The women protest, referencing their own situation, which does not correspond to what they find to be an idealized, bourgeois notion of home. The vignettes suggest that a successful transformation of Chilean social and political life would entail recognizing, valuing, and activating the multiplicity of present experiences, ideas, and imaginations. These negotiations reflect the realities of the social project of the Allende years as much as they contain a German Jewish filmmaker's utopian ideas in the frames of a semi-fictional film. The result of a fruitful collaboration with Chilean avant-garde artists, politicians, and members of an enthusiastic population who all opened their doors to Lilienthal, *La Victoria* was Lilienthal's coming home.

## Epilogue

*La Victoria* and *Palomita blanca* set out to record the Allende era as wide-ranging modernization program only to become an epitaph to a failed social experiment. In a plot instigated by the general-in-chief of the Chilean Army, Augusto Pinochet, military forces toppled the UP government on September 11, 1973 in an act that left the incumbent president dead. The self-appointed government reinstated former class privileges and powers and persecuted Communists and Allende partisans in most violent ways. The country became a testing ground for a fully-fledged neoliberal social and economic system with the help of the so-called Chicago Boys. As part of the overarching political repression, the seeds of a vivid and critical film culture were destroyed. *Palomita blanca*, which was to premiere on Chile's Independence Day on September 18, was instead banned by the fascist regime. Ruiz, with a visa that Lilienthal obtained for him, managed to leave Chile in October 1974, one of approximately one million fellow Chilean citizens who would turn into émigrés. After a sojourn in West Germany, where he made *Mensch verstreut und Welt verkehrt* (*The Scattered Body and the World Upside Down*, 1975), which was produced by *Das kleine Fernsehspiel*, he settled in France permanently. *La Victoria* had its premiere at the Berlin Film Festival in June 1973. It was scheduled to air on ZDF at the end of that year, but the channel reacted to the devastating news from Chile by broadcasting *La Victoria* on September 17. Only after the country returned to democracy in 1989 would the films become accessible to Chilean audiences. The negatives of *Palomita blanca*, which had been thought lost since the coup d'état, were discovered under a staircase in the offices where Chile Films had operated. The film had its belated opening event in 1992 in the Viña del Mar Film Festival and was received with standing ovations. Its cinema release reached an astonishing one hundred thousand viewers. In the same year, the Goethe-Institut in Santiago organized a screening that consisted of Lilienthal's *Es herrscht Ruhe im Land*, *David* (1979), and *Der Radfahrer von San Cristóbal* (1987), but it did not include *La Victoria*.[17] The film was first seen at the 2003 Valparaíso Film Festival and had its official cinema premiere in 2020. *Palomita blanca* was restored and digitalized in 2017 and has since received renewed scholarly attention.[18]

Revolutionary acts, communal art projects, and socialist critiques alike, *La Victoria* and *Palomita blanca* zoom in on the aims, urges, and desires of different social groups. Because of the decades-long time lag between production and exhibition, the film material is "marked by an air of untimeliness" (López-Vicuña 2017, 159–60). Today, the films produce alienation in some spectators who feel uneasy about their ideological overtones, especially because the legacy of the UP government as well as that of socialism remains a contentious issue in Chile and elsewhere. To others, the films represent loss and recovery of the country's best talents and creative minds. While Ruiz never looked back on his last Chilean film (Cáceres 2019, 273), Lilienthal recalls *La Victoria* as linked to a filmmaking practice that captured a community in the making (Sandberg 2021, 166–68). In this spirit, the revisiting of *La Victoria* next to *Palomita blanca* is a productive case of crossing East-West and North-South boundaries to discover NGC afresh through the eyes of different cultural-political agents, and in different aesthetic and artistic sites.

## Notes

1 Lilienthal worked with photographer Michael Ballhaus and editor Heidi Genée as well as with actors Hanna Schygulla and Hanns Zischler, among others, in his various films.

2 Claudia Sandberg, "Die frühen Fernseharbeiten von Peter Lilienthal: Ein jüdischer Remigrant im Westdeutschland der Nachkriegszeit," in *Jüdischer Film: Ein neues Forschungsfeld im deutschsprachigen Raum*, ed. Lea Wohl von Haselberg and Lucy Alejandra Pizaña Pérez (Munich: text+kritik, 2022): 207–25.

3 Hans Günther Pflaum and Hans Helmut Prinzler, *Cinema in the Federal Republic of Germany: The New German Film Origins and Present Situation, with a Section on GDR Cinema* (Bonn: Internationes, 1993), 94.

4 For an extensive analysis of Lilienthal's Latin American films and connections, see Sandberg 2021.

5 Claudia Sandberg, "*Das kleine Fernsehspiel*: Model of a TV-Avantgarde," in *The German Cinema Book*, 2nd ed., ed. Tim Bergfelder, Erica Carter, Deniz Göktürk, and Claudia Sandberg (London: BFI, 2020): 331–33.

6 The 1967 Viña del Mar Film Festival invited commercial and independent filmmakers from all over the continent to screen their films and take part in workshops, debates, and lectures. In what film historians acknowledge as a foundational event of New Latin American cinema, this festival saw a convergence of ideas by artists that provided a theoretical framework for a new way to think and utilize the genre of film. The filmmakers met in Viña two years later to present their first films.

7 Hans Ehrmann, "Chile's Six Films, Three Quite Good; Red-Slanted Regime a New Factor," *Variety*, January 1971.

8 Antonio Skármeta was a longtime friend of Lilienthal's who participated in almost all his Latin American films as consultant, scriptwriter, and/or actor.

9 Manuel Bermúdez, "Silvio Caiozzi: La aventura de cine como destino," *Archipelago: Revista Cultura de Nuestra America* 11.43 (2004): 38–40, http://revistas.unam.mx/index.php/archipielago/article/view/19679/0.

10 Ruiz was critical of this expensive and highly competitive casting call, which was advertised in all nationally circulating newspapers. The director filmed the interviews and used this material to make a documentary. *Palomilla brava* (*Bad Girl*, 1973) observes and criticizes this large-scale marketing campaign. Unfortunately, the film is lost. For details see Cáceres (2019, 227–33).

11 Margaret Power, "Class and Gender in the Anti-Allende Women's Movement: Chile 1970–1973," *Social Politics* 7.3 (2000): 289–308, https://doi.org/10.1093/sp/7.3.289.

12 Christina Gerhardt, "Helke Sander's dffb Films and West Germany's Feminist Movement," in *Celluloid Revolt: German Screen Cultures and the Long 1968*, ed. Christian Gerhardt and Marco Abel (Rochester: Camden House, 2019), 69–86.

13 Lisa Baldez, *Why Women Protest: Women's Movement in Chile* (Cambridge: Cambridge University Press, 2002), 11.

14 Ruiz's *La telenovela errante* (*The Wandering Soap Opera*, 1990) focuses on the idea of Chilean reality having become a soap opera. Valeria de los Ríos claims that this trope appeared first in *Palomita blanca* (2019, 9).

15 For squatter settlements in Chile and Peru and their high level of planning and organization and other current housing and educational projects, see Daniel Goldrich, Raymond B. Pratt, and C. R. Schuller, "The Political Integration of Lower-Class Urban Settlements in Chile and Peru," *Studies in Comparative International Development* 3 (1967): 3–22, https://doi.org/10.1007/BF02800606.

16 Janet L. Finn, "*La Victoria*: Claiming Memory, History, and Justice in a Santiago Población," *Journal of Community Practice* 13.3 (2005): 9–31, https://doi.org/10.1300/J125v13n03_02.

17 Goethe-Institut, press release on the retrospective of Lilienthal's films at the Seventh Film Festival in Valparaíso, 2003.

18 Felipe Blanco, "*Palomita blanca*: Televisión inconclusa," *laFuga* 21 (2018), https://lafuga.cl/palomita-blanca/885.

## Works Cited

Barría Troncoso, Alfredo. 2011. *El espejo quebrado: Memorias de cine de Allende y la Unidad Popular*. Santiago: uqbar.

Barr-Melej, Patrick. 2017. *Psychedelic Chile: Youth, Counterculture, and Politics on the Road to Socialism and Dictatorship*. Chapel Hill: University of North Carolina Press.

Cáceres, Yenny. 2019. *Los años chilenos de Raúl Ruiz*. Santiago: Catalonia.

Cornejo, Tomás. 2013. "Filmar a contrapelo: el cine de Helvio Soto durante la Unidad Popular." *Atenea* 508: 13–29. http://dx.doi.org/10.4067/S0718-04622013000200002.

Cortínez, Verónica, and Manfred Engelbert. 2011. *La Tristeza de los tigres y los misterios de Raúl Ruiz*. Santiago: Cuarto Propio.

Davidson, John. 1993. "As Others Put Plays upon the Stage: *Aguirre*, Neo-colonialism, and the New German Cinema." *New German Critique* 60 (Autumn): 101–30.

Elsaesser, Thomas. 1989. *New German Cinema: A History*. London: BFI.

Goddard, Michael. 2013. *The Cinema of Raúl Ruiz: Impossible Cartographies*. New York: Columbia University Press.

González, Rodrigo. 2020. "La Unidad Popular según Raúl Ruiz." *La Tercera*, May 9.

Kracauer, Siegfried. 1977. "Die kleinen Ladenmädchen gehen ins Kino." In *Das Ornament der* Masse, 279–94. Frankfurt: Suhrkamp.

Lilienthal, Peter. 1984. Discussion with artists at the Akademie der Künste Ost about his film *Das Autogramm*, November 20.

———. 2006. "In paradiesischen Zeiten. Interview mit Peter Lilienthal." Interview by Egon Netenjakob. In *Es geht auch anders: Gespräche über Leben, Film und Fernsehen*, edited by Egon Netenjakob, 99–120. Berlin: Bertz+Fischer.

Littin, Miguel, 1976. "Interview with Miguel Littin." Interview by Jean-René Huleu, Pascal Kane, and Ignacio Ramonet. In *Chilean Cinema*, edited by Michael Chanan, 53–65. London: BFI. First published in *Cahiers du cinéma* (1974): 251–52.

López-Vicuña, Ignacio. 2009. "Raúl Ruiz's Lost Chilean Film: Memory and Multiplicity in *Palomita blanca*." *Studies in Hispanic Cinemas* 6.2: 111–24.

———. 2017. "Raúl Ruiz's Lost Chilean Film: Memory and Multiplicity in *Palomita blanca*." In *Raul Ruiz's Cinema of Inquiry*, edited by Ignacio

López-Vicuña and Andreea Marinescu, 159–76. Detroit: Wayne State University Press.

Prager, Brad. 2020. "Constructing Authorship: Werner Herzog Is His Films." In *The German Cinema Book*, 2nd ed., edited by Tim Bergfelder, Erica Carter, Deniz Göktürk, and Claudia Sandberg, 231–41. London: BFI.

Ríos, Valeria de los. 2019. *Metamorfosis: Aproximaciones al cine y a poética de Raúl Ruiz*. Santiago: metals pesados.

Ruiz, Raúl. 1970. "Dialogo con Raul Ruiz." Interview by Enrique Lihn and Federico Schopf. *Nueva Atenea* 423 (July–September): 58–65.

Sandberg, Claudia. *Peter Lilienthal: A Cinema of Exile and Resistance*. New York. Berghahn Books, 2021.

Shiel, Mark, 2006. *Italian Neorealism: Rebuilding the Cinematic City*. London: Wallflower.

# 6

# *KATZ UND MAUS*

## A West German Project in Poland by Pohland

*John E. Davidson*

## Prologue

Hansjürgen Pohland's 1967 film adaptation of Günter Grass's *Katz und Maus* (*Cat and Mouse*, 1961), one of the early screenplay-subsidy recipients from the Kuratorium junger deutscher Film, channeled the political contradictions of the era almost immediately. Karena Niehoff, a member of the Kuratorium board, used this pun to describe the prerelease whirlwind around the film: "If one had a meticulous protocol of the behind-the-scenes events in the cat-'n'-mouse game . . . that has been going or went on for months around the film *Cat and Mouse*, one could distill out an image of the Federal Republic's internal politics down to the last detail."[1] Of course, it should come as no surprise that an adaptation of one of the foundational examples of *Vergangenheitsbewältigung*—coming to terms with the Nazi past—caused such consternation. The participation of Willy Brandt's sons, coupled with the contemporaneous formation of the Grand Coalition, virtually ensured that this film would be—and, when considered at all, continues to be—seen through the lens of "bundesdeutscher Innenpolitik" (internal Federal Republic politics). The two most recent scholarly treatments tacitly continue that trend: Enno Stahl contends that Pohland's film is more adequate to its contemporary German society and memory politics than Grass's novella; Magdalena Saryusz-Wolska argues that the film belongs to the New German Cinema because of its engagement with *Vergangenheitsbewältigung* and thus has been unfairly excluded from consideration among key works in that canon.[2] Both those contributions make strong cases for enshrining Pohland's *Cat and Mouse* as a key text in mid-1960s West German cultural politics.

The origins of the present essay are rooted in a different question: whether that tight focus on the Federal Republic's internal and/or cultural politics obscures a broader landscape to which this film belongs. A number of things prompted this question, among them Pohland's insistence on shooting in Gdańsk; Grass's engagement with the area's multiethnic history in the "Danziger Trilogy" and beyond; early attempts by the production company to recruit Andrzej Wajda as director (and his apparent interest); the film's nearly unique standing as a West German/Polish co-production; reports that the team from "Polski Film" played ambiguous roles in the filming; the rumored interest in incorporating the filming of Stanislaw Rózewicz's *Westerplatte* (1967) into the frame story of *Cat and Mouse*; and, perhaps more obliquely, the appearance of puppets that seem a potential link to the avant-garde art and film scene in Eastern Europe. In what follows I suggest that investigating the final version of Pohland's film in the framework of contemporary Poland, its historical traces of the war, and the backdrop of collaborations that breached the Iron Curtain refocuses our attention on the politics of German *Vergangenheitsbewältigung* as an international activity. *Cat and Mouse* stands alone among the early films of New German Cinema in taking this approach.

To set the stage for an internationalized analysis of *Cat and Mouse*, I begin by placing it in the orbit of the two Adenauer-era films co-produced with and shot in Poland by Artur Brauner and then Kurt Ulrich. My investigation uncovers aspects about these international co-productions crossing the West-East divide that point in four perhaps unsurprising but nonetheless important directions: (1) to continuities (at least on the FRG side) in the "relatively unregulated bilateral cooperation" that was already being bureaucratically replaced in Western European co-productions (Bergfelder 2005, 55); (2) to producers' interests that were primary over directors' artistic concerns; (3) to hard currency that was as important as overt political considerations during the production process; (4) to the fact that participation in the co-production did not lead inevitably to distribution or reception as a co-produced work—in other words, politics trumped earning potential *after* the film was completed. The following section briefly sketches the historical and film-historical contexts surrounding the three co-productions filmed in Poland between 1949 and 1968, which represent not just three different types of feature films but also three models of co-production. Aleksander Ford's *Ósmy dzień tygodnia* (*Der achte Wochentag / The Eighth Day of the Week*, 1958), a naturalistic, socially critical melodrama, is an almost entirely Polish project with significant German financial backing.[3] Victor Vicas's *Jons und Erdme* (*Jons and Erdme*, 1959), a contribution to the dark German-Heimat genre with an inexplicably hopeful conclusion, is a West German production (with a second, minor Italian co-producer) that was filmed almost entirely in Poland. *Cat and Mouse* is an art film that represented a more significant integration between the national co-producers. Despite these distinctions, my discussion in the following section will highlight how the primary producers' overall desires for international exposure take advantage of a relative "permeability of the Iron Curtain" (Frieberg 2019, 5) prior to filming but conclude that this permeability leads to contradictory results during their films' circulation. Laying that groundwork allows me to turn to a close analysis of *Cat and Mouse* in the final section that makes sense of Pohland's travel to Poland.

## The Relative Limits of "Permeability"

Although memory of the Nazi war of aggression and its immediate aftermath is always a baseline, the historical and film-historical background to this chapter begins at the "Polish October" of 1956, the period after Nikita Khrushchev had denounced Josef Stalin and during which Władysław Gomułka solidified his leadership of the People's Republic of Poland. In the international cultural contextualization that concerns this volume, the Polish October was marked most notably through an increased recognition for the Catholic Church and an increased role for individual Catholic intellectuals, who acted as leading liaisons with West Germany. Out of these relationships grew greater press and television contact, with West German journalists often traveling to and in some cases living in Poland, especially Warsaw.[4] These journalists and artists served as de facto public-relations representatives and were very much impressed with the intellectual openness in Poland: their sense was that, from the perspective of the FRG, Poland was Eastern, but looking from the East Bloc, it was much closer to the West than the GDR. The Polish October saw an uptick of local artistic freedom as well, reflected especially in the visual arts and in the productions of the so-called Polish Film School, which often dealt with World War II and its aftereffects. While for much of the 1950s only short films were seen in the FRG (the Oberhausen Festival's "Path to Our Neighbors" series was key in this regard), a few representatives of the Polish Film School made an impression. For example, Andrzej Wajda's *Kanał* (*Sewer*, 1957) won Silver at Cannes in 1957 but was somewhat less well received when it premiered in West Germany in 1958.[5] Other examples that drew attention in the Federal Republic because of their treatment of the German-Polish war history include Wajda's *Popiół i diament* (*Ashes and Diamonds*, 1958), Jerzy Kawalerowicz's *Prawdziwy koniec wielkiej wojny* (*The Real End of the Great War*, 1957), and Tadeusz Konwicki's *Ostatni dzien lata* (*The Last Day of Summer*, 1958).

Behind the Iron Curtain, Poland's cultural influence was felt both before the Polish October and after the "rollback" that followed.[6] However, despite the deep engagement in the East Bloc with Polish art and letters in general, and cinema specifically, Polish films were seen *less* frequently in East Germany than West. Two reasons seem primary here: the Oder-Neisse border was a problem as much in public sentiment as in political discourse on both sides; beyond that, "Gomułka's return raised the question of the legitimacy of [working with] East Germany's SED regime" (Borodzeij 1996, 64–65).[7] In one case, a Polish movie about the bombing of Dresden was filmed in the GDR but only shown in the Bonn Republic.[8] Roman Polański's first feature, *Nóż w wodzie* (*Knife in the Water*, 1962), was an exception that received a good deal of press as *Messer im Wasser* on both sides of the inner-German border. In the 1960s the distribution and reception of Polish films in the FRG expanded greatly, while remaining minuscule in the GDR, according to Margarete Wach (2011). That expansion was built primarily on increased international recognition but was perhaps also eased by the publicity around a pair of co-productions from the late 1950s that had attempted to make it big on West German screens and beyond.

The first was Ford's *The Eighth Day of the Week*. An avowed Communist, Ford had organized a Polish film crew within the USSR's forces during World War II and then briefly became the head of Film Polski in its aftermath. Immediately following Hitler's defeat, he made

*Majdanek—cmentarzysko Europy* (*Majdanek: Cemetery of Europe*, 1945), a documentary that marked his first post-Nazi-era success. From that point on, and throughout his career until his suicide in 1980, he concentrated primarily on the pain and sacrifice of the Polish people in wartime. At the point when his protégés Wajda and Polański garnered notice as the new Polish School in film, and the postwar aftermath segued fully into the realities of the Cold War, Ford shifted his attention briefly to the plight of contemporary Poles in Warsaw. His pet project was adapting Marek Hłasko's short story "Ósmy dzień tygodnia" ("The Eighth Day of the Week"). Despite Ford's strong reputation in the Polish film world, he struggled mightily with this undertaking until he secured backing from Brauner's CCC film company out of West Berlin, which enabled the completion of *The Eighth Day of the Week* in 1957 and its premiere in 1958. The film starred Zbigniew Cybulski (the lead from Wajda's *Ashes and Diamonds* who was sometimes known as the Polish James Dean) and was unique as a West German/Polish feature co-production to that point. The film boasted two relatively well-known German figures: Sonja Ziemann, who was trying to blaze a trail to more serious fare than her *Heimatfilm* roles had allowed and was also romantically involved with Hłasko.[9] Bum Krüger was the second German, a supporting-character actor quite popular in the 1950s and '60s. Despite these two actors, *The Eighth Day of the Week* was a thoroughly Polish production except for Brauner's involvement.

Brauner originally came from and kept contacts in Łódź, where Ford had held a professorship since 1949, which facilitated the connection between the two. Partnering with two lions of the Polish cultural scene, and bringing hard currency to the proceedings, CCC was able to get the adaptation made in a political and fiscal climate that Ford and Hłasko had not been able to negotiate on their own. Brauner was interested in the area and its history, but his primary drive here was a twofold push to become the conduit for material out of Poland in worldwide distribution and to open new markets for distributing his German productions. The success of this plan was mixed at best. After the film was completed, the Polish authorities deemed it too dark a representation of contemporary life under socialism. The plot revolves around an unmarried couple who have no private space to consummate their relationship amid a dire housing shortage. Ironically, the main character is a young architect making plans for building the bright socialist future. This borderline dystopian, alcohol-saturated environment cannot even be escaped with the couple's fantasy night spent alone after being locked in a department store after hours. Although some cuts were made in the film to appease them, the Polish authorities refused to let the film screen as a Polish/German entry at Cannes, which was a blow to Brauner's plans. Then, without consultation, he entered it in the Venice Biennale as a *West German* production, which garnered him both a bit of critical acclaim and the ire of Polish officials. In the face of this reaction, Brauner eventually decided not to push his worldwide distribution plans, more or less renouncing not only profits but even the chance of recovering full costs for *The Eighth Day of the Week*. He did this in the hope of future cooperation and greater profit through the culturally permeable Iron Curtain. That cooperation never really materialized.[10]

Kurt Ulrich, a producer based in Berlin, had a different plan than Brauner for looping Poland into his firm's internationalization, one that centered in part on a Sudermann novel adaptation scripted by Robert Stemmle. To make *Jons and Erdme* (subtitled *Die Frau des Anderen / The Other Man's Wife*), he went east for a cheap staging ground where his company could hold court and have a virtual monopoly on the attention of the Western press in Warsaw. Ulrich had managed to sign two international stars from Federico Fellini's acclaimed *La Strada* (1954), Giulietta Masina and Richard Baseheart. Among the FRG's established stars and budding actors in the mix were Carl Raddatz, Gert Fröbe, and Karin Baal. Victor Vicas, a rising talent, directed this dark and extremely wet *Heimat* fare, which was shot almost entirely on location in the villages and moors outside of Warsaw. The choice to film in the East was a unique one for the producer, given that Ulrich Film had arisen out of the Berolina firm in 1957 and concentrated exclusively on Western sites and themes.[11] Clearly, the expense of the star cast and crew for *Jons and Erdme* made shooting remotely but cheaply attractive, and Film Polski was added to the team. Ulrich gambled that the oddity of this group working in Poland would draw enough attention to garner (close to free) publicity that would pay off in the end.

Part of Ulrich's plan was successful. The West German intelligentsia in Warsaw took notice, and Western journalists made several trips into Poland to cover the shooting. The lead actress, who would injure herself badly during the filming but carry on heroically, drew particular interest. There was much speculation about whether "die Masina" would be able to continue physically or to set her roots firmly enough in Pomeranian soil and speech to pull off her role in the film. Warsaw itself, where the crew and the journalists were housed, received a good bit of positive press in the process as well, and so the Poles got more than just an influx of Western cash out of the deal.[12] Ultimately, however, the return on the investment and effort could not have met Ulrich's hopes, for the curiosity shown during filming failed to drum up sustained interest following the premiere in Frankfurt am Main in September 1959. The reception in the press was tepid at best, with no strong positive responses and most reviews highlighting a range of complaints, finding that the film was too long, ponderous, and convoluted; Masina, although a great actress, was out of her element; Baseheart was too distant; Raddatz was too old or too unbelievable as an explosively violent drunk; and there was too much rain. The domestic box office was mediocre, and there was no worldwide distribution. Ulrich had contracted Masina to do three projects with his company, but she only made one other (Julien Duvivier's *Das kunstseidene Mädchen / The Artificial-Silk Girl*, 1960), backing out of *Die Dreigroschenoper* (*Three-Penny Opera*, 1962) because the previous two collaborations were not successful.[13] Most important, the international market never opened up for *Jons and Erdme*, and so Poland did not serve as a gateway to global growth for Kurt Ulrich Film or its other productions.

The contract that Ulrich had signed with Film Polski to "co-produce" *Jons and Erdme* in 1959 did, however, become the basis of one further West German/Polish co-production. A redlined version of that *Leistungsvertrag* (agreement for services) became the template for Pohland's agreement with the Polish authorities for *Cat and Mouse*, which he had been angling to adapt and shoot in Gdańsk since Grass's novella appeared in 1961. Thus, the genesis of this third West German/Polish co-production is more tightly grouped with the previous two than its eventual release date (1967) indicates. An Oberhausen Manifesto signatory, Pohland epitomizes those in New German Cinema whose "antipathy to 'Daddy's cinema' centered primarily on the fact that it was 'Daddy's' and only secondarily on its merits" (Bergfelder 2005, 2). He had some experience directing but then moved more into production with the founding of Modern Art Film. The company had gotten an agreement to film the book early, in part because of the promised participation of the well-respected Walter Henn as writer and director. Another factor was the artistic focus and critical success of

*Tobby* (1961), the story of a jazz musician in Berlin who resists the lure of international travel and fame to remain a true "Yatzer" in his familiar Berlin haunts. The Grass adaptation would not be Pohland's first international foray: in 1963 as producer, he took an entourage to California to film Michael Pfleghar's *Die Tote von Beverly Hills* (*The Dead Girl of Beverly Hills*, 1964). In making this film "that broke all the conventions" (Groh 2019), he took full advantage of the "crazy European" label given his crew by the Los Angeles press to move in and out of the scene, play fast and loose with financial arrangements, and disregard union requirements in order to work on the cheap.[14] In the wake of these two eye-catching films in the early 1960s, some strong interest in Pohland's *Cat and Mouse* developed, but it took a long time to get rolling and seemed ill-fated. After making a trip to Gdańsk to scout locations and producing a preliminary treatment with Pohland, Henn died early in 1963. A new director/screenwriter had to be found. Andrzej Wajda was contacted and expressed some interest but at the time was committed elsewhere. Meanwhile, another screenplay was generated but elicited such negative reactions (from Grass, among others) that Henn's original draft treatment became the basis for moving forward.[15] Later, Wajda became free and offered to do the project but had to be refused, because Modern Art Film's co-production/funding agreements had become dependent on engaging a West German director. So Pohland stepped in himself.

The filming did not go any more smoothly than the pre-production phases: Grass objected to some choices in the screenplay, such as the reduced role of Catholicism and the removal of scenes in the Marienkirche (Basilica of St. Mary of the Assumption of the Blessed Virgin Mary), and voiced as much.[16] Jean-Gil Chodziesner-Bonne, the assistant cameraman, had to drive the rushes to West Berlin every filming day, develop them, and then call to indicate whether they had come out.[17] Well-known cabaret satirist Wolfgang Neuss, who had played the male lead in *The Dead Girl of Beverly Hills*, was cast in *Cat and Mouse* as the "older" Pilenz and became particularly difficult, disappearing for extended stretches.[18] This retarded the already slow pace of filming, and some wondered what they were doing in Poland for so long. Neuss quipped bitingly that the director had managed to film Gdańsk as a relatively passable approximation of Lübeck, perhaps a sarcastic gesture to the number of expatriated Danziger in that other Hanseatic city, where the Bund der Vertriebenen (Confederation of

Displaced Persons) was grounded in 1957; however, it just as likely was meant to imply that the location shooting adds nothing to the fabric of the film.

While the satirist has a point in some regards, the very fact that this trans–Iron Curtain co-production was taking place at all should not be underestimated, and the film that stems from it of necessity bears traces of Gdańsk that are not inconsequential. In the remainder of this essay, I suggest that the prerelease (and subsequent) skirmishes placing Pohland's *Cat and Mouse* within "bundesdeutscher Innen(kultur)politik" have obscured from view moments of aesthetic apprehension that the film opens up through traveling to engage with German memory *in Poland*. This examination retroactively uncovers a complex grappling with the nascent project of *Vergangenheitsbewältigung* shaped as a necessary, yet in some ways self-deluding, *international* undertaking. In that sense the choices of this director/producer made *Cat and Mouse* a truer co-production in terms of real engagement than its two predecessors, even if its co-production partner "Rytm" was largely a "beard."[19]

## Pilenz's Progress

*Cat and Mouse* opens on a quietly humming crowd seated in an elevated set of stands, the slightly high-angled shot centered on a woman of roughly sixty holding a pamphlet suggesting that these are displaced "Germans" from Danzig. As the camera pans right across a banner declaring that "the Danziger fights for freedom and justice," the anticipatory murmuring is broken by a voice from the PA system: "Attention . . . Joachim Mahlke, Knight's Cross recipient and former student at the Conrad High School in Danzig Langfuhr, is being sought by his one-time classmate Pilenz." The camera continues to pan across a ceremonially decorated stage in the distance of the arched hall and then stops to frame another banner on the opposite upper deck reading, "Homeland—eternal bond." This beginning scene echoes the ending of Grass's novella but also signals a change in direction at the outset of Pohland's film. Rather than a meeting of those who had received that military honor, these are *Heimatvertriebene*, the self-declared displaced Germans of Danzig, and that shift brackets out the war experience in two ways. First, the public-address announcement points the viewer back to Pilenz's and Mahlke's school days in the complicated ethnic and political arrangement of the city following the Treaty of Versailles and beyond, moving away from any implied continuity in military institutions.[20] Instead, the implied continuity here is in the reactionary sense of *Heimat* that remains unbroken from the end of World War I to the present, at least in this gathering of the displaced, which marks a second shift away from Grass's text. The mise-en-scène underscores the shift. The lettering is distinctly old-fashioned (Sütterlin-like) and the iconography somewhat archaic, while the costuming is postwar, if unstylish. At best, an indistinct geo-temporal location serves as the point of origin in this search for Mahlke, who cannot be found in the contemporary Federal Republic, although similar spirits clearly still haunt such gatherings. The film uses this opening to develop tensions beyond questions about the search for Mahlke. Its concern, I suggest in the following discussion of the film's opening and closing segments, is just as much with Pilenz as a "tourist" in Gdańsk now as a German in Danzig "back then."

After the brief opening with the *Heimatvertriebenen*, *Cat and Mouse* jumps into a sprint through the countryside to Poland that eschews any actual border crossing, a montage that erases differences between the countries and their histories. The frame of reference now is privileged Western travel, conceptually recasting the conquest and occupation of the *Blitzkrieg* in a more benign guise.[21] In this montage, the adult Pilenz speeds along in a Fiat Spider convertible, several shots distinctly showing its West German license tag.[22] A narrator intones in voice-over: "Zwanzig Jahre nach dem Kriege *reist* ein Deutscher in die Stadt seiner Jugend, nach Danzig, und er sieht diese Stadt, die jetzt Gdańsk heisst, wie sie heute ist."[23] Pilenz is a German actor on his way to play in a Polish film, but at no time does the film show us his work activity. The narrator informs us that memory is always a matter of the past encased in the present, which is why this German will appear as a grown man in the company of companions from his youth. Unlike the film's opening sequence, which varies and repositions the ending of Grass's novella, this journey is an addition by the filmmakers that introduces the idea of contemporary travel, which in itself calls up current geopolitical configurations in a manner that the novella does not. The year is 1966. The montage is brisk, set to an upbeat, bebop-like jazz soundtrack composed by Hungarian-born guitarist Attila Zoller.[24] The Fiat passes a statue of the Virgin Mary in a field, the car-mounted camera fixing on it in a pan as the car speeds past. The carefree sense of the sequence is broken by a cut to a black cat in the road, followed by a brief take through the windshield of the cat (a cardboard cutout), now on the car's hood, which brings the car and the music to a screeching halt. These two figures—the Virgin and the caricatured cat—both offer objects for obsessive belief in the film: the Virgin being the medium for Mahlke's idiosyncratic faith; the cat providing the vehicle for exploring Pilenz's pilgrimage toward his hero, "the Great Mahlke," and the sense of partial responsibility that he bears for his idol's deeds and fate.[25]

The motoring montage continues until a sharp turn focuses the traveling camera on a sign announcing Gdańsk, a gesture to Polish autonomy that also designates it as the stage for this attempt at redemption through the conceptual rear projection of *Vergangenheitsbewältigung*. As the car enters the city, the montage continues, varying between shots that depict the deep marks on Gdańsk left by brushes with the German past: the historic structures of the former Hanseatic city; areas seemingly still devastated from the war; and modern structures that clearly have been erected in areas where that devastation has been cleared away. Moving first through the city's outskirts, the montage captures postwar shopping halls

FIGURE 6.1. *Cat and Mouse*—The cat on the convertible. (Screengrab)

with big glass windows and a pair of high-rise apartment complexes. The tempo here is similar to that of moving through the Polish countryside. Shots that pan and track from the car increase the sense of dynamic pace, while the takes continue to change about every other second. A longer take fixes on the city's most recognizable traditional landmark, the Krantor (the Crane Gate) on the inner harbor, as the vehicle carries the camera around the waterfront. This more historical, well-preserved section then gives way to images of the adjacent bomb-damaged buildings that remain a physical reminder of the war and the claims of Germans to this as "Heimat." Several shots present the reconstructed Marienkirche, where the Mahlke of the novella pursued his cult worship of the Virgin. The city itself has not yet forgotten the German presence, and the film—despite the German-centric reminiscence driving the storyline—continually presents a city that exists in the present and not in Pilenz's memory.

These opening segments correspond to Grass's sense of the two qualifications that the adaptation of the novella needed to meet, which he expressed in an exchange with Pohland: a presentation satisfying to older readers who knew the book; and a form speaking to younger filmgoers who did not.[26] Announcing Pilenz's search for Mahlke by traveling to the Danzig of his youth, the opening speaks to Grass's first desire; the contemporary gestures to the Charta der deutschen Heimatvertriebenen (Charter of German Homeland-Expellees, founded in 1950), the driving montage, the modern jazz soundtrack, and the sign to "Gdańsk" meet the second. The two sequences opening *Cat and Mouse* embody the contradictions inherent in this project of *Vergangenheitsbewältigung*. On the one hand, Pohland's film reenacts the erasure of Poles and Poland that is at the heart of the history with which the novella ostensibly wants to come to terms. The final shots of the drive to and into the city establish this when another sign announces the entrance into Langfuhr, a predominantly German area in the Danzig of Pilenz's and Mahlke's childhood. There is no sign to Wrzeszcz, as the district has been known since, and archival materials indicate that Pohland hoped to replace all Polish signs with German ones.[27] On the other hand, the location shooting in contemporary Gdańsk and the insistence on Pilenz as a figure of the present consistently confront the film's viewers with the contradictory nature of such a search for history through the personal past explored from the present. Not long after passing the Langfuhr sign, the montage ends in Sopot with the Fiat pulling up in front of the Grand Hotel, where the viewer watches Pilenz hoist his four bags of luggage out of the car, which solidifies his image as a Western visitor. However, the next scene shows Pilenz parking the Spider in front of their old school, where he begins his encounter with the past, which marks the last time the car appears. With the Western-traveler motif firmly established in the present, the film turns Pilenz's attention to confronting the past, while the viewer (in the phrase the narrator used to introduce the traveler) continues to "see the city as it is today."

Pilenz's progress into his past has been relatively easy up to this point, and the next portion of the film in Langfuhr seems drawn from his memory, concentrating on the school and the wrecked minesweeper *Rybitwa* as Mahlke learns to swim and develops his dedicated following. But the "adult" Pilenz regresses, with Neuss increasingly acting his role in the manner of an infantilized acolyte of Mahlke, while the backdrop of contemporary Gdańsk concretizes as a physical locality of the present. Increasingly the viewer is confronted with traveling shots of Polish signs on buildings, East Bloc cars, trucks, trams, and modern pedestrians looking at archaic German uniforms and directly at the camera that films them. After Pilenz's hero purloins the Knight's Cross and disappears from the scene, his "summer without Mahlke" is evoked through images of contemporary Gdańsk seen from the windows of the streetcar that takes him to the beach. He is intrigued to see his friend return to town, but the separation has broken the previous spell, which becomes clear when a manic Mahlke recites the exploits leading to his own receipt of the Knight's Cross. Filmed under the boardwalk with a hand-held camera that circles left to right in close-ups of the individual faces, this take ends in a medium two-shot showing

FIGURE 6.2. *Cat and Mouse*—The traveler arrives. (Screengrab)

both the uniformed soldier's self-absorption and the lack of reaction by the "schoolboy," Pilenz. His breathless hero worship has dissipated, although he is still willing to help his friend stage his speech as a returning hero at the Conradinum; however, when that opportunity fails to materialize, and Mahlke is disinclined to return to the front, Pilenz becomes dismissive, looking to sever their contact quickly. As the war hero recites the speech that he would have given at the Conradinum, Pilenz rows him to hide on the wreck and once there is eager to be off: "Na mach schon, ich muss nach Hause" ("Hurry up, I have to get home"). In a knowingly cutting response, Mahlke turns to an idiom that closes the circle on the film's depiction of Pilenz as a traveler: "Na schön, *Reisende* soll man nicht aufhalten."[28] This response to the idea of "going home" reintroduces the tropes that began the film: "going home" either aligns Pilenz with the reactionary *Heimatvertriebenen* or gestures to the return voyage of the touristic traveler.[29]

The final moments after Mahlke disappears below deck resolve that tension: Pilenz's project is *both* touristic and anchored in Gdańsk. Quick takes as he broods in several places on the minesweeper show him waiting after pounding out his "can-o-pen-er" message on the ship's hull. Then a

FIGURE 6.3. *Cat and Mouse*—The opening of the final take. (Screengrab)

FIGURE 6.4. *Cat and Mouse*—The end of the final take. (Screengrab)

cut jumps to Pilenz on the *Rybitwa* at a later time, signaled by a different outfit (a vacationer's matching light-colored shorts and shirt) and the appearance of a modern motorboat in the place where the rowboat was previously tied. The German looks at the hole through which Mahlke had disappeared, then climbs into the boat, and the film's final high-angle shot follows Pilenz speeding around and away from the wreck. While very different in its content, this shot bookends with the opening at the gathering of *Heimatvertriebenen* through its formal aspects: it begins fixed on a single figure from a high angle and then pans nearly 180 degrees to the right across a scene to expose the full context of the setting. Here the movement ends by framing the fancy craft between the Polish past of the minesweeper and the present of the beach full of bathers at Brzezno until, after several seconds, the boat is obscured by the ship. The composition is telling: a piece of the ship damaged in World War II looms overlarge in the foreground, while in the distance the curve of the beach mirrors the path and wake of Pilenz's craft, which itself lines up with an industrial tower spewing smoke in the far background of Westerplatte before a cut-to-black shows "Ende." No jazz soundtrack implies a journey out of Poland or back to Germany; the style of the speedboat recalls the traveler's trip to town, but the freedom of the convertible on the road has been exchanged for the vessel that cannot leave the harbor. Pilenz's progress has taken him to Gdańsk, but it is not the Celestial City of a mastered past. The traveler "disappears" above the water just as Mahlke disappeared beneath it toward the end of the war: a German presence ghosting within the geopolitical situation of contemporary Poland.

Pohland's co-produced film, shot in Poland, went quickly into relative obscurity, in part because the contemporary reception had had the wind taken out of its sails by preemptive conversations about "bundesdeutsche Innenpolitik." Yet, by neither pretending to be about Poland nor maintaining a presence in Germany, *Cat and Mouse* opens a broader view on the project of coming to terms with the past than any other early film in the New German Cinema. It makes palpable a reality that was in part of Mahlke's and Pilenzs' (and Grass's) making, even though Pohland's Gdańsk is as unmoved by Pilenz's trip as it is by Mahlke's failure to surface. It envelops them both and mutes the music of carelessly self-absorbed, self-fashioning *Vergangenheitsbewältigung*. In an era that was beginning to insist on the individual's personal history as a key to political memory, this film suggests that coming to terms with the national past remains a collectively *international* undertaking.

## Notes

For their assistance in researching this article, special thanks to Agnieszka Polanowska of the National Film Archive in Warsaw; Regina Hoffmann, Lisa Roth, Diana Kluge, and Julia Riedel of the Stiftung Deutsche Kinemathek; and Mareike Palmeira at the Modern Art Film Archiv.

1 *Süddeutsche Zeitung*, February 8, 1967; unless otherwise noted, translations in this article are the author's.
2 See Enno Stahl, *Für die Katz und wider die Maus: Pohlands Film nach Grass* (Berlin: Verbrecher Verlag, 2012); and Magdalena Saryusz-Wolska, "New German Cinema's Forgotten Film: Hansjürgen Pohland's *Katz und Maus*," *German Life and Letters* 66.1 (January 2013): 111–25. On the (lack of) images of Poles and Polish films in German films before the *Wende* (political turn), see also chapter 3 in Randall Halle, *The Europeanization of Cinema: Interzones and Imaginative Communities* (Champagne-Urbana: University of Illinois Press, 2014).
3 In his important study of popular international co-productions, Tim Bergfelder describes this as the model for West German/Swedish productions such as the *Pippi Longstocking* adaptations (2005, 65). He devotes a chapter to Brauner and CCC, which contains a brief reference to *The Eighth Day of the Week* as a "commercially risky" project with the "potential of enormous publicity beyond German borders" (107). This is *International Adventures*' only mention of the three films discussed in this essay.

4 Television journalists and reportage were significant here. A particularly important undertaking was the 1959 West German TV filming of the fifteenth anniversary of the Warsaw Uprising, a moment of cooperation that attempted to solidify Poland's heroic self-image. See Frieberg 2019, especially chapter 3.

5 Adam Krzemiński and Damien Thiriet, "Warschauer Aufstand: Ruinen der Festung," in *20 Deutsch-Polnische Erinnerungsorte*, ed. Hans Henning Hahn and Robert Traba (Paderborn: Ferdinand Schöningh, 2017), 239–72, here 254–55.

6 Tatjana Kossinova, "Die polnischen Ereignissen von 1956—in den Augen sowjetischer Dissidenten," in *Das Jahr 1956 in Ostmitteleuropa*, ed. Hans Henning Hahn and Heinrich Olschowsky, trans. Klaus Marten (Berlin: Akademie Verlag, 1996), 172–87, here 178.

7 See also Stefan Wolle, "Polen und die DDR im Jahre 1956," in Hahn and Olschowsky, *Das Jahr 1956 in Ostmitteleuropa*, 46–58.

8 That film was Jan Rybkowski's *Dziś w nocy umrze miasto* (*Heute Nacht stirbt eine Stadt / Tonight a City Dies*, 1961). Aleksander Ford's *Krzyżacy* (*Knights of the Teutonic Order*, 1960) was an exception in that it was shown in the GDR but not the FRG (Wach 2011). Later, Rybkowski's *Kiedy miłość była zbrodnią* (*Rassenschande / When Love Was a Crime*, 1968) had its premiere on West German television (WDR) but was never shown in Poland because of its pro-German depictions. See Eugeniusz Cezary Kröl, "Gesellschaftliche und politische Grundlagen des Bildes der Deutschen im polnischen Spielfilm nach dem Zweiten Weltkrieg," in *Deutschland und Polen: Filmische Grenzen und Nachbarschaften*, ed. Konrad Klejsa and Schamma Schahadat (Marburg: Schüren, 2011), 33–44.

9 Ziemann also worked with Brauner's company in an Italian "white telephone" co-production in 1956 (Bergfelder 2005, 125–26).

10 Brauner's CCC and Ford would, however, later work together on an English-language German/Israeli co-production about the Warsaw pedagogue Janusz Korczak, who voluntarily accompanied the children from his orphanage to Treblinka. Wulf Kansteiner describes *The Martyr* (1974) as an "overly sentimental film [that] painted a simplistic, heroic picture of Korczak" (Kansteiner 2006, 121).

11 Perhaps the height of these were the high jinks of O.W. Fischer in the second remakes of two "Peter Voss" films.

12 For an example of positive press, see, for example, Kurt Habernoll, "Ein westdeutscher Film entsteht hinter dem Eisernen Vorhang" *Tagesspiegel*, May 17, 1959.

13 Masina was well advised here, as Staudte's *Three-Penny Opera* was a complete financial and critical flop (Bergfelder 2005, 78).

14 Although she had sold the rights to her late husband's work, Valerie von Martens objected strenuously to the end product of this Curt Goetz adaptation. "Die Tote von Beverly Hills," Stiftung Deutsche Kinemathek (SDK) Schriftgutarchiv.

15 According to documents in the Pohland material in the SDK's Schriftgutarchiv, this became a potential sticking point in getting the screenplay subvention from the Kuratorium, which more than once asked for an attestation that Pohland was the sole author of the "Drehbuch" (that attestation was given but seems to stretch the truth). Interestingly, the unmarked Polish-language shooting script on file at the Nation Film Archive in Warsaw lists Walter Henn as the creator (personal communication with Agnieszka Polanowska at the Filmoteka Narodowa, June 28, 2019).

16 Undated letter from Grass to Pohland, SDK Schriftgutarchiv. The film does contain some images of the Marienkirche; however, more striking is a B-roll insert of an archaic church bearing the inscription "966–1966" above the door. The former is the year associated with the Christianizing of the "Polens" (more than a decade before Gdańsk was formally founded), while the millennial anniversary announced on the portal echoes with the empire of a thousand years desired by the Nazis.

17 Jean-Gil Chodziesner-Bonne, "Erinnerungen und Impressionen zu den Dreharbeiten von *Katz und Maus* im Sommer 1966 in Gdynia nahe Sopot," interview recorded in Replonges, January 13, 2017, Modern Art Film Archiv.

18 Early treatments also had scenes with a "young" Pilenz, but that role was not filled and fell out of the script before the shooting finally began ("Katz und Maus," SDK Schriftgutarchiv).

19 Personal communication with Agnieszka Polanowska at the Filmoteka Narodowa, June 28, 2019.

20 Grass's novella specifically describes this as a meeting of war survivors who bore the Knight's Cross, at which a band from the Bundeswehr was playing (1961, 188–89). In the screenplay for the film, it is identified as a 1958 meeting of the Bund der Heimatvertriebenen in Münster.

21 One shot captures a vast group of mounted equestrians banking through a field as the Fiat powers by, perhaps recasting the futile (and largely mythical) charges of Polish cavalry against mechanized troops in the September Campaign.

22 This was the Sport Spider version of the 124 on loan from the Fiat company, according to cameraman Chodziesner-Bonne ("Erinnerungen

und Impressionen zu den Dreharbeiten von *Katz und Maus*"), who could travel by car through the GDR because of his French passport and thus was tasked with picking it up in Heilbronn in early summer 1966. In the framework of filming *Cat and Mouse*, not just Pilenz's Fiat but all the vehicles driven by the company filming in and around Gdańsk made quite the spectacle of Western consumer luxury.

23 "Twenty years after the war, a German *travels* to the city of his youth, to Danzig, and sees the city, which is now called Gdańsk, the way it is today" (emphasis added).

24 An Austrian citizen, Zoller played in Vienna and then Berlin before moving permanently to the United States in 1959. Zoller worked from the script when composing, linking the music to the fabric of the story rather than the rhythm of the edits.

25 The narrator notes in describing the search for Mahlke: "an dessen Schicksal [Pilenz] Mitschuld trägt" ("for whose fate [Pilenz] shares complicity").

26 Undated letter, Grass to Pohland, "Katz und Maus," SDK Schriftgutarchiv.

27 It is clear from the finished film that this erasure was not pursued consistently. Polish infuses the mise-en-scène through building names, signs on commercial vehicles, and end stations on tramcars. As a side note, the Polish Wrzeszcz itself gestures to tensions in Polish history in its slight variation from the Kashubian Wrzészcz.

28 Emphasis added. Literally, this means "Oh, then, one shouldn't detain *travelers*." This idiom appears in Grass's novella but in a different context: in response to Pilenz's protestations that Old Man Kreft had limited the rowboat rental to ninety minutes. Manheim translates it more colloquially and accurately: "Ok, never detain a busy man" (181).

29 The original screenplay contains segments devoted to exiting Danzig that do not appear in the final film version.

## Works Cited

Bergfelder, Tim. 2005. *International Adventures: German Popular Cinema and Europeans Co-Productions in the 1960s*. Oxford: Berghahn Books.

Borodzeij, Wlodzimierz. 1996. "Die Beziehung Polen-DDR im Spiegel der Akten des polnischen Außenministeriums." In *Das Jahr 1956 in Ostmitteleuropa*, edited by Hans Henning Hahn and Heinrich Olschowsky, translated by Klaus Marten, 58–67. Berlin: Akademie Verlag.

Duvivier, Julien, dir. 1960. *Das kunstseidene Mädchen* (*The Artificial-Silk Girl*). Kurt Ulrich Film.

Fellini, Federico, dir. 1954. *La Strada*. Paramount Pictures.

Ford, Aleksander, dir. 1945. *Majdanek—cmentarzysko Europy* (*Majdanek: Friedhof Europas / Majdanek: Cemetery of Europe*). Documentary filmed with the Red Army.

———. 1958. *Ósmy dzień tygodnia* (*Der achte Wochentag / The Eighth Day of the Week*). CCC-Film and Film Polski.

———. 1960. *Krzyżacy* (*Kreuzritter / Knights of the Teutonic Order*). Zespol Filmowy.

———. 1974. *Sie sind frei, Dr. Korczak* (*The Martyr*). CCC Film and Bar Kochba Film (Tel Aviv).

Frieberg, Annika. 2019. *Peace at All Costs: Catholic Intellectuals, Journalists, and Media in Postwar Polish-German Reconciliation*. Oxford: Berghahn Books.

Grass, Günter. 1991. *Cat and Mouse*. Translated by Ralph Manheim. New York: Harcourt. First published in 1961.

Groh, Thomas. 2019. "Ein Film, der sämtliche Konventionen brach." *Der Tagesspiegel* 11.10.

Kansteiner, Wulf. 2006. *In Pursuit of German Memory: History, Television, and Politics After Auschwitz*. Athens: Ohio University Press.

Kawalerowicz, Jerzy, dir. 1957. *Prawdziwy koniec wielkiej wojny* (*The Real End of the Great War*). Film Polski.

Konwicki, Tadeusz, dir. 1958. *Ostatni dzien lata* (*The Last Day of Summer*). Zespol Filmowy.

Marischka, Georg, dir. 1959. *Peter Voss, der Held des Tages* (*Peter Voss, Hero of the Day*). Kurt Ulrich Film.

Pfleghar, Michael, dir. 1964. *Die Tote von Beverly Hills* (*The Dead Girl of Beverly Hills*). Modern Art Film.

Pohland, Hansjürgen, dir. 1961. *Tobby*. Modern Art Film.

———. 1967. *Katz und Maus* (*Cat and Mouse*). Modern Art Film.

Polański, Roman, dir. 1962. *Nóż w wodzie* (*Messer im Wasser / Knife in the Water*). Zespol Filmowy.

Rózewicz, Stanislaw, dir. 1967. *Westerplatte*. Zespol Filmowy.

Rybkowski, Jan, dir. 1961. *Dziś w nocy umrze miasto* (*Heute Nacht stirbt eine Stadt / Tonight a City Dies*). Film Polski.

———. 1968. *Kiedy miłość była zbrodnią* (*Rassenschande*, aka *Als Liebe ein Verbrechen war / When Love Was a Crime*). Film Polski.

Staudte, Wolfgang, dir. 1962. *Die Dreigroschenoper* (*The Three-Penny Opera*). Kurt Ulrich Film and C.E.C. (Paris).

Vicas, Victor, dir. 1959. *Jons und Erdme* (*Jons and Erdme*). Kurt Ulrich Film and Film Polski.

Wach, Margarete. 2011. "Deutsch-Polnische Kopruduktionen seit 1957 vor dem Hintergrund des Vertriebs und der Rezeption polnischer Filme in Deutschland." In *Deutschland und Polen: Filmische Grenzen und Nachbarschaften*, edited by Konrad Klejsa and Schamma Schahadat, 127–49. Marburg: Schüren.

Wajda, Andrzej, dir. 1957. *Kanał* (*Sewer*). KADR.

———. 1958. *Popiół i diament* (*Ashes and Diamonds*). KADR.

# 7

# BABELSBERG FREEDOMS

## The Films of the Babelsberg Film School, European New Waves, and New German Cinema

*Ilka Brombach*

*Translated by Christopher Etheredge, Marco Abel, and Jaimey Fisher*

In this essay, I will discuss student films made at the East German film school in Babelsberg, which I would like to situate within the context of several European new waves, including New German Cinema. In particular, I will focus on films that were made between 1956 and 1967, a period that constitutes the immediate prehistory and also overlaps with the beginning of New German Cinema. These films allow us to see how, roughly at the time when a new wave emerged in West Germany (the FRG), one formed in East Germany (the GDR) as well, which, like its West German counterpart, positioned itself as part of the European—indeed, global—movement of new waves.

The student films made at the Babelsberg film school constitute a largely unknown group of works that film historians have barely begun to study. As I hope to show, however, these films are especially well suited to closing a film-historical gap concerning how scholars understand East German cinema's relation to the history of the new waves. Scholars have tended to assume that, in the GDR, the emergence of a new wave was either entirely prevented or exclusively limited to the so-called *Verbotsfilme* (also known as "Rabbit Films," meaning banned films) of 1965.[1] Carefully attending to the student films allows us to show that there were multiple attempts at forging a GDR new wave and that such attempts unfolded over a longer period of time, even though, due to the prevailing cultural and political conditions, they did not directly address a public in the form of a manifesto.

If we consider the student films made at the Babelsberg film school as evidence of an emerging early new wave in the GDR, then we can place them next to New German Cinema in order to sketch a *German-German* film history within the various transnational contexts that this volume seeks to foreground. In doing so, I take my cue from the discipline of history, in which this approach to studying inner-German division is well established.

## Film Schools and New Waves

It is no coincidence that the products of a film school are particularly relevant in this context, for such institutions enjoy a special status within developed film cultures. While they are primarily places where filmmaking is taught, they also are alternative sites of film production. Most of the time, in Europe, anyway, they are state-run and not directly a branch of the film industry; they are frequently one part of the state-subsidized art academies and are therefore committed to the principles of artistic freedom and academic autonomy. In other words, film production at film schools was, and is, often relatively independent from the prevailing politico-regulatory and/or socioeconomic conditions, thereby offering generally freer spaces for experimentation. Film schools could therefore serve as important settings for emergent new waves, as was famously the case, for example, in Łódź and in Prague. Such schools were, moreover, frequently founded in the context and in the spirit of the new waves, as is the case with the West German film academies in Berlin (dffb) and Munich (HFF).

To what extent does this hold true for the film school of the GDR as well?

What I shall be terming the "Babelsberg film school" (for simplicity's sake) was founded in 1954 as the Deutsche Hochschule für Filmkunst (DHF, or German University for Film Art), which would later become Hochschule für Film und Fernsehen "Konrad Wolf" (HFF, "Konrad Wolf" or Academy for Film and Television "Konrad Wolf").[2] It was the first German film school, founded nine years after the end of the Second

World War and seven years before the Wall went up. Its founding, then, is, first and foremost an aspect of the early GDR context—of the GDR's cultural politics of the 1950s and of East Germany's postwar film culture. In 1946, DEFA, the East German state-owned film studio, began producing films, with Wolfgang Staudte's *Die Mörder sind unter uns* (*The Murderers Are among Us*, 1946) the earliest postwar feature. From the early 1950s on, the number of film productions declined. Feature films tended to be in the vein of socialist realism, political documentaries, and/or prestige films expressive of the Stalinist cultural politics of the time.

With a lack of audience interest in such features, talk of a crisis of DEFA cinema grew—concerns parallel and, in some ways, similar to what occurred in West Germany. For example, cited in this critical discourse were the films' reliance on the old UFA style, constraining political demands, and the new medium of television. In response, the ZK (central committee) of the GDR's dominant SED (Socialist Unity Party) passed a resolution in 1952 on the "Aufschwung der fortschritlichen deutschen Filmkunst" ("uplift of the progressive German film art") and decided "Maßnahmen zur systematischen Nachwuchsschulung nach sowjetischem Vorbild" ("measures to systematically train the new generation following the Soviet model") (Baumert 1979, 47). From its opening in 1954 (until 1990, when it was incorporated into unified Germany's academic system), the Babelsberg film school was the only training site for filmmakers in the GDR, housed in mansions near the DEFA (erstwhile UFA) studios and thus from 1961 (the year the Berlin Wall was built) in the border region near Griebnitzsee.

The foundational structure and principles of the new film school point beyond the GDR's immediate borders, suggesting a thoroughly transnational underpinning. Its organizational structure, for example, was copied from the film schools in Moscow and Prague. Teaching was based on the principles of the classic studio system, divided by trade in the subjects of directing, cinematography, scriptwriting, acting, and production; for the purposes of film exercises, teams formed, drawing their members from the various subject areas. In this respect, training at the DHF differed from film academies such as the dffb (Deutsche Film und Fernsehakademie Berlin / German Film and Television Academy Berlin) in West Berlin, which were founded only later, in the context of the new waves, and took their cues more openly from auteurism.

FIGURE 7.1. Film student Peter Brand on the terrace of the Babelsberg film school (where he studied cinematography from 1954 to 1958), with a view of Griebnitzsee (at the time the border between Potsdam and West Berlin), ca. 1956.

In other respects, however, training at Babelsberg was comparable to that of its contemporaries. Rather than emphasizing auteurism, one self-consciously thought of the school as an art school—the University for Film *Art*. This shaped the curriculum, which featured seminars on the histories of film, literature, and art as well as on acting, drawing, and photography, which were obligatory for all tracks. Many students in the various trades were therefore intent on developing integrated ways of working: directing students wrote their own scripts; cinematography students realized their own directing projects, and so on. Furthermore, film history played a special role in all this: students were exposed to films from German and international film history as well as to many contemporary films from around the world. International films, vetted by the DEFA foreign trade office and often not shown in regular cinemas, were generally sent for one day to the film school, where students could then watch them at screenings every Monday. As a result, the film school enjoyed a privileged situation within the otherwise restrictive media environment of the GDR, at least as far as reception was concerned.[3]

Film production was more constrained, especially with any allusions to international models. Similar to the state censorship to which DEFA was subjected, all stages of film production were carefully monitored, so that, when in doubt, authorities could (and would) intervene as early as script development or intercede after the first cut. In rare cases, finished films could be denied final approval—which could have grave consequences for a student's prospects for future employment (see Brombach 2016). Last but not least, the activities of SED-party groups (*Parteigruppen*; the smallest organizational units of the SED [Socialist Unity Party] in companies and institutions) as well as surveillance by the Stasi within the film school were part of the state's control and censorship measures. Nevertheless, compared to the situation at the DEFA studio, the film school offered considerably more liberties, since it produced films "only" for purposes of educating the next generation of GDR filmmakers, rather than for distribution beyond the school's confines. Beyond the occasional film festival or television screening, these works remained mostly out of sight within the broader GDR public sphere.

At the beginning of the 1960s, however, the Babelsberg film school exerted significant influence on GDR film culture, very much in the spirit of a generational change. Its first graduates, for example, directors such as Hermann Zschoche, Kurt Tetzlaff, Ingrid Reschke, and Jürgen Böttcher, as well as cinematographers such as Christian Lehmann and Wolfgang Dietzel, switched over to the DEFA studios (and later to GDR television). Their presence there effected a different understanding of film, which initially triggered resentment among the old guard that had learned filmmaking by *making* films, without the benefit of attending a film school. While Babelsberg graduates did not have much practical experience, they had considerable knowledge of film history; and many of them rejected the old UFA style that was still shaping DEFA cinema.[4]

Ever since its founding and in greater numbers since the 1970s, Babelsberg was attended not only by students from East Germany but also by students from Eastern Europe. Moreover, attendance occasionally included students from Western nations but, above all, students from the so-called Global South, who were trained in the GDR under a politics of "international solidarity."[5] After graduation, most of them returned to their countries of origin; their films form another chapter (one for which I do not have space herein) in the history of alternative film movements, pointing beyond the more narrow confines of the German and in particular East German context.

## Babelsberg Student Films and German-German Film History

Where can, and should, one begin with a German-German approach to these films?

In contrast to contemporary historical research, film studies after 1990 primarily approached the postwar cinema of the two Germanys separately. This is likely due to the controversies within DEFA research during the 1990s, which debated the degree to which DEFA films should be understood as an isolated body of work that was defined by political repression and censorship. In contemporary historical research, however, historians of West and East Germany, following Christoph Kleßmann, have long considered the relationship of the two Germanys through the framework of an "asymmetrically intertwined and parallel history" (Kleßman, Misselwitz, and Wichert 1999, 12): although the two states developed in opposite directions due to the mutual demarcation of the two systems, they were in this negative relation simultaneously oriented toward each other. Subsequent research in both social and cultural history has explored numerous aspects of East German society within state structures in ways that aim to move beyond a reductive model of unidimensional state repression.[6] This also goes for research on German-German media and film culture that heeds a dynamic of simultaneous division and proximity, of simultaneous competition and exchange. This kind of research has included, in particular, investigations of the two Germanys' film festivals and television as they unfolded under the influence of the Cold War.[7] But this broadening of a German-German perspective has not hitherto included, as it has in contemporary history, the European and extra-European contexts of film and media culture.[8] In exploring new wave films from a German-German-European perspective, then, one can build on research that examines GDR cinema from 1965, or, more precisely, from 1961 to 1965, in terms of a new start, or *Aufbruch*.[9]

For these reasons, I will explore below six East-German student films from the years 1956 to 1967. My analysis aims to reconstruct how they, like other new waves, unfolded in dialogue with Italian neorealism and how they also, shortly thereafter, were in communication with the first new wave films from Eastern Europe, rather than, as with New German Cinema, with those from Western Europe. I will undertake this reconstruction with recourse to documents from the Babelsberg film school and oral histories as well as by engaging in comparative film analysis, addressing important aspects of these films such as their themes of the transformation of gender relations and generational shifts, which were also typical of the new waves. But I will analyze such familiar themes within their East German contexts and therefore regard them as unfolding somewhat differently than in New German Cinema. I will also highlight labor as a theme that played an important role in the cinema of East Germany and Eastern Europe. Additionally, I will discuss the filmic and artistic traditions that these films invoke. These traditions diverge from those at work in New German Cinema, but I will also elucidate these films' formal aspects, such as the particular role the documentary form assumed at the film school, which can be understood as a commonality with New German Cinema. Finally, I will investigate the relevance of censorship and political directives for these films, not least to take up a contested issue in DEFA research concerning the question of whether East German films can, in the context of the new waves, be considered a film movement that rejected conventions and authorities. In short, the individual analyses are meant to demonstrate that a conceptual triangle composed of films from East Germany, New German Cinema, and the various European new waves is required to write a German German film history of this epoch.

## *Auf einem Bahnsteig* (*On a Train Platform*, 1957) and *Ladri di biciclette* (*Bicycle Thieves*, 1948)

Let's begin with Kurt Tetzlaff's 1957 documentary short, *Auf einem Bahnsteig*, which illustrates the intensive reception of Italian neorealism at the Babelsberg film school in the 1950s and 1960s.[10] The school was practically *the* site for the reception of neorealism in the GDR that, as in other European film cultures, initiated a kind of cinematic awakening.

In the 1950s, Italian films were shown neither in GDR cinemas nor at the film school. As Soviet cultural policy was implemented in the early

GDR, Italian neorealism was problematized and condemned as "critical realism" (in contrast to socialist realism, which was supposed to portray socialist reality positively).[11] Many GDR film students initially saw these neorealist films illegally in West Berlin—the Berlin Wall was not yet up—at the Filmbühne am Steinplatz, the West Berlin cinema that had the "Italians" in its program. Despite various controls, the film school was unable to stop these cineastic border crossings; numerous reports from contemporary witnesses record that on some evenings not only half of the Babelsberg student body but also the lecturers met at the Filmbühne.[12] The young lecturer Bernhard Thieme and the directing student Jürgen Böttcher enforced that neorealist films were shown and discussed in seminars at the school.[13] Party files of the time confirm that the school's administration permitted the screenings in order to curb these many illegal trips to West Berlin.[14] Then, in the 1960s, the most important Italian films were included in the film school's curriculum, with their prints kept in the archive for repeated viewings. However, *Auf einem Bahnsteig* can be considered paradigmatic also because of its documentary form.

The film school's educational concept, especially its focus on documentary films, existed from its founding until the fall of the Berlin Wall. At first, in the 1950s and well into the 1960s, the school faced material shortages common in the early postwar period. Above all, there was a shortage of equipment (cameras, editing suites, and lighting), which is why theoretical instruction predominated. Students could make only three short films during their course of study, at least two of which had to be documentaries because their production costs were lower than for feature films. But what was initially merely a stopgap measure was eventually incorporated into the mandatory curriculum, and students were trained exclusively in documentary filmmaking during their first two years of study. Accordingly, successive generations of Babelsberg students recorded the everyday as well as the working world across the GDR, creating street scenes in both the cities and the provinces as well as individual and group portraits of people from all occupational groups and social classes. Thus, the creative encounter with the models of European cinemas, and especially those of Italian neorealism, often took place in the medium of documentary film. Tetzlaff's film exercise is a good example of this.

*Auf einem Bahnsteig* is a short, four-minute milieu study shot at the Ostkreuz train station in Berlin Friedrichshain. It captures in snapshots a piece of proletarian Berlin in 1957: on a workday, early evening, workers drink a beer on their way home and watch women; two boys push each other around at a kiosk. When the next train pulls in, the boys steal a few returnable bottles unnoticed. The film tests some elements of the Italian models. The motif of theft and the train station as a setting are taken from Vittorio De Sica's *Bicycle Thieves*. Tetzlaff also tried his hand at the Italian method of shooting with nonprofessional actors and on original locations. In preparation for the shoot, he had spent multiple afternoons observing the train station, arranged to meet some passersby for the day of the shoot, and rehearsed short scenes with fellow students, which they then acted out on location among the people waiting at the station. The film therefore mixes staged and observed scenes. The film's temporal framing is inspired by De Sica (and also by Fred Zinnemann's *High Noon* [1952]): a certain period of time, in Tetzlaff's case the time between two trains, functions as a dramaturgical bracket.[15]

Tetzlaff's film exercise is thus an example of the reception of neorealism in GDR film, in that the artistic and political mission of the film in the context of the 1950s is to take up neorealism—officially banned but admired by cineastes—at all. But the film is also interesting because it points ahead to a development of DEFA documentary film—of which Tetzlaff was later one of the most important protagonists—toward a consciously poetic, aesthetically ambitious documentary film. In fact, with *Auf einem Bahnsteig*'s neorealist feature film elements, he tests the narrative possibilities of documentary film, especially with scenic storytelling and cinematic montage. And while short-film exercises dispensed with the soundtrack to save material, Tetzlaff uses this limitation productively: instead of a voice-over, obligatory in 1950s DEFA documentaries for the purposes of offering political and ideological explanations, Tetzlaff makes the (silent) images speak for themselves.

*Auf einem Bahnsteig* can thus be considered a first, quiet step taken by some GDR documentary filmmakers toward more aesthetically ambitious filmmaking—which put them at some remove from the political-propagandistic documentaries of the early DEFA. Focusing on the artistic and aesthetic was attractive to these filmmakers because it allowed them to distance themselves from GDR cultural-political demands for partisan documentary films, whose primary aims were to influence and educate. (Of course, from time to time they were forced to make such works anyway.) In pursuing less political, more poetic purposes, however, these filmmakers also took a direction away from the decidedly political films of the European documentary film movements of the 1960s and 1970s, such as cinéma vérité and direct cinema, with their emphatic understandings of the public (and counter-public) sphere, authenticity, and free speech.

What does a comparison of such a film with New German Cinema show us? The role of documentary at the Babelsberg film school confirms something to which Thomas Elsaesser and Michael Wedel have pointed in the context of New German Cinema: that while the standard film histories of the new waves tend to focus on feature films, documentaries also played a key role in the emergence of New German Cinema. Wedel underscores the importance of the Munich Group DOK59 for the prehistory of the Oberhausen Manifesto, and he sketches a "poetics of documentary" (2011, 363) as a key trait of New German Cinema in the oeuvres of many of its representatives.[16]

## *Der Elefant von Hoyerswerda* (*The Elephant of Hoyerswerda*, 1959), the Socialist *Aufbaufilm*, and the Traditions of European Photography and Painting

Christian Lehmann's graduation film *Der Elefant von Hoyerswerda* deals, like many other student films of the time, with one of the most politically favored themes—that of labor and workers.[17] In the 1950s, GDR cultural policy had enforced the original Soviet art doctrine of socialist realism, including the demand for art to be partisan (understood as siding with the working class).[18] Workers were to be portrayed accordingly in films; concurrently, from the early 1950s on, DEFA documentaries propagandistically presented stories of the reconstruction of East German industry after World War II.

With *Der Elefant von Hoyerswerda*, Lehmann (later one of the most important cameramen of DEFA documentaries) initially follows up on these (*Wieder-*)*Aufbaufilme* (reconstruction films). The film observes construction work in Hoyerswerda, Saxony, where a residential district is being projected for the employees of the newly built Schwarze Pumpe gas combine (the largest lignite refining plant in the world at the time). A gantry crane, the "Elephant of Hoyerswerda," assembles the first large-scale slabs in the GDR. One sees how buildings are put together and façades are scaffolded, how crane drivers, bricklayers, and carpenters do their work, and, in the end, how the workers' families move into the new apartments. In this way, the narrative arc also corresponds to the Soviet and GDR documentaries of the 1930s through the 1950s, which staged successes in industrialization, housing construction, and the formation of a new socialist society.

What is interesting is how Lehmann's film realizes the theme in terms of visual aesthetics. Along the outlined narrative arc, it alternates between long shots of the architecture and the summer construction site, on the one hand, and close-ups and semi-close-ups of the workers' faces and bodies, on the other. Lehmann had studied photography at the Leipziger Hochschule für Grafik und Buchkunst (Academy of Fine Arts Leipzig) before studying cinematography; his experience as a photographer and his reception of various photographic traditions and styles impacted his camera work. The way in which he brings symmetries and structures as well as light and shadow into the frame in his shots of architecture, for example, resembles the photography of the New Objectivity, in particular Albert Renger-Patzsch.

The shots of the workers allow for an even wider range of associations in terms of models from film, photography, and painting. An important point of reference for the depiction of working people and everyday situations, for example, was certainly social documentary photography, which was greatly admired by the camera students of Lehmann's cohort; the visit to the photo and traveling exhibition "The Family of Man" in 1955 in West Berlin was one of the most formative art experiences of his generation.[19] Likewise, the films of Italian neorealism served as a point of reference, as their portrayals of the so-called common people and their everyday lives were enthusiastically received. More important, however, especially for Lehmann's diploma film, was probably the DEFA documentary film *Turbine I* (Joop Huisken, 1953), which belonged to the series of documentaries about production and industry. However, instead of heroic images of the "heroes of labor" and finished construction projects, Huisken focused on the detailed observation of the tangible work performance of industrial workers. Lehmann's worker sequences take a similar approach but—more than Huisken's—use images of individual faces and hand movements, thus also illustrating the competence of individual workers. In addition, as in the architectural shots, Lehmann works discreetly with image composition, especially with light and shadow. He thus treats the work's subject as one worthy of art (without aestheticizing it), very similar to what one knows from realist paintings. The fact that Lehmann then actually "rediscovers" Gustave Caillebotte's *Les raboteurs de parquet* (1875) speaks to this interpretation.

The aesthetic strategy as a whole—the individualizing depiction of work and skills as well as the artistic handling of the subjects of work that emphasizes image composition—significantly differs from the usual DEFA documentaries about industry and production and relates only ambivalently to the film's more propagandistic narrative arc. It draws on traditions of prewar and modern photography and art, especially on realism and documentary, which treated the subject of labor in the context of questions of social equality in the sense of more generally egalitarian worldviews rather than of Communism.

*Der Elefant von Hoyerswerda*, then, is a heterogeneous work. On the one hand, it meets national (GDR-specific), historically conditioned political standards (thus it is censored art in the broadest sense); on the other hand, it expands against the backdrop of a very multifaceted European artistic tradition—in this case, the representation of labor. Whether the film's freer visual aesthetic counteracts the adapted narrative or remains in broad agreement with it cannot be ascertained from the film alone, as both levels are equally present in the film.

If one looks from these films back to those of New German Cinema, two things are particularly interesting. First, by tracing the artistic traditions that are relevant here—including those of the Frankfurt School and Brecht, which were both important to New German Cinema—we can see how one could pose more precise questions and develop a more differentiated model, especially if embracing a German-German-European perspective on these matters. This is also true of the related question of the break from "Daddy's cinema." If, in film schools, Italian neorealism was a key point of departure—one that opened up a whole spectrum of narrative, stylistic, and shooting techniques that were opposed to the classical studio film—then the Babelsberg film school was, somewhat differently, interested in neorealism because students could connect to these films in terms of both their content and general philosophy: as a Marxist-informed reaction to fascism, the Italian films chose ordinary people as their protagonists. What attracted the film students to these neorealist films was precisely the association of a formal renewal with a leftist, Marxist attitude:

FIGURES 7.2 AND 7.3. *Der Elefant von Hoyerswerda*—Workers (Screengrab), and Gustave Caillebotte, *Les raboteurs de parquet*.

neorealism offered the students a way to elude, or to create space within, the directives of East German cultural politics, with its normative models of social realism.

## *Notwendige Lehrjahre* (*Necessary Apprenticeship Years*, 1960) and *Путёвка в жизнь* (*Road to Life*, 1931)

With his graduation documentary *Notwendige Lehrjahre*, even Jürgen Böttcher, who had been, as noted above, a significant force in the reception of neorealism at film school, managed to serve a politically opportune subject—one that seems, from today's perspective, problematic.[20] The film concerns a *Jugendwerkhof* (youth work camp) in Thuringia, a state institution that serves as a home for young delinquents, with the explicit aim of making them productive members of society. From today's perspective, these youth work camps make for one of the darkest chapters of East German history, given that, as institutions of discipline, they abused and even broke their young inmates, at least since the 1964 founding of the youth work camp at Torgau. But at the time, the youth work camp "Rudolf Harbig" in Römhild, in which Böttcher shot, was a kind of model project. The later head of the Youth Department in the Ministry for National Education (*Volksbildung*), Eberhard Mannschatz, promoted the institutional pedagogy of Anton Makarenko and introduced his methods for work, training, culture, and education in the collective after 1955.[21]

Bötttcher's film offers a voice-over that largely takes the perspective of the authoritarian, East German educational institute. The problem, so the voice-over suggests, is that of young criminals who are difficult to educate, having grown up with bad role models in the challenging conditions of the postwar era. By bad role models, the film means Western youth culture, which was widely accessible, at least partially, to the young in the East. Given this context, the home is postulated as a necessary educational measure. The scenes of training, work, and leisure of the youths in the home are, however, depicted in the spirit of Makarenko: the film shows traditional academics and vocational training, the active development of skills, an organized and engaging framework, opportunities to participate in governance of the home, and teachers open to discussing disagreements. The commentary links, one could say, the contradictory notions of an authoritarian and a reformed education.

In addition to the voice-over and these scenes of everyday life, the film depicts a theater project that Böttcher himself initiated during the filming at the home—Böttcher even hired an actor, Katharina Lind, as a teacher for it. With her, the youths develop improvised scenes in the style of Brecht, in which the consequences of one's home life play out and then are absorbed into the documentary's narrative. These scenes suggest a number of revealing associations from film history.

First, in a citation that Böttcher intended, *Notwendige Lehrjahre* refers to a Soviet feature of the 1930s that was a filmic trailblazer for Makarenko's pedagogy—one that was, because of its work with young nonprofessional actors, a neorealist film *avant la lettre*.[22] This film was Nikolai Ekk's *Путёвка в жизнь* (*Road to Life*) about the homes of Makarenko, shot with an ensemble of young former pupils whose joy in acting and tremendous expressiveness still impress today. Like Ekk, Böttcher propagates Makarenko's pedagogy, an education emphasizing responsibility and collective self-organization, and also like Ekk, Böttcher works with nonprofessional actors, who reenact their own biographical experiences. Formally, Böttcher's film develops in this way another type of documentary film that focuses on the aesthetic and the artistic. He uses the film to challenge the creativity of his protagonists, to show that they are acting—and thus solving conflicts and reflecting on and shaping their lives. The film and its creative protagonists thus encounter each other as equals on the levels of art and free play.

As for content, however, certain moments prove problematic, especially those theatrical scenes in which the young play out conflicts from the recent past, scenes in which violence, sadism, and hierarchies among the youths unfold. If we look at these scenes from today's perspective—with our knowledge about the GDR's youth work camps—they seem like a message in a bottle or scenes of Freudian displacement: the instances of juvenile violence that are played out and then overcome in the scenes seem to stand in for the violence of the teachers and the educational methods that the film and theater project render both visible and invisible.

The relationship of this film to the new waves and to New German Cinema is multifaceted. The motif of young criminals can be found in films of all eras. Films such as François Truffaut's *Les quatre cents coups*

(*The 400 Blows*, 1959) and Alexander Kluge's *Abschied von Gestern* (*Yesterday's Girl*, 1966) mark the theme of generational conflict and even explicit generational break. One can interpret the fact that Böttcher is referring not to Truffaut but, via Brecht, to Ekk in a number of ways, first of all as confirmation that Eastern European cinema served as a more important point of reference for East Germany films than the French New Wave. And distinguishing it from other European or West German films is how the film's attitude toward its protagonists varies: whereas in the voice-over the film expresses a sense of pedagogical superiority and, in turn, the need for the protagonists to subordinate themselves to sociopolitical imperatives, it also meets them at eye level in the playful theatrical scenes. Yet that Böttcher is referring to Brecht, as Kluge and many representatives of New German Cinema are doing, underscores the commonalities of the two German cinemas.

## *Barfuß und ohne Hut* (*Bare-Footed and without Hat*, 1964) and *Le joli mai* (*The Lovely Month of May*, 1963)

Böttcher developed this approach to a creative interaction between protagonists and film after his studies in his documentaries, including *Barfuß und ohne Hut*, one of the first interview films in the GDR that follows Chris Marker's *The Lovely Month of May* (the model for an interview film at the time). Böttcher's film shows teenagers or young adults spending their vacation on the Baltic Sea beach in Prerow in August 1964, interviewing, among others, a professional driver apprentice at the Berlin transport company who would like to study music, his friend who works for the railroad as a shunter, students from the College of Pedagogy in Karl-Marx-Stadt, and a car mechanic apprentice who would like to join the navy—young people of various professions and educational paths who are asked about their future plans and observed on the beach.

The idea of "translating" the Parisian May as an August day at the Baltic Sea is elegant, and not only because the Baltic Sea was the (accessible) place of longing for young people in the GDR. Vacations there at the campgrounds and on the beach were largely free of regulation: Böttcher stages beach life in a way that compensates for the fact that, within the

FIGURES 7.4 AND 7.5. *Barfuß und ohne Hut*—A young couple at the beach, and a couple in *The Lovely Month of May*. (Screengrab)

regimented GDR public sphere, interviews could not be conducted with the same openness, conjuring an interesting parallel to Marker's making his film the favored medium for an open exchange about politics and life plans. In fact, Böttcher critically refers to the existing conditions only at a few moments, such as when a student talks about wanting to become a teacher in order to change the traditional relationship between students and teachers or when another reports his desire to join the navy in order to see the world (which, two years after the Wall was built, was actually only possible with the navy). Böttcher's "lovely August" must therefore convey the mood of departure differently than Marker's. He does this by placing scenes of beach life next to the interviews, showing the young people playing guitar, building sandcastles, and dancing at night. The scenes of sensuality and creativity convey a moment of freedom that the film and its protagonists share. In this way, the film is also an expression of the brief phase of liberalization in GDR politics and film policy at the beginning of the 1960s.

## *Sommergäste bei Majakowski* (*Summer Guests at Majakowski*, 1967) and *Le joli mai*

Volker Koepp and Alexander Ziebell's student film *Sommergäste bei Majakowski* also refers directly to *The Lovely Month of May* (and to *Barfuß und ohne Hut*).[23] The film's political background, however, is the tense situation after the Eleventh Plenum of the Central Committee of the SED in 1965, the so-called *Kahlschlagplenum*, at which the liberal, reformist course of the 1960s was reversed and—with a ban on the entire annual production of DEFA—an example was made of cinema. At the same time, the Czechoslovak reform experiment of the Prague Spring—the outcome of which was not yet certain—was being closely watched. Given this context, it is likely that Koepp and Ziebell's documentary about a journey through the Soviet Union in the footsteps of the poet Vladimir Mayakovsky was made out of both caution and euphoria. The subject matter—the most important poet of the Russian October Revolution and his abiding significance—expresses a cautious disposition toward the prevailing political circumstances. The film's approach to its subject matter, however, is diametrically opposed to such a cautious attitude. Quotes from

Mayakovsky's poems are spoken (by Manfred Krug) off-screen, including the well-known verse that the revolution is a matter for the youth, while the images show young people on the Black Sea and in the streets of Moscow. The revolution that Mayakovsky evokes in his poems becomes, in the montage of image and sound, the awakening of Koepp and Ziebell's generation. The film's provocation was, of course, recognized at the film school. As punishment, Koepp then had to shoot his next film exercise on the subject of labor in the form of a young workers' brigade.

Apart from the provocation, however, *Sommergäste bei Majakowski* opens up another variant of the artistic documentary film, one that Koepp developed further in the course of his career and in which literary passages are quoted or in which Koepp's commentary attains distinctly literary qualities. In this, too, Koepp follows Marker, whose off-camera commentaries in *The Lovely Month of May* offer their own literary-essayistic qualities. Here, too, it is interesting to relate the Babelsberg films to the films of New German Cinema. In both cinemas, there was an intensive reception of Marker; in the case of New German Cinema, as is well known, the most prominent examples are the films of Harun Farocki and Hartmut Bitomsky. Their films belong to the essay film—the "intellectual brothers of the documentary film." The East German counterpart would be—in this metaphor—the sensual, poetic sister: Böttcher and Koepp, inspired by Marker, developed documentaries that deploy elements of literature and art, expressing a sense of potential freedom and independence that is grounded in the aesthetic.

## *Wir spielen Hochzeit* (*We Play Marriage*, 1964) and *O něčem jiném* (*Something Different*, 1963)

Finally, I would like to discuss Klausdieter Roth's student film *Wir spielen Hochzeit*.[24] Like the Marker interpretations just discussed, the film is shaped by the optimism of the 1960s. Roth belongs to the cohort that was able to see the first films of the Czech New Wave at the Babelsberg film school.[25] A young lecturer in film history, Christiane Mückenberger, procured film prints from Prague and screened them in her seminars.[26] In the spirit of this awakening, Roth and fellow students, including Rainer Simon and Iwanka Grabtschewa, founded the Kollektiv 63 and pushed for

FIGURES 7.6 AND 7.7. *Sommergäste bei Majakowski*—Revolution is a matter for youth. (Screengrab)

more student control in the shared governance of the school. *Wir spielen Hochzeit* reflects on the relationship between the sexes. In theme and composition, it resembles Vera Chytilová's early Czech New Wave film, *Something Different*.

Roth's film is insightful for different reasons than the films discussed so far. For one, it mixes documentary and feature film scenes and is one of the few student films to undertake formal experiments of this kind. Together with his feature and graduation film *Ritter des Regens* (*Knights of the Rain*, 1965), it can be considered in the context of GDR feature films of the 1960s that negotiate the theme of love against the background of emancipation and social liberalization.[27] Telling the story of a love relationship—from getting to know each other and the strong emotions at the beginning to the everyday life of marriage to the disappointment and separation at the end—Roth mixes documentary observations (of passersby on the street, newly in love, first without, then with, children) and play scenes (of marriage and divorce), while casting the roles of husband and wife with various actors.

*Wir spielen Hochzeit* demonstrates how our love life obeys traditional cultural patterns; the cinematic arrangement is designed as a sequence of varying scenes that follow the progression from infatuation to marriage to, finally, married life with children according to conventional gender roles. In this, it echoes Chytilová's film, which recounts (in its first episode) the story of a woman who flees her marriage, with its many conventions and hierarchical gendered relationship, only to return to her husband and continue her old life. As Roth does in his film, Chytilová plays with small discontinuities in the scenes (the woman is seen in one image with a certain hairstyle or dress, in the next with another), thereby foregrounding a tension between individual behavioral routines and cultural patterns.

It is interesting that the films neither formulate a major critique of conventions nor promise liberation. If anything, they are about a certain liberalization of conditions, which is primarily visible in the cinematic design's small escapes from the conventions of storytelling. Chytilová's and Roth's films, as well as other DEFA films about love, could therefore be considered less radical than their Western European counterparts. One could speculate about Roth that the moral ideas still prevalent in the GDR at this time would have worked as indirect censorship and thus caused him to question the role of heterosexual relationships, marriage, and family only

FIGURES 7.8 AND 7.9. *Wir spielen Hochzeit*—children play family, and *Something Different*—family scene. (Screengrab)

in a humorously ironic way, without fundamentally querying how they might underpin a society based on a desire for collectivity and cohesion.

Analogously, the film's experimental narrative form could also be considered less radical, for it is playful and reflective rather than challenging and critical; in this, one could certainly see an echo of the cultural-political verdict against formalism, which went in concert with the advocacy of classical narrative. But this moderate experiment could just as well be read as a reflection of the demand for GDR films not to be elitist and instead to be comprehensible, that is, not to address solely cineastes but everyone. The cautious, reflective treatment of the themes of emancipation and love could, in turn, also be understood as an attempt to depict relationships as worth changing but always valuable. Or one could see in it a kind of admission of not yet being able to foresee and evaluate the consequences of emancipation that began in the 1960s. In any case, it would be worthwhile to compare in greater detail the films of New German Cinema, the GDR films, and the films of the new waves regarding such topics.[28]

## Conclusion

One can see how the films from the Babelsberg film school discussed herein offer a multiplicity of formal and narrative aspects that could be characterized as a kind of East German new wave. The traits include references to neorealism and other new waves, their aesthetic-formal strategies, and a series of themes typical of the new waves, including generational conflict and gender relations. At this basic level of an affinity with the European new waves, these student films and the films of New German Cinema can be read in terms of a German-German and European film history.

Via detailed film analysis and comparison, a whole range of both commonalities and differences between the two film movements becomes clear. The differences between the cinema of the two Germanys is not based on strategies of competition and demarcation, as contemporary historical research has shown for many areas of German-German politics as well as for cultural and social history. One can instead conclude that the two film movements developed in a parallel manner, at least during the time period that I have analyzed in this essay. Their respective filmic counterparts were in Europe, not in the "other" Germany—and for East German films, they were especially in Eastern Europe, where similar social realities and cultural-political givens formed the conditions for filmmaking.

The need for East German cinema to cope with censorship and politically motivated directives does distinguish the two German film movements, as it profoundly marked the films of East Germany. Moreover, due to the German-German situation of a media-technical and linguistic public sphere that was simultaneously indivisible and yet riven by competition, censorship and political directives affected these East German films even more than other Eastern European new waves. In my view, then, the student films show how the film schools were not only relatively free spaces for cinematic experimentation but also spheres in which filmmakers could practice coping with the complexities of the political and formal guidelines. Strategies for constructively engaging the guidelines, circumventing or developing them further, were probed. As a result, the films were partially an amalgam of different, even contradictory artistic and thematic positions.

At the same time, a closer comparative look at New German Cinema and East German cinema promises new insights into their respective handling of filmic and artistic traditions—of the break with some traditions and the engagement with others. One could ask, for example, what the status of classical narrative was, given that traditional production methods, in the sense of the crafts and the guidelines, were taught and followed at the Babelsberg film school, whereas the origins of New German Cinema lay beyond a school or studio structure. Perhaps ignorance and rupture sometimes went hand in hand. Furthermore, one could ask: how did the reception of Brecht leave its (divergent) marks on both movements? And: how did both sides develop a formally highly self-conscious kind of documentary, yet with different tendencies? This study, I hope, has sketched a possible range of new paths for exploring a German-German film history in the context of the European new waves.

## Notes

1 See, for example, Thomas Christen, "Kaninchenfilme und Kahlschlag: Die verbotene Welle in der DDR," in *Einführung in die Filmgeschichte*, vol. 2: *Vom Neorealismus bis zu den Neuen Wellen: filmische Erneuerungsbewegungen, 1945–1968*, ed. Christen Thomas (Marburg: Schüren, 2016), 362–84.

2 Today it is called the Filmuniversität Babelsberg KONRAD WOLF.

3 Film festivals, especially the Internationale Leipziger Dokumentar- und Kurzfilmwoche, to which lecturers and students traveled annually,

provided them with an additional opportunity to orient themselves within international cinema. Of course, they were also able to watch international films that *Westfernsehen* (West German television) broadcasted. See, for example, Elisabeth Prommer and Andy Räder, "Kinogrenzgänger im geteilten Deutschland (1949–1961): Filmgeschmack, Nutzung und Motive des Kinobesuchs," in Wedel, Byg, and Räder (2013, 131–47); and Franziska Kuschel, *Schwarzhörer, Schwarzseher und heimliche Leser: Die DDR und die Westmedien* (Göttingen: Wallstein Verlag, 2016).

4 See, for example, *Filmwissenschaftliche Mitteilungen*, February 1965.

5 See Ilka Brombach, "Filme ausländischer Student*innen an der Hochschule für Film und Fernsehen 'Konrad Wolf,'" in *In deutscher Gesellschaft: Passagen-Werke ausländischer Filmemacher*innen 1962–1992*, ed. Tobias Hering and Tilman Baumgärtel (Bundeszentrale für politische Bildung, 2018), https://www.bpb.de/lernen/filmbildung/274740/filme-auslaendischer-student-innen-an-der-hochschule-fuer-film-und-fernsehen-konrad-wolf/.

6 See Frank Wolff, "In der Teilung vereint: Neue Ansätze der deutsch-deutschen Zeitgeschichte," Archiv für Sozialgeschichte 58 (2018), 353–391; Ulrich Mählert and Frank Möller, eds., *Abgrenzung und Verflechtung. Das geteilte Deutschland in der zeithistorischen Debatte* (Berlin: Metropol Verlag, 2008); and Hermann Wentker, "Zwischen Abgrenzung und Verflechtung: deutsch-deutsche Geschichte nach 1945, 2005," https://www.bpb.de/shop/zeitschriften/apuz/29301/zwischen-abgrenzung-und-verflechtung-deutsch-deutsche-geschichte-nach-1945/.

7 See, for example, Heather L. Gumbert, *Envisioning Socialism: Television and the Cold War in the German Democratic Republic* (Ann Arbor: University of Michigan Press, 2014); and Kötzing 2013.

8 For contemporary history, see, for example, Thomas Lindenberger, "Ist die DDR ausgeforscht? Phasen, Trends und ein optimistischer Ausblick," *Aus Politik und Zeitgeschichte*, 2014, https://www.bpb.de/shop/zeitschriften/apuz/185600/ist-die-ddr-ausgeforscht-phasen-trends-und-ein-optimistischer-ausblick/. For scholarship that examines DEFA cinema from an international (not merely German-German) perspective, see Wedel, Byg, and Räder 2013.

9 Henning Wrage, *Die Zeit der Kunst: Literatur, Film und Fernsehen in der DDR der 1960er Jahre. Eine Kulturgeschichte in Beispielen* (Heidelberg: Universitätsverlag 2009); Thomas Christen, "Kaninchenfilme und Kahlschlag: Die verbotene Welle in der DDR," in *Einführung in die Filmgeschichte*, vol. 2: *Vom Neorealismus bis zu den Neuen Wellen: filmische*

*Erneuerungsbewegungen, 1945–1968*, ed. Thomas Christen (Marburg: Schüren, 2016), 362–84.

10 The film was published in *Babelsberger Freiheiten: Filme der Hochschule für Film und Fernsehen "Konrad Wolf," 1957–1990*, 2 DVDs, ed. Ilka Brombach (Berlin: absolut Medien, 2018).

11 This occurred, for example, at the first film conference in 1952, convened by the Central Committee of the SED.

12 See, for example, Kurt Tetzlaff, "Interview with Christiane Mückenberger: 'Wir waren besessen von der Arbeit,'" in *Das Prinzip Neugier. DEFA Dokumentarfilmer erzählen*, ed. Christiane Mückenberger, Ingrid Poss, and Anne Richter (Berlin: Neues Leben Verlag, 2012), 156–76, here 163.

13 Ilka Brombach, interview with Jürgen Böttcher, Berlin, October 27, 2015, not published.

14 See file of the SED party group of the film school: "Bericht der Parteiorganisation der Deutschen Hochschule für Film und Fernsehen über die Erfüllung der Aufgabenstellung des 30. Plenums Zentralkomitees, vom 9.7.1957," Federal Archives (Bundesarchiv), Berlin, BArch 2115/57.

15 For Zinnemann's influence, Ilka Brombach and Chris Wahl, interview with Kurt Tetzlaff, Berlin, March 10, 2015, not published.

16 See also Thomas Elsaesser, *Der Neue Deutsche Film: Von den Anfängen bis zu den neunziger Jahren* (Munich: Heyne, 1994).

17 Published in *Babelsberger Freiheiten: Filme der Hochschule für Film und Fernsehen "Konrad Wolf," 1957–1990.*

18 The film conferences convened by the Central Committee of the SED in 1952 and 1958 served this purpose in film and in other fields.

19 See Christian Lehmann, "Interview with Peter Badel: Im Gespräch mit Christian Lehmann. Wahrscheinlich einer unserer schönsten Berufe überhaupt," in *Kamera läuft: DEFA-Kameraleute im Gespräch*, ed. Peter Badel (Berlin: Defa-Stiftung, 2007).

20 Jürgen Böttcher, *Der Sekretär* & *Ein Weimarfilm*, 2 DVDs, Edition Filmmuseum 103 (2016).

21 Isabel Schmid, *Jugendwerkhöfe in Thüringen Sozialistische Umerziehung zwischen: Anspruch und Realität* (Erfurt: Landeszentrale für politische Bildung Thüringen, 2014), https://www.lztthueringen.de/media/abzug_jwk_innenteil_030614.pdf.

22 For Böttcher's intended citation, Ilka Brombach, interview with Jürgen Böttcher, Berlin, October 27, 2015.

23 Published in *Babelsberger Freiheiten: Filme der Hochschule für Film und Fernsehen "Konrad Wolf," 1957–1990.*

24 Published in *Babelsberger Freiheiten: Filme der Hochschule für Film und Fernsehen "Konrad Wolf," 1957–1990.*
25 Klausdieter Roth, "Interview with Ralf Schenk: Die Träume eines Motorradhelden. Ein Gespräch mit Dieter Roth und Egon Schlegel," in *apropos: Film 2001—Das Jahrbuch der DEFA-Stiftung*, ed. Erika Richter and Ralf Schenk (Berlin: Defa-Stiftung, 2001).
26 Christiane Mückenberger, in Axel Geiß, *Jahrgänge—Gesprächsrunden 40 Jahre HFF, 1968–1972*, video footage Hochschule für Film und Fernesehen (HFF), produced by TV channel RBB in 1994.
27 In the course of the Eleventh Plenum of the Central Committee of the SED in 1965, *Knights of the Rain* (directed jointly with Egon Schlegel) was banned; the film copy was not archived.
28 A similar approach toward Eastern European films of the new waves is evident in Dominik Graf and Lisa Gotto, *Kino unter Druck: Filmkultur hinter dem Eisernen Vorhang* (Berlin: Alexander Verlag, 2021).

## Works Cited

Baumert, Heinz. 1979. "Gründungsgeschichten." *Filmwissenschaftliche Beiträge* 1.79: 46–58.

Brombach, Ilka. 2016. "Dokumente III: Die Auswirkungen des 11. Plenums auf die Filmhochschule Babelsberg." In *Deutschland 1966: Filmische Perspektiven in Ost und West*, edited by Conni Betz, Julia Pattis, and Rainer Rother, 96–108. Berlin: Bertz + Fischer Verlag.

Kleßmann, Christoph, Hans-Jürgen Misselwitz, and Günter Wichert. 1999. "Vorwort." In *Deutsche Vergangenheiten—eine gemeinsame Herausforderung. Der schwierige Umgang mit der doppelten Nachkriegsgeschichte*, 9–14. Berlin: Ch. Links Verlag.

Kötzing, Andreas. 2013. *Kultur- und Filmpolitik im Kalten Krieg: Die Filmfestivals von Leipzig und Oberhausen in gesamtdeutscher Perspektive, 1954–1972*. Göttingen: Wallstein Verlag.

Wedel, Michael. 2011. *Filmgeschichte als Krisengeschichte.: Schnitte und Spuren durch den deutschen Film*. Bielefeld: transcript Verlag.

Wedel, Michael, Barton Byg, and Andy Räder, eds. 2013. *DEFA international: Grenzüberschreitende Filmbeziehungen vor und nach dem Mauerbau*. Wiesbaden: Springer VS.

# 8

# THE ULM SCHOOL AND FEMINIST FILM HISTORY

*Hester Baer*

Recalling the singular impact on the New German Cinema of the Ulm School of Design (Hochschule für Gestaltung; HfG), where he was a founding director of West Germany's very first film school, Alexander Kluge asserts, "There is an official history of the so-called New German Cinema and an underground one. The so-called New German Cinema is measured in public by its most successful films. However, the roots of this success lie in its branching sidelines. These sidelines were the consistent focus of the [Ulm Film] Institute from 1962 to 1980" (1980, 5). Founded in 1962 as a direct result of the Oberhausen Manifesto, the Department of Film Design (Abteilung für Filmgestaltung) operated under the umbrella of the HfG, which had been established in 1953 as the successor institution of the Bauhaus; in a reprise of the Bauhaus's fate, the HfG was closed by the state for political reasons in 1968. (The film department continued to operate independently after that date as the renamed Institut für Filmgestaltung, but it no longer trained students in the same way.) Although short-lived, the Ulm School developed a distinctive film pedagogy combining an engagement with critical theory and an emphasis on the creation of formally rigorous "miniatures" imprinted with an authorial vision. This approach, which emphasized the role of cinema in creating a counter-public sphere (*Gegenöffentlichkeit*), left a lasting influence on the German film landscape of the 1970s and 1980s, visible especially in the films directed by the department's faculty, Kluge and Edgar Reitz, but also in the work of prominent women filmmakers Claudia von Alemann, Jeanine

Meerapfel, and Ula Stöckl. Among the first to engage the Ulm model of filmmaking in noteworthy ways—and the only graduates of the school who went on to make feature-length narrative films for the cinema—Alemann, Meerapfel, and Stöckl all contributed significantly to the emergence of the feminist film project in West Germany, itself a central component of the New German Cinema (NGC).

The project of developing a (feminist) counter-cinema germinated at the Ulm School, yet its roots there, along with the features of Alemann, Meerapfel, and Stöckl, have remained less well known—overshadowed by the influence of the Deutsche Film- und Fernsehakademie Berlin (dffb) and more internationally familiar directors including Helke Sander, Helma Sanders-Brahms, and Margarethe von Trotta—for at least two main reasons. First, as Thomas Elsaesser has suggested, the feminist film movement in Germany gained recognition by establishing a common program that presented women's films as "issue-oriented" in connection with their primary source for funding and means of distribution and exhibition: television.[1] By contrast, even as they developed a novel feminist aesthetics in the form and content of their films, the women directors who trained at Ulm positioned themselves as film authors in line with the Ulm model, and (at least initially) eschewed what they viewed as a pigeonholing of their work as women's films (*Frauenfilme*).

Second, as John Davidson (1999) has shown, the NGC emerged as a coherent body of work—what he terms a "genre"—in large part through its international reception, which was predicated on the notion that these films were exemplars of national-cultural representation. Accordingly, the films of Sander, Sanders-Brahms, and von Trotta were hailed abroad not least due to their specific attention to the unique trajectory of German history in the twentieth century. Here too, the pioneering feminist work of Alemann, Meerapfel, and Stöckl falls outside the parameters of what Kent Casper and Susan E. Linville refer to as "the pervasive cinematic typology of Germans" (1985, 251), even as their films reflect a critical approach to the German past and present.

This chapter reconsiders the relationship between the widely recognized (international) success films of the NGC and its lesser-known "branching sidelines" by returning to the significant legacy of the Ulm School and its marginalized contributions to feminist film history. I examine how the work of Alemann, Meerapfel, and Stöckl defies conventional paradigms that have structured our understanding of the NGC, including authorship, issue-orientation, and forms of national-cultural representation, and I dwell especially on the way their films manifest direct engagement with global contexts: Alemann in a focus on the radical movements associated with global 1968; Meerapfel in an autobiographical exploration of her own family's history as refugees from Nazi Germany to Argentina (followed by her own immigration to the postwar Federal Republic); and Stöckl in films that draw heavily on her own formative experiences in France and England in the 1960s and in Italy during the 1970s.

Noteworthy for their multilingualism and hybrid formal approach, the features of Alemann, Meerapfel, and Stöckl exemplify transnationalism along multiple registers, even as they have remained less visible abroad than their more "typologically German" counterparts. Rather than exploring the intersections of the NGC and its global contexts via a comparison of German films and their international equivalents, then, this chapter probes the conditions of possibility that enabled the international success of particular films and directors in the first place, while also reframing attention to the global significance of several key filmmakers whose work has been neglected.

## The New German Cinema and Feminist Film History

Among the twenty-six young filmmakers who signed the Oberhausen Manifesto in 1962, there were no women; as Claudia Lenssen observes, "At the time, the right to artistic self-realization in film had obvious masculine connotations, and the cultural power to control its interpretation was solidly anchored in patriarchal rituals" (2012, 239). Nonetheless, one of the signal trajectories that eventually came out of the concerted attempt to break with "Daddy's cinema" and create a new foundation for filmmaking was the development of a critical women's cinema and feminist film culture in West Germany, whose flourishing was without parallel in global cinema of the era. As Julia Knight notes, "The decisive breakthrough came in 1977" (1992, 11), when at least five prominent women directors debuted their first feature films, several of which won major prizes; by the 1980s, in Elsaesser's estimation, the Federal Republic possessed "proportionally more women filmmakers than any other film-producing country" (1989,

185).[2] While initially overlooked within scholarship, women directors and feminist film came to comprise a concerted focus of critical approaches to German film in general and a key sphere for considering the genre of NGC specifically, both at home and abroad.[3]

Likewise, attention to international developments in feminist cinema formed a crucial horizon for the self-understanding of German feminist filmmakers. In 1973, Alemann and Sander convened the First International Women's Film Seminar in West Berlin, where they screened forty-five women-directed films (mostly documentaries) from seven countries organized in four thematic sections: women, work, and collective action; women and media representation; abortion rights, sexuality, and women's roles; and the women's movement in Europe and the United States. The participants, including fifteen invited directors from abroad, engaged in critical discussion of both the films on view and their own experiences with filmmaking; the result was a mutual decision among the West German filmmakers "to exchange information about their projects and production options more than had been the case before, and to better coordinate the distribution and political work of their films" (Alemann and Sander, quoted in Möhrmann 1980, 31). While this event was thus crucial for the collective organization of women filmmakers—a collectivity that proved to be a necessary precursor for the broader recognition of their work—as Renate Möhrmann notes, "The filmmakers were motivated less by aesthetic interest than by social engagement" (27). That is, insofar as the organized women's movement provided a political framework for the emergence of feminist film culture in West Germany, it fostered the orientation of feminist cinema (both narrative and documentary) toward social issues. In the course of the 1970s, film—even more than literature or journalism—quickly became the most important venue for exploring and representing women's oppression and for envisioning and expressing an alternative feminist consciousness.

In 1974, Sander founded *frauen und film*, the first feminist film journal in Europe, which further contributed to this work by pursuing the double mandate of "investigating the way patriarchal culture operates in the medium of film" and "recognizing and defining an emergent feminist culture and taking up and further developing the questions it poses" (*frauen und film* 1975, 3). If critical attention to feminist film was largely shaped by the context of the second-wave women's movement—visible in the tendency to privilege politics over aesthetics and to overlook the work of certain filmmakers—then *frauen und film* consistently sought to complicate the picture. In 1977, the journal published special sections devoted to four established women filmmakers who "do not come from the women's movement and take an ambivalent or distanced attitude toward it": Stöckl, Sanders-Brahms, Erika Runge, and Dore O. (*frauen und film* 1977, 2). This ostensibly distanced attitude can be attributed to the fact that all four women had begun their filmmaking careers before the consolidation of the organized women's movement (typically dated to Sander's speech on behalf of the Action Council for Women's Liberation at a September 1968 meeting of the Socialist German Student Organization [SDS]); they subsequently felt misrecognized by the movement and/or their work diverged from the feminist film project's emphasis on social engagement. As Stöckl explained in an interview included in the special section devoted to her in *frauen und film*, "I was always interested in women's themes, as the films themselves document, and the specific ways in which one ultimately becomes identified with a movement can be manifold" (Hiller, Lenssen, and Strempel, 1977, 8).[4] Even so, the journal's concerted engagement with the work of women filmmakers from outside the women's movement demonstrates the extent to which, already in the 1970s, a particular conception of feminist cinema predominated that tended to obscure other roots and "branching sidelines."

This conception derived not least from the centrality of Sander, who united in one charismatic persona the face of both the women's movement and the feminist film project and who was crucially responsible for the prominent role that film played in shaping a feminist counterpublic in West Germany. Sander enrolled in the dffb in 1966, the year it opened. Although she came from an international background—she began her career as a theater director in Finland, where she also worked in television—upon her return to Germany, her work increasingly focused on domestic issues. Driven by her own untenable position as a single mother and a filmmaker, Sander embraced political activism by spearheading the movement to establish *Kinderläden*, cooperative childcare centers that would help alleviate the double burden women faced. The *Kinderläden* movement in turn led to the founding of the Action Council, which later developed into the broad-based women's movement.

Madeleine Bernstorff (n.d.) has pointed out the dffb's initial difficulties in recruiting women, especially in comparison to Ulm; Sander was among only three women in the first class of thirty-five admitted students. However, the emphasis on political filmmaking at the dffb, as well as its proximity to the key events of 1968—which significantly informed many of the student films produced there over the following decade—fueled its importance for feminist developments. As Christina Gerhardt notes, "The early dffb's filmmaking documented the political actions [of the SDS and of student protests] and also sought to put forward a counter-message, thereby supporting the social movements politically and acting, de facto, as their mass media arm" (2019, 69). Sander's early documentary films produced at the dffb were no exception, addressing topics closely connected to her own political activism. Her most well-known film of the period, *Brecht die Macht der Manipulateure* (*Break the Power of the Manipulators*, 1968), which was shot together with Ulrich Knaudt, Skip Norman, and Harun Farocki, presents a detailed critique of the manipulative practices of the mainstream news media, especially the Springer Press. Sander's other films made at the dffb show a consistent preoccupation with the problems of childcare and early childhood education, women's double burden as workers and parents, and their subjective experiences of sexism; they also experiment with formal techniques for conveying these themes. These early films indubitably demonstrate, as Gerhardt asserts, that "West Germany's feminism, be it politically or cinematically regarded, did not start in the late seventies, but in the late sixties" (2019, 83).

Following her graduation, Sander continued to make documentaries on topics crucial to second-wave feminism, including women and work and birth control, before debuting her first feature, *Die allseitig reduzierte Persönlichkeit—Redupers* (*The All Around Reduced Personality*, 1977), which went on to become the most well-known German feminist film. With its autofictional portrayal of freelance photographer and single mother Edda Chiemnyjewski (played by Sander), *Redupers* makes visible the political dimensions of private life. At the same time, the film's meta-critical narrative about a women's photography project documenting contemporary Berlin employs the city's geopolitical partition, symbolized by the Wall, as a potent metaphor for the divisions that shape social life and for the concomitant naturalization of (women's) oppression. As Kaja Silverman has described it, "*Redupers* makes the wall a signifier for psychic as well as ideological, political, and geographical boundaries. It functions there as a metaphor for sexual difference, for the subjective limits articulated by the existing symbolic order both in East and West. The wall thus designates the discursive boundaries which separate residents not only of the same country and language, but of the same partitioned space" (1983, 10). By engaging divided Berlin as a figure for social divisions and sexual difference—indeed, as a metaphor for the limits of the symbolic order—*Redupers* distilled a critical connection between the "special status" of postwar German identity and ideology itself, a connection that came to predominate in both feminist films and the NGC more broadly.

## The Ulm School and Feminist Film

The central significance of Sander and her films to the development and visibility of West German feminism has shaped an abiding focus among scholars and critics on the convergence of feminist cinema and national-cultural representation. Yet a closer look at the Ulm School reveals another trajectory of West German feminist filmmaking, one that intersects with its more successful counterpart while also exhibiting more concerted engagement with global contexts. Given the provincial location of Ulm, a small southwestern town far from the metropoles, this engagement may seem surprising. However, the status of the HfG as the successor to the Bauhaus, with its substantial legacy as a harbinger of international style, attracted students and faculty from all over the world and fostered a cosmopolitan atmosphere; the school's conscious embrace of this legacy provides one explanation for the fact that women studied there in relatively high numbers. As Alemann, who enrolled at Ulm in 1964, recalls, "The ratio of women [*Frauenquote*] was impressively high at the time. Six of twenty students in the Department of Film Design were women: Ula Stöckl, Marion Zemann, Jeanine Meerapfel, Recha Jungmann, Ursula Wenzel, and me" (2014, 34).[5]

The HfG Ulm was founded in 1953 by Inge Scholl, Otl Aicher, and Max Bill. Scholl, the older sister of Hans and Sophie Scholl, who were murdered by the Nazis for their role in the White Rose student resistance movement against the Third Reich, established the Scholl Siblings Foundation in 1950 with the express intention of providing funding for an independent school of design. Scholl's husband Aicher, a graphic designer, taught at the school, which was directed by Bill, an architect and designer who had studied at the Dessau Bauhaus. Ad hoc film courses were offered at the HfG beginning in the late 1950s. Following the Oberhausen Manifesto, which demanded "the creation of an intellectual center for film, in which new generations can be trained and in which theoretical work and developmental work have their place," a formal course of film studies was established with the founding of the Abteilung für Filmgestaltung in 1962. Under the direction of Oberhausen signatories Kluge, Reitz, and Detten Schleiermacher, the school offered training grounded on the principle of combining education in film theory, research, and praxis.

The writings of the Frankfurt School provided a significant theoretical anchoring for film education at the HfG, which sought to develop a conception of cinema in opposition to the culture industry. Daniela Sannwald describes this conception in her comprehensive history of the Ulm Film School: "Like literature and science, film should constitute a form of knowledge and imagination that orients itself to reality as a whole" (1997, 96). As Kluge put it in "Die Utopie Film," in which he outlined his pedagogical principles, film's potential to intervene in reality, together with its mass basis, entails a special responsibility on the part of the filmmaker; for this reason, "film education cannot be technical training alone" but must include the cultivation of a conscience "in intellectual, artistic, economic, and political regards" (1964, 1140). In a companion piece to Kluge's titled "Utopie Kino," also written in the 1960s, Reitz likewise describes the conception of cinema that informed his teaching in Ulm: he conceives of a new "analytical film" that is not bound by a formal style but rather aims to dismantle conventional categories and methods of filmmaking, adopting a range of techniques to facilitate its analysis of reality. As Reitz explains, "According to Adorno, until now most films are nothing more than 'propaganda for the world as it exists', a world that is not subject to transformation. [The analytical film] deconstructs the existing world into its various elements; once these have been liberated from the constraining circumstances and stereotypes associated with them, the imagination can begin to engage with them again" (1983, 18). Accordingly, hands-on education at the HfG cultivated competency in the use of cameras, lighting, editing, and producing, and students were encouraged to develop their own aesthetic approaches to unmasking reality through film.

The emphasis on developing formal-aesthetic techniques to deconstruct and imaginatively intervene into reality, the focus on fostering an authorial vision linked to one's intellectual and political conscience, and the cultivation of a DIY approach to filmmaking all proved to be particularly influential for the women filmmakers training at Ulm (and, ultimately, for the NGC as a whole). These principles importantly encouraged students to incorporate and interrogate their own subjectivity in their filmmaking; as Sannwald points out, even Stöckl's earliest student films make visible "a maxim of the later so-called *Frauenfilm* . . . : to always make one's own reality an integral part of any cinematic statement" (1997, 137).

Experimentation with this approach was significantly facilitated by one of the key pedagogical innovations of film education at Ulm: the production of so-called miniatures. Very short films that presented coherent dramaturgical units, miniatures explored everyday life and social reality, often in ways that linked the personal and the political. Stöckl's *Musiker Weber* (*The Musician Weber*, 1963), for example, draws on the life of her father to examine the role of the Nazi past in the present. A musician in the Ulm City Orchestra and a follower of the Nazi cause who served at the front beginning in 1941, Stöckl's father survived the war but struggled to find gainful employment again after receiving a two-year *Berufsverbot* (employment ban) as part of denazification proceedings. On a formal level, *Musiker Weber* engages with the question of how film represents interiority, and the relation between objective reality and subjective perception, by unspooling the same images twice, accompanied first by an impersonal voice-over narrating events in the life of the musician and then again by a first-person narration of the same events.

The creation of miniatures presented a solution to the budgetary constraints of independent filmmaking, while also demanding of students close attention to the economy of form; eventually, miniatures could also be stitched together into longer works. As Stöckl later explained, "Thinking in miniatures enables you, even if you don't have money for a full feature film—which might consist of twenty-five or thirty miniatures—just to begin and to build onto that beginning later. For me, miniatures represent the principle of hope" (quoted in Sannwald 1997, 103). The form of the miniature is visible not only in many of the documentary shorts produced at Ulm but also, notably, in the patchwork style that underpins the later features of Ulm-trained directors.

Enabling the integration of analytical units, in Reitz's sense, into a narrative plot development while also foregrounding the process of artistic

FIGURE 8.1. *The Musician Weber*—The musician Weber on his bicycle. (Screengrab)

production, the miniature principle became a creative affordance for women directors. As Sannwald remarks of Stöckl's graduation film *Neun Leben hat die Katze* (*The Cat Has Nine Lives*, 1968), which exploited the concept of the miniature to make an aesthetic virtue of the low-budget context in which it was produced, "jumping between situations—the eschewal of linearity—corresponds to the life paths of the main protagonists," two women navigating the process of self-realization in tension with patriarchal institutions and norms (1997, 184). Indeed, the radical vision of *The Cat Has Nine Lives*, now regarded as the first West German feminist film, derives not least from the way Stöckl intertwines a political critique of normative temporalities with the aesthetic eschewal of continuity and linear narrative.

Although strictly speaking the miniature was abandoned as a pedagogical tool in 1964 in favor of the short film, the first student films of Alemann and Meerapfel nonetheless reflect an engagement with the miniature principle in their formal and thematic construction. Alemann's *Einfach* (*Simple*, 1965) is a five-minute experimental documentary that zooms in on the difficulties of performing ostensibly simple everyday activities (opening a can, threading a needle); the film disrupts the alignment of femininity and domesticity even as it reflects on issues of accessibility and design that were widely discussed at the HfG.[6] Meerapfel's *Abstand* (*Distance*, 1966) interrogates the relationship between the filmmaker and her boyfriend, fellow Ulm student Hartmut Kirste, calling into question the authenticity of their romantic feelings (and conventions of heterosexual coupledom more broadly) while also using voice-over in self-reflexive ways to unmask the role of women's authorship in the film's construction.

Recalling the influence of Ulm's pedagogy on her filmmaking, Meerapfel explains: "Kluge always said, one should narrate things one knows. He also always tried to get me interested in doing something about Latin America. And I think I ended up telling stories about women because I know a lot more about them than I do about the fate of men, because women shaped me and because I am a woman" (quoted in Sannwald 1997, 194). Not only did the Ulm model promote a style of filmmaking that drew overt connections between subjectivity and reality, urging women to draw on their experience well before the feminist motto "The personal is political" became widespread, but, as Meerapfel indicates, Kluge (and Reitz) also encouraged specific attention to global contexts. This attention took different forms, including an embrace of multilingualism, the casting of non-German actors, attention to the intersections of local, national, and global paradigms, and reflection on international and intercultural autobiographical experiences. Often the transnational dimensions of films by Ulm-trained women directors offered specific vectors for engagement with global feminisms.

## Feminist Filmmakers of the Ulm School and Their Global Contexts

Among the women filmmakers who trained at Ulm, Alemann, Meerapfel, and Stöckl stand out for their significant contributions to feminist film history. All three filmmakers have devoted themselves to activism on behalf of women filmmakers: Alemann catalyzed the women's film movement together with Sander, and both Meerapfel and Stöckl were founding members of the Association of Women Film Workers. All three have also been involved in the resurgent twenty-first-century campaign for gender equity and diversity in the German film industry spearheaded by the feminist group Pro Quote Film (PQF), which Meerapfel has supported as president of the Akademie der Künste in Berlin (2015–24). Alemann, Meerapfel, and Stöckl have further contributed to educating the next generation of filmmakers through their professorships at universities and film academies.

However, it is through their films that all three have left their most significant imprint on the history of feminist cinema. Alemann is the director of numerous documentaries on a broad range of internationally oriented topics. As Bernstorff has noted, "Very few (women) filmmakers in West Germany pursued their interest in international political issues through such an engagement as von Alemann did" (2019, 92). In May 1968, Alemann visited Paris, where she shot the film *Das ist nur der Anfang—der Kampf geht weiter* (*This Is Only the Beginning—the Struggle Continues*, 1969), a commission for the West German public broadcaster WDR that both documents the student-led revolution and examines the role of film "as a weapon of political struggle" (Alemann 2014, 35). Her subsequent documentaries focus on the intersections of feminism and anti-imperialism, including *Kathleen und Eldridge Cleaver in Algerien* (*Kathleen and Eldridge Cleaver in Algeria*, 1970), *Germaine Greer* (1970), *Anti-imperialistische Frauenkonferenz in Toronto* (*Anti-Imperialist Women's Conference in Toronto*, 1971), *Aus eigener Kraft—Frauen in Vietnam* (*Through Their Own Efforts—Women in Vietnam*, 1971), and *Filme der Sonne und der Nacht—Ariane Mnouchkine* (*Films of the Sun and the Night*, 1977). Alemann also worked on collaborative films about the women's movement and the wages for housework campaign—*Das schwache Geschlecht muss stärker werden* (*The Weak Sex Must Become Stronger*, 1970)—and about Namibia (*Namibia*, 1973). Her long-form documentary *Es kommt darauf an, sie zu verändern* (*The Point Is to Change It*, 1973) focuses on the oppressive conditions faced by women workers in the West German metal industry.

Although her political activism drove Alemann's prolific period of documentary filmmaking in the 1970s, her earliest films eschewed generic boundaries—in line with Ulm's emphasis on the production of analytical films—blurring narrative and nonnarrative forms. The experimental film *Fundvogel* (*Foundling-Bird*, 1968), for instance, employs the voice-over narration of a Grimms' fairy tale as the structuring device for a dreamlike exploration of childhood war trauma. Exhibiting a collage-like approach and a formal emphasis on the relation of sound and image, *Fundvogel* constitutes an aesthetic precursor to Alemann's feature *Die Reise nach Lyon* (*Blind Spot*, 1980), among the most aesthetically important works to emerge from the feminist film project.

*Blind Spot* was originally conceived of as a costume drama about the nineteenth-century French-Peruvian socialist feminist Flora Tristan. When Alemann was unable to raise the large budget that film required, she reimagined the project as a contemporary narrative that follows the historian Elisabeth (played by the American actress and daughter of a German Jewish refugee Rebecca Pauly), who travels to Lyon in search of Tristan's traces. Elisabeth's quest to connect to the utopian promise embodied by Tristan—who wrote about the oppression of the working classes before Marx and also theorized women's subjection in patriarchy—leads her to archives, bookstores, and historical sites such as the locus of the silk weavers' revolt where she roots out facts about Tristan's life in Lyon. However, this quest also takes the form of a search for affective proximity to Tristan, with whom Elisabeth closely identifies, through the use of assistive technologies, especially a tape recorder, to capture the ambient sounds and atmospheric residue of the city that Tristan once inhabited. Anticipating the style of today's Berlin School of filmmaking, *Blind Spot* consists largely of static long takes of Lyon that depict the city's emptiness in August punctuated by a spare use of sound, dominated by Elisabeth's voice-over, intermingling German narration with French dialogue. Even as the film imagines (French) history as a locus of feminist "identity construction for women who must embark on the long path into the historic future" (Hoff 1981, 13), it also offers a paradigmatic narrative about working through the objective and subjective layers of an unresolved past that resonates with the NGC's focus on *Vergangenheitsbewältigung* (working through of the past) in the German context.

Meerapfel is known especially for her development of a woman-centered "autoethnographic aesthetic" (Linville 1998, 111) across multiple features and documentaries, and her films likewise investigate the intersections of public and personal histories with an emphasis on the legacies of fascism in the postwar period. Born in Buenos Aires to a French Catholic mother and a German Jewish father, Meerapfel studied journalism and worked as a freelance reporter in Argentina before enrolling at Ulm. Her 1968 documentary *Regionalzeitung* (*Regional Newspaper*), completed

FIGURE 8.2. *Blind Spot*—Elisabeth with tape recorder in Lyon. (Screengrab)

at the HfG, critically examines the production process of the Ulm-based *Schwäbische Donau-Zeitung*, probing the politicized decision-making that informs editorial and reporting choices of this daily newspaper with an emphasis on the intersections of international, national, and local issues. In 1969, together with several Ulm classmates, Meerapfel co-founded the filmmaking collective Epplewoi Motion Pictures, whose experimental films—which remained unfinished at the time but were completed years later—included *Zwickel auf Bizyckel* and *Am Ama Am Amazonas*. Following the dissolution of the collective, Meerapfel worked as a journalist while developing her first feature, *Malou* (1981), a formally inventive autofiction portraying the quest of a young Jewish woman living in West Berlin to comprehend the life and legacy of her mother, played by Ingrid Caven, whose name (Malou) the film bears.

Throughout the 1980s and 1990s, Meerapfel's work, which often included international co-productions, embraced both fictional and non-fictional modes to explore the lives of Jews living in divided Berlin (*Im Land meiner Eltern* [*In the Country of My Parents*, 1981]); the everyday

FIGURE 8.3. *Malou*—Ingrid Caven. (Screengrab)

racism experienced by Turkish migrants to West Germany (*Die Kümmeltürkin geht* [*Melek Leaves*, 1985]); and the psychological consequences of the Argentine military dictatorship (*Desembarcos—Es gibt kein Vergessen* [*When Memory Speaks*, 1989]). Meerapfel's narrative features often employ intercultural love stories to engage with questions of identity, memory, and history, as in *Die Verliebten* (*The Lovers*, 1987), *Annas Sommer* (*Anna's Summer*, 2001), and *Der deutsche Freund* (*The German Friend*, 2012).

*Malou* likewise depicts the vexed relationship between the Jewish protagonist Hannah (Grischa Huber), who grew up in Argentina, and her German husband Martin (Helmut Griem). As Hannah tells Martin in a letter, "I talk in your language, with your friends, in your country. Do you understand, Martin? I have everything, but I'm confused. . . . My mother gave up her language, her religion, her heritage, everything, for a man. I don't want that to happen to me. I'm afraid, and I'm looking for . . . her and for myself." This search begins with an inventory of objects that index Malou's past and trigger a series of imaginative flashbacks and actual journeys to the stations of Malou's life: Strasbourg, where she was born and met Hannah's father Paul while performing in a nightclub; Sulzweier, in southwestern Germany, where she lived with Paul's wealthy, assimilated family after their marriage; Amsterdam, where they flee after the Nazis take over and where Hannah is born; and Buenos Aires, where they finally settle and where Malou, turning to alcohol after Paul leaves her, eventually dies in penury. These excursions are juxtaposed with scenes from the present day, in which Hannah engages dialogically with her mother's inheritance as she seeks to determine her own identity, sense of self, and place in the world. Described by Linville as a form of "multicultural heteroglossia," the collage aesthetic of *Malou* engages with diverse genres, languages, and locations: "The multiple cultural and geographic spaces inhabited by women in *Malou* give rise to a sense of displacement that is considerably less metaphoric than that evinced" in NGC films by Wim Wenders, Werner Herzog, and others (1998, 127).

Following her groundbreaking debut with *The Cat Has Nine Lives*, Stöckl went on to become one of the most prolific directors of feminist feature films in the Federal Republic, premiering more than ten between 1968 and 1992. While her films span a range of genres and forms, they are united by the attempt to imagine alternatives to heteropatriarchy and to offer "radical other models of relationships, sexuality, and identity," prompting recent critics to find queer traces in Stöckl's oeuvre (Ashraf, 2019, 98). Her experimental film *Die Geschichten vom Kübelkind* (*Tales of the Dumpster Kid*, 1971), a collaboration with Reitz, is a case in point: it comprises a series of twenty-five shorts—they could be exhibited in any order, according to audience preference—about a child who is born from a placenta discarded in a hospital garbage can; emerging full-grown and without knowledge of gender roles, the dumpster kid embarks on adventures, many of them sexual, that satirically call attention to social norms.

Before she became the country's first woman film student, Stöckl had escaped the restrictive atmosphere of West Germany in the 1950s, working in Paris and London, first as an au pair and later as a secretary. In France, she experienced firsthand the political turmoil surrounding the Algerian War of Independence and began to reckon with the Nazi past; in the home of her employers in England, she saw images of Auschwitz for the first time. These experiences not only motivated Stöckl's turn to filmmaking but also infused many of her films, which, although less overtly attentive to global politics than Alemann's and Meerapfel's, nonetheless similarly evidence multilingualism and engage with transnational contexts. Stöckl regularly cast non-German actors in her films, including the French-born Kristine de Loup, who stars in both *The Cat Has Nine Lives*, a film that includes extensive dialogue in both German and French, and *Tales of the Dumpster Kid*. Stöckl's interest in troubling nationalism is perhaps most evident in *Das alte Lied* (*The Old Song*, 1992), the first feature by a Western director shot in the post-Wall GDR and a co-production with DEFA, which offers a prescient take on property disputes and memory contests in the context of both the *Wende* and the Nazi past.

While shooting Werner Schroeter's *Palermo oder Wolfsburg* (*Palermo or Wolfsburg*, 1980), a film in which she acted, Stöckl met and befriended the Italian actress Ida Di Benedetto, whom she later cast as the lead in *Der Schlaf der Vernunft* (*Sleep of Reason*, 1984), which reimagines the Medea story in contemporary West Berlin. Di Benedetto, who spoke no German, learned the substantial dialogue for the film phonetically. Her character, Dr. Dea Janssen, is a gynecologist conducting research on the harmful biological effects of birth control pills manufactured by a pharmaceutical conglomerate run by the nefarious Erdmann, who profits from controlling women's bodies. Dea's husband Reinhard works for Erdmann; he has also moved in with Erdmann's daughter Johanna, his lover, who also happens to be Dea's medical partner. Dea's mother, who speaks only Italian, lives with her, as do Dea's teenage daughters. While her mother supports Dea by cooking and cleaning for the family, Dea's daughters rebel against her by watching TV all day; one of them also takes birth control pills and even appears in an advertisement for the pill in defiance of her mother. Stöckl's poetic language, featuring black-and-white cinematography, abrupt cuts, and disjunction between sound and image, deftly blurs the lines between dreams and reality to give formal expression to Dea's struggle to assert herself in the face of these vexed relationships: "By purging her rage in her dreams, by taking vengeance to the fullest measure," Dea is able to separate herself—like her namesake Medea—from the marital, familial, and professional bonds that oppress her (Johnson 1993, 101). As an immigrant and a woman, Dea refuses to adapt to the expectations of mainstream German society, and her rich imaginative life offers an avenue for self-determination outside of heteropatriarchal and dominant cultural norms.

Driven by their training in Ulm and their diverse commitments to feminist, anti-authoritarian, and leftist politics, Alemann, Meerapfel, and Stöckl stand out for the way they embrace both narrative and documentary filmmaking, often scrambling the conventions of fiction and nonfiction film and combining elements of both in their works; all three filmmakers have also worked collaboratively, coauthoring films with other directors and in collectives. Certainly the sui generis quality of their films, together with their collaborative efforts, have contributed to the fact that they have received less recognition as auteurs than their more internationally visible counterparts. If Alemann, Meerapfel, and Stöckl defy received notions of authorship pinned to NGC, their films (especially their features) also often flout the ostensible issue-orientation of women's filmmaking. Instead, their films exhibit what Alison Butler has called "a feminist politics of location [by situating women's] identity in dynamic historical situations, to reveal the imbrication of technologies of gender with those of local, national and international power" (2002, 91). The elaboration of this politics of location aligns with the NGC's critical engagement with Germanness, but the filmmakers' embrace of global contexts beyond the dominant paradigm of national-cultural representation paradoxically contributed to their limited reception beyond the borders of West Germany in the 1970s and 1980s. As Patricia White points out, "Dominant conceptualizations of cinema organized around national movements, waves, and auteurs often minimize or misrecognize the significance of women filmmakers' participation and the questions of representation—both aesthetic and political—that it raises" (2015, 7). Renewed attention to the transnational feminist vision articulated by Alemann, Meerapfel, and Stöckl not only is long overdue but also compels a broader reconsideration of the generic contours of the NGC.

## Notes

All translations from the German are my own. This chapter builds on research first published in my book on Ula Stöckl's *Neun Leben hat die Katze* (*The Cat Has Nine Lives*, 1968) and borrows some material and formulations used there. See Baer 2022.

1 In *New German Cinema*, Elsaesser explores a critical tendency to distinguish between "author-oriented films (where the emphasis is on self-expression, or the implied audience is the international, art house spectator) and issue-oriented films (dealing with social problems or

controversial issues aimed at home audiences)" (1989, 52); because West German television, "with its voracious appetite for issues," constituted the main source of funding for women filmmakers, their films tended to fall into the latter category. See also Elsaesser, "Touching Base: Some German Women Directors in the 1980s" (2005, 219–30).

2 Feature films by Heidi Genée, Ulrike Ottinger, Sander, Sanders-Brahms, and von Trotta debuted in 1977. Notably, the films that won prizes both focused on German history filtered through the lens of male literary authors: Genée's *Grete Minde*, an adaptation of the novella by Theodor Fontane, and Sanders-Brahms's *Heinrich*, based on the life of Heinrich von Kleist.

3 Key publications that drew attention to feminist film as a major component of NGC include Renate Möhrmann's *Die Frau mit der Kamera* (1980); Elsaesser's *New German Cinema* (1989); Renate Fischetti's *Das Neue Kino* (1992); Julia Knight's *Women and the New German Cinema* (1992); and Sandra Frieden et al., eds., *Gender and German Cinema: Feminist Interventions*, vol. 1: *Gender and Representation in New German Cinema* (1993). Also significant was the attention of journals including *frauen und film*, *New German Critique*, *Jump Cut*, and *Camera Obscura*, as well as the emphasis on German cinema within Anglophone feminist film theory. See, for example, E. Ann Kaplan, *Women and Film: Both Sides of the Camera* (1983); Teresa de Lauretis, *Technologies of Gender* (1987); and Judith Mayne, *The Woman at the Keyhole* (1990).

4 The founding of the Verband der Filmarbeiterinnen (Association of Women Film Workers) in 1979 in many ways resolved the divisions among women directors from "inside" or "outside" the women's movement that had characterized the early years of the feminist film project, since it aimed to bring together all women involved in filmmaking to demand better conditions. Stöckl and Sanders-Brahms were both involved in the campaign, which was organized by Hildegard Westbeld, Christiane Kaltenbach, and Petra Haffter. More than eighty women film workers signed the association's manifesto, which demanded equity in film funding, jobs and training spots, and committee assignments, as well as support for the distribution and exhibition of women's films. See "The Manifesto of Women Film Workers (1979)" (1988).

5 Among the thirty-one students who studied film at Ulm between 1959 and 1968, ten were women. See Schubert and Maus (2012, 207).

6 Alemann took up this premise again in her award-winning 1981 film *Das Frauenzimmer* (*The Women's Room*), a satirical take on housework.

## Works Cited

Alemann, Claudia von. 2014. "Wir wollten alles und das sofort." In *Wie haben Sie das gemacht? Aufzeichnungen von Frauen und Filmen*, edited by Claudia Lenssen and Bettina Schoeller-Boujou, 32–37. Marburg: Schüren.

Ashraf, Toby. 2019. "Verunsicherungen: Keine Ehe, keine Wahrheit, kein Junge—Queere Spuren im Werk von Ula Stöckl." In *Ula Stöckl*, edited by Claudia Lenssen, 87–99. Munich: edition text + kritik.

Baer, Hester. 2022. *The Cat Has Nine Lives*. German Film Classics. Rochester, NY: Camden House.

Bernstorff, Madeleine. 2019. "Film Feminisms in West German Cinema: A Public Sphere for Feminist Politics." In *Celluloid Revolt: German Screen Cultures and the Long 1968*, edited by Christina Gerhardt and Marco Abel, 87–104. Rochester, NY: Camden House.

———. N.d. "Feminismen an der dffb 1966–1985." https://dffb-archiv.de/editorial/feminismen-dffb-1966-85. Accessed July 25, 2023.

Butler, Alison. 2002. *Women's Cinema: The Contested Screen*. London: Wallflower.

Casper, Kent, and Susan E. Linville. 1985. "Nazi Reframes: Negative Stereotyping in American Reviews of New German Films," *Literature/Film Quarterly* 13.4: 250–57.

Davidson, John. 1999. *De-Territorializing the New German Cinema*. Minneapolis: University of Minnesota Press.

de Lauretis, Teresa. 1987. *Technologies of Gender: Essays on Theory, Film, and Fiction*. Bloomington: Indiana University Press.

Elsaesser, Thomas. 1989. *New German Cinema: A History*. New Brunswick, NJ: Rutgers University Press.

———. 2005. *European Cinema: Face to Face with Hollywood*. Amsterdam: Amsterdam University Press.

Fischetti, Renate. 1992. *Das Neue Kino: Acht Porträts von deutschen Regisseurinnen*. Frankfurt: tende.

*frauen und film*. 1975. "Das Programm für *frauen und film*." 6: 3–15.

———. 1977. "Vorwort." 12: 2.

Frieden, Sandra, et al., eds. 1993. *Gender and German Cinema: Feminist Interventions*. Vol. 1: *Gender and Representation in New German Cinema*. Providence: Berg.

Gerhardt, Christina. 2019. "Helke Sander's dffb Films and West Germany's Feminist Movement." In *Celluloid Revolt: German Screen Cultures and the Long 1968*, edited by Christina Gerhardt and Marco Abel, 69–86. Rochester, NY: Camden House.

Hiller, Eva, Claudia Lenssen, and Gesine Strempel. 1977. "Gespräch mit Ula Stöckl." *frauen und film* 12: 3–11.

Hoff, Claudia. 1981. "Auf der Suche nach der verlorenen Flora Tristan: Die 'Reise nach Lyon' von Claudia von Alemann." *frauen und film* 27: 13–18.

Johnson, Sheila. 1993. "Modern Medea (*Reason Asleep*)." In *Gender and German Cinema: Feminist Interventions*, vol. 1: *Gender and Representation in New German Cinema*, edited by Sandra Frieden et al., 93–110. Providence: Berg.

Kaplan, E. Ann. 1983. *Women and Film: Both Sides of the Camera*. New York: Methuen.

Kluge, Alexander. 1964. "Die Utopie Film." *Merkur* 18: 1135–46.

———. 1980. "Ein Hauptansatz des Ulmer Instituts." In *Ulmer Dramaturgien: Reibungsverluste*, edited by Klaus Eder and Alexander Kluge, 5–7. Munich: Carl Hanser.

Knight, Julia. 1992. *Women and the New German Cinema*. London: Verso.

Lenssen, Claudia. 2012. "Gruppenbild ohne Dame: Wo waren Frauen am 28.2.1962." In *Provokation der Wirklichkeit: Das Oberhausener Manifest und die Folgen*, edited by Ralph Eue and Lars Henrik Gass, 239–45. Munich: edition text + kritik.

Linville, Susan E. 1998. *Feminism, Film, Fascism: Women's Auto/Biographical Film in Postwar Germany*. Austin: University of Texas Press.

"The Manifesto of Women Film Workers (1979)." 1988. In *West German Filmmakers on Film: Visions and Voices*, edited by Eric Rentschler, 5–6. New York: Holmes & Meier.

Mayne, Judith. 1990. *The Woman at the Keyhole*. Bloomington: Indiana University Press.

Möhrmann, Renate. 1980. *Die Frau mit der Kamera: Filmemacherinnen in der Bundesrepublik Deutschland*. Munich: Carl Hanser.

Reitz, Edgar. 1983. "Utopie Kino (1963–65)." In *Liebe zu Kino: Utopien und Gedanken zum Autorenfilm 1962–1983*, 12–31. Cologne: Verlag Köln.

Sannwald, Daniela. 1997. *Von der Filmkrise zum Neuen Deutschen Film: Filmausbildung an der Hochschule für Gestaltung Ulm, 1958–1968*. Berlin: Wissenschaftsverlag Volker Spiess.

Schubert, Peter, and Monika Maus, eds. 2012. *Rückblicke: Die Abteilung Film—Institut für Filmgestaltung an der hfg Ulm 1960–1968*. Ulm: Club Off.

Silverman, Kaja. 1983. "Helke Sander and the Will to Change." *Discourse* 6: 10–30.

White, Patricia. 2015. *Women's Cinema, World Cinema: Projecting Contemporary Feminisms*. Durham: Duke University Press.

# 9

# ON DEBILITY IN HELMA SANDERS-BRAHMS'S *DIE BERÜHRTE*

*Ervin Malakaj*

Helma Sanders-Brahms's *Die Berührte* (*No Mercy, No Future*, 1981) was inspired by a letter the director received from a stranger. Rita G., the letter's named author, recounted details about her sexual relations with over eighty men. Reflecting on the letter's contents, Sanders-Brahms foregrounds Rita's social context: "What was scandalous for those around this young woman (parents, psychiatrist, etc.) was the fact that [her sexual partners] were members of the lowest social class: vagrants, guest workers, Black, and disabled men" (Sanders-Brahms and Rita G. 1981, 173).[1] Rita's written account indeed conveys the details of her parents' extremely negative response to her sexual life: her mother is repulsed by it and even temporarily leaves town, while Rita's disapproving father convinces his daughter to check into a mental health clinic. Regarding her institutionalization, Rita notes, "When I walked out of the specialist's office, my father was gone, and I was soon admitted to a closed ward" (178). Rita's account is thus about the symbiotic relationship between institutionalization and the scandal-averse context she traverses. The letter relays in gruesome detail the strategic maiming of Rita's body in order to suppress her sexual urges and unsanctioned relations in service of maintaining the status quo. "I was dragged up the stairs and into bed and forcibly given pills and injected with drugs. . . . At the mercy of the woman doctor and the staff, I was robbed of all human dignity" (178).

The adaptation of this material in *No Mercy, No Future* stages a grotesque commentary on the effects of self-actualization in a violent system of power. At the tail end of the 1960s and '70s women's rights movement, Sanders-Brahms's aesthetic repertoire in the film does not present affirmative futures for women's liberation through agency. Instead, it offers strategic debility as widespread, tightly orchestrated, and institutionalized technology devised to suppress a self-actualization that the broader system of power in the film views as pathological. In this chapter, I will outline what is at stake in this aesthetic outlook for women's liberation by situating the film in a broader context of feminist filmmaking in Central Europe. My aim is to outline how the film both draws on and irritates received feminist film discourse and aesthetic practices. While the plot of *No Mercy, No Future* studies women's daily routines under heterocapitalist patriarchy in the spirit of similar investments that mark feminist filmmaking of its period (and Sanders-Brahms's own earlier films), it does not celebrate agential prowess in this process (see Malakaj 2019). Instead, the film paints agential regimens as toxic alternatives to women's self-actualization in a system that continually refines processes of debilitation to control unruly bodies. The film's concern with strategic debilitation is in fact less inspired by a politics through which it aims to imagine how to overcome systemic violence than it is committed to show strategic debilitation as an insurmountable feature of power.

Consequently, as I will show below, *No Mercy, No Future* offers an equally somber and troubling outlook on the impossibility of union and collective struggles against the forces of debilitating power. While the persistent attempts of the title character Veronika (Elisabeth Stepanek) to secure affirmative relationships reveal the struggles of other people broken by the system—for example, the senescent, disabled, and working-class men of color—in the film such encounters culminate in depictions of lustful intimacy that objectify Veronika as the ultimate conquest for these men. This representational strategy casts the male characters of color as particularly virile. Here, I will examine in detail Veronika's relationship with Demba (Jorge Reis)—a Ghanaian man Veronika meets on the street and whom she seeks to marry—with regard to her investment in his virility. I will show how Demba's characterization not only draws on the stereotype of the sexually aggressive Black man but also collides with how Demba's racialized body becomes the ultimate sign of the impolitic in the domain of Veronika's parents (for more information on the impolitic, see Gorfinkel 2012). Although Sanders-Brahms's *No Mercy, No Future* lodges a critique of strategic debility through which she at times aims to articulate something akin to intersectional struggles against heterosexist and racist oppression, this vision fails when considering the representational strategies of the men of color in the film.

## The Routines of Daily Life in Feminist Filmmaking: *Jeanne Dielman*

In her now canonical essay "Feminism and Film," Helke Sander outlines the aesthetic commitments of feminist filmmaking of her era by foregrounding women directors' roles in developing new cinematic regimes required to articulate the material conditions for women's lives under heteropatriarchy. Through her paradigmatic understanding of feminist filmmaking—that is, "We [women] must first learn to see with our own eyes and not through the mediation of others"—she articulates a main criticism of the West German film establishment (2004, 219). The institution of West German film was, in her critique, predominantly a male domain that denied women access to cinematic self-actualization. For Sander, this context was characterized by bad labor conditions underpinning women's filmmaking. Much like the efforts of the broader women's movement, in which "only gargantuan efforts to gather individual insights piece by piece" were initiated "to examine our fragmented history from the point of view of women's interests," so too was the broader project of feminist filmmaking less an organized movement defined by strategic division of labor than a matter of clusters of individuals advancing projects that collectively sought women's liberation (219).

The archive of feminist filmmaking was consequently made up of a range of films variously aligned with the women's rights movement. Sander notes that some feminist film productions actively aimed "to contribute to social campaigns . . . all born of the desire to support the women's movement in such a way as to have an immediate effect" (2004, 220). Her filmmaking is an example here. In *Macht die Pille frei?* (*Does the Pill Liberate?*, 1973), Sander aligns with an aesthetic-political program advanced by a number of her contemporary filmmakers such as Ingrid Oppermann, Gardi Deppe, and Sabine Eckhard, whose work articulated a critique of paragraph 218 of the West German Basic Law, which criminalized abortion

(Knight 1992, 76–79). Such examples of what is called the *cinéma militant*, which in Gertrud Koch's assessment was a cinematic practice "intended to produce an activist oppositional public sphere, addressed to a particular oppressed group," saw film as an instrument by which to imagine an affirmative communality that grows out of and stimulates further political agitation (2004, 277).

However, Sander also recognizes other types of feminist filmmaking that did not always explicitly align with the political missions of the broader women's movement. In fact, she notes that the type of political filmmaking required to aid women's rights discourse "often distracts from women artists' own projects, which are more complicated" (2004, 220). For Sander, the focus of this other type of feminist filmmaking begins and ends with women themselves. Such labor entails a reinvention of cinematic regimes by recognizing the burdens that women's bodies had to bear on-screen, in particular with regard to eroticization and sexualization: "Nude bodies and sexual organs play a role, these being filmed not to awaken erotic feelings in men nor to be sexually neutral or medically functional, but rather to picture the female body so as to lead women into the blank regions of unexplored subjectivity" (221). Here, feminist film offers moments in which women can envision unrealized potential for themselves and for other women. In the writing of Sander's contemporary filmmaker Jutta Brückner, these types of films "are searches for traces" that index an "affirmation of identity . . . [through] hopeful stories looking forward to a self-confident life, in which one can feel and think at the same time" (2004, 238–39). As such, feminist filmmaking takes on the role of "signposts on the road to a gradual liberation of individual and collective creativity" (240). In the assessment of filmmakers such as Brückner (and by extension Sander), feminist filmmaking engenders semi-utopian aesthetic visions for women filmmakers, performers, and audiences whereby these can imagine different worlds, different potentials for themselves on a path toward liberation.

Material considerations about the conditions for production, but also the place of self-study and determination through an aesthetic praxis centered on the experiences of women, inform the visual and narrative regimes of feminist filmmaking. These are expressed in the structures of feeling characterizing feminist film theory, which regularly convey frustration about the material conditions for filmmaking. Sander, for instance, speaks of "desperate attempts" in discussing women directors' struggles to secure funding for their work (1974, 16). At the same time, these material considerations are articulated in the storylines of women's filmmaking themselves. Margarethe von Trotta describes this aesthetic practice as one characterized by a collapse of the private and the public: "We stand up in public for what we think in private and are not so able and eager to make compromises" (1988, 90; see also Gerhardt 2019, 78–80). In practice, this commitment takes various forms. Gertrud Koch has noted that the genre of documentary, which was formally invested in archiving women's subjective experiences of the everyday, helped shape a radical feminist subjective aesthetic by centering the daily lives of women (1981, 49). Nondocumentary feminist filmmaking deployed visual and narrative strategies pertaining to the private/public dialectic that similarly studied the rhythms qualifying women's daily subjective experience. Drawing on the French film critic Claudine Herrmann, Judith Mayne has noted how "some women filmmakers have resolutely insisted upon the representation of real time" (1981, 36). Such "realist" investment—frequently expressed through, for example, stationary camera use and long takes—rejects received editing and camera use praxes in order to reveal temporal structures of women's experiences historically neglected in cinema.

Chantal Akerman's work famously exemplifies such commitment to studying the daily routines of women. In particular her film *Jeanne Dielman, 23 Quai de Commerce, 1018 Bruxelles* (1975) has been hailed as model of "focusing on what has traditionally been marginal" in foregrounding parts of women's lived experience historically deemed outside of the purview of cinematic representation (Mayne 1981, 37). I would like to examine what is at stake in this film with regard to the study of daily routines by way of framing my discussion of *No Mercy, No Future*. If, following Sander and Brückner, feminist film is invested in utopian longing by embedding within it the traces of a more affirmative future for women, and if the cinematic study of women's daily experiences, lives, and rhythms articulates this (as exemplified by Akerman's film), then *No Mercy, No Future* draws on this representational strategy but does so by denying affirmative futures leading to women's liberation.

Akerman has on numerous occasions expressed her mission to study women's routines through her cinema. In a 1976 interview she notes, "I give space to things which were never, almost never, shown in that way, like the daily gestures of a woman. They are the lowest in the hierarchy of film images" (Bergstrom 1977, 118). Instead of glamorized cinematography of women orchestrated primarily in service of the heterosexual male gaze and the patriarchal superstructure that it serves, Akerman is drawn to the quotidian. Akerman's cinema explicitly engages with structures of cinematic time through which she seeks to resonate with audiences, specifically women. The long takes surveying the title character's quotidian routines form an essential part of the formal repertoire, which enables audiences to linger on and contemplate the effects of privatized gestures. Ultra-realism, which is Akerman's term to describe effects of formal preoccupation with quotidian experiences that can be generalized and thus applied to the experiences of other women, offers a means by which women audiences can envision alternative futures—in the spirit of the traces that Brückner considers in her writing about feminist film aesthetics (Akerman, Alemann, and Hurst 1976, 36).

*Jeanne Dielman* chronicles the quotidian life of the film's eponymous character (Delphine Seyrig), a widowed mother. Spread across three days, the film, primarily set in Jeanne's apartment, offers insights into her household routines, pastime activities, and her sex work. Routine-focused, contemplative cinematography defines *Jeanne Dielman* (see Kuhn 1994, 167–68). For instance, the first day features a sequence in which Jeanne serves a dinner she prepared for her and her son Sylvain (Jan Decorte). Spanning twelve minutes, the sequence features shots in which Jeanne oscillates between the kitchen and dining room to set up the dinner table and reheat and serve the food she prepared earlier. Each set of actions is shot with a stationary camera. For example, when Jeanne enters the kitchen, she is captured in a medium shot (see figure 9.1). Nestled between the kitchen table and the stove, she opens a drawer to take out a serving spoon, grabs one plate, moves into the space between the kitchen sink and the oven, and spoons the food onto the plate. Jeanne then repeats the action for the second plate. The stationary camera permits viewers to observe in their entire duration the gestures Akerman mentions in her interviews. Because the camera lingers on this tight space through which Jeanne maneuvers, viewers observe as she prepares not one but two plates and have unobstructed, unmanipulated access to these actions in that they are not divided into discrete shots but shown in a continual take.

FIGURE 9.1. *Jeanne Dielman*—Jeanne plating the entrée for dinner in the kitchen. (Screengrab)

Such patterning of daily rhythms in the film through a focus on minutiae is juxtaposed with Jeanne's traversing Brussels's cityscape as part of her daily chores. Trips to the convenience store, post office, and tailor offer visual space in which her resolute commute to support daily life at home finds expression. In this regard, Jeanne's search of a replacement button for her son's jacket takes her to the department store. A long shot in which a stationary camera observes an escalator carrying a series of women one by one into view opens the sequence. Jeanne is positioned in a line of other women who are going about their daily lives. As with the scenes in her apartment, each of the shots conveying her traversing the outside world is characterized by a lingering camera that permits viewers to study quotidian rhythms, favoring daily gestures over more spectacular plot strategies. Such an investment in the quotidian has been described by Ivone Margulies as an "aesthetics of homogeneity" qualified by the cinematographic and narrative sameness underpinning individual scenes (1996, 80). However, the patterns of daily rhythms conveying sameness in Jeanne's life position viewers to ponder how fragile the world order is from the perspective of the film's protagonist (78). This becomes particularly prominent by the third day, when what appears to be a stable routine culminates in a scene in which a client forcefully resists her attempts to repel him. Once he climaxes and rolls off her, Jeanne stabs him in the neck with a scissors.

The aesthetic concerns with daily routines in *Jeanne Dielman* were immediately interesting for feminist West German filmmaking and film theory. In an interview, the cinematographer Babette Mangolte, who worked with Akerman on *Jeanne Dielman*, notes that the West German television industry became interested in funding Akerman's *News from Home* (1976) as a result of the critical success of *Jeanne Dielman* across Europe, in particular among feminist circles (Bergstrom 2019, 41). Akerman's interview with the leading West German feminist film journal *frauen und film* praises the film for its investment in an "agonizing slowness and precision" in order to enact a commentary on the affective regimes for viewers who can study the "small inaccuracies" that come to distort the fragile routines of Jeanne's everyday life (Akerman, Alemann, and Hurst 1976, 32). Moreover, Akerman's work regularly features in the reflections on feminist film theory proliferating in *frauen und film*. Karola Gramann and Heide Schlüpmann, for instance, write enthusiastically about Akerman's influence on feminist filmmaking in modeling formal means by which to subvert voyeuristic visual regimes through minimalist hyperrealism (1979, 45).

Considering the impact of Akerman's aesthetic praxis on feminist film theory in West Germany, *Jeanne Dielman* offers a useful framework for a discussion of Sanders-Brahms's *No Mercy, No Future*. The careful engagement with women's routines engraved in the visual and narrative rhythms of the film was seen as an embodiment of a liberatory feminist film praxis. The contemplative opportunities afforded by the long takes studying Jeanne's gestures, as well as the fragility of the routines in which the title character invests so much, stage a scenario wherein women viewers especially can glean the frustrations that in some capacity might reflect their own daily patterns. This, in turn, could stimulate utopian longing for a better time and place.

## Debilitation and the Tempering of Self-Actualization in *No Mercy, No Future*

Sanders-Brahms's *No Mercy, No Future* rejects any affirmative capacities that grow out of agential prowess. The contemporaneous West German feminist criticism of the film overwhelmingly rejected its glum outlook for women's self-actualization. In a 1982 review of the film in the women's magazine *Emma*, wherein she rehearses racist and antisemitic tropes later typical of her public writing, Alice Schwarzer laments the film's unbearable victimization of the woman's body robbed of "every bit of dignity and strength" (1982, 307). In Schwarzer's assessment, *No Mercy, No Future* not only romanticizes women as "dehumanized creatures who suffer instead of experiencing" but also advances a grotesque vision of woman-to-woman solidarity: "Coldness and deceit are generally the prominent features of women who appear next to the heroine in this film—by the way, always only in passing" (307). For Schwarzer, Sanders-Brahms herself is nothing but a "sadist who wants to drown her own gender in the cesspool of masochism" (307). Gertrud Koch's 1981 review in the *Frankfurter Rundschau* similarly indicts the film for its gratuitous emplotment of women's suffering: "Few films by women show violence against women, rape, and social oppression as a pure, passive story of suffering, let alone as an inescapable destiny of femininity" (quoted in Schwarzer 1982, 306). Whereas Akerman's film offers moments for reflection that reach beyond the stultifying pressures of Jeanne's daily life—and features a woman not in search of men for fulfillment—*No Mercy, No Future* offers the opposite through its preoccupation with debility.

Scholarship on debility draws on the tradition of biopolitical discourse famously catalyzed by Michel Foucault. His writing on sovereignty has been particularly productive for scholars interested in the technologies of power orchestrated in order to administer life. Through his discussion of sovereignty—that is, "the right to take life or let live"—Foucault outlines the distinctions between sovereign agency and biopower (2003, 240). Whereas the sovereign's claim to power lies in having access to decisions over life and death, biopolitics, in Foucault's understanding, is more generative. As Lauren Berlant has noted, "The difference between sovereign agency under a regime of sovereignty and under a regime of biopower . . . can be thought of as a distinction between individual life and collective living on" (2011, 97). Berlant then theorizes how, under neoliberal-biopolitical regimes, the subject's experience of the world is defined by "ongoingness, getting by, and living on," a collection of circumstances simultaneously characterized by reproducing life (that is, conditioned behavior that propels subjects forward) as they are an indicator of what Berlant calls "slow death" (99–100). As "a condition of being worn out by the activity of reproducing life" under the auspices of biopower, slow death helps bring into view the effects of biopower on the bodies and populations it targets (100). As an analytical category, slow death helps articulate how the daily habits of populations—temporal structures, behavioral patterns, and recurring investments—serve biopolitical ends.

Drawing on the work of Berlant, Jasbir Puar has expounded how biopolitical regimes deploy strategic debilitation as a sanctioned mechanism by which to maintain public "health" as a means to control populations. While Berlant shows how under biopolitical regimes "living increasingly becomes a scene of the administration, discipline, and recalibration of what constitutes health" (2011, 97), Puar discusses debility as a "slow wearing down" that "maintains the precarity of certain bodies and populations precisely through making them available for maiming" (2017, xiv, xvii). As a technology for population control, debility then reproduces sanctioned life by stifling the unruliness of unwanted bodies. Biopolitical control, here, is less about eliminating populations and more about maintaining them in the service of proliferating—and indeed refining—an ongoingness in place to serve power. As Puar notes, "Maiming is a source of value extraction from populations" in that a debilitated body can be more receptive to the principles of biopolitical governmentality (xviii).

It is in the spirit of dramatizing Veronika's slow death and strategic debilitation that Sanders-Brahms's film relinquishes an affirmative vision for feminist self-determination. *No Mercy, No Future* indeed offers a critique of biopolitical governmentality of unruly bodies by deploying feminist aesthetics—even if these, in the assessment of Koch and Schwarzer, indict feminist solidarity politics. In the film, personal agency is less about self-actualization than it is a technology of slow death. It is not a means by which to seize control of life toward more affirmative futures for the woman protagonist or a means to achieve intersectional solidarities among white women and men of color; instead it is a mechanism by which the replication of life contributes to a slow undoing of the feminist subject in the service of hegemony.

Some of the contemporary reviews of *No Mercy, No Future* indeed came to celebrate the film's political prowess. Jill Forbes's review for *Monthly Film Bulletin*, for instance, praises Sanders-Brahms's entwinement of Veronika's fragmentedness as expressed through episodes of mental distress and her own suicide attempts through cutting with the fragmentation of Cold War–era Berlin—the splitting of the city by means of a wall (1982, 80). However, the political commentary in the film reaches beyond the politics articulated in Forbes's review. The film is not so much concerned with Veronika's personal struggles as expressed by toxic behavior stimulated by East/West division politics as it is with articulating how her body and her person are part of an assemblage of nonaffirmative power structures. These structures not only enable her traversing through the city (a privilege afforded by her social class) and govern her desires (her search for Christ as embodied in most men she encounters) but through debilitation also regulate her body and thus maintain her within the purview of biopolitics (her institutionalization and medicalization).

The complex assemblage of the effects of power begins to come into view upon closer examination of Veronika's daily patterns, in which she seeks self-actualization and experiences harm as a result. Take, for instance, a sequence of events relayed in the film's opening. An early scene shows the protagonist at a holiday party. Disenchanted by the festivities dominated by wealthy white West Germans from her own habitus, Veronika cheers up as an unnamed Asian man enters the ballroom and takes a seat next to her. As they begin to dance, a long shot shows a man in the costume of St. Nicholas dancing around them, as though surveilling their activity.

In the next scene, Veronika is on the subway, presumably on the way home from the festivities. She is seated across from an elderly man while three younger men extend their arms toward her (see figure 9.2). Their silver-painted faces and simultaneous gestures cast them as robotic figures making advances toward her in an unappealing fashion. The elderly man, whose face is painted gold, winks at her and waves her over to signal his advance. Veronika responds affirmatively. In the following scene, the two enter an attic storage space with an unmade bed. The unnamed man continues his advances and then lies on top of Veronika. The scene cuts to his climax, shortly after which Veronika pushes him off, stunned into desperation by what has just happened. The man's commentary and Veronika's reaction suggest that the sexual violence in the scene may indicate this is the first time she has had intercourse with a man.

In comparison to *Jeanne Dielman*, which displays the protagonist's daily life in order to subvert voyeurism and to facilitate reflection in the service of ideas aligned with women's liberation, the depiction of routines

FIGURE 9.2. *No Mercy, No Future*—Veronika on the subway. (Screengrab)

in *No Mercy, No Future* features an onslaught of Veronika's failed attempts to discover herself, her urges, and her future outlook. Starting with the scene at the holiday party, the sequence of events conditions a pattern for Veronika's search throughout West Berlin for idealized male companionship or other means for self-actualization. The scene of racialized and exoticized excitement at the dance stimulates her companionship with men cast as nonnormative from the perspective of the heterosexual, white, appropriately aged, able-bodied, Christian men surrounding her at the party. This white hegemonic context seems unappealing to Veronika, for whom a possible relation with a man of color becomes a bridge to another habitus at the same time as it becomes a site for severe scrutiny by a Christian saint. Her subsequent relation with an elderly man results in a traumatic transition into the world of sex, which in that moment of the film is only possible in the remote, unideal location of the attic. The remainder of the film features similar challenges. However, these accumulated experiences do not collectively help advance Veronika's movement into more affirmative terrains but rather collectively enact the twofold premise of self-actualization under biopolitics. On the one hand, these ventures index a possible affirmative outlook for Veronika's self-actualization. In that she is adamantly pursuing men in search of ideal companionship, the recurring attempts signal a potential hope, whereby each new relation might reveal itself to be the right one. This is an affective cycle of behavior effectively characterized by Berlantian ongoingness. On the other hand, the search itself becomes her slow undoing. Each attempt to reach beyond the habitus, which offers no premise for good living, faces scrutiny by the governing forces and slowly harms her body as various institutions of power aim to subdue her.

When Veronika attempts to stage political protest, biopolitical force begins to become extremely legible in the film. Following her traumatic encounter with the elderly man, Veronika is in her room, knitting and listening to the radio. The news report announces US president Reagan's support of the El Salvadorian government during the Salvadorian Civil War. Veronika grabs the radio and ventures outside the parameters of a US military training ground. She takes off her clothes and lies on the snow-covered field naked. Immediately thereafter, a group of US soldiers detains her and brings her to a mental health clinic. Under the auspices of nurses there, she is first warmed up in a bathtub but then restrained to a bed. Finally, a close-up shot shows a medical professional injecting Veronika with a drug, presumably to further subdue her (see figure 9.3). The military intervention is not a cause of death to Veronika. The film presents these soldiers' intervention not as an act meant to annihilate Veronika's protesting body but rather as one to pass her on to the medical professionals who will subdue her. Just like her self-actualization attempt with unidealized men, characterized by harm and surveillance, Veronika's self-actualization attempt through political action faces military force that exposes her body to pharmacological maiming.

Veronika will face the force of medical institutions over and over again throughout *No Mercy, No Future*. These experiences become particularly potent once they converge with the institutions of her family, the neighborhood watch, and the church. The authority of such an assemblage of vectors of power is most pronounced in their efficient surveillance and subsequent debilitation of the protagonist following her attempt to marry Demba, a guest worker whom she met on the street. Demba confesses to Veronika that he was left homeless after losing his job. Veronika offers to help, and the two find a rundown hotel. Demba proves persistent in a conversation in which Veronika tells him that the doctor instructed her to abstain from sex following an abortion lest she sustain harm. Veronika

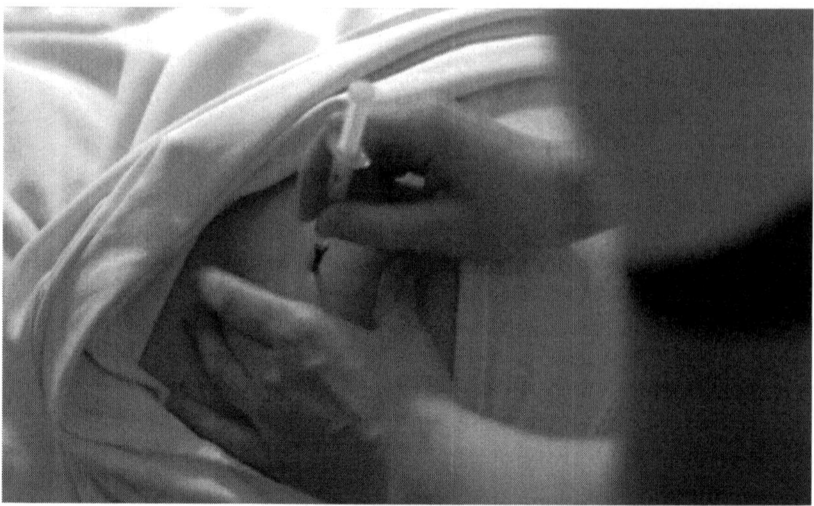

FIGURE 9.3. *No Mercy, No Future*—Veronika is pharmacologically subdued. (Screengrab)

gives in. After a long sex scene, the two are covered in the blood emanating from Veronika's body. In the following scene, Demba and Veronika go to a church to get married. Veronika, in her street clothes, happily escorts Demba, dressed in a pristine white suit, into the church (see figure 9.4). Following a series of questions about proper paperwork required to get married, the church official phones Veronika's father and soon afterward declines to marry the couple. In the next scene, the couple is at Veronika's family home, where her mother is disgusted at the sight of the two. Her father, though surprised, initially tolerates their union and allows them to stay in the house temporarily, albeit in separate rooms. Demba is in the basement, where he feels put aside like a disposable object. Shortly after Veronika convinces him to meet her in her bedroom, her father and a group of men forcefully abduct, institutionalize, and finally pharmacologically subdue her. Demba, who tries to help her, is left behind. Veronika's father pays him off, and Demba leaves the house.

Veronika's investment in Demba gives rise to conflicting readings about possible intersectional solidarity. Initially, their union might appear mutually beneficial. As much as Veronika seeks a means to escape her habitus through marriage, Demba is afforded a chance to remedy his

FIGURE 9.4. *No Mercy, No Future*—Veronika and Demba wait to get married. (Screengrab)

precarious situation through their union. The tenuousness of the context in which they met notwithstanding, both approach the prospect of union affirmatively. However, each wears the other out. The sex upon which Demba insists exacerbates the wound Veronika sustained as a result of her abortion, literally covering her in blood as a result, and jeopardizes her future health. Also, although he initially tries to help her as she is being institutionalized, Demba leaves and is never seen again after her father pays him off. Then again, Veronika's insistence on marriage exposes Demba to the vulgar racism characterizing the way the church official and Veronika's parents respond to Demba's Blackness (see figure 9.5). He feels the pressures of being used by Veronika to wage her battles against her habitus, a racialized violence most explicitly articulated when he takes a seat in a chair ornamented with caricatured, racialized Black figures "propping" up the rests of the chair in Veronika's room.

At each juncture, the couple's investment in hopeful futures is nothing but cruelly optimistic ongoingness that exposes both to severe harm and subsequent surveillance. The material consequences of this slow death of the body are shown primarily through Veronika. At the end of the film, the effects of the medicalization enact schizophrenic visions that alter her relationship to the world even as they subdue her. We know from the

FIGURE 9.5. *No Mercy, No Future*—Veronika, Demba, and Veronika's father. (Screengrab)

film's opening that the doctors have pronounced Veronika almost healed. But this "healthy" status is nothing but an indication of the suppression of her attempts at self-actualization. However, Demba's experience of the episodes is also marked by severe violence through being the recipient of racist rejection, which consequently registers on his body, even if not in the form of an open wound. Both are subject to and eventually relegated back into whatever station it is they were not supposed to have left: Veronika's impulses to actualization are subdued, while Demba is sent away from her parents' house.

## Conclusion

In an interview with Harlan Kennedy, Sanders-Brahms comments on the extreme representational strategies characterizing Veronika's sex scene with Demba: "I knew that this scene, in normal film terms, goes on 'too long.' . . . But I did it deliberately. I wanted the audiences to become caught up in the spiral of suffering that Rita G. is in" (Kennedy 1982, 21). That is, whereas shot duration as expressed through the long take comprised a central formal component in the aesthetic repertoire that helped articulate feminist utopian aesthetics in *Jeanne Dielman*, the scene's duration in *No Mercy, No Future* aims to produce a shock politics that stultifies audiences in apprehending the sexual violence Veronika endures in the scene. That feminist film criticism in West Germany took issue with the film's relishing in the suffering of the protagonist registers here in Sanders-Brahms's own admittance that woman's suffering was indeed the main representational goal in this scene and throughout the film. In articulating the harmful effects sustained by Veronika's investment in ongoingness, however, Sanders-Brahms not only expresses that the power structures administering life are too omnipresent for feminist self-actualization to take ground without sustaining harm to women's bodies but also draws on racist tropes to do so. Demba's plight under this regime of power finds expression in the film, but his character's function is to serve as the ultimate cipher of the impolitic, which ushers in the most severe collaboration between assemblages of power to sanction and control Veronika.

One of the most successful and widely recognized woman filmmakers of the 1970s whose work shaped both feminist film discourse and contributed to the broader impulses of the New German Cinema, Sanders-Brahms created representational strategies in *No Mercy, No Future* that offer a somber outlook for the capacities of film to envision futures aiding liberation movements (Möhrmann 1980, 141–42). Comparing the film to *Jeanne Dielman* yields in which ways Sanders-Brahms draws on received feminist cinematic language and where she departs from it. If, as Katie Trumpener has noted, the New German Cinema was "particularly interested in the way individual subjectivity was shaped by the institutions of state and the institutions of art," then *No Mercy, No Future* indeed carries forward the movement's investment in its considerations of the limitations of individual self-actualization under biopolitics (1989, 40).

## Note

1 All translations from German are my own.

## Works Cited

Akerman, Chantal, Claudia Alemann, and Heike Hurst. 1976. "Interview mit Chantal Akerman." *frauen und film* 7: 32–37.

Bergstrom, Janet. 1977. "Chantal Akerman on *Jeanne Dielman*: Excerpts from an Interview with *Camera Obscura*, November 1976." *Camera Obscura* 1.2: 115–21.

———. 2019. "With Chantal in New York in the 1970s: An Interview with Babette Mangolte." *Camera Obscura* 34.1: 31–57.

Berlant, Lauren. 2011. *Cruel Optimism*. Durham: Duke University Press.

Brückner, Jutta. 2004. "Women's Films Are Searches for Traces (1981)." Translated by Antje Masten. In *German Essays on Film*, edited by Richard W. McCormick and Alison Guenther-Pal, 237–41. New York: Continuum.

Forbes, Jill. 1982. "Berührte, Die (No Mercy No Future)." *Monthly Film Bulletin* 49: 79–80.

Foucault, Michel. 2003. *Society Must Be Defended: Lectures at the College de France*. Edited by Mauro Bertani et al. Translated by David Macey. New York: Picador.

Gerhardt, Christina. 2019. "Helke Sander's dffb Films and West Germany's Feminist Movement." In *Celluloid Revolt: German Screen Cultures and the Long 1968*, edited by Christina Gerhardt and Marco Abel, 69–86. Rochester, NY: Camden House.

Gorfinkel, Elena. 2012. "Impossible, Impolitic: *Ali: Fear Eats the Soul* and Fassbinder's Asynchronous Bodies." In *A Companion to Rainer Werner Fassbinder*, edited by Brigitte Peucker, 502–15. London: Wiley-Blackwell.

Gramann, Karola, and Heide Schlüpmann. 1979. "Raus aus den Prokrustesbetten! Die Diskussionsbeiträge des 'Women's Event' Edinburgh 1979." *frauen und film* 22: 36–47.

Kennedy, Harlan. 1982. "Assignment in Berlin: Festival Report and Werner Herzog's *Fitzcarraldo*." *Film Comment* 18.3: 20–23.

Knight, Julia. 1992. *Women and the New German Cinema*. London: Verso.

Koch, Gertrud. 1981. "Von den Schwierigkeiten im Umgang mit der Autonomie." *frauen und film* 31: 49–51.

———. 2004. "Ex-Changing the Gaze: Re-Visioning Feminist Film Theory." In *German Essays on Film*, edited by Richard W. McCormick and Alison Guenther-Pal, 275–90. New York: Continuum.

Kuhn, Annette. 1994. *Women's Pictures: Feminism and Cinema*. London: Verso.

Malakaj, Ervin. 2019. "Cruel Optimism, Post-1968 Nostalgia, and the Limits of Political Activism in Helma Sanders-Brahms's *Unter dem Pfllaster ist der Strand*." In *Celluloid Revolt: German Screen Cultures and the Long 1968*, edited by Christina Gerhardt and Marco Abel, 237–52. Rochester, NY: Camden House.

Margulies, Ivone. 1996. *Nothing Happens: Chantal Akerman's Hyperrealist Everyday*. Durham: Duke University Press.

Mayne, Judith. 1981. "The Woman at the Keyhole: Women's Cinema and Feminist Criticism." *New German Critique* 23: 27–43.

Möhrmann, Renate. 1980. *Die Frau mit der Kamera: Filmemacherinnen in der Bundesrepublik Deutschland*. Munich: Hanser.

Puar, Jasbir K. 2017. *The Right to Maim: Debility, Capacity, Disability*. Durham: Duke University Press.

Sander, Helke. 1974. "Nimmt man dir das schwert, dann greife zum knüppel." *frauen und film* 1: 12–48.

———. 2004. "Feminism and Film (1977)." Translated by Ramona Curry. In *German Essays on Film*, edited by Richard W. McCormick and Alison Guenther-Pal, 215–22. New York: Continuum.

Sanders-Brahms, Helma, and Rita G. 1981. "Die Berührte." In *Sex & Lust: Verführung—Schönheit–Liebe—Gewalt*, edited by Arno Widmann, 173–80. Berlin: Ästhetik und Kommunikation Verlags-GmbH.

Schwarzer, Alice. 1982. "Die Unwürdige." In *Mit Leidenschaft: Texte 1968–1982*, 303–9. Hamburg: Rowohlt.

Trumpener, Katie. 1989. "Reconstructing the New German Cinema: Social Subjects and Critical Documentaries." *New German Critique* 18: 37–53.

von Trotta, Margarethe. 1988. "Female Film Aesthetics (1982)." In *West German Filmmakers on Film: Visions and Voices*, edited by Eric Rentschler, 89–90. New York: Holmes & Meier.

# 10

# ENIGMATIC SOUNDSCAPES

## Werner Herzog's *Kaspar Hauser* and Jane Campion's *The Piano*

*MARGARET STRAIR*

## SOUNDSCAPES IN NEW GERMAN CINEMA AND WORLD CINEMA

The spaces in which the films of New German Cinema take place serve less to instantiate a particular historical moment than to emphasize displacement—whether of nation, values, or even time itself.[1] New German Cinema posits a national cinema precisely through attempting to refract its own understanding of the nation through a post–World War II lens.[2] With stories focused on protagonists who are "alienated from their social surroundings and lack a clear sense of Self or a feeling of collective belonging" and stories that explore "the theme of not belonging, of not belonging to the place where one is supposed to belong that is home or Heimat" (Scharf 2008, viii), the question of coming to terms with a nation's past is relocated into subjective encounters with the world that defamiliarize the familiar. This move and the displacements it entails are partially grounded self-reflexively in the filmic medium: images displace ourselves to ourselves and, to invoke Stanley Cavell, rely on a sense of making things foreign to ourselves.[3]

Images alone, however, are not the only means by which these displacements occur. In exploring transnational perspectives within world cinema, Nataša Durovičovà notes the ability of sound in film to both reinforce and undo a sense of specificity and national space, inducing a disorientation that simultaneously places and displaces viewers (2009,

91). For Durovičovà, sound assumes features of an omnipresent force that shapes the spaces it occupies. For contemporary audiences, this is realized through a passive entrance of audiences into the circulation of spaces of other nations and other languages (94). While Durovičovà focuses chiefly on the global circulation and exhibition of foreign-language films, she also discusses sound's ability to function as a destabilizing force by which audiences both delineate their own spaces and disrupt them—and, in a way, cross borders. Much like the cultural/historical dimensions of New German Cinema, and the body of images one encounters in cinema, sound—diegetic and nondiegetic—displaces.

Werner Herzog's *Kaspar Hauser: Jeder für sich und Gott gegen alle* (*The Enigma of Kaspar Hauser*, 1974) tells the story of such displacements through the film's soundscape. The film sharpens awareness of both the visual and acoustic specificity of a culture and nation and stages means by which they may be disrupted. When the eponymous protagonist crosses into the confusingly sonorous society of nineteenth-century Germany, he describes his transition from being kept isolated for years in the silence of a cellar as a particularly hard one. The silence that had once marked Kaspar's "purity of being" (Peucker 1995, 89) is relinquished, replaced by a comparatively complex and noisy social order—an order of specific rules, proscribed and institutionalized modes of communication and artistic expression that constrict and render him an "outsider within," ultimately leading to his murder.[4] Much of the film, as described by Kaja Silverman, is the story of a failed story—of the failed use of language and the inability to construct or sustain any form of narrative (1981–82, 73), whether in Kaspar's writing or speaking. To speak through Silverman's Lacanian reading, such a failure is the inability to fall into the paternal, symbolic order that consists of difference and language rendered through the paternal signifier (75). Understanding Kaspar's enigma as a failure of language, textuality, and narrative displaces Kaspar, "the outsider within," and his intuitive modes of self-expression that are at odds with those of the dominant social order and gendered norms. He is, as Les Wright shows, an allegory for New German Cinema's "search for identity" complicated through the "problem of collective trauma denied through deliberate cultural amnesia" (1998, 319), that amnesia being the inability to find one's own narrative. Kaspar's search for narrative and identity under these conditions and the failure of a linguistic mode of self-expression open up other dimensions of the filmic medium to view aspects of his displacement that are dependent on sound. Indeed, diegetic and nondiegetic sound perform gestures beyond language, while simultaneously destabilizing and rendering wholly inadequate solely visual and narrative means for telling his story. If Herzog lamented the lack of images to fully represent the complexities of the present, the dynamic built between sound and image in *Kaspar Hauser* begins to reconceptualize their syncretism and move toward more convoluted modes of representation and narrative.

Although *Kaspar Hauser*'s soundtrack chiefly consists of classical compositions, it is rather homogenous by comparison with other films of New German Cinema, whose disjointed soundtracks feature a mixture of musical genres. Caryl Flinn argues that these heterogeneous soundtracks undo the unifying function of music in film sound scores and "complicate a notion of history that would pass off as seamless, with the present neatly and unproblematically detached from its past" (2004, 4), which Herzog achieves through other means in the soundscape. Whether through Kaspar's tenuous grasp on the German language or his own musical practice at the piano, Kaspar engages in his own messy negotiation of cultural binaries and practices and their sonic boundaries, all of which culminate in his inability to integrate into his surroundings and account for his past using the narrative means available in his present social environs. Furthermore, the borders between diegetic and nondiegetic sound Herzog utilizes in the film's sound design and in nonnarrative dream sequences in the film complicate modes of self-representation in and through the filmic medium. Rather than depicting a past and a present seamlessly detached from one another, tensions across the diegetic and nondiegetic soundscape reveal the struggle to articulate the past through means in the present and the impossibility of doing so. But most significantly, it shows the importance of sound for staging alternatives that are not yet fully available for understanding the past.

Turning from images to sound to understand Kaspar's role as an outsider within targets other aspects of his identity and its connection with the film's soundscape. His apparent genderlessness contours his position as an outsider within by linking his expressive capacities beyond the reach of language, which positions him increasingly at fraught boundaries between the diegetic and nondiegetic elements of the film, between different gendered phases of psycho-social development and sexuality in a social order where those roles are clearly demarcated along the masculine-feminine binary. According to Lacanian and Kristevan thought, the nonlinguistic and acoustic modes of representation toward which he has an affinity and which Herzog privileges in the film's sound design are coded as feminine and, in Kristevan semiotics, as the maternal, despite his presenting as masculine. Raya Morag explains Kaspar's genderlessness as a clear disavowal of the Hitlerian and Nazi imagery of masculinity and sexuality (2011, 476), and I argue the film's soundscape and the borders Kaspar navigates when he crosses into German society and culture from silence show the limited efficacy of such a disavowal.

Displaying "a deep suspicion of the forms conventionally used to express history and a profound sense of alienation from national culture" (Cook 1993, xiii), feminist filmmaking of the 1990s somewhat more optimistically stages the possibility of female protagonists finding themselves through "an act of transgression": transgressing boundaries between "national and international, home and abroad, masculine and feminine" (xiv). In this more contemporary film landscape, sound too functions as a critical means of staging displacements, homelessness, and alienation, as well as visiting past and enduring oppressions. Jane Campion's *The Piano* (1993) provides one example, in which the fraught colonial New Zealand setting where the protagonist Ada McGrath (Holly Hunter) finds herself is compounded by both Ada's acoustic experience of the world around her and the film's use of nondiegetic sound. Like *Kaspar Hauser*, *The Piano* relies on depictions of aesthetic experiences focalized through the protagonist to forge distinct spaces and soundscapes that also show the outsider within. Ada, like Kaspar, plays the piano and assumes a different acoustic stance toward the world in which she lives than the other characters in the film. Her positionality as a white, Scottish woman who does not speak situates her similarly to Kaspar, as an outsider within, but she is implicated differently in the colonial structures that shape the film and its soundscape. Ada's complicity with oppressive structures, when understood as expressed through the film's sound design and soundtrack, shows the challenges of understanding an individual's position in New Zealand's colonial past. This complexity is compounded by an attempt to view history from the perspective of a female protagonist who finds herself between several borders in the filmic medium and the cultural landscape of the film.

Both Kaspar's and Ada's interactions with their films' soundscapes through the interplay of diegetic and nondiegetic sound point toward the capacity of an individual's acoustic relationship to the world to disrupt, reshape, or reinforce borders and binaries of a social order and their identities within it. Each protagonist's experience reveals how spaces can be disrupted, formed, and participated in through audiovisual means and how sound is instrumental in confronting and articulating the cruelty of those orders by rendering these protagonists outsiders within. Viewed in conjunction with *The Piano*, Herzog's rendering of Kaspar's story participates in a gesture toward a cultural feature that would later be used to rethink world cinema—its polyvalence, which according to Shekhar Deshpande and Meta Mazaj "is about seeing the world from the perspective of the periphery" and displacing "the relationship between the center and the periphery" (2018, 30). While world cinema's polyvalence acknowledges the different perspectives of a particular film reception, one might liken Kaspar's experience of the culture in which he finds himself to partaking in attempted shifts in perspective, facilitated through crossing over into European society. For Kaspar, crossing sonic borders in the diegesis and the audiovisual borders in the filmic medium brings him from the periphery to a center that is elusive or unstable: a failed story is a failed attempt at both reaching this center and accounting for one's history. But it is only a failure by relying on narrative means that insist on a hyper-local and national as well as gendered specificity, which the mise-en-scène will uphold but the soundscape begins to undo. In this way, New German Cinema, at least as represented by one of its most famous examples, unearths the potential of linking aesthetic experience with a broader transnational project of cinema, which can be scaled and reflected in the experiences of individuals navigating their acoustic environments and their histories.

## *Kaspar Hauser's* Soundscapes and Visuals of Displacement

In a 1974 interview, Herzog likens Kaspar to a passion figure within a film divided into the stations of a passion play. Eschewing the pedagogical emphasis of François Truffaut's *L'enfant sauvage* (*The Wild Child*, 1970), Herzog utilizes a subtler approach to telling Kaspar's "story of abuses"

(Ames 2014, 27). It unfolds over tensions between the sonic and visual spaces of the film, deploying all elements of the filmic medium to depict a phenomenological encounter between Kaspar and the world in which he finds himself. In this "anti-*Bildungsroman*" (Corrigan 1994, 134), sound and image converge to expose limitations to the diegetic sound of the social order and consequently gesture beyond both the narrative capacities of sound and the filmic medium and the social order in which Kaspar fails to fit. It is a story about language, in which sound and silence are coded through complex interactions with images inside and outside of the film's narrative.[5] Tensions between the diegetic and nondiegetic soundscapes fully expose us to the displacements that occur—to the contours of Kaspar's enigma, the reaches of that enigma into the other elements of his life, and film's role in shaping that enigma. Undoubtedly, Kaspar's relationship to diegetic and nondiegetic sound reveals him as both an agent of and subject to displacement, an enigmatic role that no other character assumes.

Responding to a comment on the presence of outsiders in his films, Herzog locates in Kaspar and Kaspar-like figures an ability to disrupt the social order in which they find themselves: "I always felt that a figure like Kaspar Hauser was not an outsider. He is at the center; he manages to retain his unblemished human dignity while everyone around him seems to be so hideously conditioned. These people, transformed as they are into domesticated pigs or members of the bourgeois society, are the bizarre ones, not Kaspar" (Cronin 2002, 68).[6] From the beginning, Kaspar is positioned as a figure through which displacements may be viewed that manifest in the upturning of key binaries that govern modes of self-expression and communication accepted within the predominating social order and consequently reveal the violence of that order. The elevation of the "the sensual, physical, and corporeal" over the "verbal, rhetoric, and certain modes of reasoning," as Brad Prager (2007, 18) phrases this tendency in Herzog's opus, is one way by which order is destabilized. In terms of the soundscape, this binary is upheld and is delivered in the diegesis through Kaspar's speech patterns compared to those of the other protagonists and his relationship to music. There is a marked difference between Kaspar's accent and monotonous intonation while fumbling through the German language and those of the other characters to reinforce the cultural dissonance between Kaspar and those around him.

This binary is also revealed in Kaspar's detrimental relationship to diegetic music, which ossifies his position as an outsider. When embedded in the diegesis, music operates as a mode of expression that remains chiefly foreign to Kaspar. When he encounters Florian (Popul Vuh's Florian Fricke) at the piano as the blind man who plays and sings unorthodox music, he tells his caregiver Professor Daumer (Walter Ladengast): "I feel [the music] strongly in my breast, I feel so suddenly old."[7] Compared with language, music offers Kaspar the appeal of immediacy (Peucker 1995, 89), which is also reflected in his response to Florian's composition. Kaspar's understanding of his own challenges playing the piano has a similar tenor, referencing his body: "Why is everything so difficult for me? Why can't one play the piano like breathing?" Music affects yet eludes Kaspar—it possesses ethereality and expressivity that is irreproducible and occluded by his own physicality and corporeality. Later, when Kaspar performs on the piano at court, he is unable to play the rehearsed scales and songs, producing a cacophony that resembles his speech. And tellingly, following his performance, he attempts to strip off his clothing as an act of displaying his corporeality in refusing to be, as Herzog puts it, "boxed in" (Cronin 2002, 112). Relatedly, sound constitutes part of a cultural institution that continues to demonize and torture him: church music is stripped of its religious and spiritual significance for Kaspar; he calls it "screaming," which causes him to flee a church. His failure to produce and later comprehend music signifies not only his disjointed relationship to the surrounding culture but also his inability to escape a corporeal and deeply sensuous orientation to the world.

However, the film's nondiegetic sound suggests another orientation to the soundscape by inverting much of what the diegetic music does, adding complexity to the soundscape and Kaspar's relationship to it. Part of the film's opening sequences through its combination of text, image, and sound introduces a paradox emblematic of the film's use of nondiegetic sound. A line of text, "Don't you hear this horrid screaming all around, that one calls silence?," which invokes Georg Büchner's *Lenz*, emerges on-screen as Pachabel's Canon plays over a windswept grain field.[8] Silence in the diegesis is aligned with the expressivity of nondiegetic music and promises a meaning that cannot be ciphered without a convergence of sound, image, and text all at once.[9] Whereas diegetic music functions like the language Kaspar fails to grasp, nondiegetic music gestures toward an entirely different way of perceiving the world (figure 10.1).

One sequence that draws out the expressive capacity of nondiegetic music and this ironic bend is Kaspar's dreamscape of the Caucasus Mountains after he explains to Professor Daumer that he has started to dream after having not done so prior to being brought into society. This sequence deploys nondiegetic music in a compelling way, showcases a complexity beyond the irony of the opening sequence, and adds another layer to Kaspar's inscrutability. Following Kaspar's declaration "I dreamed of the Caucasus Mountains," the dreamscape itself is a synthesis of sound (in this case, the musical underscoring of Albinoni's Adagio in G Minor) and image (a static shot over which the camera hovers) that opens a dimension to Kaspar's character that is wholly distinct in appearance and tone from other parts of the diegesis (figure 10.2).[10]

In such moments, as Silverman observes, the "visual diegesis fractures" (1981–82, 89) are shaped by both the diegetic and nondiegetic components of the film. The dreamscape illustrates how music and sound operate simultaneously as unbound yet structuring elements, at once beholden to and free from diegetic conventions. On the one hand, nondiegetic music lacks the spatiotemporal barriers of the visual that situate the music even further outside of narration and any frames of restriction

FIGURE 10.1. *The Enigma of Kaspar Hauser*—Text, image, and sound converge onscreen prior to cutting to Kaspar in his cell. (Screengrab)

FIGURE 10.2. *The Enigma of Kaspar Hauser*—Kaspar's dreamscape of the Caucasus Mountains, underscored with Albinoni's Adagio in G Minor. The music crescendos from near silence from the close-up of Kaspar's face to the images of the dreamscape. (Screengrab)

(Chion 1994, 67). On the other hand, the meeting of sound and image can evolve into a syncretism that reins in the unbounded nature of sound. As Herzog himself indicates, "Certain pieces of music . . . , when heard alongside particular images, reveal the inner qualities of the scene to the spectator. The perspective changes but not the image itself. A scene might not be logical in a narrative way, but sometimes when music is added it starts to acquire an internal logic" (Cronin 2002, 116). This suggests that the boundaries between image and sound are not impermeable: the image anchors the sound just as sound animates the image, and images underscored with music assume features that separate them from the surrounding flow of the narrative with their own added internal cohesion. While Herzog's images, such as those present in the dream sequence, are essential to opening up other spaces in the film, pairing them with sound gives this space an entirely unique character.

This dual tendency of the nondiegetic music to be beyond and yet interacting with the image adds an ambivalence to the role of sound: when paired with images, nondiegetic music is never solely beyond but also never completely within narration. Thus, as liberating as nondiegetic music is, seemingly outside of language, it also has its limitations, given the audiovisual nature of cinema. Peucker explains that the visuals of the dream sequences so central to the film itself "do not necessarily declare themselves in narrative terms," and thus they become "so personal and enigmatic" that these sequences are "beyond the reach of words" (1986, 111). A mix of narrative and nonnarrative visual elements requires us to look at the sonic spaces in the film differently from one another and yet recognize their interactions.[11] The efficacy and potency of the music in this sequence, as a counter to the diegetic music, sound, and language Herzog uses, require that the distinction between diegetic and nondiegetic material be maintained. The nondiegetic music is forced into a syncretism with an image that never quite satisfactorily provides clear answers about Kaspar but that nonetheless succeeds in pointing beyond the diegesis for answers about Kaspar and even the impossibility of finding them. While this sequence succeeds in depicting what Corrigan describes as a space "where the outside is also the center" (1994, 141), it also struggles with the fact that outside, once it becomes a center, is not cipherable and is still beyond any means of comprehension.

Through Kaspar's acoustic relationship with the culture in which he finds himself, we experience the foreignness of the sensory, symbolic, and affective dimensions of the world to which he is brought. Whereas Durovičovà describes the character of language—whether located in the mise-en-scène, intertitles, or synchronized sound—to tie images to a particular time and place (2009, 92), nondiegetic music as deployed by Herzog undoes what language does and performs another kind of displacement of Kaspar by displacing the acoustic specificity of the culture in which he tries to assimilate. Seen here, the soundscape only deepens his enigma and his undecipherable character. It deepens because of the constant gesture outward beyond the means of representation available to him and beyond the cultural coordinates of senses, affect, and corporeality on which Kaspar fails to be mapped in any uniform way. The failure Kaspar suffers in the end is clear: after his disastrous appearance he once again returns to the piano in the privacy of Daumer's home, unable to reproduce the progress he had previously made.

Herzog's cinematographic project is rooted in a kind of irony that forces one to grapple with multiple dimensions to any set of seeming oppositions, which according to Corrigan is an irony that "may very well subvert any binary distinctions" (1986, 14). If music is representative of a structure-giving practice on one level, it does something different, though not diametrically opposed, on the other. It is precisely this kind of irony that pushes us outward beyond our means of representation, only to in fact be ensnared in their deficiencies. For Kaspar, this is a failure to cross into and assimilate into European society and to become a fully assimilated male within the social order. Kaspar's experience may well subvert binary distinctions, thus asserting himself beyond a given social order, beyond language, because no order of the sonic landscape of the film accounts for his enigma. Taken in the context of the project of New German Cinema, this kind of irony emerges by displacing a sense of national identity, turning elements of cultural tradition and institutions in on themselves, to render them foreign and even dangerous. Being "homeless at home" or the "outsider within" is a deep irony in this film, compounded by the burden of a history that is present but inarticulable.

## Campion's *The Piano*, Borders, and Sonically Ambiguous Spaces

The imperative to reconceptualize the binary oppositions that structure social and psychological orders undergirds feminist thought.[12] Through his attempts at navigating such binaries, Kaspar became something of a figurehead for a call by Helke Sander for feminist filmmakers in the late 1970s to "learn to see with their own eyes": "Women today find themselves in a situation which is perhaps best comparable to Kaspar Hauser or the wild child. They must learn to see with their own eyes, and not the mediation of others" (1982, 50). The binaries subverted in *Kaspar Hauser*, however, create visuals and a narrative of ambiguity that result in their upholding: the binaries Kaspar navigates are already positioned in a certain proximity to one another both in the filmic diegesis and in the filmic medium itself. The entanglements of sound and image, masculine and feminine, as well as diegetic and nondiegetic sound, make it impossible to extricate oneself from their tensions, just as Kaspar himself is unable to do. Later films on a global scale similarly utilize a suspicion of traditional modes of expression but will not necessarily fall into the "anti-*Bildungsroman*" tendencies of *Kaspar Hauser*. They utilize a conspicuously global scale that places greater conceptual distance and space between the binaries navigated through their protagonist's transgressive social, political, and aesthetic experiences. A part of this is tied to the displacements that surround the historical instances of the film itself: whereas Herzog relocates the postwar experience into a nineteenth-century society setting, *The Piano* is set in New Zealand's colonial period and revisits that time through a different set of cultural coordinates and questions such as postcolonial theory and postmodernism of the early 1990s (Margolis 2000, 25). But, like Herzog, Campion uses sound as a mechanism that disrupts a protagonist's fundamental orientation of being at home, which is complicated through other factors belonging to the time in which the film was made: crossing between "home and abroad, national and international" and, when thinking of the filmic medium itself, between "mainstream and art cinema" (Cook 1993, xiv, quoted in Margolis 2000, 25). For Campion, the ambiguous space created through these crossings, amplified through film sound, reinterprets yet fails to fully reconcile with an oppressive colonial past.

In *The Piano*, sonic displacements reflect the protagonist's shifting agency and her conformation to or divergence from the world around her. The plot unfolds around Ada, a widowed Scottish woman and pianist who does not speak and finds herself thousands of miles away in an arranged marriage to Alistair Stewart (Sam Neill) in colonized Aotearoa (New Zealand). It follows her and her daughter Flora's interactions with the Māori and Ada's affair with George Baines (Harvey Keitel), their neighbor. Ada's relations with her environment, devoid of dialogue at first and facilitated through the piano, her notepad, and her daughter's translations of her sign language, are complicated by other cultural interactions taking place across the film and inevitably spilling over into the film's soundscape.

In keeping with the power of music, *The Piano* assigns music the ability "to short-circuit language and somehow evoke raw, unmediated feeling" (Allen 2000, 44) in a decisively less ambivalent way than *Kaspar Hauser* does. Ebert (1993) describes the film as "peculiar and haunting" and "not about particular characters but a whole universe of feeling," an effect constituted by a complicated soundscape that utilizes visuals rife with geographic, cultural, and political displacements, opening viewers to the affective states allowed by these displacements. If Kaspar Hauser's story ultimately denies a pathway for agency to escape the abundant cruelty of his given social order, Ada's story ends, on the one hand, optimistically in that it seemingly fulfills that mission: she finds her voice in a way that releases her from her surroundings and a coerced marriage; on the other hand, however, her story fails deeply in another way: it fails, through the soundscape, to excise Ada from a colonial enterprise and the male gaze.

The role of music and sound in this film and Ada's interactions with these elements are also notably shaped by Julia Kristeva's theories of language and Laura Mulvey's notion of the feminine gaze, whereby music bisects the occlusive, patriarchal order of language, the film's visuals, and the world depicted on-screen.[13] Just as Kaspar's enigma is reinforced by his inability to assimilate into the patriarchal order of narrative, Ada too remains something of an enigma to those around her, if not to the audience privy to her voice-overs. Sound interacts with the identities of these characters differently depending on their complicity and participation in their respective cultural frameworks and histories. Other factors beyond gender impact Ada's interactions with the film's soundscape and underscore conspicuous structures of power and oppression that determine Ada's own quest for language and agency. One cannot, for example, overlook the omnipresence of the white gaze and colonized imagery that both inspired and permeate the film. Campion cites both seeing old photographs of Māori women in European clothing and Emily Brontë's *Wuthering Heights* (1847) as inspiration for the film, transposing a European Romantic aesthetic onto a colonized landscape.[14] Campion's film has come under criticism (Margolis 2000, 19) for this colonized aesthetic and its depiction of the Māori people, highlighting the problematics of the crossing of physical and cultural borders in the film's visuals.[15]

These remarks, however, carry significance in the film's soundscape and ways to understand Ada's relationship to it through depicting oppositions that fail to be fully reconciled: she is both woman and colonist—both oppressed and oppressor—and neither clearly inside nor clearly outside, just as both the music produced in the film and her voice are similarly in sonically ambiguous spaces. As Kathleen McHugh has argued, Ada's voice-over at the beginning of the film about being married off to Alistair Stewart opens up an ambiguous sonic space, while also explicating her role as a commodity in a patriarchal and colonial environment: "Ada's statement simultaneously positions her as object of exchange (between her father and Stewart) and as a subject possessed of a colonial imaginary—she voices Stewart's proprietary relation to New Zealand. It also registers perspective and complexity of the film's narration. Though Campion received a lot of criticism for her representation of the Māori, her film nevertheless exercises an ongoing commentary on colonialism and its link to patriarchy, repression, and the containment and confinement of western women who nevertheless embody and perpetuate this proprietary ethos" (2001, 202). Since sound is the primary aesthetic means that marks her engagement with her surroundings, it too assumes the ambiguities of Ada's social positioning as visually and sonically depicted in the filmic medium. In the voice-over, the voice describing her origins and her silence is called "the mind's eye." Thus sound already performs an important epistemological gesture traversing opposing binaries: "*The Piano* opens to view the mind's eye; film as unfixable movement between subjective and objective, translucent and opaque" (Jacobs 1994, 770). Through creating from the beginning a space of aesthetic and social ambiguity, the film already sonically portrays the difficulties in crossing borders and attempts at doing so that trouble binaries in Ada's dual complicity and victimhood.

Other aesthetic ambiguities in the film's soundscape and images are compounded by the landscape and geographic, cultural, and political displacements. The most powerful vehicle by which this is recognizable is the music Ada plays on her piano and the film's nondiegetic music. The nondiegetic music represents displacements that make it difficult to pin down historical or geographic specificity: music for the film composed by Michael Nyman integrates modern components and traditional music from the period.[16] Ada's own compositions, which strike those around her as strange, draw on compositional features that are not strictly Romantic, as Claudia Gorbman remarks (1999, 52). Most compelling of these is "Ada's theme," which recurs throughout the film. For example, when Ada is taken to the beach where her piano was left after it had been deemed too heavy to carry, she begins playing it through the slats in the crate in which it has been kept. The music continues to underscore the scene as Ada and Flora walk on the beach, becoming nondiegetic music (figure 10.3).

A second instance occurs when Stewart violently cuts off Ada's finger with an ax in retaliation for her continued affair (although it isn't sexual at this stage) with Baines. As Gorbman describes the common musical underscoring of these scenes: "The film disregards the paradigm of music as illustration. . . . *The Piano* keeps its music fresh, so to speak, not functioning leitmotivically [*sic*] with fixed or even evolving signification. Instead, in eluding fixed meanings, the cues contribute to the film's impression of depth, openness, and psychological ambiguity" (1999, 53). In short, there is no one way to read the nondiegetic music, as it too is folded into a murky position of being both subjective and objective, inside and outside of diegesis.

As both a metaphorical and instrumental prop, the piano in Kaspar's story has a far more limited meaning and significance than it does in Ada's—at various points throughout the film, her story is directly and literally tied to the piano, and it is sustained as a key mode of self-expression that is denied in Kaspar's story. The piano as a prop belongs to a network of meanings and functions that shift throughout the film, which Campion herself describes (quoted in Hardy 1999, 62). Ann Hardy understands this in terms of the piano's use and perception by different characters: "Indeed, the central object and metaphor in the film itself, the piano, is placed to

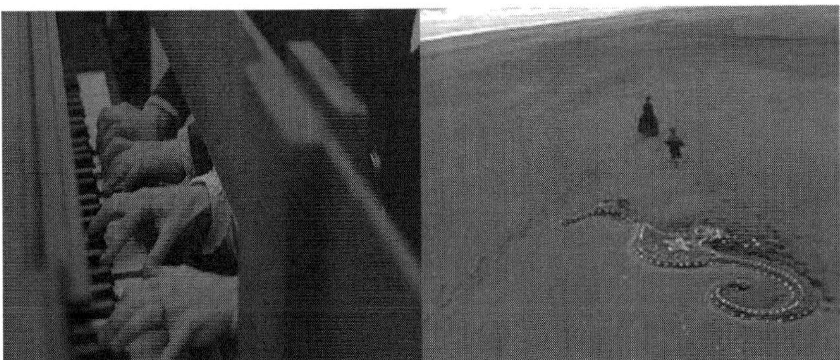

FIGURE 10.3. *The Piano*—Ada playing the piano, with the music becoming nondiegetic as the scene progresses. (Screengrab)

reflect that one entity-many meanings strategy. An object with a very specific iconic density and shape, it nonetheless produces one of the most evanescent forms of human expression. As a symbolic entity, the piano is polysemic, a producer of different meanings . . . for everyone in the film who sees it and uses it" (1999, 62). The physical presence of the piano makes it harder for Ada to fully extricate herself from the judgments and gazes of others and is initially a tool Baines employs to seduce her, but it is also her primary means of autonomy.

Additionally, the piano's physical presence is both anchored deeply in the diegesis and directly participates outside of the diegesis and outside of language. This is visible in the concluding sequences of the film, which have come under a high degree of criticism, most notably for their failure to conform to a wholly feminist interpretation. Originally intended to depict Ada's death (Childs 2013), the penultimate sequence shows Ada, Baines, and Flora leaving for Nelson with her piano on a boat steered by Māori. Following Ada's request to have the piano thrown overboard, she is tangled in the rope and submerged underwater with the instrument, but she manages to free herself and resurface. Her voice-over in the epilogue returns to the scene of submersion: "At night, I think of my piano in its ocean grave. And sometimes myself floating above it. Down there everything is so still and silent that it lulls me to sleep. It is a weird lullaby, and so it is, it is mine. There is a silence, we're happy, no sound" (figure 10.4).

FIGURE 10.4. *The Piano*—Ada's body tied to and suspended above the submerged piano in the epilogue. (Screengrab)

The otherworldly, subaquatic silence beyond the colonized landscape is her own language, and yet she is literally tied to the piano in that revelation. It seems, then, that the piano fully lives up to its status of doubled meaning: both liberating and lethal, the piano is how Ada extricates herself from her social and cultural environs but is also her end.

Had Campion kept the original ending with Ada suspended in her grave underwater paired with the voice-over at the end retrospectively reflecting on her submersion, the story told would have other implications. Ada's experiences reveal the struggle for agency articulated through the sonic landscape and how, when imbricated in a colonial setting, the nature of that agency, even if attainable to some degree, is both restricted and adulterated. If the patriarchy and colonialism are linked together, then Ada's relationship to music and the film's soundscape is one means by which such intermingling is both visible and audible. In the end, it is only the silence of a fictionalized aquatic grave, a dream that conjures a world within a world, that extricates her from the colonial enterprise. And in that world, there is no sound to delineate the borders crossed or to create ambiguously coded spaces.

## Sound and Challenging the Past

Spatial and historical displacements in both these films are realized and compounded through sonic displacements, as sound performs seemingly contradictory actions: it both limits and opens spaces and thereby heightens awareness of audiovisual and national spaces through their creation and disruption. As Jacques Attali observers: "Noise is inscribed from the start within the panoply of power. Equivalent to the articulation of space, [noise] indicates the limit of territory and the way to make one's self heard within it" (quoted in Durovičovà 2009, 90). This characterization resonates across Ada's and Kaspar's stories: each struggles to look for that articulation beyond merely speech and to utilize other means to delineate spaces and make themselves heard within them. And both struggle to do so in their respective stories with the means of expression available to them, though for different reasons, alluding to other spaces beyond both narration and the filmic medium in which such expressions might be possible.

However, Kaspar's story about the persistence of his enigma uncovers a pessimism in New German Cinema that fails to offer any redemptive pathway that would allow "the outsider within" to grasp its present and past. The film's soundscape and Kaspar's interaction with it tell the story of a cinema, of a nation, attempting to confront itself, though perhaps, like Kaspar, not quite ready or able to do so. The synthesis of key sound and image pairings shows a far rougher attempt at reconceptualizing social, aesthetic, and historical binaries than Campion's in *The Piano*. These displacements are never quite enough for someone to fully extricate themselves from a culture and its history; they offer means by which such an onerous task might be accomplished but still fail in varying degrees. The new orientations opened through the soundscape in *Kaspar Hauser* are self-reflexive, but they line Herzog's film up with tendencies that far exceed the parameters of New German Cinema alone, in which displacements through sound reveal the challenges of coming to terms with one's past, wherever that may be, and the silence that befalls one when one is unable to.

## Notes

1 The introduction to Timothy Corrigan's *New German Film: The Displaced Image* (1994) describes New German Cinema as a genre of displacements.

2 Corrigan expounds the role of history in *New German Film* (1994) and in the introduction to *The Films of Werner Herzog: Between Mirage and History* (1986, 7), as does Julia Knight in the introduction to *New German Cinema: Images of a Generation* (2004).

3 Stanley Cavell, *The World Viewed* (Cambridge, MA: Harvard University Press, 1977).

4 Scharf (2008, 150) draws on the phrase "outsider within" to characterize both Kaspar's experiences and a motif within New German Cinema.

5 Silverman 1981–82; Van Wert 1986; Peucker 1986; and Prager 2007 use language as a primary means for understanding Kaspar's inaccessibility. I focus on the acoustic dimension of Kaspar's experiences (not limited to language) throughout the film.

6 Scharf (2008, 150) elevates this to the question of national identity and belonging explicitly: "Hence, Kaspar is depicted as an 'outsider' within or an 'insider' outside who is ultimately destroyed due to—in national identity terms—the programmatic impossibility of his performative (in

its negative sense) identity position marked by personal/social 'homelessness' and resulting from the highly ambiguous relationship between the individual and his social realm."

7 Translations of German from the film are mine.
8 Prager (2007, 63) and Peucker (1986) discuss the literary origins of this quotation and the status of literary texts in Herzog's films.
9 Van Wert (1986, 69) calls silence in Herzog's films "musical" and notes how it functions as rests between music. I instead note their similarities.
10 Hillman (2012, 171) calls this an unconscious dimension. Corrigan (1994, 132, 141) discusses long static shots in *Kaspar Hauser* as "keys to Herzog's own cinematic vision and the alternative space he wishes to present."
11 Peucker (1986, 107) and Corrigan (1986, 11) identify interactions between the narrative and nonnarrative in Herzog's opus.
12 Sandra Frieden, Richard W. McCormick, Vibeke R. Petersen, and Laurie Melissa Vogelsang, eds., *Gender and German Cinema: Feminist Interventions*, vol. 1: *Gender and Representation in New German Cinema* (Providence, RI: Berg, 1993), iii.
13 For further discussion of the feminine and music in Campion's film, see Bihlmayer 2003.
14 Jane Campion, "New Again," an interview by Katherine Dieckmann and Michael Tabb, *Interview Magazine*, January 1992, https://www.interviewmagazine.com/film/new-again-jane-campion.
15 Margolis explores the question of New Zealand heritage in this film and situates the film's production and reception within attempts at grappling with legacies of colonialism in New Zealand.
16 Gorbman 1999 discusses different musical sources and inspirations for music in *The Piano*, including the stylistics.

## Works Cited

Allen, Richard. 2000. "Female Sexuality, Creativity and Desire in *The Piano*." In *Piano Lessons: Approaches to "The Piano,"* edited by Felicity Coombs and Suzanne Gemmell, 44–63. Sidney, Australia: John Libbey.

Ames, Eric, ed. 2014. *Werner Herzog: Interviews*. Jackson: University of Mississippi Press.

Bihlmayer, Jaimey. 2003. "Jane Campion's *The Piano*: The Female Gaze, the Speculum and the Chora within the H(y)st(e)rical Film." *Essays in Philosophy: A Biennial Journal* 4.1: np.

Childs, Ben. 2013. "Jane Campion Wanted a Bleaker Ending for *The Piano*." *Guardian*, July 8. https://www.theguardian.com/film/2013/jul/08/jane-campion-bleak-ending-the-piano.

Chion, Michel. 1994. *Audio-Vision: Sound on Screen*. Edited and translated by Claudia Gorbman. New York: Columbia University Press.

Cook, Pam. 1993. "Border Crossings: Women and Film in Context." In *A Sight and Sound Reader*, edited by Pam Cook and Philip Dodd, x–xxiii. Philadelphia: Temple University Press.

Corrigan, Timothy. 1986. Introduction to *The Films of Werner Herzog: Between Mirage and History*, edited by Timothy Corrigan, 1–19. New York: Methuen.

———. 1994. *New German Film: The Displaced Image*. Bloomington: Indiana University Press.

Cronin, Paul. 2002. *Herzog on Herzog*. London: Farber & Farber.

Deshpande, Shekhar, and Meta Mazaj. 2018. *World Cinema: A Critical Introduction*. New York: Routledge.

Durovičovà, Nataša. 2009. "Vector, Flow, Zone: Towards A History of Cinematic Translation." In *World Cinemas, Transnational Perspectives*, edited by Nataša Durovičovà and Kathleen Newman, 90–120. New York: Routledge.

Ebert, Roger. 1993. "*The Piano*." Review of *The Piano*, by Jane Campion. *RogerEbert.com*, November. https://www.rogerebert.com/reviews/the-piano-1993.

Flinn, Caryl. 2004. *The New German Cinema: Music, History, and the Matter of Style*. Berkeley: University of California Press.

Gorbman, Claudia. 1999. "Music in *The Piano*." In *Jane Campion's "The Piano,"* edited by Harriet Margolis, 42–58. Cambridge: Cambridge University Press.

Hardy, Ann. 1999. "The Last Patriarch." In *Jane Campion's "The Piano,"* edited by Harriet Margolis, 59–84. Cambridge: Cambridge University Press.

Hillman, Roger. 2012. "Coming to Our Senses: The Viewer and Herzog's Sonic Worlds." In *A Companion to Werner Herzog*, edited by Brad Prager, 168–86. Oxford: Wiley-Blackwell.

Jacobs, Carol. 1994. "Playing Jane Campion's Piano: Politically." *MLN* 109.5: 757–85.

Knight, Julia. 2004. *New German Cinema: Images of a Generation*. London: Wallflower Press.

Margolis, Harriet. 2000. Introduction to *Jane Campion's "The Piano,"* edited by Harriet Margolis, 1–42. Cambridge: Cambridge University Press.

McHugh, Kathleen. 2001. "Sounds That Creep inside You: Female Narration and Voiceover in Jane Campion's *The Piano*." *Style* 25.2: 193–218.

Morag, Raya. 2011. "Post-Trauma, Post-Queer: The Hitlerian Imago and New German Cinema." *New Review of Film and Television Studies* 9.4 (December): 472–92.

Peucker, Brigitte. 1986. "Writing and Literature in the Films of Werner Herzog." In *The Films of Werner Herzog: Between Mirage and History*, edited by Timothy Corrigan, 105–18. New York: Methuen.

———. 1995. *Incorporating Images: Film and the Rival Arts*. Princeton: Princeton University Press.

Prager, Brad. 2007. *Aesthetic Ecstasy and Truth: The Films of Werner Herzog*. London: Wildflower.

Sander, Helke. 1982. "Feminism and Film." Translated by Ramona Curry. *Jump Cut* 27: 49–50.

Scharf, Inga. 2008. *Nation and Identity in New German Cinema: Homeless at Home*. New York: Routledge.

Silverman, Kaja. 1981–82. "Kaspar Hauser's 'Terrible Fall' into Narrative." *New German Critique* 24–25: 73–93.

Van Wert, William. 1986. "Last Words: Observations on a New Language." In *The Films of Werner Herzog: Between Mirage and History*, edited by Timothy Corrigan, 51–71. New York: Methuen.

Wright, Les. 1998. "The Cycle of German Gay Coming-Out Films, 1970–1994." In *Queering the Canon: Defying Sights in German Literature and Culture*, edited by Christoph Lorey and John L. Plews, 311–39. Columbia, SC: Camden House.

11

# NEW HOLLYWOOD FASSBINDER

## Genre and Gender in Sam Peckinpah's *Cross of Iron* and Rainer Werner Fassbinder's *Querelle*

*Ian Fleishman*

As actor turned producer Dieter Schidor recalls, before agreeing to allow Jean Genet's *Querelle de Brest* (1947) to be adapted for the screen, Genet's publisher, Gallimard, "demanded the confirmation of an internationally recognized director. Since I had heard through many channels that Genet admired Sam Peckinpah's films, I did not go to Fassbinder but traveled instead to San Francisco to speak to Peckinpah" (1982, 7).[1] Well before Fassbinder, then, Peckinpah himself signed on as putative director for *Querelle* (1982), becoming the first in an illustrious list of potential auteurs approached, at different stages, to head the project: John Schlesinger, Roman Polański, and Martin Scorsese, among others. Also under consideration at later moments were Werner Schroeter and Bernardo Bertolucci; Schroeter even cowrote an early draft of the script with Burkhard Driest but didn't have the commercial name recognition necessary to secure funding for the project.[2] This constellation invites us, perhaps, to consider Fassbinder's *Querelle*, often understood to be the dying breath of the New *German* Cinema, in relation to New *Hollywood* and as of a piece with contemporary art cinema transnationally.

"It is not ironic," comments Christopher Sharrett, "that Peckinpah was a favorite director of Jean Genet." Rather, the kind of "male-oriented action-adventure fiction" for which Peckinpah was known "has as its basic subtext the description of a gay utopia where the male libido is unfettered and takes directions both destructive and liberatory" (1998, 91, 90).

New Hollywood's affinity for reworking such masculine genres (the gangster film, the western) is well documented.[3] The collaboration between Schidor and Burkhard Driest, whose company Planet-Film ultimately produced *Querelle*, in fact began on the set of Peckinpah's war film *Cross of Iron* (1977), as both actors have roles in both pictures.[4] (The earlier film also includes a number of actors who are part of Fassbinder's stable, including Klaus Löwitsch, who plays Corporal Krüger, and Roger Fritz, who plays Triebig.) In what follows, I'll probe the imbrication of genre—taken in the broad sense of predictable narrative paradigms—and gender across the Atlantic divide in *Cross of Iron* and *Querelle*, specifically examining the characters of Corporal Steiner in the first and Lieutenant Seblon in the second as indexes of the codes of authority (read: authorship), masculinity, and homosocial community symptomatized by each film.

Building on Paul Schrader's distinction between American movies (where people solve a problem) and European films (where they probe a dilemma), Thomas Elsaesser notes "the inability of the New Hollywood protagonist to take on the symbolic mandate that classical Hollywood narrative addressed to its heroes: to pursue a goal or respond to a challenge" (2004a, 63). Elsewhere, Elsaesser implicitly characterizes this as a perceived *feminization* of narrative convention: "the predicament of mainstream [American] cinema, when . . . attempting to represent in narrative-dramatic form the contradictions in American society, while having as its language only the behaviorist code of direct action and raw emotion, devised for an altogether different philosophy of life or masculine ideal" (2004b, 283). In Elsaesser's account, as its allegiances shift to less goal-oriented narratives, the New Hollywood *Autorenfilm* adopts from art cinema its "aimless, depressive or (self-)destructive" protagonists—this anxiety being, in turn, symptomatic of broader cultural sentiment in the 1970s: "The new behavioral norms of males . . . show the masculinist ethic in crisis. . . . At the same time, we can look at these ragged patterns of response as a 'working through' of the dislocations caused by the Vietnam war, and recognize in them the traumatic after-shocks to self-image and self-esteem" (2004a, 31, 63). Elsaesser's apt descriptions of the narrative form and character archetypes of American new wave filmmaking point to a double crisis at its core: a crisis of national consciousness (corresponding roughly to Elsaesser's pathos of failure) and a concomitant disruption of traditional conceptions of masculinity (personified in the unmotivated hero). Seduced but also discomfited by such new possibilities for his male protagonists, encoded, at least in *Cross of Iron*, as homosexuality, Peckinpah's work struggles within and against generic expectations; Fassbinder's, on the other hand, elevates masculine passivity to a desideratum, with important implications for the model of narrative closure, (masculine) authorship, and national belonging each film would appear to suggest in relation to New Hollywood and New German Cinema more globally.

## Peckinpah

Both films examined here are, fittingly, fundamentally international undertakings. Adapted from Willi Heinrich's novel *Das geduldige Fleisch* (*The Willing Flesh*, 1955), *Cross of Iron* was a British–West German co-production primarily shot on location in the former Yugoslavia. It features an international cast of American, English, and European actors speaking in a sometimes confusing hodgepodge of assorted accents. *Cross of Iron* premiered in West Germany, where it had the highest-grossing box office since *The Sound of Music* (1965), unlike in the United States, where it was a critical and commercial flop. Similarly, Fassbinder's *Querelle*, which debuted in Paris, was a co-production between France and West Germany with an equally international cast sloppily dubbed into English. Closing the loop, the war scenes in Fassbinder's *Lili Marleen* (1981) are, in fact, cobbled together out of unused footage shot by Peckinpah for *Cross of Iron*.

It has often been noted that New Hollywood Cinema in general and *Cross of Iron* in particular tacitly equate American disillusionment during and following the war in Vietnam to European despair following the Second World War. Perhaps most significant, given the argument I am making, the central thesis of Raya Morag's volume dedicated to crises of masculinity in New German Cinema and New Hollywood–era films is that "the defeated male takes the place of defeat" in the Second World War and the war in Vietnam (2009, 18). At a certain moment, Elsaesser similarly comes to read New Hollywood through Gilles Deleuze's description of European cinema, revealing these crises of diminished masculinity and national defeat to be running themes across European and American new wave cinemas: "The Deleuzian schema, applied to Hollywood of the 1970s, brings us back to the purported European influence, but now mediated by specifically American crises—the war in Vietnam, the corruption of the offices of state, the changing nature of post-industrial society—which would then correspond to the no less or even more traumatic experience of Europe after WWII and the Holocaust, reverberating, according to Deleuze, in neorealism (Rossellini, Antonioni), the nouvelle vague (Godard, Rivette) and the New German cinema (Wenders, Fassbinder)" (2004a, 65). More immediately, as Andrew Britton glosses the historical backdrop of New Hollywood: "For the first time, an active mass defeatism existed in a Western capitalist country during wartime" (2008b, 75). Of *Cross of Iron*, specifically, Britton contends that "the film is about Vietnam [and] can be so in the way it is only because it is ostensibly about the retreat of the German army from the Soviets in 1943" (92). But if *Cross of Iron*—which depicts the retreat of German forces from the eastern front—indeed allegorizes the contemporary conflict through its manifest historical subject matter, it does so by allowing an oddly sanitized form of fascism to represent the American perspective.

Indispensable to this metonymic displacement is the shared imaginary of an all-male homosocial community, a masculinist fantasy linking fascism to genres such as the war film more generally. The perplexing association in the cultural imagination between fascism and homosexuality has long since been established, most painstakingly by Andrew Hewitt, who highlights the tendency of each to stand in tacitly for the other (1996, 9).[5] Britton, who addresses the homoerotic subtext of *Cross of Iron* in two essays, at first dismisses this "popular belief that every member of the Nazi Party was gay, and that fascism and gayness are virtually synonymous"—but then arguably comes close to resuscitating an altered version of it when he implies that the film's fear of Communism and its closetedness or homophobia are linked: "It is crucial to our sense of the film's significance that its political despair and its inability fully to confront its sexual themes are intimately related to one another" (2008a, 287, 2008b, 95).[6] Taking a broader view, David Greven notes that "while homosexuality informs several important New Hollywood films, it is only intermittently treated in explicit fashion. . . . Diegetically, homosexuality is relegated to the margins, yet shown to be a pervasive, implicit threat registered within the larger crisis in masculinity at the center of so many 1970s films. Not just registering this crisis, New Hollywood films strove to make sense of the shifting, unstable state of masculinity in the decade" (2013, 11). Perhaps it is more accurate, then, to speak of condensation (*Verdichtung*) in *Cross of Iron*: a collapse, in multiple senses, of homosexuality, fascism, national belonging, and gender norms.

In any event, as Britton has it, it is precisely "the war [that] is the necessary condition for the existence of the 'world without women' which provides the male group with its basis" (2008b, 93). Fassbinder's *Querelle* famously only has one significant female role, the brothel keeper Lysiane (Jeanne Moreau), whom Fassbinder insisted embodied for him the woman as such. Similarly, other than a group of (quite literally) castrating female Russian soldiers toward the end of *Cross of Iron*, its only female figure is a nurse, Eva (Senta Berger), with whom Steiner has an aborted affair, choosing instead his company of men. Britton comments insightfully on how these moments relate to one another: "Steiner needs the war, Eva implies, because it provides a setting for, and justifies, the commitment to men which would otherwise be recognized as sexual; . . . she introduces a disturbance which must also, through the Russian women-soldiers, be exorcized" (2009b, 94).[7] War, in this account, is but a necessary pretext for an otherwise disavowed homosocial erotic bonding.

As Britton notes, Peckinpah alternately highlights and performatively represses this element, setting loose but then ultimately policing any underlying same-sex desire. An early sequence, for instance, introducing the audience to Steiner's platoon, portrays one soldier kissing another aggressively on the lips as a means of calming a hysterical outburst. This moment is crosscut with a deliciously sinister scene in which the devious Captain Stranksy, observing an act of affection between two soldiers, Triebig and Keppler, inveigles a confession of homosexuality that he exploits throughout the remainder of the film. While Peckinpah scholarship has commented on the scene, the ambivalence of the entrapment has never, to my knowledge, been noted: Stransky elicits the confession through a ruse of seduction (the phrase "world without women" is, in fact, his, its delivery palpably exuding lechery), and even while threatening to out the other soldiers, he lasciviously repeats the caress he had witnessed earlier. This subterfuge is not dissimilar to how the film, framed through Steiner's gaze, gaybaits its viewer, enjoining but then punishing cathexis in the young men under his watch through the cruel death of almost every member of the unit.

More largely, it ought to be acknowledged that Stranksy embodies all the clichéd attributes of "the vicious, European, aristocratic gay man"

(Britton 2009a, 88), thus painting a blurry, phobic, cultural portrait of "homosexuality" divorced from—and in unsteady opposition to—same-sex desire or sexual activity.[8] It is significant that the possibility of this character's gayness is never fully foreclosed, as the main narrative tension is between the rugged, manly Steiner and the well-bred sissy Stransky. As so often in Peckinpah, Steiner and Stransky refigure the common New Hollywood trope of "the male couple ganging up to escape society and women" as a form of enmity (Elsaesser 2004b, 286).[9] *The Wild Bunch* (1969), for instance, and *Pat Garret and Billy the Kid* (1973) both center around an outlaw pursued by his former partner, with undeniable romantic undertones and all the affective charge one might expect from jilted lovers. There is a similarly romantic quality to the fraught past between Dundee (Charlton Heston) and Tyreen (Richard Harris) in *Major Dundee* (1965).[10] But in Steiner's stubborn but glorified refusal to "submit" to Stranksy's authority, the specter of homosexuality doubly looms as both the impetus (personified in Stransky) and the instrument (incarnated in Triebig) of this antagonism.

It should be noted, then, that the most cathartic violence in the film occurs when Steiner vindictively and excessively guns down the overtly homosexual Triebig in front of his paramour. This act of vengeance is preceded by a variation on a recurring montage interspersing the many fallen soldiers with those still on the battlefield and terminating with the young Russian boy whose life Steiner had unsuccessfully attempted to spare at the conclusion of the film's first act. If the brutal overkill of machine-gun fire with which Steiner does away with Triebig is typical of the director, its gratuitous reprisal in slow motion, clouds of smoke billowing behind James Coburn as he is shot from a low angle, is *classic* Peckinpah.

What renders the moment even more pornographic is the utterly superfluous stabbing of Triebig's body by another soldier, as if the entirety of the homosocial community must join together in the exorcism (by an act of penetration no less) of the vampiric homo*sexual* element. Tellingly, this also appears to relieve Steiner from his duty to his remaining men, whom he abandons immediately hereafter. Gabrielle Murray has insisted that, "in certain works like . . . *Cross of Iron* . . . a utopian impulse exists at the heart of violent action" (2004, 2). Simultaneously consummating and disavowing same-sex desire, the orgiastic release of Triebig's murder is the closest *Cross of Iron* will come to fulfilling its underlying vision of a masculinist utopia.

FIGURE 11.1. *Cross of Iron*—James Coburn as Steiner. (Screengrab)

Peckinpah had apparently intended the film to conclude with Steiner and Stranksy coming to realize, as David Weddle phrases it, "that the masculine mythology of glorious conquest and grace under pressure was a sham" and disappearing together into the fog of war as if riding off into the sunset at the end of a western (1994, 56).[11] Instead, in a razor-sharp ending that was, for financial reasons, largely improvised, Steiner takes an improbably paternalistic revenge, an education cum symbolic castration: his chilling laugh reverberating over the film's final images as he watches Stranksy struggle and fail to reload his weapon. That Stranksy would be subjected to this impotence and humiliation but not the ruthless on-screen execution of Triebig points to a paradox in the film's treatment of male homosexuality: through the tough love Steiner shows to Stranksy, the supposed virtue of the brute masculine ideal is rehabilitated, but the utopian possibility the film had implicitly posited for the homosocial community collapses under its performative repudiation of same-sex desire. By the same gesture the film retracts the narrative satisfaction it had just provided through the death of Triebig, opting instead for an open and ambivalent ending. Perhaps unready fully to countenance the sexual politics of the male-oriented genre film or to escape its unspoken prescriptions for masculinity, Peckinpah has his protagonist nihilistically affirm the meaninglessness of violence for its own sake.[12]

## FASSBINDER

Joanne Leal sees New German Cinema as a wholesale rejection of Hollywood masculinity: "When the first post-war generation developed its own New German Cinema, this represented not only a rejection of 'Opas Kino' but also a refusal of its conservative models of masculinity. American cinema became in this context . . . a significant point of reference not only in the attempt to revitalize West German cinema but also to reconceptualize a West German masculinity conceived with reference to its American counterpart" (2012, 60–61). Hester Baer, focusing on the West German films that were the target of critique of the Oberhausen Manifesto, takes a dimmer view, aligning authorship with an attempt at *renewed* manliness and arguing that "the push for a New German Cinema . . . was predicated on a gender realignment . . . an embrace of the new wave, with its associations of virile masculinity. Signed by a cadre of angry young men, the 'Oberhausen Manifesto' clearly reproduced this correlation of the avant-garde and masculinity and thus appeared to initiate a transition in both film authorship and representation" (2009, 264).[13] Negotiating with typical panache between these two extremes, Fassbinder's *Querelle* can be understood to "out" the closeted elements—same-sex desire, the libidinal investment in violence, a fascination with fascism—informing works like Peckinpah's, deconstructing the mythologies on which New Hollywood machismo is based through the hyperbolic imitation of a kind of inverted drag performance.[14] After all, *Querelle* takes as its ambiguously parodic point of departure something akin to New Hollywood's wantonly violent and fiercely solitary male protagonist: Fassbinder's antihero, true to Genet's novel, murders without reason or discernible motivation.

While *Querelle* was ultimately filmed entirely in studio in Berlin, Schidor's initial intention appears to have been to shoot the film in the United States, "with New Orleans as Brest, the American navy instead of French merchant vessels [but] [t]he producers and studios in Hollywood thought I was crazy" (Schidor 1982, 8). Just as *Cross of Iron* explores American society through the foil of the German military, *Querelle*, as originally conceived, would have transplanted its French setting into the context of the American armed forces. Absent this military aspect, however, the bloodshed in *Querelle* is denied any pretense of narrative purpose. Asked whether violence is the main theme of the film, Fassbinder rather fuzzily replies: "One must descend into the deepest depths of this society in order to free himself for a new one or to be able to free himself" (quoted in Schidor 2004, 621). Fassbinder's protagonist thus gives himself over entirely to the darkest instincts habitually imputed to the male libido, worryingly perpetuating a form of what Richard Slotkin has influentially identified as the redemptive "regeneration through violence" central to the mythology of the American frontier and the structure of the western (1973).[15] While hardly a genre film in any obvious sense, through its exaggerated Village People–esque costuming (the sailor in stripes and clichéd cap, the leather-clad cop, the officer adorned with epaulets, the hard hat–donning mason), Fassbinder's film seems in equal parts a celebration and a send-up of gender *as* genre.

And if gay sex in *Querelle* feels as readily available as in a porno, punctuating the rather scrambled plot with soft-core asides corresponding, in a very real sense, to Peckinpah's battle sequences,[16] Genet biographer Edmund White is nonetheless not far off when he famously describes the source text as "a violent story of homosexual love among heterosexual men" (1993, 290).[17] Fassbinder comes to a similar conclusion when he insists that "in *Querelle*, though, homosexuality isn't an issue at all" (quoted in Schidor 2004, 621). Fassbinder's film indeed so readily and so thoroughly naturalizes a primary bisexuality in a world (almost) without women that the very identity category of the homosexual all but vanishes. If the violence of wartime provides a necessary narrative pretext for Peckinpah's exploration of homosocial bonding, Fassbinder's *Querelle* desublimates this violence into what it arguably always represented: an erotic charge between men. In so doing, *Querelle* perhaps reveals the whole question of homosexuality to be but a smoke screen for larger political concerns—merely a symbolic meeting point between crises of masculinity and community.

It seems to be this aspect of the film that constitutes, for Fassbinder, a utopian endeavor. Asked by Schidor in the final hours of his life why he would have chosen to make *Querelle* immediately after three films focusing on women (*Lili Marleen* and *Lola* in 1981, *Die Sehnsucht der Veronika Voss* the following year), Fassbinder replies: "Those weren't women's films I was making but rather films about society, *whereas Querelle is really a utopian endeavor in opposition to society*. That's where I want to mark the distinction rather than between women's films / men's films. These [earlier] films were meant to depict society as precisely as possible. That works better with women. But *Querelle* is about an attempt at a society that might still be wonderful despite all its repulsiveness" (quoted in Schidor 2004, 617; my emphasis). Barely concealed in this assertion is the implication that women are trapped in the society in which they find themselves whereas men have the capacity, at least, to break free through an exploration and an embrace of all that is abject in that society. But if Peckinpah's incapacity to face the homoerotic undertones of his subject matter unflinchingly ultimately leads him into nihilism, Fassbinder's foregrounding of this aspect flirts with fascism, as he himself readily admits: "Every conceivable utopia of course harbors the danger of fascoid moments" (quoted in Schidor 1992, 617). Geneviève Sellier has noted the difficulty of French Nouvelle Vague auteurs to accept the fact that "heroic virility" has become "associated with the most retrograde of political values": "It is as if the creator in our culture, even when he is sincerely 'on the left,' could not fantasmatically affirm himself except in the mode of the most traditional of virile values: physical courage, the refusal of all social or affective ties, and the confrontation with death" (2009, 144). Similarly, Fassbinder surprisingly affirms the masculinist code of virile action as a perilous but necessary path toward building a better world.

It is perhaps possible to isolate the exact moment where the film attempts to sublate its own entanglement with fascist violence into another form of homosocial utopia in one of the final and climactic exchanges between the sailor Querelle (played by Brad Davis) and his commanding officer, Lieutenant Seblon (Franco Nero), who serves as a quasi-extradiegetic figure and supplementary narrator throughout. Discovering Seblon's dictaphone, which in an earlier version of the script had alternately been a telescope and a camera, Querelle becomes privy to the officer's most intimate and most violent fantasies:

> But loved by Querelle, I would be loved by every sailor in France. Because Querelle is a compendium of all their masculine and naïve virtues. If I desire authority, this admirable form which evokes love and fear, then I must awaken a feeling for this authority in the heart of the sailors. They ought to love me, I want to be their father. And injure them. I shall mark them. They will hate me. In the face of their misery, I shall remain unmoved. More and more, the feeling of perfect power will fill my being.

If this first half of Seblon's recorded soliloquy intermingles emphatically fascist power fantasies of authority, violence, and homosexual desire coalescing around Querelle, who serves synecdochically for masculinity as such, this dream is revealed to be a sham the moment Seblon appears on-screen:

> Having conquered my compassion, I shall be strong and sad when I regard my pathetic disguise. I know that I will never leave Querelle. My whole life will be dedicated to him. When I suffer, I cannot believe in God. In pain, all I can count on is myself and the misfortune for which I have someone else to thank.

At this point, Querelle pulls a knife on Seblon, who commands him with an almost erotic fervor to stab him but is saved by the continued playback of the dictaphone:

> We have Jesus to thank that we are able to glorify humility. For he made it the sign of the divine. The godhead in our innermost depths. For why should we renounce the violence of this world? If this godhead is to confront violence, then it must be strong if it is to achieve the victory. And humility can only be born of humiliation, otherwise it is nothing but vanity.

This monologue is Fassbinder's film at its most didactic, and through Querelle's on-screen reaction the audience is instructed, perhaps, as to how we ourselves are intended to interpret and respond to this switch point between an eroticized sadism and a no less masculine masochism. Kaja Silverman notably almost entirely elides *Querelle* from her analysis of masochistic and utopian, feminist masculinity in Fassbinder because, contrary to her preferred model—as Roy Grundmann insists—*Querelle* "deidealizes masculinity without dephallicizing it" (Silverman 1982; Grundmann 2012, 582). Such an embrace of male passivity as I am sketching here might, then, bring *Querelle* into unexpected alignment with more frequently studied works by Fassbinder and those focused on by Silverman.

Hector Kollias (2006), among others, has demonstrated how Genet's novel already associated passivity with virility by dint of the affirmation of abjection in bottoming. In Fassbinder's adaptation, Seblon's elevation of passivity is apparently supposed to be contagious. Initially, the officer is physically subordinated to Querelle, standing at the bottom of the staircase and shot from a high angle. But as the background monologue continues toward its surprising deus ex machina in an incongruous evocation of Christ, the camera rises, as if Seblon were growing in stature, and tracks in on Querelle, who visibly melts in reaction to the words he is hearing. A supple tilt down Brad Davis's taut body to the knife he is holding suggests, as do so many other shots throughout the film, that Seblon's is the narrative perspective, implicating the viewer as well in homoerotic desire; the extreme low angle from which Querelle is shot (an inversion of the image of Steiner standing over the corpse of Triebig) as he follows the instruction to put away his knife serves as visual confirmation of Seblon's assertion that the greatest power in the face of violence resides in abdicating control. This is further confirmed by the film's dénouement, as Querelle chases Seblon up a staircase to the brothel, begging to be laid across his legs like a *pietà*.

In a dramatic departure from the novel, Seblon and Querelle thus come to the reconciliation lacking, mutatis mutandis, between the odd couple Steiner and Stranksy—unexpectedly providing the satisfaction of limited narrative resolution missing at the open end of *Cross of Iron*. Hesitantly, then, and not unproblematically, *Querelle* might also hint at the variety of redemptive marriage plots through which myths of regenerative violence sustain themselves—the kind of happily-ever-after Murray (2004) insists that Peckinpah's films refuse. Even in its taking homosexuality for granted and its paean to passivity, Fassbinder's film appears unable entirely to escape received tropes of masculinity.

## Auteur Erased

"The paradox of the New Hollywood," writes Elsaesser, "was that the loss of confidence of the nation . . . did little to stifle the energies . . . of young filmmakers. They registered the moral malaise, but it did not blunt their appetite for stylistic or formal experiment" (2004a, 31). Thus Elsaesser appears to intimate that this new American investment in formal innovation might in some sense respond precisely to a crisis in the masculinist ethic, as if European avant-gardism could serve as a compensatory mechanism for the loss of compelling (meta)narratives (63). Just as Baer (2009)

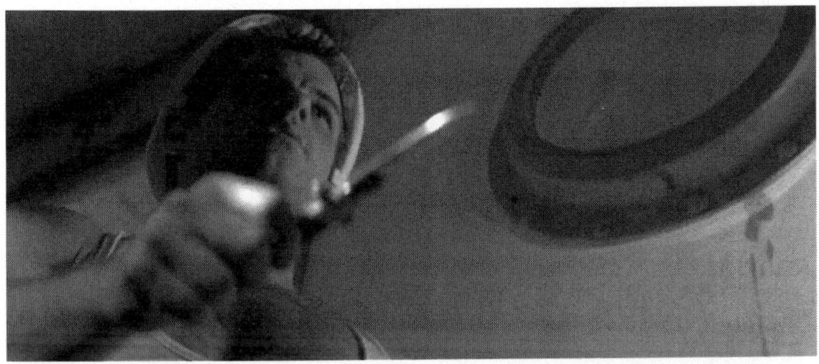

FIGURES 11.2 AND 11.3. *Querelle*—Querelle with knife confronting Seblon. (Screengrabs)

has compellingly excavated the masculinist impulse behind the emphasis on auteurism among the signatories of the Oberhausen Manifesto, one might conclude that, if New Hollywood is indeed the site of a (re)negotiation of national and masculine ideals through a shift in narrative form, then, in this light, the attempt to transpose a European model of the (at least in this context, most often male) art cinema auteur into a Hollywood studio setting might be rightly viewed as the unsteady self-assertion of a wounded or self-questioning masculinity. Ironically, this doubt will only be compounded by an auteurist narrative model, which seldom provides the reassuring closure of masculine genres but rather fundamentally tends to upend it.

Asked in his final interview whether he had ever been tempted to work in Hollywood or "to create a kind of German Hollywood," Fassbinder recalls: "At one point that was my explicit thinking. What I want is a Hollywood cinema, a cinema that is as wonderful and universally understandable as Hollywood, but at the same time not as mendacious" (quoted in Schidor 2004, 622). If the European influence lends artistic autonomy but also an unfamiliar and often uncomfortable sense of narrative openness to New Hollywood endeavors, Fassbinder's ideal for a new German cinema would seem to be to meet America halfway, having recourse to the legibility and universality of Hollywood even in a work as obviously avant-garde as *Querelle.*

This desire points to a potentially telling, if subtle, chiasmus in the approach to authorship decipherable in Peckinpah and Fassbinder: both obliquely attempt to lay bare the gender implications of the genre film, but whereas this leaves Peckinpah with only the hollowed-out husks of the cultural values a war movie traditionally represents, it puts Fassbinder's film in the position of advocating the institution of *new* values it can only vaguely and insufficiently distinguish from a Hollywood happy ending. Leal makes a similar claim with specific regard to Fassbinder's treatment of masculinity:

> Fassbinder is . . . criticizing what are presented as "Americanized" gender identities. . . . The Western patriarchal gender norms reinforced by classic Hollywood cinema are regarded as anachronistic, not overly fluid but on the contrary dangerously rigid. Fassbinder does not, however, propose a German substitute for the gender dynamics he critiques. In what might appear to be a largely negative conclusion, the experiences of his characters suggest that there is in fact no alternative to their enforced performance of debilitating but authoritative gender roles. It is, of course, possible to frame positively the proposition that there is no such thing as an "authentic" masculinity, German or otherwise. Indeed, Fassbinder's anti-Hollywood gesture consists precisely in his subversive exposure of the performative nature of gender identities, something classic cinema attempts to hide by insisting on the "regulatory fiction" of the naturalness of the gender norms it promotes. (2012, 68)[18]

But while Leal is right to emphasize the ineluctability of normative gender paradigms as they appear in Fassbinder, the deconstruction of gender in his films is not, as this would seem to imply, reducible to Brechtian estrangement or parody by hyperbole. It also reposes, in *Querelle* at least, on the paradoxical—and, admittedly, perhaps not entirely persuasive or coherent—equation of virility and passivity and on a relinquishing of (narrative) control that also entail the potential for self-deconstruction or even self-destruction.

Both films discussed here conclude, after all, with an enigmatic unraveling: Peckinpah's with Stranksy being fired upon by the same cherubic actor who had played the slain Russian boy at the heart of the initial conflict with Steiner; Fassbinder's with an image almost indistinguishably played in reverse and the indecipherable declaration that the titular figure never existed to begin with. It is worth noting that the two protagonists I have examined serve not only as filmic focalizers but, more pointedly, as "auteur" figures: Steiner through his association with the trippy montage sequences illustrating his inner turmoil (thus aligning him with montage, with the ordering of images itself),[19] Seblon through his overt position as sometimes narrator and consistent cinematic voyeur. As diegetic stand-ins for notoriously difficult directors both nearing the bottom of a downward spiral of self-destructive behavior discernible in their final films, these figures testify, perhaps, to the difficulties inherent in authorial experimentation within the strict constraints of the only available models of masculinity.[20]

## Notes

1 Unless otherwise noted, all translations are my own.

2 As Thomas Elsaesser notes, it was only with the success of *Die Ehe der Maria Braun* in New York and Paris that Fassbinder became a viable contender in this lineup: "It gave Fassbinder the chance to outbid Werner Schroeter by allowing Dieter Schidor, the producer and originator of the project, to conclude a contract with Gaumont for co-financing *Querelle*, and thus ensure world-wide distribution for what would become his last film" (1996, 99).

3 Alexander Horwath, for instance, speaks of the dual genealogy of Hollywood cinema: on the one hand, the genre film or B-film in the vein of Roger Corman and, on the other, the "acknowledged debt" to the "modernist elements" inherited from European art cinema (2003, 83). For the overlap in personnel between New Hollywood and European new wave cinemas, see Horwath 2003, 87.

4 For Schidor's account of the beginnings of Planet-Film and of *Querelle* on the set of *Cross of Iron*, see his interview with Kurt Raab (Raab and Peters 1982, 333–46, especially 337).

5 See also Halberstam 2011.

6 Britton would seem to prefer an egalitarian homosociality in the American tradition of Herman Melville or Walt Whitman, whom he sees aligned with Sergei Eisenstein.

7 Bernard F. Dukore (2012) compares the figure played by Senta Berger in this film to the one she played in *Major Dundee* (1965).

8 Britton's phrase here refers not to Stranksy but rather to a character from Steve Carver's *Drum* (1976). Britton does not seem to regard Stransky as coded homosexual, referring instead to Triebig as "a gay Machiavel," although Stransky is inarguably the mastermind behind the betrayal of the homosocial unit (2009b, 94).

9 On the example of *Easy Rider*, which Elsaesser reads as paradigmatic for New Hollywood, he connects the "double male lead" and, more pointedly, "the sentimental love story of the all-male couple" directly to the "open-ended, loose-structured narrative, so often imitated since" (2004b, 286). For Paryz, who similarly alludes to male same-sex couple formations in more than one of Peckinpah's films, it is Steiner's subordinate, Schnurrbart, who acts as his "wife" and "mother" to the platoon (2011, 330). One might see Colonel Brandt (played by James Mason) and Captain Kiesel (David Warner) as another such couple. As Cordell Strug points out: "Brandt himself would be an adequate hero for a war story; add Kiesel, with his cynical outsider's detachment, and you have a decent pair of ordinary heroes who complement each other: figures of integrity and competence, with no illusions" (2012, 144–45).

10 For a discussion of such homoerotics across Peckinpah's oeuvre, see Sharrett 2014.

11 Marek Paryz reads *Cross of Iron* as an example of "the symbolic narrative paradigm of the post-Western" (2011, 322). More pointedly, Paryz, following Will Wright, describes the film as exemplary of the "professional Western": "This group of strong men, formed as a fighting unit, comes to exist independently and apart from society. . . . The social values of justice, order and peaceful domesticity have been replaced by a clear commitment to strength, skill, enjoyment of the battle and masculine companionship" (Wright 1975, 86, quoted in Paryz 2011, 323). Similarly, Drehli Robnik (2004) reads New Hollywood war films as allegories of post-Fordist production.

12 For Elsaesser, the violence or machismo of New Hollywood protagonists merely reflects varying degrees of panic: "the defensive gesture of a self-alienated male in a society he does not understand and over which he has no control" (2004b, 283). See also, in the same volume, Martin 2004.
13 See especially Baer's chapter on Herbert Vesley's *Das Brot der frühen Jahre* (1962) (2009, 257–77).
14 We might see this as akin to the kind of parody by exaggeration of masculinity Jack Halberstam (1998) identifies in the practice of drag kinging.
15 Slotkin's findings (1992) have often been discussed in the context of Peckinpah, most extensively by Murray in *This Wounded Cinema* (2004). Slotkin himself has a chapter on Peckinpah's *The Wild Bunch* in light of the My Lai massacre in Vietnam.
16 Al LaValley, for instance, sees the film as negotiating between "the art house film and the independent and/or gay cinema, even gay pornography" (1994, 133). This is, on its own, a potentially utopian aspect of the film. Steven Marcus (1966), for instance, has coined the term *pornotopia* to describe the constant and easy availability of sexual activity in pornography. Rich Cante and Angelo Restivo (2004) have further elaborated this concept with specific regard to gay pornography. As early as 1989, Linda Williams applies Richard Dyer's categories of utopianism in the movie musical to her analysis of pornography, examining "utopian 'numbers' [sex scenes] that represent solutions to narrative problems" (1999, 270). A few years later, Dyer himself notes how "the effective multiplication of sex acts through elaborate narrativity [in gay porn] is an analogue for a (utopian) model of a gay sexual lifestyle that combines basic romanticism with an easy acceptance of promiscuity" (1992, 130). Dyer's thinking is also one of the key theoretical perspectives informing Murray's treatment of violence and utopia in Peckinpah (Murray 2004, especially 71–72). For a more thorough discussion of the links between this pornographic utopianism and fascism, see Fleishman 2021, 2022.
17 As Caryl Flinn summarizes: "*Querelle* produces a queer male community that appears to be organized around sameness yet is not, its group irreducible to a single identity. Scarcely characters, or even gay characters, these male figures seem to embody tensions and charges that move in a number of different directions at once, directions not adequately covered by categories of sex" (2012, 325).
18 Grundmann concurs that while *Querelle* "stops short of envisioning concrete alternative communities (a fortunate aspect, no doubt, since many such visions tend to be idealizing), the transformation of the self that it depicts is so radical that it also requires us to rethink the relation between

self and others—indeed it asks us to rethink relationality as a very mode. In this sense, *Querelle* shifts the emphasis from existing alternative communities to hypothetical modes of communal alterity" (2012, 589).

19 Curiously, in the scandalous *Straw Dogs* (1971), it is the figure of Amy Sumner (Susan George) whose traumatized mental state during and following her rape dictates the associative editing of such sequences. Within the highly complex and profoundly problematic gender politics of this film, it is perhaps possible, on a meta-reflective level, to identify a kind of lover's quarrel between such a muddled feminized montage and the meticulous masculinized mise-en-scène or cinematography represented by the Rube Goldberg domestic defenses David Sumner (Dustin Hoffmann) orchestrates in the film's climactic sequence.

20 As Cordell Strug notes of Peckinpah's final films, for instance: "It was hard not to view them through the haze of stories about Peckinpah's deterioration" (2012, 137). Regarding Fassbinder's work on *Querelle*, Jürgen Trimborn comments: "If he had up until this point always been the master of his powers for all of his films, now for the first time control over his film and also over himself was slipping out of his hands" (2012, 388).

## Works Cited


Baer, Hester. 2009. *Dismantling the Dream Factory: Gender, German Cinema, and the Postwar Quest for a New Film Language*. New York: Berghahn Books, 2009.

Britton, Andrew. 2009a. "Sexuality and Power; or, The Two Others (1977–1978)." In *Britton on Film: The Complete Film Criticism of Andrew Britton*, edited by Barry Keith Grant, 287–311. Detroit: Wayne State University Press.

———. 2009b. "Sideshows: Hollywood in Vietnam (1981)." In *Britton on Film: The Complete Film Criticism of Andrew Britton*, edited by Barry Keith Grant, 74–96. Detroit: Wayne State University Press.

Cante, Rich, and Angelo Restivo. 2004. "The Cultural-Aesthetic Specificities of All-Male Moving-Image Pornography." In *Porn Studies*, edited by Linda Williams, 142–66. Durham: Duke University Press.

Dukore, Bernard F. 2012. "Make War, Not Love: Sam Peckinpah's *Major Dundee* and *Cross of Iron*." *Journal of Film and Video* 64.6 (Winter): 50–56.

Dyer, Richard. 1992. "Coming to Terms: Gay Pornography." In *Only Entertainment*, 121–34. London: Routledge.

Elsaesser, Thomas.1996. *Fassbinder's Germany: History, Identity, Subject.* Amsterdam: Amsterdam University Press.

———. 2004a. "American Auteur Cinema: The Last—or First?—Picture Show?" In *The Last Great American Picture Show: New Hollywood Cinema in the 1970s*, edited by Thomas Elsaesser, Alexander Horwath, and Noel King, 37–69. Amsterdam: Amsterdam University Press.

———. 2004b. "The Pathos of Failure: American Films in the 1970s: Notes on the Unmotivated Hero." In *The Last Great American Picture Show: New Hollywood Cinema in the 1970s*, edited by Thomas Elsaesser, Alexander Horwath, and Noel King, 279–92. Amsterdam: Amsterdam University Press.

Fleishman, Ian. 2021. "'Naturgeil': Homo-Eco-Erotic Utopianism in Hitler Youth Film Propaganda and 'Boy Scout' Porn." *Colloquia Germanica* 53.2–3: 269–88.

———. 2022. "Rolf Hammerschmidt's *Boytropolis* and the Ethno-Ecological Imaginary." *Environmental Humanities* 14.3: 680–98.

Flinn, Caryl. 2012. "Declined Invitations: Repetition in Fassbinder's Queer 'Monomusical.'" In *A Companion to Rainer Werner Fassbinder*, edited by Brigitte Peucker, 313–32. Chichester: Wiley Blackwell.

Greven, David. 2013. *Psycho-Sexual: Male Desire in Hitchcock, DePalma, Scorsese and Friedkin*. Austin: University of Texas Press.

Grundmann, Roy. 2012. "*Querelle*'s Finality." In *A Companion to Rainer Werner Fassbinder*, edited by Brigitte Peucker, 579–603. Chichester: Wiley Blackwell.

Halberstam, Jack. 1998. *Female Masculinity*. Durham: Duke University Press.

———. 2011. "'The Killer in Me Is the Killer in You': Homosexuality and Fascism." In *The Art of Queer Failure*, 147–71. Durham: Duke University Press.

Hewitt, Andrew. 1996. *Political Inversions: Homosexuality, Fascism and the Modernist Imaginary*. Stanford: Stanford University Press.

Horwath, Alexander. 2004. "A Walking Contradiction (Partly Truth and Partly Fiction)." In *The Last Great American Picture Show: New Hollywood Cinema in the 1970s*, edited by Thomas Elsaesser, Alexander Horwath, and Noel King, 83–105. Amsterdam: Amsterdam University Press.

Kollias, Hector. 2006. "Jean Genet's Queer Origins: A Reading of *Querelle de Brest*." *French Studies* 60.4: 479–88.

LaValley, Al. 1994. "The Gay Liberation of Rainer Werner Fassbinder: Male Subjectivity, Male Bodies, Male Lovers." *New German Critique* 63 (Autumn): 108–37.

Leal, Joanne. 2012. "American Cinema and the Construction of Masculinity in Film in the Federal Republic After 1945." *German Life and Letters* 65.1: 59–72.

Marcus, Steven. 1966. "Conclusion: Pornotopia." In *The Other Victorians: A Study of Sexuality and Pornography in Mid-Nineteenth-Century England*, 266–86. New York: Basic Books.

Martin, Adrian. 2004. "Grim Fascination: *Fingers*, James Toback and 1970s American Cinema." In *The Last Great American Picture Show: New Hollywood Cinema in the 1970s*, edited by Thomas Elsaesser, Alexander Horwath, and Noel King, 309–32. Amsterdam: Amsterdam University Press.

Morag, Raya. 2009. *Defeated Masculinity: Post-Traumatic Cinema and the Aftermath of War*. New York: Peter Lang.

Murray, Gabrielle. 2004. *This Wounded Cinema, This Wounded Life: Violence and Utopia in the Films of Sam Peckinpah*. Westport, CT: Praeger, 2004.

Paryz, Marek. 2011. "The Poetics and Politics of the Post-Western: The Western Topoi and Archetypes in Sam Peckinpah's War Film *Cross of Iron*." In *Projecting Words, Writing Images: Intersections of the Textual and the Visual in American Cultural Practices*, edited by John R. Leo and Marek Paryz, 321–35. Newcastle upon Tyne: Cambridge Scholars.

Raab, Kurt, and Karsten Peters. 1982. *Die Sehnsucht des Rainer Werner Fassbinder*. Munich: Bertelsmann Verlag.

Robnik, Drehli. 2004. "Allegories of Post-Fordism in 1970s New Hollywood: Countercultural Combat Films, Conspiracy Thrillers as Genre Recycling." In *The Last Great American Picture Show: New Hollywood Cinema in the 1970s*, edited by Thomas Elsaesser, Alexander Horwath, and Noel King, 333–58. Amsterdam: Amsterdam University Press.

Schidor, Dieter. 1982. "Vorwort des Herausgebers." In *Querelle-Filmbuch*, by Rainer Werner Fassbinder, edited by Dieter Schidor, 7–9. Munich: Schirmer-Mosel.

———. 2004. "'Ich mußte mein Leben gelebt haben, um diesen Film machen zu können': Rainer Werner Fassbinder über *Querelle*." In *Fassbinder über Fassbinder: Die ungekürtzten Interviews*, edited by Robert Fischer, 617–24. Frankfurt: Verlag der Autoren, 2004.

Sellier, Geneviève. 2009. *Masculine Singular: French New Wave Cinema.* Translated by Kristin Ross. Durham: Duke University Press, 2009.

Sharrett, Christopher. 1998. "Peckinpah the Radical: The Politics of *The Wild Bunch*." In *Sam Peckinpah's "The Wild Bunch,"* edited by Stephen Prince, 79–103. Cambridge: Cambridge University Press.

———. 2014. "*Bring Me the Head of Alfredo Garcia*: Peckinpah the Dramatist." *Film International*, July 8. http://filmint.nu/?p=12659.

Silverman, Kaja, "Masochistic Ecstasy and the Ruination of Masculinity in Fassbinder's Cinema." In *Male Subjectivity at the Margins*, 214–96. New York: Routledge.

Slotkin, Richard. 1973. *Regeneration through Violence: The Mythology of the American Frontier, 1600–1860*. Middletown, CT: Wesleyan University Press.

———. 1992. "Cross-Over Point: The Mylai Massacre, *The Wild Bunch* and the Demoralization of America, 1969–1972." In *Gunfighter Nation: The Myth of the Frontier in Twentieth-Century America*, 578–623. New York: Maxwell Macmillan International.

Strug, Cordell. 2012. "Human Striving, Human Strife: Sam Peckinpah and the Journey of the Soul." In *Peckinpah Today: New Essays on the Films of Sam Peckinpah*, edited by Michael Bliss, 137–46. Carbondale: Southern Illinois University Press.

Trimborn, Jürgen. 2012. *Ein Tag ist ein Jahr ist ein Leben: Rainer Werner Fassbinder: Die Biographie*. Berlin: Propyläen.

Weddle, David. 1994. *"If They Move . . . Kill 'Em": The Life and Times of Sam Peckinpah*. New York: Grove.

White, Edmund. 1993. *Genet: A Biography*. New York: Knopf.

Williams, Linda. 1999. *Hard Core: Power, Pleasure and the "Frenzy of the Visible."* Berkeley: University of California Press.

Wright, Will. 1975. *Six Guns and Society: A Structural Study of the Western.* Berkeley: University of California Press.

# 12

# INSTITUTIONALIZING PASSION AS SHOCKS TO THE SYSTEM

## Michel Foucault and Anti-Psychiatry in Werner Schroeter's *Day of the Idiots* and Milos Forman's *One Flew over the Cuckoo's Nest*

*Jaimey Fisher*

The press kit for Werner Schroeter's *Tag der Idioten* (*Day of the Idiots*, 1981) offers something unusual for such marketing materials: extensive citations from an already world-famous philosopher-historian, Michel Foucault. Mentions made of such a thinker are unusual enough in these kinds of materials, but what makes these references particularly remarkable is that Foucault was commenting directly on the West German filmmaker—and not only remarking on Schroeter, but comparing him favorably, for instance, to the global auteur Ingmar Bergman. Even if Foucault would likely resist the construction of facile hierarchies, he declares Schroeter's foregrounding of the psychology of women more convincing than Bergman's (Foucault and Schroeter 2018, 185). The press kit quotes both from a piece in which Foucault writes extensively about Schroeter's cinema ("The Nondisciplinary Camera vs. Sade," 1972) and from a published conversation between the French philosopher and the West German filmmaker from December 1981, two and a half years before Foucault's death and right around the time Schroeter had just completed *Day of the Idiots*. In Schroeter's published autobiography, *Days of Twilight, Nights of Frenzy* (*Tage im Dämmer, Nächte im Rausch: Autobiographie*, 2011/2017), in which he discusses Foucault and their points of contact for several pages, Schroeter recounts that he even floated a book-length series of such conversations with the philosopher to publishers, who passed.

If these pieces by Foucault, the press kit, and Schroeter's autobiography underscore cross-border influence and engagement, then this curious constellation highlights something telling about Schroeter's career: his films were conspicuously global in their content and orientation—much more so than those of many directors of New German Cinema, at whose margins he worked.[1] His films, for instance, manifest the recurring New German Cinema interest in the United States and US popular culture, as with his planned Marylin Monroe project that ended up producing the very different *Willow Springs* (1973), shot in Southern California with German and American actors, as well as his interest in the New York avant-garde, for example, in casting Candy Darling in *The Death of Maria Malibran* (*Der Tod der Maria Malibran*, 1972), affirming his attraction to Andy Warhol and the Factory. From some of his earlier works, like *Salomé* (1971, shot in Lebanon) to his most famous films *Nel Regno di Napoli* (*The Kingdom of Naples*, 1978) and *Palermo oder Wolfsburg* (1980) to his later-period shoots in (then) Czechoslovakia, France, and Portugal, Schroeter worked in, and engaged with, multiple non-German cultures. His was not merely a touristic frequenting of foreign places: for example, Schroeter, who spent a year in Naples as a teenager, had a deeper experience and engagement with Italy than the many famous German artists who had visited and made work there. Finally, but probably most abidingly in his career, Schroeter repeatedly manifested in his plots, productions, and general approach an engagement with European and global culture, not least with European theater, art cinema, and especially opera. His early and long-lasting interest in/inspiration by Greek American diva Maria Callas, for example, is a central part of his career and, as he recounts it, his emotional life.

This transnational orientation and cross-border creativity garnered him early and sustained praise in West Germany, although it likely diminished his profile in the United States, where expectations for German cinema seemed (and seem) to be more that such films engage German national themes, especially the German national past (Grundmann 2018, 24). Schroeter was arguably more celebrated by the West German critical and industrial establishment at this mid- and late 1970s time than his friend Rainer Werner Fassbinder, with Schroeter's winning the Golden Bear at the Berlin Film Festival in 1980 and multiple Filmbänder in Gold (West Germany's top prize for a film director at the time, for *The Kingdom of Naples*, *Day of the Idiots*, and *Malina* [1990])—and that success, of course, rested on far fewer films than Fassbinder's. But despite his emphatically global orientation and extensive domestic recognition, his international profile has never come close to approaching that of Fassbinder, Werner Herzog, or Wim Wenders. *Day of the Idiots* is an intriguing case in point: with its public premiere at the Hof Film Festival in October 1981 and then theatrical run starting in March 1982, the film was widely praised and won Schroeter one of his Filmbänder in Gold—but the film is hardly discussed or analyzed now, even as interest in Schroeter has grown, modestly, in recent years.[2]

The press kit and autobiography confirm how Schroeter's *Day of the Idiots* was, typically, well imbricated in the currents of European thought and culture at the time, especially in Foucault's thinking on madness and its treatment in modernity. Foucault himself was, of course, well versed in and thoroughly influenced by German-language traditions, including by a key Hegelian mentor, Jean Hippolyte, as well as by German phenomenology; he was obsessed at one point with Hermann Broch; and, probably above all, he was impressed by Friedrich Nietzsche, the reading of whom Foucault saw as a watershed in his intellectual development (Macey 2019, 34). Foucault's interest in and opining on Schroeter may not be such a surprise, as Foucault also had extensive firsthand experience of West Germany and its culture, having directed the Institut Français in Hamburg between 1958 and 1960, after stints in Sweden and then Warsaw. His interest in European avant-garde and art cinema circuits resonates with his engagement in aesthetic resistance to the disciplinary mechanisms of modern thinking and society. Even if his later thinking arced somewhat away from aesthetic resistance toward political activism, his investment in the limit-experiences in the arts had been there from the beginning (in his 1963 book on avant-garde writer Raymond Roussel, for instance) and, if his interest in Schroeter is any indication, right through to the end of his life.

*Day of the Idiots* has been largely neglected in the recent revival of interest in Schroeter in part, I think, because it resists or exceeds the prevailing interpretations of his complex aesthetic approaches. Even if Schroeter's work generally does display key elements of queer aesthetics, as Alice Kuzniar (2000) and Roy Grundmann (2018) have argued persuasively, or of an "allegorical gaze," as Michelle Langford (2006) has convincingly explored, it is notable that none of these scholars has much to say about *Day of the Idiots*. The film, indeed, depicts lesbian desire and polymorphous erotic pleasures (pace Kuzniar and Grundmann), and it does marshal moments of tableau composition, gesture-laden expression, and allegorical decay (à la Langford), but *Day of the Idiots* nonetheless—as is so often the case with Schroeter's work—seems up to something else besides. In this essay, I explore how illuminating the transnational currents and contexts around this dense and largely neglected film prove. Such cross-border intellectual and cinematic currents and contexts elucidate the film's unusual status within Schroeter's oeuvre, with *Day of the Idiots*, in turn, simultaneously elaborating and varying these intellectual and cinematic trends.

Using Foucault's interest in Schroeter, and Schroeter's in Foucault, as an entrée, I explore *Day of the Idiots* in the context of the transnational anti-psychiatry movement that built, in part, on Foucault's first major work, *Histoire de la folie à l'âge classique* (*History of Madness in the Classical Age*). This movement included not only this, Foucault's breakthrough work, but also the work of prominent psychiatrists like R. D. Laing and David Cooper in the English-speaking world and Franco Basaglia in Italy. In addition to his discussion of Foucault, Schroeter cites these three anti-psychiatry psychiatrists as he details his interest in and realization of *Day of the Idiots*. Although the anti-psychiatry movement has been largely forgotten, these transnational intellectual currents manifested in a key theme of the new waves globally around this time: madness not so much as a malady of the individual but more as a metaphor for the malaise of modern societies. Within the new waves, this mode of manufactured madness focused, in particular, on the psychological struggles of especially younger people in the face of modern society—not least in Frederick Wiseman's breakthrough (and soon banned) documentary *Titicut Follies* (1967) and then, just a few years before *Day of the Idiots*, in Milos Forman's *One Flew over the Cuckoo's Nest*, which was both the second top-grossing film and most Oscar-winning film of its year (1975—and that despite opening in November). Although Schroeter does not mention Forman's film—particularly odd, given the profile of *Cuckoo's Nest* and that *Day* was shot in Prague, Forman's former hometown—reviews at the time tied the two, and there are, as this essay aims to elucidate, many similarities as well as telling differences between the films (see, for example, Jeremias 1982). Taken together, these films of the late 1960s and 1970s, *Titicut Follies* and *One Flew over the Cuckoo's Nest*, indicate a very different direction than the more trusting depictions of mental health professionals in films of the late 1940s and 1950s (see, for example, Walker 1993; Polan 1986). As in Foucault's work, these later, clearly more critical films undertake a dual engagement with characters' mental experiences: they depict the questionable medical practices around modern psychological "health" and diagnose characters' mental struggles as manifesting broader maladies of the Enlightenment and the modernity it ushered in. Such depictions reveal notable themes of the new cinematic waves crashing around the world and therefore a crucial link between Schroeter's unusual work and broader global currents.

## *Day of the Idiots*—Transnational Art Cinema and Thought

The majority of the early conversation between Schroeter and Foucault is taken up with the nature of "passion," which Foucault, in Schroeter's work, contrasts to other films' more familiar and ubiquitous "love" (Foucault and Schroeter 2018, 179). Foucault's distinction might seem odd, even academic, but it is well woven into the conceptual constellation of his history of madness, since being mad was inextricably entwined with passion before the modernization of madness as mental health. Foucault, in fact, argues that passion, in that it crosses and interweaves "the body and soul," actually formed the basis for the "very possibility" of (historical) madness (1988, 97). As he draws this distinction between passion and love in his conversation with Schroeter, Foucault explains how he sees passion operating in the director's work: "What is passion? It's a state; it's something that just happens to you, takes hold of you, and seizes you by both shoulders. It doesn't stop and doesn't begin anywhere. In fact, you have no idea where it's coming from. . . . It's a constantly mobile state, but it doesn't move to a given point. . . . It's simply that in these situations of passion, you are not yourself" (Foucault and Schroeter 2018, 179–80). Foucault's characterization of passion as an alternative economy and mode of feeling sounds very much like the "affect" of the recent affective turn—in such passages, one witnesses how interwoven his thought is with Deleuze's (likely a case of mutual and reciprocal influence). In the case of *Day of the Idiots*, one can similarly see how the modernization and institutionalization of madness categorize and confine such alternative modes of emoting and feeling.

In their conversation, Foucault and Schroeter then move to discuss their current amorous passions, and it is precisely such passions interwoven with madness, and the blurry boundaries between them, with which Carol (Carole Bouquet) contends throughout *Day of the Idiots*. In Schroeter's fragmentary, often surreal character study of Carol, her central struggle arises from her passion for her consistently oblivious lover, Alexander, who remains elusive, narratively and emotionally, throughout the film. In *Day*'s plot, Schroeter's interests focus much more—and rather typically for Schroeter's work—on female passions rather than on either the object of desire or a couple's actual interactions: this plot, typically, is more about an individual's experience of passion than conventional love or romance. Carol's obsession with Alexander and his feelings, or lack thereof, for her is confirmed throughout *Day* with an unusual editing device deployed throughout: Schroeter cuts abruptly to apparently internal diegetic, close-up insert shots of Alexander's face looking directly at the camera, a shot asynchronous to other events on the screen before or after. They seem to be internal or subjective shots of Carol, as her mind inevitably turns again to him, no matter where she is or what she is doing. Her passion for him takes hold of her, with "no idea where it's coming from," as Foucault puts it (Foucault and Schroeter 2018, 179–80). In these abrupt inserts, Alexander's expression is one of silence and slight bemusement, extending the inscrutability of his feelings and Carol's inability to read them. The film's early episodes, which introduce these inserts, signal her inability to navigate her extreme passion within her relationship with him. Although her desire for him is straight, her inability to manage this alternative economy of desire and passion is queer—a central theme of Schroeter's work generally, as Grundmann has elaborated (2018, 10–12)—and many of the desires Carol will encounter in her fellow patients in the institution are conspicuously queer and decidedly outré.

The film's opening establishes this dense constellation, with Carol's extreme passion already intercut and interwoven with madness and its institutionalization in modern societies. In fact, the film's opening scene shoots the exterior of the mental institution—through its high fence—where Carol will soon end up. In Schroeter's introduction to her, in the film's second scene, Carol has woken up agitated in her lover's apartment while he sleeps on, a foreshadowing of their relationship throughout the film: viewers hear, via voice-over, a tortured monologue in her head vent about her lover's inscrutability while she darts around the apartment disquieted and eventually destructive. Saying (internally diegetically, perhaps in an echo of Büchner's *Danton Death*) she would like to cut out a piece of Alexander's head and replace it with a windowpane—just to see what he feels about her—she throws the contents of his large desktop on the floor. Soon thereafter, as he sleeps on unperturbed, she is emptying his closet and tearing up his clothes. The combination of inner monologue and outer aggression serves as a stark indication of her struggles with inner mental states and outer social environment, key themes of interior versus exterior experience explored throughout the film. These themes are materialized in visual motifs that Schroeter shows throughout—doorways and windows that provide unstable interfaces between individuals and their contexts. After around twenty minutes of Carol's erratic behavior, the plot takes a sudden turn toward the institutional when, by accusing an innocent woman of terrorist activity, Carol deliberately has herself remanded to the mental facility with which the film mysteriously opened. There she experiences the exuberant anarchy of the institution's other patient-inmates. Her doctor becomes convinced that she is psychologically sound and should be discharged, but the voices in her head and sudden visions make her question where she does belong.

Schroeter's Carol Schneider is played by the twenty-three-year-old Carole Bouquet, whose casting confirms the director's emphatically European orientation. A French actor who had broken through as (one half of) Conchita in Luis Bunuel's *That Obscure Object of Desire* (1977) at age nineteen and then appeared in Betrand Blier's *Buffet froid* (1979), her transnational stardom would, in the same year, 1981, of *Day of the Idiots*, be cemented by her performance as the main "Bond girl" love interest in *For Your Eyes Only*, the twelfth film in the UK's most successful film series ever (and still one of its main box office draws). Needless to say, it is unusual for a German art cinema, even avant-garde filmmaker to work with, as his protagonist, an actor with such an international and commercial profile.

Notably, Schroeter would also work with Isabelle Huppert, affirming his European reputation and transnational orientation. Bouquet went on to be one of France's best-known actresses and celebrities, including becoming a high-profile fashion model (like Catharine Deneuve) for Chanel, thus extra-filmically representing consumer objects at least as transnational as James Bond. Schroeter's work with Bouquet underscores his work's focus on female protagonists and melodrama—as Grundmann highlights, this interest in (even obsession with) women and the suffering to which society subjects them is a key link between Schroeter's work and queer cinema around the 1960s/1970s new waves (2018, 10–12). This often included a personal bond to the female actors whom his films foreground. Schroeter met Bouquet in Saint-Tropez and apparently enjoyed a substantive friendship with her that included car travels through Italy in which she, pretending to be his wife, would help him pick up young men all over the peninsula—part of her "acting test," as he recounts in his autobiography (2017, 151–52). Bouquet is dubbed throughout Schroeter's film, which works without undue distraction because viewers are often hearing the non-mouthed, stream-of-disturbed-consciousness jumble in Carol's head anyway.

## A 1970s and 1980s Movies Madness? Anti-Psychiatry, Cinematically Seen

The conspicuous characteristic common to *Day of the Idiots*, *One Flew over the Cuckoo's Nest*, and *Titicut Follies* is how all three films foreground allegedly mad characters on the margins of mental institutions, literally and metaphorically: all three chart the fate of individuals precariously institutionalized to reflect on the broader society. In this plot strategy, all three works highlight how madness and the modern confinement associated with it are malleable and even arbitrary. In this way, the films engage with allegedly ill patients to collectivize their condition, with the understanding that what afflicts the individual—long understood as a localized psychological "disease" and/or moral "failing"—often has broader historical and/or social origins. At their narrative cores, the films foreground one of the foundational insights of the anti-psychiatry movement that gained momentum in the 1960s: that those suffering from mental "illness" were frequently symptomatizing society at a particular historical moment more than their own mental challenges. The very act of creating such art engaging such patients contravenes the modern isolation of the mentally "ill" away from mainstream society, a tendency that Foucault, among others, historicized around this time. Their problems mostly emerge—according to anti-psychiatry—when and where social systems diverge from individual experience, such that conformity to the system can quickly become coercive. The agents of this conformist and coercive system, which Ken Kesey (2002) terms the sprawling "Combine" in his novel *One Flew over the Cuckoo's Nest*, are the full range of social authorities, but especially, for the purposes of the narrative, medical professionals like Dr. Spivey and Nurse Ratched in *Cuckoo's Nest* or the two doctors, Dr. Bruno and Dr. Laura, as well as Nurse Elisabeth in *Day of the Idiots*. In these critiques of psychiatry, mental health "treatments" serve more as modes of social control, materialized in "therapeutic" tools like group sessions, medication, and even more brutal bodily interventions, vividly depicted in all three films, as I shall explain.

Perhaps the main thrust of Foucault's *Histoire de la folie* (literally, *History of Madness*, usually translated as *Madness and Civilization*, 1988) is that both institutions and the diagnoses that land people there are highly contingent, that is, historically and socially produced and conditioned. For him, the way that a historical era constructs and treats madness manifests its treatment of reason's other, unreason. If the "Classical age" is that in which reason rose and ruled, then Foucault is carefully charting the role of what he terms "unreason" in this age and beyond, that is, unreason both before and after the Classical age. Foucault suggests that in the late Middle Ages and Renaissance there was a surprising recognition of the contributions of madness, as unreason, to the truth. According to Foucault, those eras supported, at least partially, the belief that one can learn about human experience and our world from madness—precisely, I would submit, the presumption of these films in their foregrounding of protagonists who might or might not be mentally "ill." There was even a "reverence and awe" for madness (Gutting 2007, 61). This means, as all three of these films assert, that madness is contiguous with "normal" life in their respective cultures, that the limits of madness are in fact artificial and renegotiated with that of the broader society over time. The mad have something to tell us because they are also us.

In his autobiography discussion of Foucault and *Day of the Idiots*, Schroeter associates his interest in the French philosopher with other key thinkers of what came to be known as the "anti-psychiatry movement," including R. D. Laing, David Cooper, and Francisco Basaglia (2017, 150–51). Schroeter observes that he had read all three, whose work led him to "reject psychology, psychoanalysis, and psychiatry" (150). He presumably did not always feel this way, as he studied psychology at the University of Cologne, studies that he soon broke off. All three figures Schroeter cites in his diaries lodged thoroughgoing critiques of modern psychiatry—in which all had trained and which they had all practiced in one form or another. All became key figures in the public profile of anti-psychiatry through their publications. Laing, for instance, is cited throughout Deleuze and Guatarri's *Anti-Oedipus* (1972)—a book that Schroeter also references in his autobiography—and David Cooper wrote the ecstatic introduction to the first English edition of Foucault's *Histoire de la folie* (translated, lamentably loosely, as *Madness and Civilization*) in 1964. It was Cooper, in fact, who popularized the term *anti-psychiatry* in his 1971 book *Psychiatry and Anti-Psychiatry*. The first English edition of *Madness and Civilization* also appeared in a series edited by Laing, "The World of Man," in which *The Order of Things* (*Les mots et choses*) and *Archeology of Knowledge* also first appeared in English—meaning that a key framework for Foucault's introduction to Anglophone audiences came through these figures and venues of the anti-psychiatry movement (Pearson 1992, 111–12). In these ways, Schroeter related Foucault's work on madness to the broader anti-psychiatric movement of the 1960s and 1970s.

As figures with whom Schroeter was familiar, Laing, Cooper, and Basaglia all rejected what was understood as the purely illness model of psychological conditions like schizophrenia. In this 1960s and 1970s moment, the anti-psychiatry movement was interwoven with philosophical, especially existential and phenomenological, trends, something undoubtedly true of Foucault's earlier work as well. For example, the focus on experience noted above, especially experience generated in an individual's conflicts with society, were at the core of these anti-psychiatric trends. Laing's *Politics of Experience* (1967) charted how madness emerged in the conflict between repressive societies and those individuals fighting that repression, extending such depictions to political dissidents—something *Day of the Idiots* also explores with the institutionalization of an alleged terrorist. Laing thought the vocabulary regularly deployed in the psychiatric community needlessly denigrated the mad, and he advocated for "therapy" to replace "treatment," as well as "client" rather than "patient" (Nasser 1995, 745). But the lasting effects of the movement were not only in the common understanding of the illness and its institutional context, but also the initiative to protect the rights of those under psychiatric care (745). Probably its greatest—and most controversial—legacy is the move away from mental institutions altogether and toward "community-based care," something with which Basaglia is closely associated. In fact, the Italian laws primarily responsible for dismantling institutions for the "mentally ill" are known as the Basaglia laws (Foot 2014, 235–49). Both Laing and Cooper thus saw modern psychiatry as complicit with political and economic normalizing forces in Western societies. Foucault, of course, offered a crucial (if, at times, wobbly) historical basis for these critiques, historicizing the conceptualization of madness as a medical condition, to be confined and discounted in mainstream society, replacing an understanding of it as a diverse mode of experience and thinking "unreason."

How could such sprawling histories and abstract discourses, even if cited in Schroeter's autobiography, be explored cinematically? One could start with the shared settings of these films: institutions committed to the care of the allegedly mentally ill. The three films are set, for the majority of their plots, in institutions at an emphatic (and narratively consequential) remove from mainstream society in which those diagnosed as mentally ill are housed, with their consent or not. The location settings of both *Titicut Follies* and *One Flew over the Cuckoo's Nest* proved central to their legacies: that *Follies* was set and shot in a state institution for the "criminally insane" led, first, to an official ban in the state of Massachusetts and, second, to eventual reforms of the system it documented (Durante 2022). For *Cuckoo's Nest*, Forman not only shot the film in an active hospital, the Oregon State Hospital, but also resided there for a time to work on the script, had the actors shadow patients, and cast some patients as extras (Forman and Novak 1993, 213–15). He even had the director of the hospital, Dr. Dean K. Brooks, play McMurphy's doctor, Dr. Spivey. Despite Kesey's novel's fantastical, even surreal tone, Forman deliberately made his approach more documentary, which likely lent the adaptation's critique even more credibility.

By focusing not only on the cognitive and behavioral diversity of the characters but also on their spatial fates, the films are, in fact, engaging one of Foucault's basic insights about the modern treatment of madness. The spatial trajectory of madness in the Classical era is central to its changing place in human experience. After the Middle Ages and the Renaissance, in which unreason was regarded as playing a role in comprehending human experience, the Classical era activated what Foucault terms the "Great Confinement" (1988, 48–74) from the mid- and late seventeenth century onward. One scholar of Foucault's work has called confinement a fundamental category of his Classical-age argument (and therefore the fundamental category of the whole book; see Gutting 2007, 66). This confinement underscores how Foucault highlights, throughout his work, the role of dynamic or heterotopic spaces, especially institutional spaces, in the history of modernity's disciplinary mechanisms. For him, space is part of the broader operations of what he would come to call a *dispositif*, or apparatus, as in the *dispositif* of the panopticon. This confinement of the mad activated the effective exclusion of unreason from the work of reason (66). A key event for Foucault related to the Great Confinement was the fading importance of the confinement of people with leprosy. During the Middle Ages, there was, according to Foucault, a rapid drop in the number suffering from the disease, such that an entire infrastructure for isolating them from mainstream society—for public health reasons—was left unutilized. The urge to confine was then displaced to the allegedly mad. In a press conference on *Day of the Idiots* in Hof where the film premiered, Schroeter abruptly and somewhat inexplicably raises the issue of those suffering from leprosy, underscoring his familiarity with Foucault's arguments about the broader social and spatial shifts surrounding madness in modernity.

## Medical Professionals and Their Dubious Powers

Like *Titicut* and *Cuckoo's Nest*, *Day of the Idiots* makes, for its borderline protagonists, key antagonists out of the attending doctors and other medical professionals, especially nurses. The ubiquity of these suspect mental health care providers underscores, in fact, how global anti-psychiatry elucidates Schroeter's complex and challenging film. All three of these films that engage with anti-psychiatry foreground doctors and their role in both diagnosis and treatment. Perhaps surprisingly, Foucault's *Histoire de la folie* does not completely condemn doctors—rather, doctors are part of a broader shift in disciplinary power coursing through the whole society, not least around unreason as it became modern madness. Foucault's later lectures specify how psychiatrists helped transform madness in society and how such transformations dovetail with the broader operations of power in society: "It seems that the major tremors that have shaken psychiatry since the end of the nineteenth century have all basically called the doctor's power into question; his power and its effect on the patient, more than his knowledge and the truth he told regarding the illness. More precisely, let us say that, from Bernheim to Laing or Basaglia, what was at stake was how the doctor's power was involved in the truth of what he said and conversely how this truth could be fabricated and compromised by his power" (2008, 341). With the medicalization of madness (in mental "health" and "illness"), doctors and nurses became key social figures through medical power rather than through medicinal knowledge. This shift in the power of doctors and other medical professionals was also due to the increasing disciplinary powers of both juridical and moral processes in modernity and their growing overlap with medicine. All three films register this power beyond the mere medical in disturbing ways, with, intriguingly, *Day of the Idiots* exploring it most subtly and in ways that prove surprisingly sympathetic to doctors, even while still critiquing medical institutions generally.

The medical personnel in both *Titicut Follies* and *One Flew over the Cuckoo's Nest* are partly sympathetic, partly terrifying. One of the more grotesque figures of Wiseman's *Follies* is the psychiatrist Dr. Ross, whom viewers watch confront a patient, Malinowski, who is protesting the hospital's abusive conditions through a hunger strike. In a horrifically memorable scene, viewers watch the doctor insert a feeding tube through the nose of the hunger-striking patient while the latter, naked and supine, is restrained by orderlies. The patient dies shortly thereafter, with Wiseman's matter-of-fact insertion of Malinowski's modest burial, underscoring the ultimate biopolitical stakes of these institutions. In *One Flew over the Cuckoo's Nest*, Nurse Ratched is the novel's and film's most conspicuous personification of coercive mental health, an embodiment of the utterly abusive psychiatric system (standing in for what Kesey, in his novel *One Flew over the Cuckoo's Nest*, called the society-wide "Combine"). The conflict between her and Randle "R. P." McMurphy serves the plot throughout as its narrative anchor, with the hassled and harried patients oscillating between them. Particularly relevant in a Foucauldian framework is the contiguity of the medical and legal regimes—in which Ratched wields shocking biopolitical power over McMurphy's legal fate, after legal officials initially passed him off to the hospital.

*Day of the Idiots* similarly foregrounds the intersection of medical professionals with both patients and legal discourse, including a protagonist patient who begs the question of what is sane, what is criminal, and what is not. It was precisely the definition and boundaries of madness that are at stake in both Foucault's historical account and in anti-psychiatry's activist reforms. As in both *Titicut Follies* and *Cuckoo's Nest*, the interplay and intersection of legal and health authorities figures centrally in the narrative. Carol is committed to the institution for informing on an alleged terrorist, Ninon (Carola Regnier), who is herself also remanded to the facility by the police late in the film. Although *Day*'s depiction of doctors and nurses cinematically affirms this moment of transnational anti-psychiatry, it also suggests the interplay of transnational intellectual currents and national cultural specificity. In fact, the narrative function of the doctors in *Day of the Idiots* negotiates between this transnational critique of health-care professionals in the medicalization of madness and a national specificity around doctors in postwar West German culture.

As Jennifer Kapczynski has outlined for the 1940s and 1950s, the doctor was a key cultural figure for Germany's coming to terms with its criminal past in the postwar years. For a war-ravaged, atrocity-committing nation, the doctor offered an (apparently) apolitical personage to help heal self and others: "In a culture consumed by a sense of collective catastrophe and guilt, the figure of the doctor assumed a paramount and paradoxical symbolic importance. . . . In postwar West Germany, it was the physician, rather than the statesman, who appeared poised to repair the damage caused by Hitler's regime" (2008, 18). It is not a surprise that the image of a doctor served as an intensified locus for West Germany's postwar coming to terms with the past, given the role that medical "science" had played in Nazi policy and propaganda, with their manifestly biopolitical metaphors, horrific medical experiments, and ultimately mass-murderous "biological" hierarchies. In the reconstructive wake of such a past after the war, Kapczynski explores how films with doctors as protagonists, like Wolfgang Staudte's *The Murderers Are among Us* (*Die Mörder sind unter uns*,

1946) or Peter Lorre's *The Lost One* (*Der Verlorene*, 1951) ushered in the era of postwar cinema. They did so with a specific diagnosis of what was ailing Germany; the turn to Nazism conveniently became a kind of no-fault collective disease from which the nation had to heal. Understanding Nazism as a disease—rather than as a horrifically realized racist and murderous intent—was self-evidently useful for a culture trying to move on. As the first postwar German feature film and one of the indelible films of the entire postwar period, *The Murderers Are among Us* achieves what Kapczynski suggests would be a "seeing cure" for the recovering Germanys.

Such a conflicted context around doctors—in the crucible of transnational critique and national appreciation—yields an even more central role for doctors and nurses in *Day* than in *Follies* or *Cuckoo's Nest*. On the one side, there are telling similarities in all three films' critique of medical professionals, while, on the other, *Day of the Idiots* balances such global critiques with the particular medical positivity of postwar West German culture. In fact, Schroeter's film realizes this intersection in part by splitting its doctor character between two psychiatrists, Dr. Bruno and Dr. Laura, a frequently debating duo whose duality embodies the critique of psychiatry, on the one hand, as well as praise of doctors in postwar West German culture, on the other. For contrastive example, if *Cuckoo's Nest* noticeably (and misogynistically) splits its medical abuses between an avuncular Dr. Spivey and punitive Nurse Ratched—with the former sympathetic but somewhat gullible and the latter aloof and increasingly brutal—Schroeter's film tellingly bifurcates the doctor his/herself.

*Day* offers the supervisory chief male doctor and a much more sympathetically depicted female psychiatrist, Dr. Laura, played by New German Cinema regular Ingrid Caven. The discussions and debates between Dr. Bruno and Dr. Laura are much more equal than those between Dr. Spivey and Nurse Ratched—these discussions in *Day* dramatize the contradictions of the growing transnational skepticism about psychiatry with West German over-investiture in the doctor as a key figure of postwar recovery. From the various script versions in the Deutschen Kinemathek, it is clear that Schroeter expanded the figure of Dr. Laura in collaboration with Caven, both as he revised the script and then actually shot it. In fact, the later versions of the script are substantially longer and substantively more engaged with Dr. Laura's opinions on how to treat sundry patients and ailments—especially, per the above, around Carol's coerced, but Dr. Laura's believes misguided, confinement. As they unfold their relationship as well as professional perspectives, the two doctors debate "illness" in psychiatry's overall approach, an increasingly important plot point in Carol's fate.

The complexity of the doctor-patient relation is highlighted early in the film in the introduction of Dr. Laura to Carol through a highly self-conscious and stylized filmmaking throughout the scene. Carol meets Dr. Laura during her in-take processing: Nurse Elisabeth compels the newly arrived patient-inmate to strip, remove jewelry, and bathe. When Carol, now naked, realizes someone in a lab coat is watching her somewhat surreptitiously from the doorway, she is not sure who Dr. Laura is: the latter refuses to greet Carol or make any formal introduction offering her title or role. To Carol's embarrassed inquiry, "What are you doing here?" Dr. Laura responds simply that she is observing her ("Ich beobachte Sie"). Schroeter ironically, almost campily, cuts to closer and closer shots of Dr. Laura's reaction to her seeing Carol, nude and about to climb into the bath, for the first time. Accompanied by the music and Caven's inscrutable visage, these close-ups recall the film's silent close-ups of Alexander that crop up earlier as diegetic inserts, apparently internal diegetic images as Carol's voice-over longs for him to articulate how he feels. Predictably, Dr. Laura takes a more than casual interest in Carol's condition. These sub-textual tensions and renegotiated basis for the doctor-patient relationship continue when Carol visits Dr. Laura in her office. Dr. Laura offers Carol wine, which the latter then pours for both of them while commenting on a model of a severed, bloodied foot between them. It is never explained why a psychiatrist would have such a model displayed in her office, particularly as it could be seen to indicate the kind of cruel treatments sometimes deployed in such institutions.

## Climactic Moments of Shock: Electricity to the Head

With their key antagonists as medical professionals, all three films explore some of the controversial treatments used in such institutions. In fact, in the two fictional films, one of the most controversial treatments, electro-convulsive therapy (ECT), is saved for climactic plot moments. There is

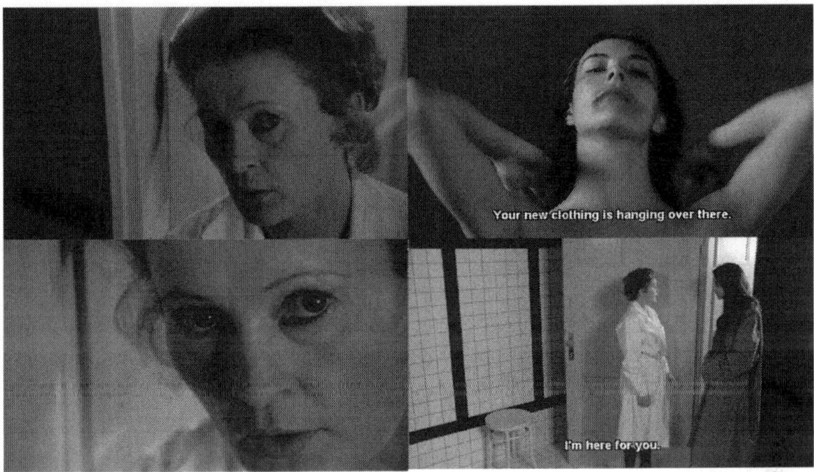


FIGURE 12.1. *The Day of the Idiots*—Dr. Laura meets the patient Carol, with erotic subtext/editing. (Screengrab)

a long history of deliberately shocking patients for medical purposes—for longer, even, than ECT has been in use. In his history of the "electrophysiological era," for instance, Sander Gilman charts the application of electricity to medical and mental ailments in the late nineteenth and early twentieth centuries, willy-nilly as these treatments may have been. The application of electrotherapies to the burgeoning field of medicine reflected the general enthusiasm for all things electric at the time. The practitioners for mental ailments included both Jean-Martin Charcot and Sigmund Freud before the latter turned, emphatically and now famously, to the "cathartic" methods of the talking cure. Before that watershed, however, some of Josef Breuer's and Freud's most famous patients, like Anna O. (Bertha Pappenheim) were treated with electrotherapy—Freud even purchased an expensive electrotherapeutic device with a loan from a wealthy friend (Gilman 2008, 343). These treatments—including for the common and overdetermined diagnosis of hysteria—were predecessors of ECT but were not yet geared to induce convulsions in patients. Indeed, the discussion unfolded around where exactly to place the electrodes on the (often vocal) muscles in question and how many volts to give the "therapy" (343). As late as the 1920s, Freud was involved in defending a colleague, Julius Wagner-Jauregg, who would go on to win the Nobel Prize for medicine, in a legal case calling into question the use of electrotherapies for "shell-shocked" soldiers of World War I. As Gilman traces, such cases foreshadow the still ongoing debate about mental illness as a set of somatic diseases requiring physical intervention or mental ones best served by psychotherapy.

If using sparks on and around putatively problematic tissue had been in use since the late 1800s, administering shocks to the temples to induce convulsions was a later innovation. Convulsive therapy by electricity was developed in 1930s Italy by psychiatrists (Ugo Cerletti and Lucio Bini) who found that shocks delivered via electrodes to the temples would induce temporary convulsions. Convulsions had formerly been induced by "insulin coma" and the "metrazol [and cadiazol] shock" for therapeutic reasons, but electricity seemed to offer a somatically less severe, more controlled intervention (Berrios 1997, 108). Apparently, perhaps because of broader optimism about electricity at the time, ECT also apparently triggered a less fearful reaction in patients than chemical interventions (109). But, as Hirshbein and Sarvananda outline, popular opinion about ECT arced from early optimism to increasing skepticism by the early 1970s to outright horror by the latter part of that decade. Initially, in the 1940s and 1950s, even popular magazines heralded the promise of the new "shock" therapy for reviving "zombie" patients or even for treating minor issues like stuttering (2008, 4). But as the therapy became more widespread in the 1950s and 1960s, opponents, including former patients, became increasingly vocal. For example, some of these public critics of the therapy liked to review how Cerletti had discovered it at a slaughterhouse, where he observed how shocks triggered seizures in pigs (Berrios 1997, 110). Others cited the abuses of the Nazis, for example, in Austrian hospitals, where ECT was added to a line-up of suspect treatments for the mentally ill, many of which resulted in the unnecessary death of the patients (Gazdag and Czech 2017, 482–88).

Given this debate, Hirshbein and Sarvananda (2008) argue that, in popular culture of the 1950s and 1960s, ECT seemed to be the most arresting synecdoche for psychiatry in general—a singular treatment that stood in for a whole field of medicine. In the popular imagination and public debate, ECT and the changing disposition toward it underscore, pointedly, the changing attitudes toward psychiatry and its patients, particularly in the era of anti-psychiatry. In his published memoir amounting to, as he terms it, a "history of ECT," Lebensohn even offers explicit advice on how to deal with anti-psychiatry and its criticisms of the procedure (1999, 173–81). In reviewing these remarkable transformations of attitudes about ECT, Lebensohn admits that Forman's *One Flew over the Cuckoo's Nest* is still the most famous representation, while Hirshbein and Sarvananda similarly argue that the "most potent image in popular culture remains" that offered by *Cuckoo's Nest*. Notably, I think, Lebensohn was writing in 1999 and Hirshbein and Sarvananda in 2008, or twenty-four and thirty-three years, respectively, after Forman's film. Hirshbein and Sarvananda suggest that *Cuckoo's Nest*'s depiction of ECT is still so relevant for the debate about psychiatric treatments because it "captures the power dynamics [people] still see as problematic" (2008, 2). It is an amazing observation in Hirshbein and Sarvananda's study of popular magazine depictions of ECT, underscoring how the most important portrayal was still Forman's film, made in 1975 but based on a 1962 novel. These power dynamics so memorably captured resonate with the changing power of medical professionals in the nineteenth and twentieth centuries, dynamics that, according to these authors, abided in Forman's film.

In *One Flew over the Cuckoo's Nest*, R. P. McMurphy is sent to the "shock shop" about an hour and twenty minutes into the film, after his first openly violent assault on the hospital's nurses. In front of Nurse Ratched, he shatters the window of the nurses' station, a thin barrier that also serves as a psychological border between the worlds of the staff and the patients. Ostensibly, he rams his hand through the window to retrieve the confiscated cigarettes of another patient, but he is also rejecting Ratched's effort to exert control over the unruly group: she had the cigarettes confiscated because they served as currency in the card-game gambling ring McMurphy had engineered. But as one patient (Danny DeVito's Martini) observes, how can they win their money back from McMurphy if she's taken their cigarettes? After smashing the window, McMurphy is subdued by the guards and is then sent to ECT with the half-Indigenous "Chief" Bromden, who had tried to help him in the resulting scrum.

The cut from the fight to ECT is remarkable for the rapid, radical disruption of McMurphy's rabble-rousing, with Forman cutting from the din of the diatribe about the cigarettes and the ensuing anarchic melee to the eerie quiet of the ECT unit. Rather unconvincingly, McMurphy is at first confused about where he has been sent, but when they recline him gently and then ominously put conductant on his temples, he attempts to

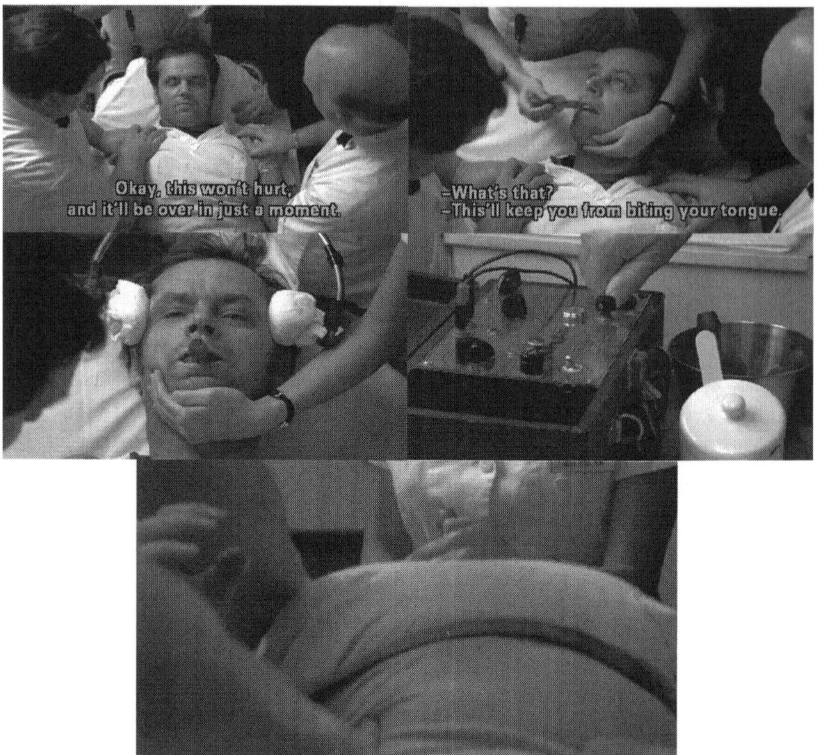


FIGURE 12.2. *One Flew over the Cuckoo's Nest*—McMurphy subjected to electroconvulsive therapy. (Screengrab)

be agreeably lighthearted ("a little dab will do you"). As he is preemptively restrained on the bed, with both leather straps and then staff preparing to hold him during the convulsions, the camera slowly zooms in on him from a low angle at his feet. The foreshortened shot offers an unusual perspective recalling the famous *Lamentation of Christ* by Andrea Mantegna (c. 1480), highlighting both McMurphy's sacrifice for the group and his imminent martyrdom.

McMurphy is subsequently subjected to psychosurgical intervention (a lobotomy), after which Bromden enacts a mercy killing on the silent, unrecognizable McMurphy. Notably, viewers do not see any of the surgery procedure itself—like Bromden, viewers witness only the results—such that the ECT sequence is the most graphically depicted psychiatric procedure of the film. Narratively speaking, it is the event that also segues to the film's final act of McMurphy's ultimate determination, and then failure, to escape. In terms of its visual strategy, however, the meticulously depicted ECT treatment is left as a synecdoche for psychiatry's most controversial techniques.

Although Schroeter did not mention *Cuckoo's Nest* in his diaries, or, as far as I know, in any interview, *Day of the Idiots* offers a very similarly staged ECT scene at a similarly watershed moment of its plot. Here, too, a vividly depicted ECT depiction segues into the film's final act, and the controversial treatment is likewise administered after a potentially rebellious deed. The key difference in Schroeter's film some seven years after *Cuckoo's Nest* is that ECT is administered not to the film's protagonist, but to the film's alleged terrorist, Ninon, whom Carol has denounced to have herself committed. From that time, the film has been fostering parallels between Carol and Ninon, who bear a marked physical resemblance to one another. Indeed, Carol and Ninon provide an example of another difficult to define yet clearly intense female relationship of the sort marking much of Schroeter's work. Of course, the other crucial difference is that a terrorist, even an alleged one, is more openly political and more openly revolutionary. If McMurphy is a contrary social force who happens to become de facto leader of his ward, his commitments seem to be primarily to gambling, to drinking, and to his sex worker friends, whereas Ninon is more overtly committed. Right before the treatment, Ninon is writing years on a black (really yellow) board: "1848+1870/71+1914+1933+1945+1967+1980+1981 = ?" These years suggest, of course, times of significant political transformation in West Germany—even aborted and/or incomplete revolutions—culminating in the two years in which the film was made (1980+1981), but amounting, in the end, only to a question mark.

After this, one of the most overtly political acts in the film, Ninon is abruptly subjected to the ECT treatment. Nurse Elisabeth suggests that the staff delay for a moment, given that Carol and Ninon are "in a circle," highlighting again the parallels and provisional solidarity between the two. But shortly thereafter, Ninon is wheeled off and subjected to the treatment in a fashion closely parallel to McMurphy: a close-up of protective mouthpiece, a cut to the footboard to show the foreshortened body, and then to high angle.

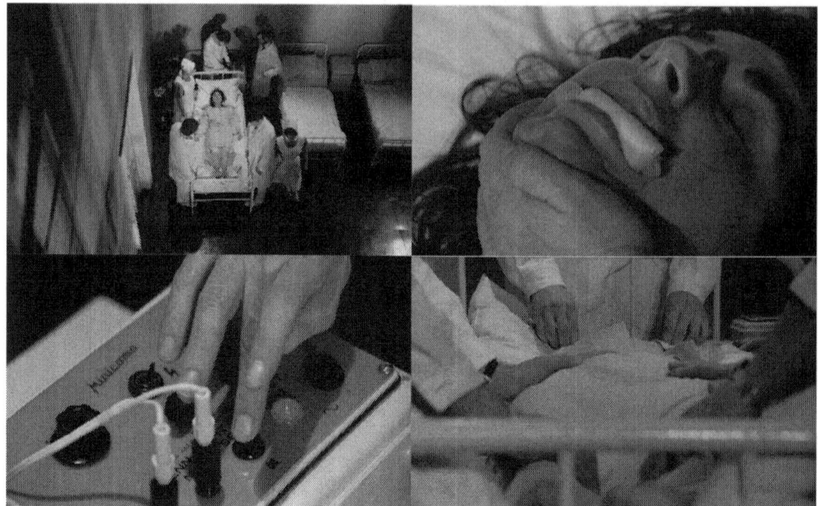

FIGURE 12.3. *Day of the Idiots*—Ninon is subjected to electroconvulsive therapy. (Screengrab)

Shortly thereafter, Carol is also framed in a similar posture, restrained as well on a gurney, for the first time in the film. Given what happened a few seconds earlier, one would expect a similar treatment to Ninon's. But then Dr. Laura appears, holding up a vial of unknown substance to Carol's temple, where the ECT electrodes would normally go. The implication—as the film does not fully detail it—would seem to be that Dr. Laura has interceded with medication instead of ECT.

## Conclusion: Dr. Laura's Last-Act Lecture on Anti-Psychiatry

Shortly after being restrained on the gurney and apparently threatened with convulsive therapy, Carol finds herself in Dr. Bruno's office discussing her continued treatment (he suggests, simply, "Musik"). Typically for the film and its complicating of (every) doctor's perspective, Dr. Laura's voice-over begins as Dr. Bruno and Carol converse, such that it becomes a sound bridge to the next scene, a classroom lecture of Dr. Laura to her patients. She discusses one of the underlying insights of the film—that "illness" is only a concept, which means that one should come to accept the needs (*Bedürfnisse*) from which the patients do not want to be freed. In this lecture, *Day of the Idiots*'s engagement with anti-psychiatry becomes even more explicit: Dr. Laura explains that her experiment in the clinic integrates "the two pillars of anti-psychiatry": first, the opening of doors (presumably of the psychiatric institutions), and, second, a reconnecting to the very reasons for the exclusion from the outer world. In her view, this helps redefine the clinic, which revisits the failures of society to address the needs of the patients. Although coming this late in the film, and standing in contrast to much of the film's previous anarchic and fragmentary depiction of the clinic, this declaration rings true to the film and its psychiatric depiction. This psychiatric depiction is one that the film expands, per Foucault's disciplinary mechanisms, to the level of society generally.

The parallels among the three films continue to their surprise conclusions—all three combine boisterous bacchanal and abrupt, even shocking deaths. For *Titicut Follies*, it is the eponymous "Follies" show, organized by the hospital guards, that brings an ironically cheerful singing and dancing to the shockingly cruel institution, devastating in the show's (and title's) highlighting of human contradictions. Through the eerily underlit song-and-dance number, the final images offer a reminder of those who have died in the brick confines of the institution. For both of the fiction films, a culminating, carefully staged party arcs to an ironic send-off for the main characters. In *One Flew over the Cuckoo's Nest*, McMurphy throws a would-be farewell party by buying off one of the guards and also arranges for young Billy to lose his virginity to one of his sex worker friends, Candy. While waiting for Billy and Candy, McMurphy fatefully falls asleep, dooming him to witness Ratched's vociferous contempt for Billy's liaison and the latter's subsequent suicide. In *Cuckoo's Nest*, the contradictions between the patients' festivities and the final, punitive lobotomy cum mercy killing complete the film's brutal emotional trajectory. In its final minutes, *Day of the Idiots* similarly contrasts a riotous concluding party, here a carnivalesque romp in costume for the patients and staff, followed by the abrupt death of the film's protagonist. In Schroeter's hands, however, the protagonist's demise is, like much of the film's take on psychiatry care, radicalized: Carol commits the suicide that she has threatened at least since the ECT scene. All three films reach a last-act crescendo of a crucible of happy convivialities and brutal externalities. Even in their conclusions, with their one-two punches of parties and subsequent death, all three films highlight the futility of any celebration in the midst of their institutions that confine people both physically and psychologically.

## Notes

1 In the recent wave of work on Schroeter, most critics locate him somewhere between underground film and New German Cinema. See, for example, Grundmann (2018, 8–9); and Langford (2006, 10).

2 In addition to the recent work done by Grundmann, Kuzniar, and Langford, the Munich Filmmuseum has been reissuing subtitled DVDs of most of Schroeter's work.

## Works Cited

Berrios, G. E. 1997. "The Scientific Origins of Electroconvulsive Therapy: A Conceptual History." *History of Psychiatry* 8: 105–19.

Durante, Salvatore B. 2022. "The Historical Significance of *Titicut Follies* in Psychiatric Treatment: An Anti-Censorship Perspective." *Psychological Reports* 126.3 (January): 1130–42.

Foot, John. 2014. "Franco Basaglia and the Radical Psychiatry Movement in Italy, 1961–78." *Critical and Radical Social Work* 2.2: 235–49.

Forman, Milos, and Jan Novak. 1993. *Turnaround: A Memoir*. New York: Villard / Random House.

Foucault, Michel. 1988. *Madness and Civilization: A History of Insanity in the Age of Reason*. Translated by Richard Howard. New York: Vintage. First published in 1961/1965.

———. 2008. "Course Summary." In *Psychiatric Power: Lectures at the Collège de France, 1973–1974*, edited by Jacques Lagrange, translated by Graham Burchell, 335–47. New York: Picador.

Foucault, Michel, and Werner Schroeter. 2018. "Werner Schroeter and Michel Foucault in Conversation (1981)." In *Foucault at the Movies*, edited by Michel Foucault, Patrice Maniglier, and Dirk Zabunyan, translated by Clare O'Farrell, 179–90. New York: Columbia University Press.

Gazdag, G., G. S. Ungvari, and H. Czech. 2017. "Mass Killing under the Guise of ECT: The Darkest Chapter in the History of Biological Psychiatry." *History of Psychiatry* 28: 482–88.

Gilman, Sander. 2008. "Electrotherapy and Mental Illness: Then and Now." *History of Psychiatry* 19.3: 339–57.

Grundmann, Roy. 2018. "The Passion of Werner Schroeter: Introduction." In *Werner Schroeter*, edited by Roy Grundman, 7–56. Vienna: Österreichisches Filmmuseum.

Gutting, Gary. 2007. "Foucault and the History of Madness." In *The Cambridge Companion to Foucault*, edited by Gary Gutting, 49–73. Cambridge: Cambridge University Press. First published in 2003.

Hirshbein, Laura, and Sharmalie Sarvananda. 2008. "History, Power, and Electricity: American Popular Magazine Accounts of Electroconvulsive Therapy, 1940–2005." *Journal of the History of the Behavioral Sciences* 44.1 (Winter): 1–18.

Jeremias, Brigitte. 1982. "Die Freiheit des Irrsinns: Schroeters *Tag der Idioten*." *Frankfurter Allgemeine Zeitung*, April 1.

Kapczynski, Jennifer. 2008. *The German Patient: Crisis and Recovery in Postwar Culture*. Ann Arbor: University of Michigan Press.

Kesey, Ken. 2002. *One Flew over the Cuckoo's Nest*. Introduction by Robert Faggen. New York: Viking. First published in 1962.

Kuzniar, Alice. 2000. *The Queer German Cinema*. Stanford: Stanford University Press.

Langford, Michelle. 2006. *Allegorical Images: Tableau, Time and Gesture in the Cinema of Werner Schroeter*. Bristol: intellect.

Lebensohn, Zigmond M. 1999. "The History of Electroconvulsive Therapy in the United States and Its Place in American Psychiatry: A Personal Memoir." *Comprehensive Psychiatry* 40.3 (May–June): 173–81.

Macey, David. 2019. *The Lives of Michel Foucault: A Biography*. New York: Verso. First published in 1993.

Nasser, Mervat. 1995. "The Rise and Fall of Anti-Psychiatry." *Psychiatric Bulletin* 19: 743–46.

Pearson, Geoffrey. 1992. "Misunderstanding Foucault." In *Rewriting the History of Madness: Studies in Foucault's "Histoire de la Folie,"* edited by Arthur Still and Irvine Velody, 110–18. New York: Routledge.

Polan, Dana. 1986. *Power and Paranoia: History, Narrative, and the American Cinema, 1940–1950*. New York: Columbia University Press.

Schroeter, Werner. 2017. *Days of Twilight, Nights of Frenzy*. Translated by Anthea Bell. Chicago: University of Chicago Press. First published in 2011.

Walker, Janet. 1993. *Couching Resistance: Women, Film, and Psychoanalytic Psychiatry*. Minneapolis: University of Minnesota Press.

# AFTERWORD

*ERIC RENTSCHLER*

## I

The editors have asked me to append some closing comments to their most timely and quite significant collection. I am glad to do so for a number of reasons, even if I would not want anyone to think of my contribution at the end of this volume as its last word or final wisdom. This is, after all, a book whose key motivation is to open up rather than close off discussion. I am altogether sympathetic to my colleagues' larger resolve, their ambitious endeavor to revisit the New German Cinema and reconsider the discursive channels in which it has previously circulated and in that way find new avenues of appreciation and understanding. Their intriguing impetus seeks to place this corpus of films within international and global contexts rather than simply considering it within the circumscribed borders of a nation's agendas and determinations.

The present undertaking continues a project initiated by John Davidson more than two decades ago in his important book, *Deterritorializing the New German Cinema*. In probing how New German films explored foreign landscapes and constructed foreign others, Davidson sought to demonstrate the pertinence of postcolonial and transnational studies for an understanding of New German Cinema. This was an essential act of redirection, for up to that point the NGC had almost without exception been considered within the context of its status as a national cinema. Specialists had invariably stressed "the Germanness of German films made by Germans" (Davidson 1999, 24), which for most North American commentators, critics and scholars alike, served as the distinctive earmark of this celebrated national cinema. In making good on his book's title, Davidson critiqued the rhetoric (both of and about) *Autorenkino* and proceeded to deterritorialize it, negotiating the liminal spaces of peripatetic features by Werner Herzog, Wim Wenders, Ulrike Ottinger, and Percy Adlon, cinematic journeys that explore foreign terrains and reflect travelers' imported itineraries. I know of few others working in German film studies (only Katie Trumpener and Randall Halle might be mentioned in the same breath), to this day, who have done so much to activate the meaning potential of the NGC beyond the national.[1] With such initiatives in mind, the prime movers of this present enterprise, quite justifiably, see a need to reflect on and both revise and broaden how scholars have conceptualized and assessed film history in the FRG as a whole during the period between the Oberhausen Manifesto and the overdetermined year of 1982—the year Rainer Werner Fassbinder died—and the dramatic demise of the movement that followed.

The undertaking is timely insofar as the so-called New German Cinema, over the last three decades, has in crucial regards become increasingly passé, losing the formidable critical cachet and scholarly allure that it once possessed. By the time that German studies at long last turned away from the constraining limits of the national and, for a variety of compelling reasons, opened its purview to more expansive post- and transnational perspectives, film scholars in the field had for the most part ceased to talk or even think about the New German Cinema. Everything of importance seemed to have been said. Indeed, the movement's heroic master narrative was well known and had come under question.[2] Its *Autorenfilm* and counter-cinema, under siege since in 1983 the West German government's leadership shifted from the left-of-center Social Democrats to the right-of-center Christian Democrats, accompanied by the auteur-adverse film legislation with its populist incentives that came with the *Wende* (political turn), likewise had become lesser priorities. To say in the 1990s that the NGC had served as a site of national self-reinvention and, more specifically, of creative renewal for German cinema was to state the obvious. If one pursued German art cinema in the aughts and teens of the new century, one invariably now turned to the Berlin School. And commentators have continued to do so into the very present, arguably to a fault, insofar as so much that is noteworthy about contemporary German cinema remains to this day woefully underestimated or overlooked.[3]

## II

The enterprise of this volume is thus both timely and significant at a moment in which the legacy of New German Cinema has come under sustained attack, most notably since 2012, the fiftieth anniversary of the Oberhausen pronouncement. One finds an abundance of reproaches in Dominik Graf's impassioned recent journeys through German genre cinema, *Verfluchte Liebe deutscher Film* (*Doomed Love*, 2016) and *Offene Wunde deutscher Film* (*Open Wounds*, 2017), both directed by Graf with Johannes Sievert. These essay films frequently refer to Klaus Lemke's "Hamburg Manifesto of 2010" in which the septuagenarian director assails the legacy of Oberhausen, its *Autorenfilm* and *Gremienkino*, and fulminates about the disaster it has wrought.[4] Alexander Kluge and his associates, with their self-serving and wildly overstated manifesto of 1962, Lemke rants, set out in the 1960s to fashion self-important serious works just like the precious essays they had written in high school to impress their teachers and please their parents. The authors of these windy and tedious tractates always knew better; Young German films were the product of *Besserwisser* that told you what to see and what and how to think. And the schoolmasterly approach of this state-subsidized cinema would have an altogether calamitous long-term effect. "We make the most beautiful cars. We have the most beautiful women," effuses Lemke in his polemic. "But our films are like tombstones. Plain. Banal. Conciliatory. Goethe-Institut" (Lemke 2010). Under the aegis of New German Cinema and as a result of its lethal fallout, he complains, the West German film scene would become dominated by directors who were "soft-skilled castrates" and producers who were "refinement junkies" (*Veredelungsjunkies*). "Weltweit," he opines, "die Toplangweiler." Which is to say, seen globally, the most boring cinema in the world.

Over the last decade, there has arisen a marked interest in contemporaries of the Oberhausener who did not share the working assumptions of the Young German Film, for example, members of the so-called Munich Group like Lemke, Roland Klick, and Rudolf Thome, to whose number we might also add, among others, Roger Fritz, Marran Gosov, May Spils, Niklaus Schilling, Martin Müller, and Rob Houwer.[5] These filmmakers, unlike their counterparts, were beholden to American genre cinema. They sought to make popular features in a variety of veins (from comedies in bohemian settings to revamped film noirs, displaced westerns, and atmospheric crime films with an erotic frisson) whose intended audience was young urban hipsters and intellectuals. Some important reassessment about this body of work is taking place; indeed, one looks forward to Marco Abel's forthcoming book on the Munich Group.[6] With valuable rediscoveries of this sort comes a welcome opportunity to rethink privileged paradigms and expand our sense of the rich nonsimultaneity to be found in West German films of the 1960s and '70s, to remember a time in which cinema programs in Schwabing allowed equal opportunity for new features by Klick and Kluge, Lemke and Peter Lilienthal, Fritz and Fassbinder, Schilling and Volker Schlöndorff, Thome and Margarethe von Trotta, Houwer and Herzog, Spils and Eckhart Schmidt, as well as Helke Sander and Helma Sanders-Brahms.

## III

Looking back and seeing the years before the Oberhausen Manifesto in a different light, the curators of an influential retrospective of postwar West German cinema from 1949 to 1963 argued that, contrary to dominant wisdom, Young German Film marked no dramatic taking leave of yesterday, that the so-called Opas Kino of the postwar years was hardly as moribund, forgettable, and unmodern as the young upstarts and leftist film critics had maintained.[7] Contrary to historians' claims that films of the Adenauer era were tame and moribund, maintained Rainer Knepperges, they were "surprising brazen, erotic, brash, frivolous, vulgar, and bizarre" (2016, 189). How could critics of the early 1960s, asked Olaf Möller, fail to see that many young directors "were following the previous generation's line more than they were breaking with it?" (2016, 16). Perhaps the promising early films of the Oberhausen signatories, all of which were viewed as Young German initial signs of life, works like Hansjürgen Pohland's *Tobby* (1961), Ferdinand Khittl's *Die Parallelstraße* (*The Parallel Street*, 1962), and Herbert Vesely's *nicht mehr fliehen* (*Stop Running*, 1962), "had more in common with the old films than they dared to admit to themselves or to each other" (17). *Maya*, an omnibus film by six aspiring directors (two of whom had signed the manifesto) that premiered in 1957, a half decade before Oberhausen, had already made it clear that it was possible "to imagine a modernising transformation from inside the industry and that there was an attempt to orchestrate this" (17). West German features of the 1950s such as Ottomar Domnick's experimental *Jonas* (1957), Harald Braun's *Der gläserne Turm* (*The Glass Tower*, 1957), and Eugen York's *Der Mann im Strom* (*Man in the River*, 1958) showed how films from the FRG "ventured into the terrain of cinema modernity, and thus demonstrated that here too it was internationally competitive, or at least wanted to be" (22).

## IV

The appellation New German Cinema was invented in the United States. One can trace it back to a Museum of Modern Art film series in 1972. The moniker became adopted and refined in the FRG and promulgated as *der Neue Deutsche Film*. The term emphasized the richness of possibility that lay in the new. In the words of the filmmakers, "The strength of German film lies in its diversity" ("Die Stärke des deutschen Films ist seine Vielfalt").[8] The phrase also conveyed a common self-understanding and a sense of collective identity ("our") that afforded a very large group of otherwise isolated young auteurs both a sense of belonging to something significant and international visibility. In crucial ways, though, the appellation was imprecise in its pretense of commonality, for there were many strong differences of opinion and conflicts of interest among the individual filmmakers. It was also misleading in the pride it presumed for itself regarding its purported openness. Its claims to diversity in fact were often belied by the New German vanguard's actual practice, especially toward women film workers.

There were in fact no women among the Oberhausen signatories. And, more significantly, with the exception of von Trotta, female directors never would assume an integral place or play a prominent role within the circles of New German filmmakers. The *Filmverlag der Autoren*, for instance, was *ein Herrenverein* (an all-men's club); its founders of 1971 consisted of thirteen men and not a single woman.[9] Prominent feminist directors like Ula Stöckl, Jutta Brückner, Ulrike Ottinger, and Sander surely never considered themselves members of this male coterie. It is illustrative to look at the numerous expressions of anger and resentment along these lines in the pages of *frauen und film*. Or, consider "The Manifesto of Women Film Workers" (1979), a document that speaks out against the marginalization and mistreatment of female colleagues by the New German filmmakers.[10] Scholarly literature often tended to overlook such acts of exclusion and view the movement as a harmonious gathering of diverse initiatives, a utopian enclave of alternative and progressive sensibilities.

It would be useful to view feminist films from West Germany within larger international dialogues. Indeed, it would be quite productive, for instance, to reread the symposia about feminist filmmaking in back issues of *New German Critique*, notably the animated conversation about female film aesthetics with, among others, Michelle Citron and B. Ruby Rich in the winter 1978 issue and, most notably, the exchange from 1982, "From Hitler to Hepburn," which appeared in a special issue on New German Cinema. In an invigorating conversation, the Berlin film critic Claudia Lenssen shares perspectives with Judith Mayne and Helen Fehervary about the production and reception of contemporary West German feminist films.[11] One might also recall the two Goethe-Institut programs of films devoted to "Women's Cinema in Germany" that circulated throughout North America in the late 1970s and early 1980s and think about their decisive impact on the nascent feminist canon as well as on film course curriculums and scholarly endeavors in the United States.

## V

The essays in this volume encourage us to return to the archive in order to both expand our knowledge base and augment our sense of possibility, to rethink accepted wisdom and factor in a larger selection of films and filmmakers, and in general to reconsider the assumptions and paradigms with which we have written German film history so that we might gain a keener awareness of what previous analyses have left out and what they have blithely underestimated or simply overlooked.

In this spirit I appreciate all of the essays in this volume as attempts to rewrite and extend our notions of West German film culture from the mid-1960s to the mid-1980s. Compelling exercises in aperture, these contributions grant attention to the work of lesser-known or underappreciated directors like Werner Schroeter, Lilienthal, Claudia von Alemann, Jeanine Meerapfel, Stöckl, and Klick. They take us beyond feature film production and elaborate, for instance, the crucial and all but unsurveyed role of animated endeavors. We become privy to a variety of otherwise underexposed sites such as the Ulm School of Design and film academies in both East and West Berlin. And an international cast of players provides a veritable gallimaufry of previously underacknowledged influences and interlocutors: D. A. Pennebaker, Raúl Ruiz, French and Belgian feminist filmmakers, Sergio Leone, Howard Hawks, Henri-Georges Clouzot, Sam Peckinpah, Jane Campion, and Miloš Forman. Indeed, in its elaboration of New German Cinema's enduring transnationality, the ensemble virtually boxes the compass, taking us to points east (be they Poland or the GDR), to Chile and New Zealand, to the Nouvelle Vague, New Hollywood, and the Italo-western.

## VI

Let me focus on two of the volume's twelve contributions as examples of its venture and say a few words about their acts of aperture. Of course, had space permitted, I could have also devoted similar attention to each of the other ten pieces. I read Ian Fleishman's analysis of Fassbinder's *Querelle* (1982) with great interest, appreciating the ways in which it stages an encounter between seemingly unlikely entities—New German Cinema and the New Hollywood—demonstrating how the fraught homosociality of Sam Peckinpah's *Cross of Iron* (1977) interrelates with the sadomasochistic homosexuality of *Querelle*. Quite compellingly, Fleishman depicts a unique transatlantic transaction whereby New Hollywood, in its post-Vietnam penchant for diminished and passive male subjects, renegotiates and recodes ideals of masculine strength by drawing on the limpid male protagonists of European art cinema, employing them as role models to represent wounded and uncertain male subjectivity. Fassbinder, in his attempt to fashion a German film that is as beautiful and well-crafted as an American production, only not as mendacious, in Fleishman's assessment meets Hollywood halfway, appropriating the legibility and universality of Peckinpah's generic feature in his garishly lit and eccentrically staged avant-garde production.

*Querelle*'s intertextual debt to *Cross of Iron* and its studious resolve to capture an international viewership catalyzed some further thoughts about another ambitious production that bears Fassbinder's name, *Lili Marleen*

(1981). Here we have an attempt to work with a larger budget, the enterprising old school producer Luggi Waltleitner, and a multinational cast that, along with Hanna Schygulla and Hark Bohm, featured Mel Ferrer and Giancarlo Giannini. Interestingly, the war-time melodrama even borrows footage from *Cross of Iron*. The terms of the dialogue in this case, however, are as different as they are provocative. Harun Farocki, no big fan of Fassbinder, called *Lili Marleen* "a real Nazi tearjerker, like the ones by Bertolucci, Visconti, Fosse" (1981, 186–87). This recasting of a Nazi-era woman's film, in which Hanna Schygulla becomes an avatar for Zarah Leander and the film as a whole a quasi-remake of the Nazi blockbuster *Die große Liebe* (*The Great Love*, 1942), updates the Adenauer era's yen for *große Stoffe* (important topics) while pillaging the arsenal of the New German retro film, in the process fueling a nascent penchant for internationalism that would later become known as *Europudding*.

Indeed, seen more widely, there is a quite provocative trajectory of West German attempts at outreach and sometimes overreach that will take us from Schlöndorff's decidedly ambitious and quite unsuccessful international co-production *Michael Kohlhaas* (1969) to his Oscar-winning *Die Blechtrommel* (*The Tin Drum*, 1979). Looking further down the road, one recalls Bernd Eichinger's earliest collaborations with New German directors like Wenders and Hans-Jürgen Syberberg, which he later eschewed as he set out to think big, both within and beyond Germany, in an entrepreneurial reliance on presold artistic properties, star-studded casts, and high-profile directors. We know that the Fassbinder of the early 1980s was also beginning to think big. He had plans to adapt Pitigrilli's novel *Cocaine* and to work with Jane Fonda on a biopic about Rosa Luxemburg. In this regard, *Querelle* was both an experiment and arguably a forerunner of the subsequent big-budgeted, internationally cast, and transnationally financed adaptations of best-selling novels engineered by Eichinger from the 1980s to his death in 2011.

It is propitious that Nora Alter brings Harun Farocki's virtually unknown *Betrogen* (*Betrayed*, 1985) into the mix. The neo noir is, as she observes, an anomaly in the director's work. Indeed, at first glance it even seems legible as a conventional television movie. And yet, in its overt references to Alfred Hitchcock and Douglas Sirk, in its "critique of the enlightened eye," as Volker Siebel points out, it is also a film with an experimental setup, and in this regard every bit as "self-referential" as

Farocki's legendary documentary essays (1998, 99). It premiered at the Hof Film Festival in the fall of 1985 on the same program as Doris Dörrie's *Männer* (*Men*). Although *Betrayed* received a markedly frosty reception, it did not altogether lack admirers. I recall critic Kraft Wetzel's words of praise in an article devoted to the responses of West German filmmakers to dramatic changes in government film-subsidy policies. Wetzel makes it clear that the derision directed at Farocki's exercise in cinephilia and necrophilia, his self-reflexive wannabe noir, was not an instance of special treatment. It was common practice at a time when commentators and spectators had become weary of anxiously ambitious *Autorenfilme*. Despite the many harsh appraisals of *Betrayed*, Wetzel remains mindful of the film's still unappreciated meaning potential. "Thirty years from now," Wetzel remarks, writing in 1986, "film historians will see this film as a big mystery" (1986, 20). Here we are, almost forty years later. Perhaps, I would suggest, the project we are in the midst of might encourage us to think of Farocki's film as a time capsule and to probe its exercise in seeing and misapprehension, its awareness that one might understand reality better and more clearly if only one is willing to take a step back. To paraphrase the director, "Maintaining one's distance means losing touch with reality in order to gain reality" (Siebel 1998, 100). And if we do so, we might very well come to consider *Betrayed* as a precursor of the Berlin School, in whose formation, especially in the work of his student and later collaborator Christian Petzold, Farocki would go on to play a seminal role.

## VII

German film history from 1962 to 1982, with the different sites it occupies and the various circumstances it invokes, offers us many puzzles and many challenges as well as many opportunities. Let me in closing briefly speak about another border that future studies of New German Cinema might want to traverse. If we switch the emphasis from the national to the international and transnational, as this collection of essays has done, we open ourselves up to a plethora of new perspectives and novel constellations. How about, though, if we not only interrogate and problematize the German dimension of the NGC but also think about this cinema's place within a larger history of the media? Take for instance, NGC's great moment of truth after 1982 and, as documented in Alexander Kluge's compendium *Bestandsaufnahme: Utopie Film* (*Taking of Stock: Utopia Film*, 1983), its confrontation with the new media and the retrospection, uncertainty, and transformation to which this reckoning gave rise. Think of the noteworthy ensemble of films from the FRG that issued from this juncture and, from a variety of perspectives, reflected on the place of film and media within the history of visual culture and cultural production at large. They offered different and, in decidedly inimitable ways, incisive considerations of film and the media, their past workings as well as unseen possibilities. Combing the history of fantasy ware and visual machinery and assessing their future prospects, they probed film's place within a more expansive array of audiovisual expressivity and what media historian Siegfried Zielinski would refer to more overarchingly as "audiovisions."[12]

Werner Nekes's *Uliisses* (1983), for instance, is a cinematic tour de force that takes its cue from Homer and James Joyce, traveling through fantasy realms while following the Odyssey of proto-cinematic possibility from ancient visual toys to early scientific experiments, from phosphorous powder to holography and laser technology, putting on ample display the director's elaborate museum of visual gadgets from past centuries. As in Nekes's subsequent prehistory of cinema, *Was geschah wirklich zwischen den Bildern* (*Film Before Film*, 1986), we find historically driven vanguard endeavors in media archaeology *avant la lettre*, films that probe the cinematic medium's place within the larger history of visual culture.

Other experimental films from the same juncture delved into the divergent shapes of contemporary media ecology and, in the process, mulled over the impact, both real and imagined, of the new media. Consider the chilling intimations of audiovisual futurity that we find in Michael Klier's video study of surveillance cameras, *Der Riese* (*The Giant*, 1982). The images here from West German big cities do not explain or comment, for they have no ax to grind. No scripted logic or artistic design determines how they function. These images are not meant to entertain or educate; they seem to show without purpose. They are the product of mute and omnipresent machines that record an array of nonplaces and figures in transit, sites of passage such as intersections, airports, train stations, junk yards, security gates, pedestrian zones, and the lanes of shopping malls. Signs of life devoid of life. This is a science fiction film without a narrative or any characters, scenes from for the most unpeopled localities that resemble the aftermath of a calamity, maybe even the end of the world. In their haunting blankness and creepy bleakness, they recall Gilles Deleuze's society of control in which discipline becomes a function of a delocalized yet ever-present and impersonal technical instrumentation. "With his montage and its musical accompaniment," writes Farocki, "Klier puts images in the subjunctive form: could these be the images of a film narrative? A productive misconstruction" (2014). Looked at today, Klier's mélange of urban prospects, the products of spying cameras that have been automatically generated in the service of unseen agencies, has an undeniably sinister aspect. Not to see the working of power is not to suggest that it does not exist. Klier's seemingly innocuous "operational images" (Farocki 2014) provide uncanny glimpses of things to come that are already there.

Or take Hellmuth Costard and Jürgen Ebert's *Echtzeit* (*Real Time*, 1983), a sobering study of sophisticated machines that simulate time and space, sketching how new technologies recode the world as virtual realities, as abstract topographies devoid of memory or feeling. What happens, the film asks, when electronically shaped images come to stand for and potentially take over the human experience of the world? Two points of focus assume the film's center stage: a couple's story and synthetic landscape images produced by a computer. The scientists Ruth and George come to fear that they are only avatars, that their persons have been body-snatched and replaced by computer programs, and that the spaces they inhabit have long since ceased to be real. Are they being both other-directed and reduced to the status of software? This, says George, "is a story that doesn't want to be one." In the words of a contemporary critic, *Real Time* above all shows how realities become illusions and how illusions become realities.[13] "Through its conversations among computer experts, through its observation of the details of microprocessor manufacture, through its discovery of a government sponsored landscape simulation, and through its narrative," argues Ann Harris, *Real Time* "uncovers and juxtaposes an array of issues which are related to realtime and which also are characteristic of theorizing about and descriptions of what is varyingly referred to as post-industrial society or the postmodern condition" (1993, 25). Here, too, yet another German reflection on the future of the media has a stunning prescience. Watching the digitized landscape images in the final sequence of *Real Time* today, one feels as if one were looking at a Google map.

Two films that Niklaus Schilling made at the start of the 1980s stand out as intriguing exercises in media ecology, explorations of cinema's future life in light of technological innovations. Just as the new government was proclaiming a dramatic film political turn and the incursion of new media confounded Schilling's colleagues, *Zeichen und Wunder* (*Signs and Wonders*, 1982) came about. This feature about television made for television was crafted for a pittance with a video camera. Six months after making it, Schilling transferred it to 16mm, in which format it was screened in the Forum at the 1982 Berlinale. "Cinema? Television? Or both?" In Schilling's assessment *Signs and Wonders* was a VHS film (2008, 40–41).[14]

*Die Frau ohne Körper und der Projektionist* (*The Woman without a Body and the Projectionist*, 1984), an electronic feature shot on video and transferred onto 35mm, presented an *amour fou* between a young projectionist and a somewhat older television commentator (hailed as the "Tele-Frau of the year"). These characters are stand-ins who counterpose celluloid dreams and video images, and in so doing enact the creative potential of recent technology.[15] The production moves between two main venues in Munich, the skyscraper that houses the TV station VETV and a small cinema (the triplex Sonnen-Filmtheater) with sparsely peopled auditoriums and a cramped projection booth. For many of Schilling's contemporaries, the film constituted a double betrayal: this first German feature made on video was co-produced by the commercial TV channel RTL. Schilling, carped Ulrich Greiner in *Die Zeit*, was not combatting the death of cinema but rather casting himself in the role of its undertaker (1984).

"How does electronic image production affect us," wondered the inveterate tinkerer Schilling, "the networking of a worldwide profusion of images?"[16] For him, video might well provide a new beginning and enable cinema to assume an electronic countenance. "It's good that cinema as we once knew it in any case no longer exists. And celluloid will disappear," he remarked, but that will not mean the end of film. In fact, we stand "to lose the last 'outposts of cinema' if we continue to leave electronic images to the people who produce advertisements and the evening news. It's important that we find a niche in these new outlets before it's too late and media interests control the international flow of images. (They will also have their own cinemas, which they will need to ensure that their interests dominate every sphere of activity)" (1984).

## VIII

As befits a book whose key impetus is aperture, its afterword ends *in media res*, with a few fragments from another possible history of New German Cinema, pieces to be put together and puzzles to be solved as we think about the pertinence of New German films for the visual culture that surrounds us and the highly mediated world in which we live.

## Notes

1 See Katie Trumpener's prescient essay regarding filmic reflections of and on German ethnocentrism, "On the Road: Labour, Ethnicity, and the 'New German Cinema' in the Age of the Multinational," *Public Culture* 2.1 (1989): 20–30; as well as "Johanna d'Arc in the Mirror of Dorian Gray: Ethnographic Recordings and the Aesthetics of the Market in Recent Films by Ulrike Ottinger," *New German Critique* 60 (1993): 77–99. See as well Randall Halle's paradigm-shifting contribution, *German Film After Germany: Toward a Transnational Aesthetic* (Urbana: University of Illinois Press, 2008). Silvia Kratzer-Julifs's UCLA dissertation of 1996, "Exile Cinema as National Cinema: Re-defining German National Cinema (1962–1995)," also intervened against the tendency to hypostatize the national dimension of NGC. Her study, alas never published, traced the endeavors of exiled directors such as Sohrab Shahid Saless who pursued careers in the FRG, carefully elaborating how displaced filmmakers fashioned German film history from the inside out. Also see Stephan K. Schindler and Lutz Koepnick, eds., *The Cosmopolitan Screen: German Cinema and the Global Imaginary* (Ann Arbor: University of Michigan Press, 2007).

2 Crucial interventions that problematized NGC's revisitations of German history were Anton Kaes's *From Hitler to Heimat: The Return of History as Film* (Cambridge, MA: Harvard University Press); and Eric Santner's *Stranded Objects: Mourning, Memory, and Film in Postwar Germany* (Ithaca: Cornell University Press, 1990).

3 A recent special issue of *New German Critique* explores various sectors of contemporary German cinema beyond the Berlin School. See Prager and Rentschler (2019, 7–8): "Many ambitious films made today in Austria and Germany have little in common with the Berlin School. . . . We would do well also to direct our attention to other sites of creative

endeavor and not assume that the Berlin School is the sole sector of German cinema worthy of critical reconnaisance."

4 For an analysis of Graf's two essay films on the demise of German genre cinema, see my article "An Elegy for German Cinema: Dominik Graf's Doomed Loves and Open Wounds," *New German Critique* 138 (November 2019): 207–33.

5 Crucial expressions of this interest include Graf and Siebert's essay films mentioned above as well as the documentary homage to the New Munich Group *Zeigen was man liebt* (*Show What You Love*, 2016) and the directorial portrait *Roland Klick: The Heart Is a Hungry Hunter* (2013).

6 See Marco Abel, *Mit Nonchalance am Abgrund: Das Kino der "Neuen Münchner Gruppe" (1964–1972)* (Bielefeld: transcript, 2024).

7 It was first screened at the Locarno Film Festival in 2016 and subsequently circulated widely, including high-profile programs and presentations in New York City and the Harvard Film Archive.

8 "Hamburger Erklärung" (1979), reprinted in *Augenzeugen: 100 Texte neuer deutscher Filmemacher*, ed. Hans Helmut Prinzler and Eric Rentschler (Frankfurt: Verlag der Autoren, 1988), 32.

9 In 2009 Arthaus released the *Filmverlag der Autoren Edition*, an extensive DVD collection of features meant both to celebrate films supported and distributed by the Filmverlag between 1968 and 1994 and, in its representative selection, to provide a comprehensive mini-history of Young and New German hallmarks. Among the fifty films on offer only four are by women: two by von Trotta (*Die bleierne Zeit / Marianne and Juliane*, 1981 and *Rosa Luxemburg*, 1985) and two by Sanders-Brahms (*Deutschland bleiche Mutter / Germany Pale Mother*, 1979 and *Manöver / Maneuver*, 1988). For a compelling portrait of the Filmverlag, undeniably conspicuous in its near lack of female presence, see Dominik Wessely's documentary *Gegenschuss: Aufbruch der Filmemacher* (*Reverse Angle: Rebellion of the Filmmakers*, 2008). A comprehensive history of the Filmverlag, arguably the most prominent German institution in the history of the NGC, still remains to be written.

10 See "The Manifesto of Women Filmmakers (1979)," in *West German Filmmakers on Film*, ed. Eric Rentschler (New York: Holmes & Meier, 1988), 5–6. In the same volume, see also Helke Sander, "Men Are Responsible That Women Become Their Enemies: Tales of Rejection," 25–30.

11 See Michelle Citron, Julia Lesage, Judith Mayne, B. Ruby Rich, and Anna Marie Taylor, "Women and Film: A Discussion of Feminist Aesthetics,"

*New German Critique* 13 (Winter 1978): 83–107; and Helen Fehervary, Claudia Lenssen, and Judith Mayne, "From Hitler to Hepburn: A Discussion of Women's Film Production and Reception," *New German Critique* 24–25 (Fall–Winter 1981–82): 172–95.

12 See Siegfried Zielinski, *Audiovisionen: Kino und Fernsehen als Zwischenspiele in der Geschichte* (Reinbek bei Hamburg: Rowohlt, 1989).

13 "*Echtzeit* von Hellmuth Costard and Jürgen Ebert: Welt am Draht," *Die Zeit*, July 8, 1983.

14 The NGC, argues Tobias Haupts, gained very little from the video market and vidéothèques. If anything, video cassettes above all served to further the American hold on the West German film market. If video stores in the FRG globalized offerings, they did so mainly by circulating Asian karate movies as well as zombie and cannibal films from Italy. See Tobias Haupts, *Die Videotek* (Bielefeld: transcript, 2014), 273–74.

15 On January 29, 1984, the German public television station ARD aired Christian Bauer and Jörg Bundschuh's film *Abschied vom Zelluloid* (*Goodbye to Celluloid*, 1984), a documentary that chronicles Schilling's work on *The Woman without a Body and the Projectionist*. At one point we hear Schilling muse, with a striking nonchalance, that "someday people will come to realize that it makes no difference which means one employs to capture images."

16 See Schilling's comments in the unpaginated German press booklet for the film.

## Works Cited

Davidson, John. 1999. *Deterritorializing the New German Cinema*. Minnesota: University of Minnesota Press.

Farocki, Harun. 1981. "Im Kino." *Filmkritik* 292 (April 1981): 186–87.

———. 2014. "Notes. Michael Klier *The Giant*, 1983," January. Neuer Berliner Kunstverein, Berlin. https://www.ercatx.org/michael-klier-the-giant-1983-by-harun-Farocki/.

Greiner, Ulrich. 1984. "Das Kino ist tot." *Die Zeit*, January 27.

Harris, Ann. 1993. "Taking Time Seriously: Technology, Politics and Filmmaking Practice in the Films of Hellmuth Costard." PhD diss., New York University.

Knepperges, Rainer. 2016. "Mama's Cinema Is Alive (and Kicking)." In *Beloved and Rejected: Cinema in the Young Federal Republic of Germany from 1949 to 1963*, edited by Claudia Dillmann and Olaf Möller, translated by Stewart Tryster et al., 188–203. Frankfurt: Deutsches Filminstitut Filmmuseum.

Lemke, Klaus. 2010. "Papas Staatskino ist tot: Hamburger Manifest von Klaus Lemke—Protest gegen das Filmfest 2010." October 1. liberalesinstitut.wordpress.com/2010/10/01/papas-staatskino-ist-tot-hamburger-manifest-von-klaus-lemke-%E2%80%93-protest-gegen-das-filmfest-2010.

Möller, Olaf. 2016. "Adenauer Country." In *Beloved and Rejected: Cinema in the Young Federal Republic of Germany from 1949 to 1963*, edited by Claudia Dillmann and Olaf Möller, translated by Stewart Tryster et al., 15–25. Frankfurt: Deutsches Filminstitut Filmmuseum.

Prager, Brad, and Eric Rentschler. 2019. "Introduction: New Prospects—After the Berlin School?" *New German Critique* 138 (November): 1–9.

Schilling, Niklaus. 1984. "Ist das Kino tot?" *Die Zeit*, February 17, n.p.

———. 2008. "Wie die Stasi mich mit Antonioni zusammenbrachte." In *Abschied vom Zelluloid?* edited by Andreas Kirchner et al., 39–52. Marburg: Schüren.

Siebel, Volker. 1998. "Rettung aus Sehnot." In *Der Ärger mit den Bildern: Die Filme von Harun Farocki*, edited by Rolf Aurich and Ulrich Kriest, 95–108. Konstanz: UVK Medien.

Wetzel, Kraft. 1986. "Wie antwortet der deutsche Film auf Zimmermann und Hollywood?" *epd Film* 3.5 (May): 16–22.

# CONTRIBUTORS

**Marco Abel** is Willa Cather Professor of English and Film Studies at the University of Nebraska–Lincoln. The author of *Violent Affect: Literature, Cinema, and Critique After Representation, The Counter-Cinema of the Berlin School* (winner of the 2014 German Studies Association Book Prize), and *Mit Nonchalance am Abgrund: Das Kino der "Neuen Münchner Gruppe" (1964–1972)*, he is the coeditor, with Chris Wahl, Michael Wedel, and Jesko Jockenhoevel, of *Im Angesicht des Fernsehens: Der Filmemacher Dominik Graf*; with Jaimey Fisher of *The Berlin School and Its Global Contexts: A Transnational Art Cinema*; with Jaimey Fisher and Aylin Bademsoy of *Christian Petzold: Interviews*; and with Christina Gerhardt of *German Screen Cultures and the Long 1968*. With Roland Végső, he coedits the University of Nebraska Press book series *Provocations*.

**Nora M. Alter** is a scholar of comparative film and media arts at Temple University in Philadelphia. She has published numerous essays on cultural and visual studies, contemporary art, and sound studies. She is the author of *Vietnam Protest Theatre: The Television War on Stage, Sound Matters, Chris Marker, The Essay Film After Fact and Fiction* and, most recently, *Harun Farocki: Forms of Intelligence*.

**Hester Baer** is professor of German and cinema and media studies at the University of Maryland. Her books include *Dismantling the Dream Factory: Gender, German Cinema, and the Postwar Quest for a New Film Language, German Cinema in the Age of Neoliberalism*, and a short monograph on West Germany's first feminist film, Ula Stöckl's 1968 *The Cat Has Nine Lives*. Baer is the coeditor, with Jill Suzanne Smith, of *Babylon Berlin, German Visual Spectacle, and Global Media Culture*. She is currently working on a new book, coauthored with Angelica Fenner: *Feminist Film History*

*Reframed: The Ulm Film School, 1962–68*. Baer currently serves as coeditor of the *German Quarterly*.

**Jennifer Lynde Barker** is a professor of film studies at Bellarmine University, where she directs the film studies minor and specializes in animation and film history and aesthetics. She also spent a year teaching in Kyoto, Japan as a Fulbright lecturer. The author of *The Aesthetics of Antifascist Film: Radical Projection*, she has published numerous articles and film reviews in *Animation: An Interdisciplinary Journal, Literature/Film Quarterly, Journal of African American Studies, MUBI Notebook, Filmihullu*, and *Cinema Scope*, among others, and curates animation programs at the Midnight Sun Film Festival. She is currently writing a book on early twentieth-century animation.

**Ilka Brombach** received her PhD in film and comparative literature from the Free University Berlin, where she worked as a researcher at the SFB 626 (Collaborative Research Center 626) on the project the Politics of Aesthetics in Western European Cinema. From 2014 to 2018, she was a researcher at the Film University Babelsberg KONRAD WOLF, working on a German Research Foundation (DFG) project on the HFF's student film archive. Since October 2020, she has served as the director of research and curation at the Film Museum Potsdam; visiting professor for Film History and Film Education for Museums at the Film University Babelsberg KONRAD WOLF; and director of the film festival moving history. She is the author of *Eine offene Geschichte des Kinos—Alexander Kluge, Rainer Werner Fassbinder, Wim Wenders, Christian Petzold, Thomas Arslan, Michael Haneke. Filmlektüren mit Jacques Rancière*; the coeditor, with Tina Kaiser, of *Über Christian Petzold*; the editor of the DVDs *Babelsberger Freiheiten: Filme der Hochschule für Film und Fernsehen "Konrad Wolf," 1957–1990*; and the coeditor, with Chris Wahl and Michael Wedel, of *Wolfgang Kohlhaase* (*Film-Konzepte* 75).

**John E. Davidson** is professor of Germanic languages and literatures and film studies at Ohio State University, where he holds a 50 percent appointment as the faculty athletics representative. As OSU's film studies director (2005–15), he served as the executive editor of *The Journal of Short Film*, a quarterly DVD publication of original artistic work from around the globe. His scholarship has appeared in such diverse venues as the *Alexander Kluge Jahrbuch*, *American Imago*, *Film and History*, *New German Critique*, *PMLA*, and *Quarterly Review of Film and Video*. Recent work in edited volumes includes "Before and Afterlives: On the Stillness of Photographs at the Outset of Adenauer Cinema," in *Photographs and German Cinema*. His current book project, supported in part by a grant from the Hans Arp Stiftung, investigates the art of the negative in the long Adenauer era.

**Jaimey Fisher** is professor of German and of cinema and digital media at the University of California, Davis. Fisher has written four books—*German Ways of War* (about German war films), *Treme*, *Christian Petzold*, and *Disciplining Germany: Youth, Reeducation, and Reconstruction After the Second World War*. He has also edited or coedited seven books or special issues, including on film (*The Berlin School and Its Global Contexts*, with Marco Abel, *Generic Histories of German Cinema: Genre and Its Deviations*, and *Collapse of the Conventional: German Cinema and Its Politics at the Turn of the Twenty-First Century*, with Brad Prager) as well as on literature and theory (*Spatial Turns: Space, Place, and Mobility in German Literary and Visual Culture*, with Barbara Mennel, and *Critical Theory: Current State and Future Prospects*, with Peter Hohendahl). He was assistant professor at Tulane University before arriving at UC Davis.

**Ian Fleishman** is the inaugural chair of the Department of Cinema and Media Studies and an associate professor in the Department of Francophone, Italian, and Germanic Studies at the University of Pennsylvania. He has published widely on subjects ranging from the Baroque to contemporary cinema and moving-image pornography. His first book, *An Aesthetics of Injury: The Narrative Wound from Baudelaire to Tarantino*, was the winner of the Northeast Modern Language Association Book Award. Along with Iggy Cortez, he is the editor of a collection of essays, *Performative Opacity in the Work of Isabelle Huppert*. His next monograph, *Flamboyant Fictions: The Failed Art of Passing*, is forthcoming.

**Ervin Malakaj** is associate professor of German studies at the University of British Columbia. He is a scholar of queer studies and German cultural history with a special focus on visual culture. His book on Richard Oswald's film *Anders als die Andern* appeared in 2023. Additionally, he is the coeditor of multiple scholarly volumes and special issues of journals focused on topics such as slapstick, print history, and queer temporalities. His ongoing work is supported by both the Alexander von Humboldt Foundation and the Social Sciences and Humanities Research Council of Canada. For his dedication to international German studies, he was awarded the 2023 DAAD Jacob and Wilhelm Grimm Prize in the junior category.

**Brad Prager** is the Catherine Paine Middlebush Chair of Humanities at the University of Missouri, where he teaches German studies and film studies. His areas of research include film history, Holocaust studies, contemporary German cinema, and the art and literature of German Romanticism. He is the author of *After the Fact: The Holocaust in Twenty-First Century Documentary Film*, *The Cinema of Werner Herzog: Aesthetic Ecstasy and Truth*, and *Aesthetic Vision and German Romanticism: Writing Images*, as well as short monographs devoted to Michael Cimino's *The Deer Hunter* and to Christian Petzold's films *Phoenix* and *Yella*. He is the coeditor of the books *Visualizing the Holocaust: Documents, Aesthetics, Memory*, *The Collapse of the Conventional: German Film and Its Politics at the Turn of the Twenty-First Century*, and *The Construction of Testimony: Claude Lanzmann's "Shoah" and Its Outtakes.*

**Eric Rentschler** is the Arthur Kingsley Porter Professor of Germanic Languages and Literatures and a faculty member of the Film and Visual Studies Program at Harvard University. His publications concentrate on German film history and theory during the Weimar Republic, the Third Reich, and the postwar, post-Wall, and postmillennial eras. His books include *West German Film in the Course of Time*, *German Film and Literature: Adaptations and Transformations*, *West German Filmmakers on Film*, *Augenzeugen: 100 Texte neuer deutscher Filmemacher* (second updated edition, with Hans Helmut Prinzler), *The Films of G. W. Pabst*, *The Ministry of Illusion: Nazi Cinema and Its Afterlife*, *Neuer Deutscher Film* (with Norbert Grob and Hans Helmut Prinzler), and *The Use and Abuse of Cinema: German Legacies from the Weimar Era to the Present*.

**Claudia Sandberg** is a film historian and filmmaker who teaches at the University of Melbourne. Her research interests include Cold War audiovisual memory, German and Latin American cinemas, and socialist film cultures. Sandberg is the author of *Peter Lilienthal: A Cinema of Exile and Resistance*, and she coedited the volumes *Contemporary Latin American Cinema: Resisting Neoliberalism?* and *The German Cinema Book*. Together with Alejandro Areal Vélez she made *Hidden Films: A Journey from Exile to Memory*, a documentary that examines the value of DEFA Chile films as audiovisual memory of the Pinochet dictatorship. Her work has appeared in anthologies and journals such as *Screenworks*, *Filmblatt*, *Journal of Latin American Cultural Studies*, and *Studies in Eastern European Cinema*.

**Margaret Strair** is a visiting assistant professor of German at Bryn Mawr College. She received her PhD in 2022 from the University of Pennsylvania with a dissertation that focused on synesthesia and intermediality in German Romantic literature. Her research interests include the interarts, visual and scientific culture, German literature and philosophy in the eighteenth and nineteenth centuries, and foreign-language education. She is also currently an assistant editor of the *Goethe Lexicon of Philosophical Concepts*.

# INDEX